Hana-Kimi

For You in Full Blossom

DISCARD

14

story and art by
HISAYA NAKAJO

HANA-KIMI
For You in Full Blossom
VOLUME 14

STORY & ART BY HISAYA NAKAJO

Translation & English Adaptation/David Ury
Touch-Up Art & Lettering/Primary Graphix
Design/Izumi Evers
Editor/Jason Thompson

Editor in Chief, Books/Alvin Lu
Editor in Chief, Magazines/Marc Weidenbaum
VP of Publishing Licensing/Rika Inouye
VP of Sales/Gonzalo Ferreyra
Sr. VP of Marketing/Liza Coppola
Publisher/Hyoe Narita

Hanazakari no Kimitachi he by Hisaya Nakajo © Hisaya Nakajo 2000
All rights reserved. First published in Japan in 2001 by HAKUSENSHA, Inc., Tokyo.
English language translation rights in America and Canada arranged with
HAKUSENSHA, Inc., Tokyo. New and adapted artwork and text © 2006 VIZ Media, LLC.
The HANA-KIMI logo is a trademark of VIZ Media, LLC. The stories, characters and
incidents mentioned in this publication are entirely fictional.

Printed in the U.S.A.

Published by VIZ Media, LLC, P.O. Box 77010, San Francisco, CA 94107

Shôjo Edition
10 9 8 7 6 5 4 3 2

First printing, October 2006
Second printing, January 2007

T 251173

www.viz.com
store.viz.com

PARENTAL ADVISORY
HANA-KIMI is rated T+ for Older Teen and is recom-
mended for ages 16 and up. Contains strong language, sexual themes and alcohol and tobacco usage.

CONTENTS

HONEY BEE

BUZZ

BUZZ

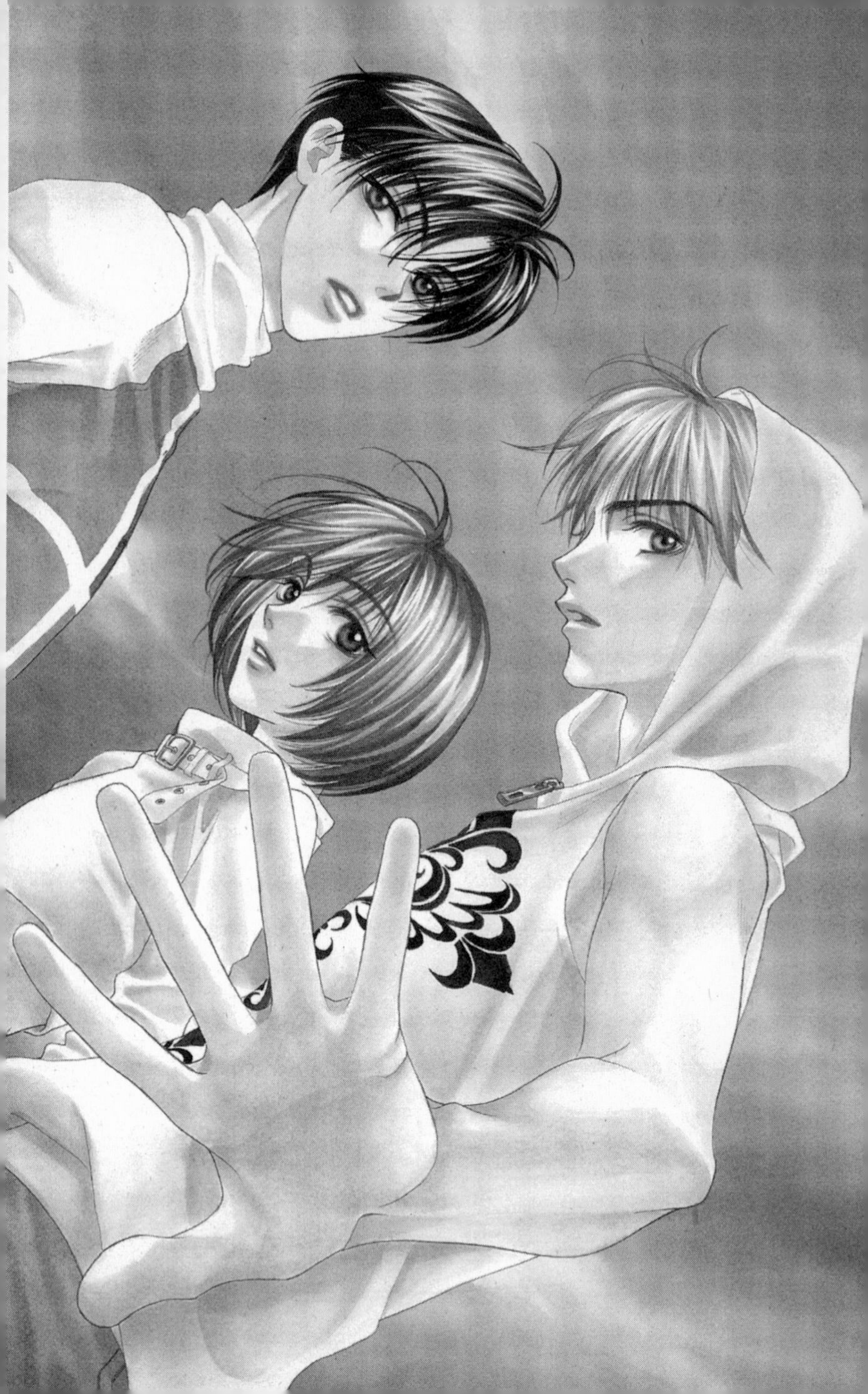

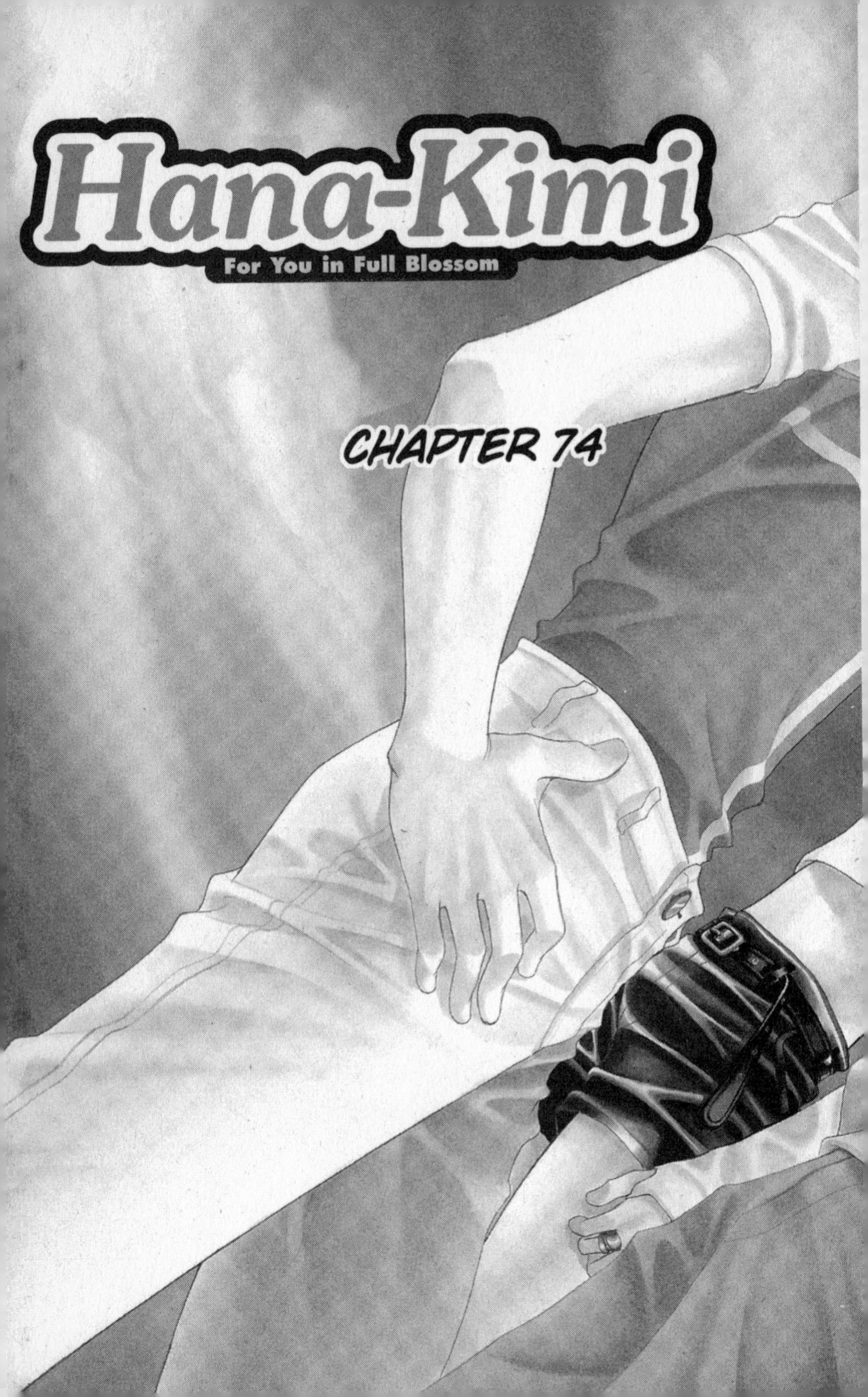
Hana-Kimi
For You in Full Blossom
CHAPTER 74

WORKER BEE

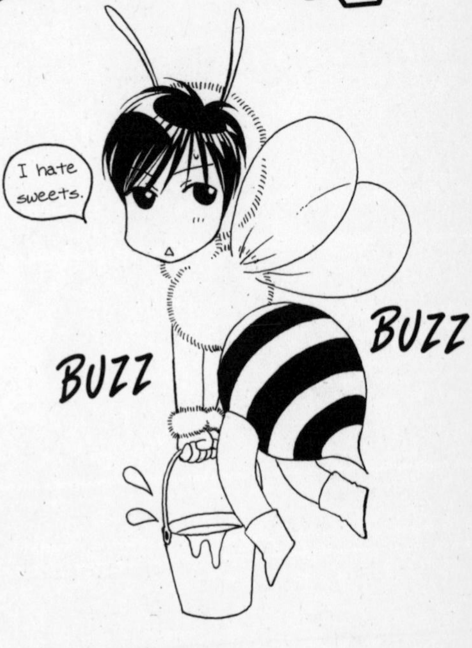

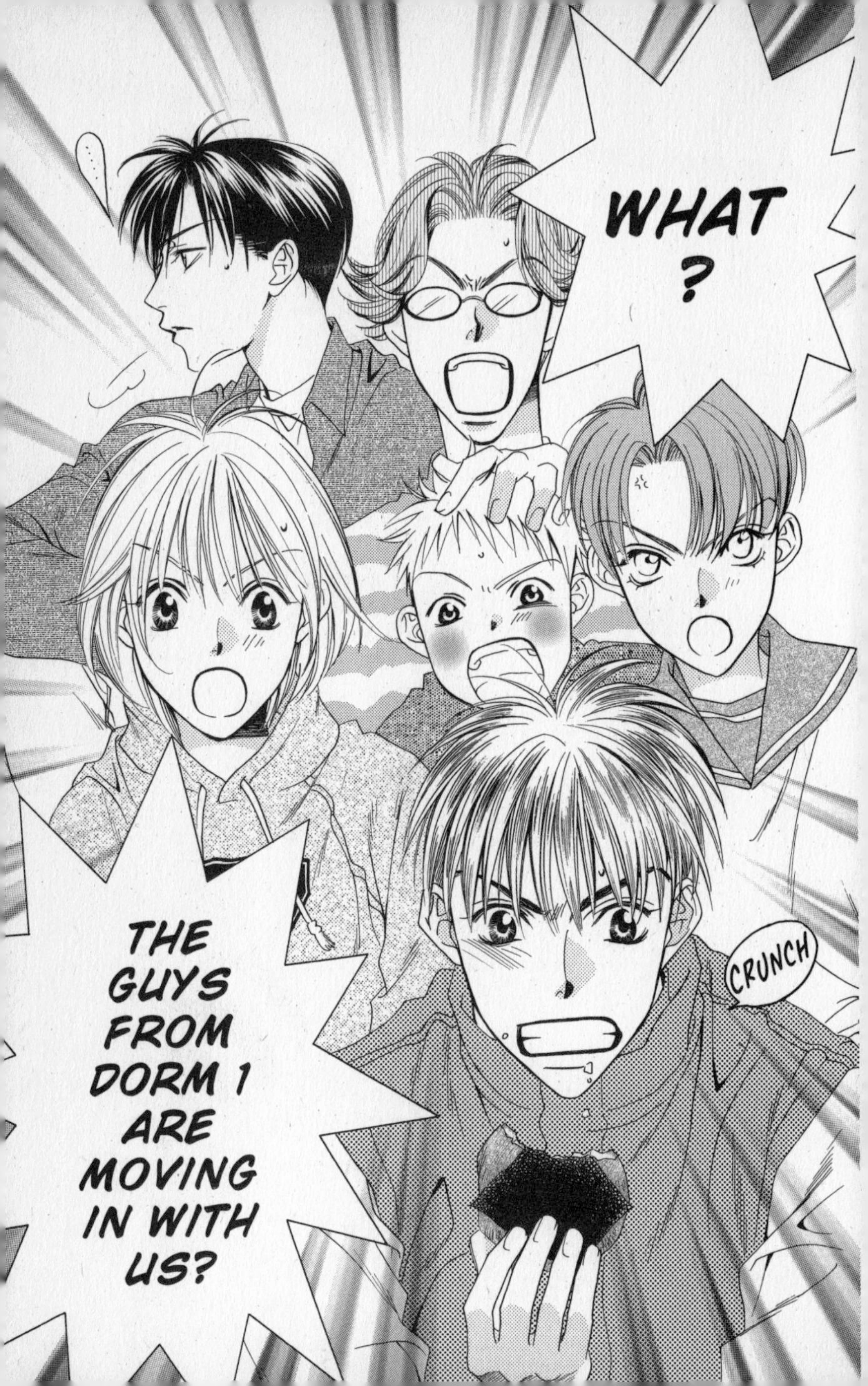
WHAT?
CRUNCH
THE GUYS FROM DORM 1 ARE MOVING IN WITH US?

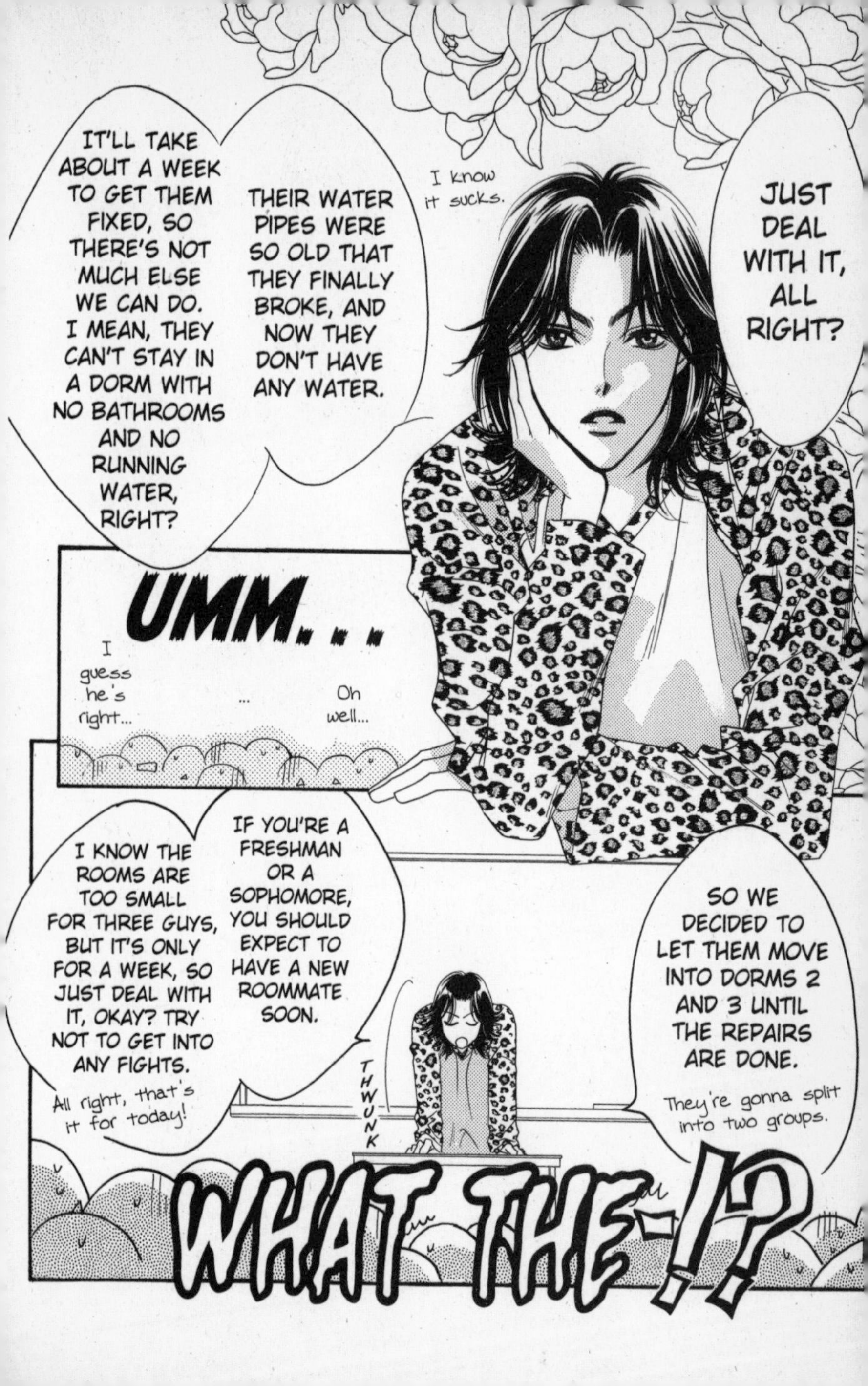
JUST DEAL WITH IT, ALL RIGHT?
I know it sucks.
THEIR WATER PIPES WERE SO OLD THAT THEY FINALLY BROKE, AND NOW THEY DON'T HAVE ANY WATER.
IT'LL TAKE ABOUT A WEEK TO GET THEM FIXED, SO THERE'S NOT MUCH ELSE WE CAN DO. I MEAN, THEY CAN'T STAY IN A DORM WITH NO BATHROOMS AND NO RUNNING WATER, RIGHT?
UMM...
Oh well...
...
I guess he's right...
SO WE DECIDED TO LET THEM MOVE INTO DORMS 2 AND 3 UNTIL THE REPAIRS ARE DONE.
They're gonna split into two groups.
THWUNK
IF YOU'RE A FRESHMAN OR A SOPHOMORE, YOU SHOULD EXPECT TO HAVE A NEW ROOMMATE SOON.
I KNOW THE ROOMS ARE TOO SMALL FOR THREE GUYS, BUT IT'S ONLY FOR A WEEK, SO JUST DEAL WITH IT, OKAY? TRY NOT TO GET INTO ANY FIGHTS.
All right, that's it for today!
WHAT THE-!?

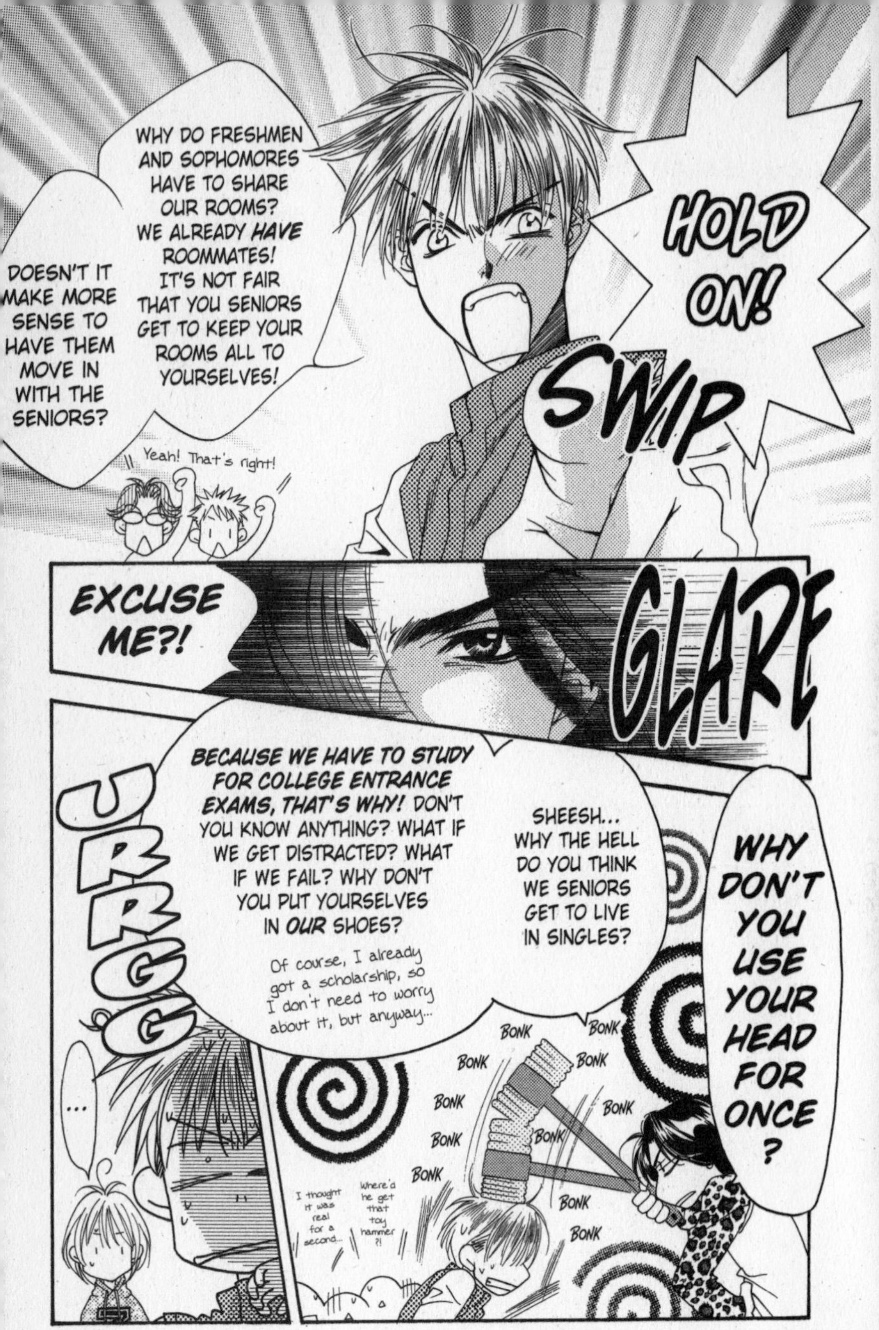
HOLD ON!
SWIP
WHY DO FRESHMEN AND SOPHOMORES HAVE TO SHARE OUR ROOMS? WE ALREADY *HAVE* ROOMMATES! IT'S NOT FAIR THAT YOU SENIORS GET TO KEEP YOUR ROOMS ALL TO YOURSELVES!
DOESN'T IT MAKE MORE SENSE TO HAVE THEM MOVE IN WITH THE SENIORS?
Yeah! That's right!
GLARE
EXCUSE ME?!
WHY DON'T YOU USE YOUR HEAD FOR ONCE?
SHEESH... WHY THE HELL DO YOU THINK WE SENIORS GET TO LIVE IN SINGLES?
BECAUSE WE HAVE TO STUDY FOR COLLEGE ENTRANCE EXAMS, THAT'S WHY! DON'T YOU KNOW ANYTHING? WHAT IF WE GET DISTRACTED? WHAT IF WE FAIL? WHY DON'T YOU PUT YOURSELVES IN *OUR* SHOES?
Of course, I already got a scholarship, so I don't need to worry about it, but anyway...
URRG
BONK BONK BONK BONK BONK BONK BONK BONK BONK BONK BONK BONK
Where'd he get that toy hammer?!
I thought it was real for a second...
...

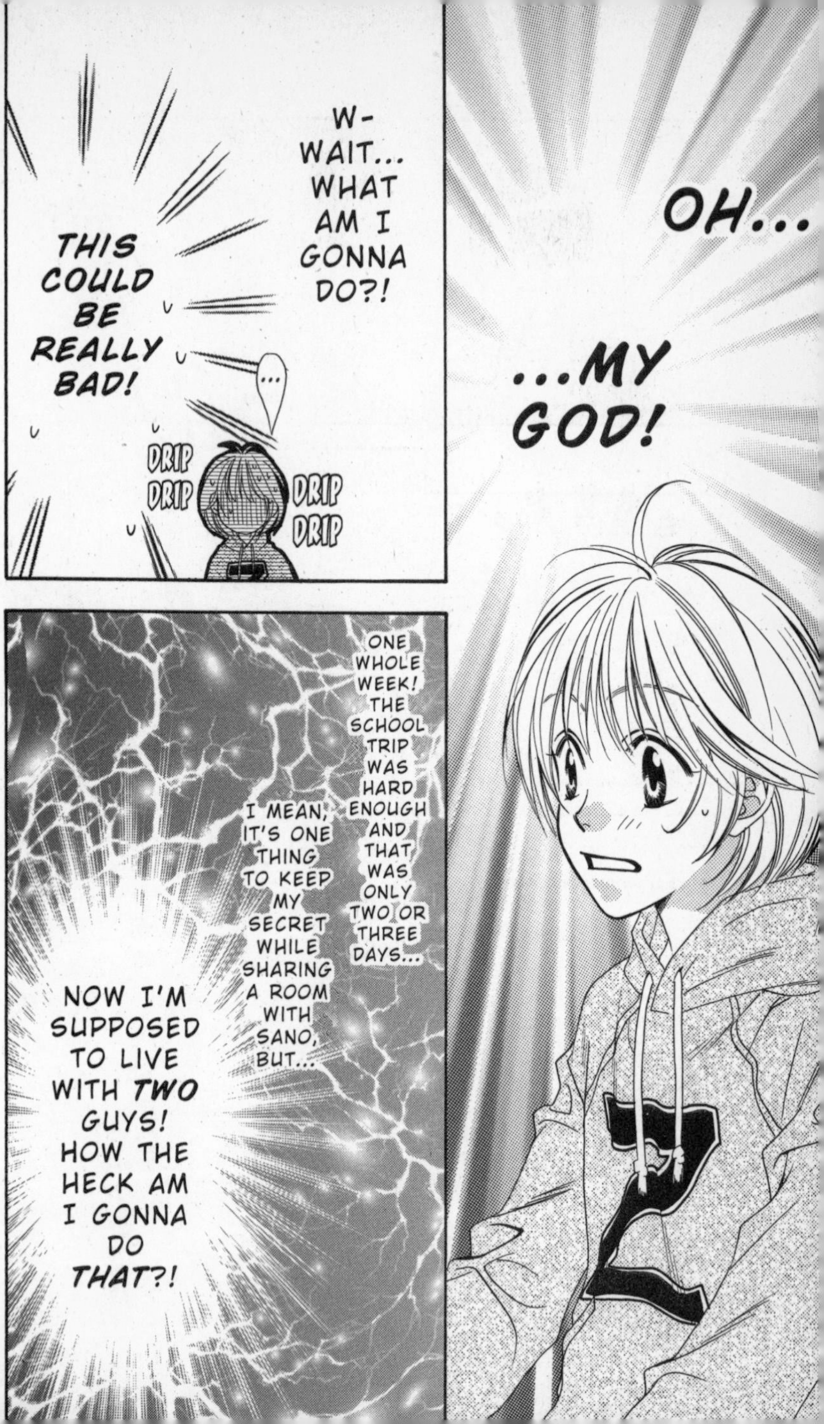
OH...
...MY GOD!
W-WAIT... WHAT AM I GONNA DO?!
THIS COULD BE REALLY BAD!
...
DRIP DRIP
DRIP DRIP
ONE WHOLE WEEK! THE SCHOOL TRIP WAS HARD ENOUGH AND THAT WAS ONLY TWO OR THREE DAYS...
I MEAN, IT'S ONE THING TO KEEP MY SECRET WHILE SHARING A ROOM WITH SANO, BUT...
NOW I'M SUPPOSED TO LIVE WITH TWO GUYS! HOW THE HECK AM I GONNA DO THAT?!

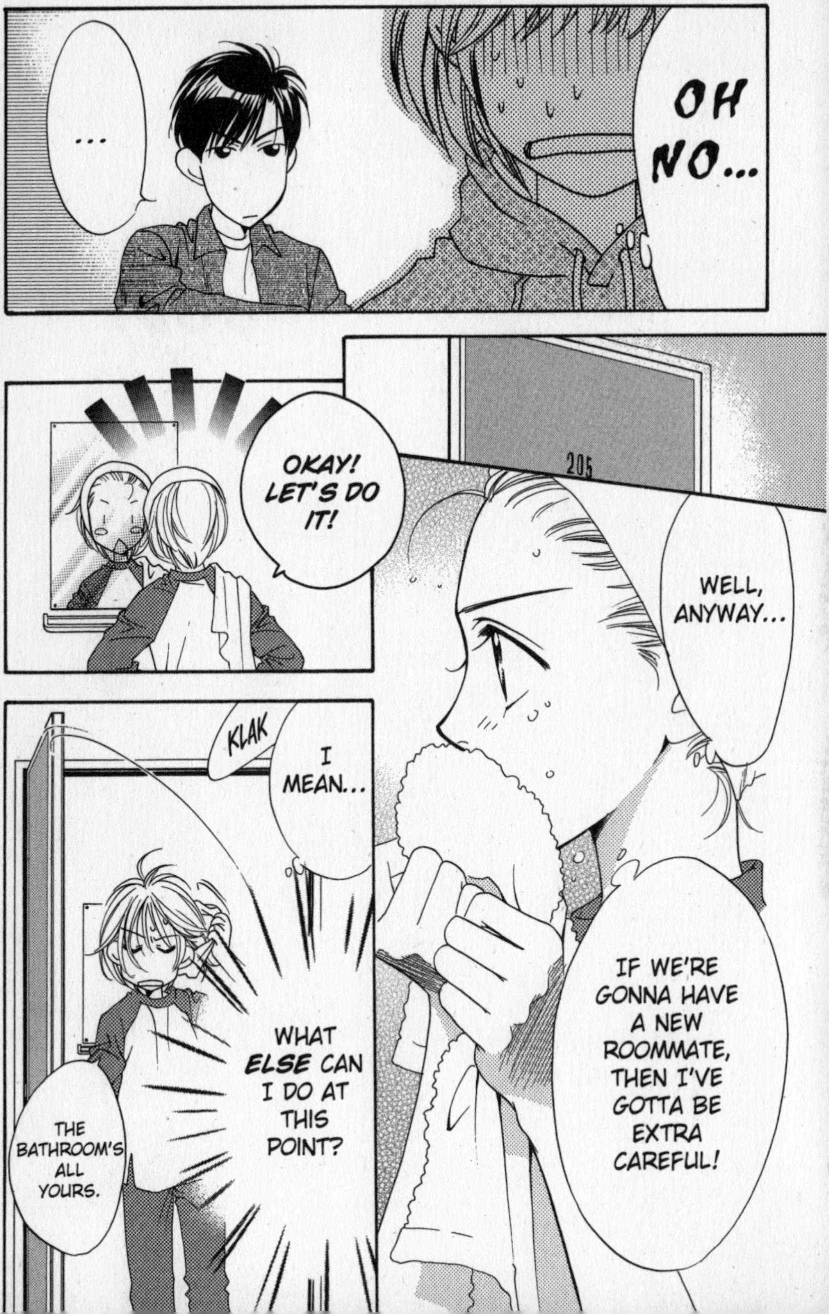
OH NO...
...
205
WELL, ANYWAY...
IF WE'RE GONNA HAVE A NEW ROOMMATE, THEN I'VE GOTTA BE EXTRA CAREFUL!
OKAY! LET'S DO IT!
KLAK
I MEAN...
WHAT ELSE CAN I DO AT THIS POINT?
THE BATHROOM'S ALL YOURS.

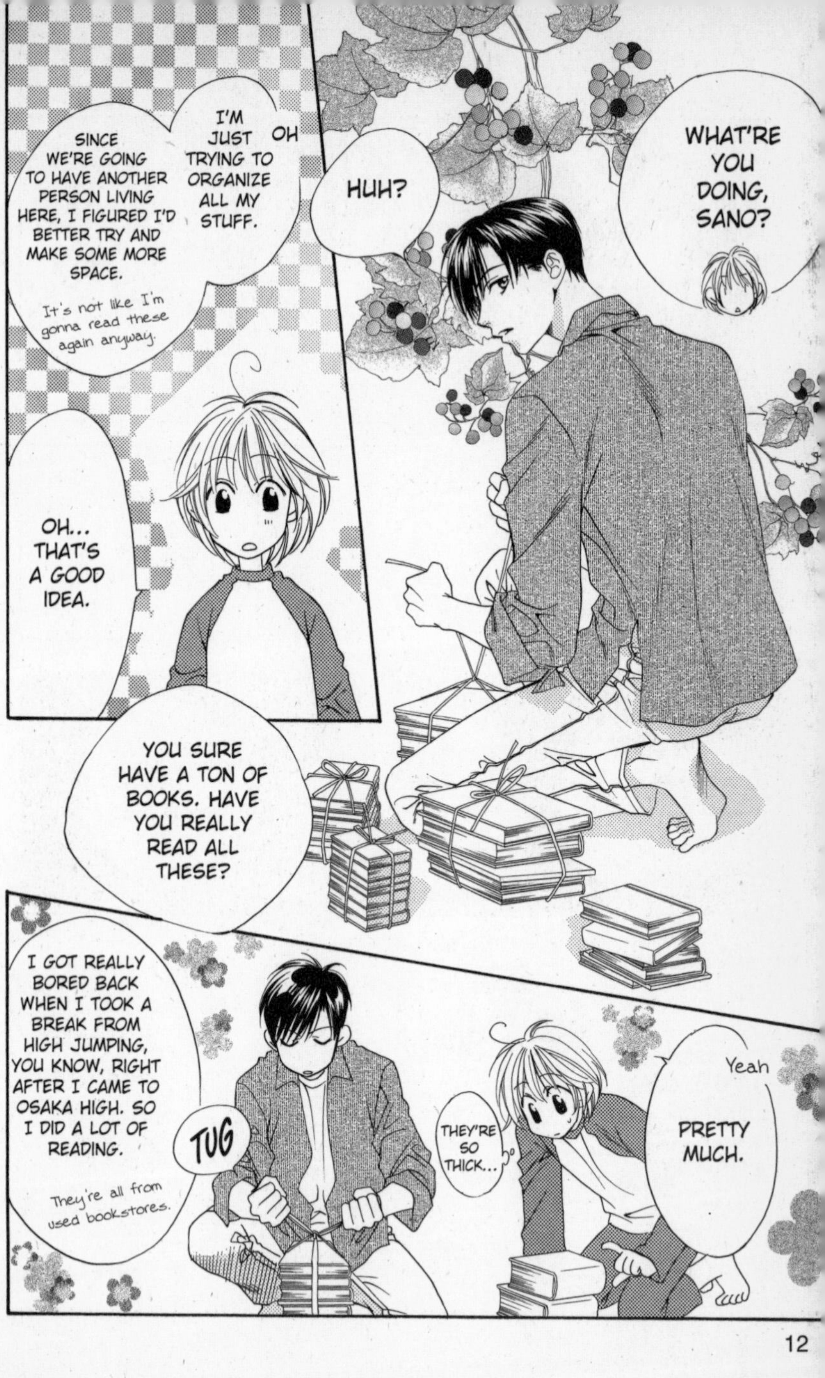
WHAT'RE YOU DOING, SANO?
HUH?
OH
I'M JUST TRYING TO ORGANIZE ALL MY STUFF.
SINCE WE'RE GOING TO HAVE ANOTHER PERSON LIVING HERE, I FIGURED I'D BETTER TRY AND MAKE SOME MORE SPACE.
It's not like I'm gonna read these again anyway.
OH... THAT'S A GOOD IDEA.
YOU SURE HAVE A TON OF BOOKS. HAVE YOU REALLY READ ALL THESE?
Yeah
PRETTY MUCH.
THEY'RE SO THICK...
TUG
I GOT REALLY BORED BACK WHEN I TOOK A BREAK FROM HIGH JUMPING, YOU KNOW, RIGHT AFTER I CAME TO OSAKA HIGH. SO I DID A LOT OF READING.
They're all from used bookstores.

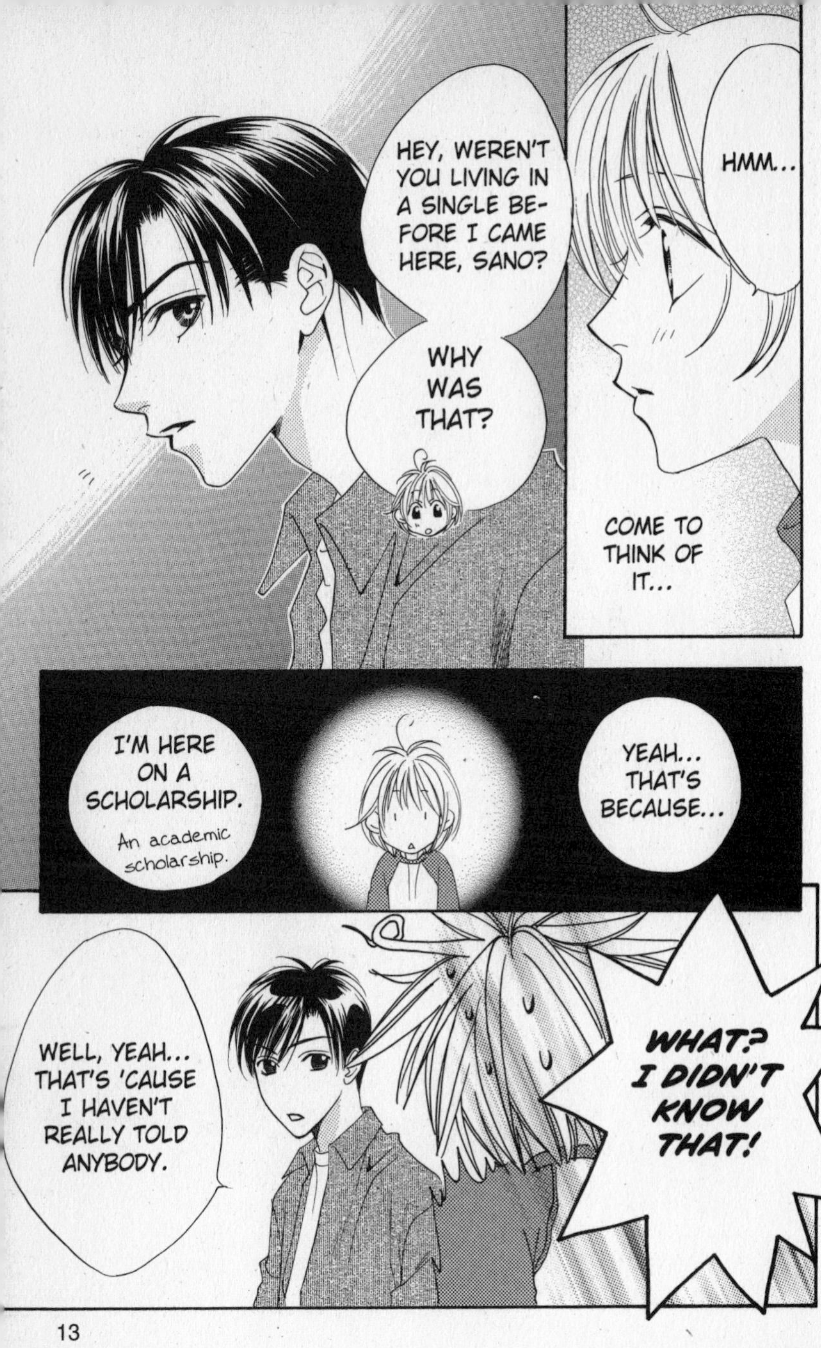
HMM...
COME TO THINK OF IT...
HEY, WEREN'T YOU LIVING IN A SINGLE BE-FORE I CAME HERE, SANO?
WHY WAS THAT?
YEAH... THAT'S BECAUSE...
I'M HERE ON A SCHOLARSHIP.
An academic scholarship.
WHAT? I DIDN'T KNOW THAT!
WELL, YEAH... THAT'S 'CAUSE I HAVEN'T REALLY TOLD ANYBODY.

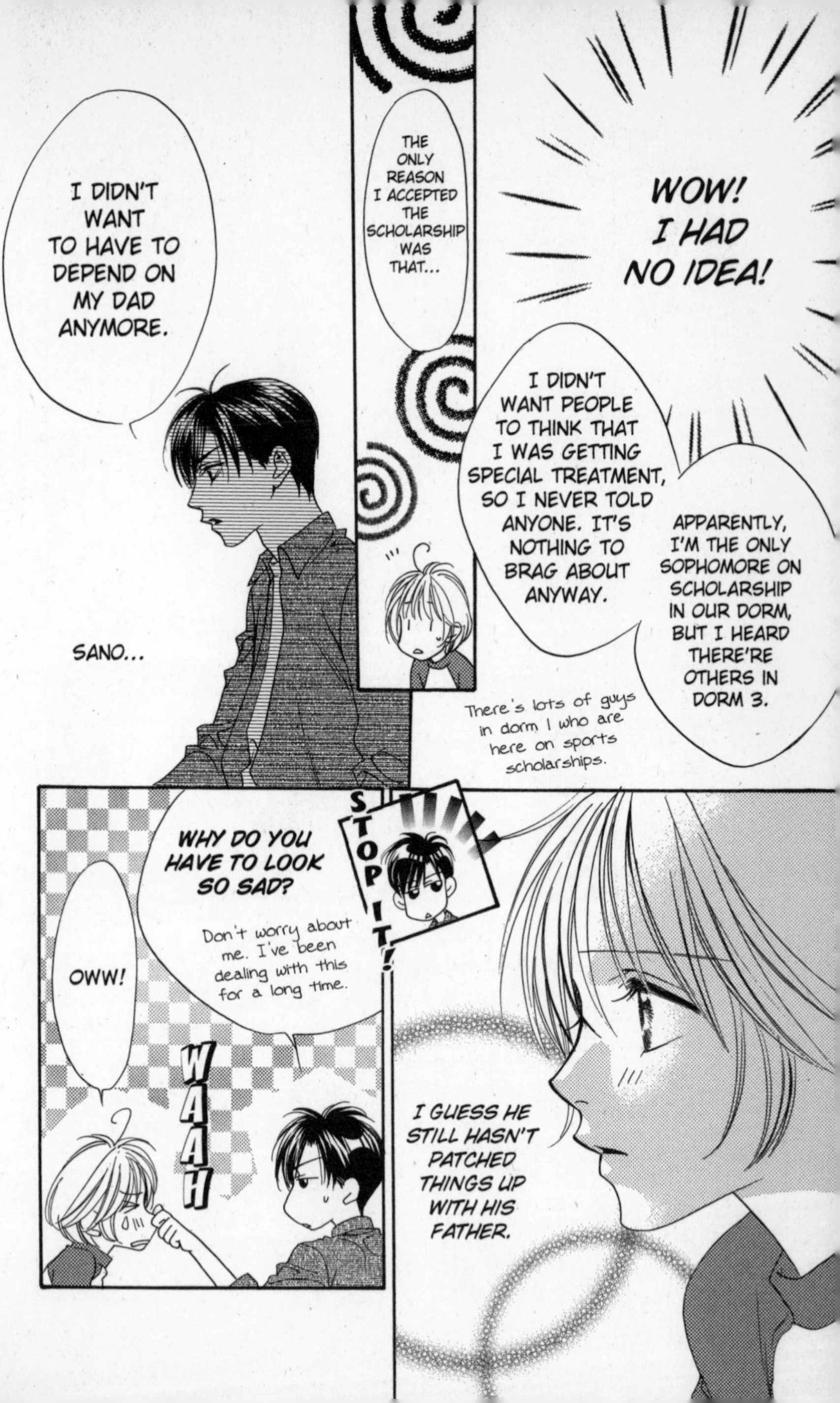
WOW! I HAD NO IDEA!
I DIDN'T WANT PEOPLE TO THINK THAT I WAS GETTING SPECIAL TREATMENT, SO I NEVER TOLD ANYONE. IT'S NOTHING TO BRAG ABOUT ANYWAY.
APPARENTLY, I'M THE ONLY SOPHOMORE ON SCHOLARSHIP IN OUR DORM, BUT I HEARD THERE'RE OTHERS IN DORM 3.
There's lots of guys in dorm 1 who are here on sports scholarships.
THE ONLY REASON I ACCEPTED THE SCHOLARSHIP WAS THAT...
I DIDN'T WANT TO HAVE TO DEPEND ON MY DAD ANYMORE.
SANO...
STOP IT!
I GUESS HE STILL HASN'T PATCHED THINGS UP WITH HIS FATHER.
WHY DO YOU HAVE TO LOOK SO SAD?
Don't worry about me. I've been dealing with this for a long time.
WAAAH
OWW!

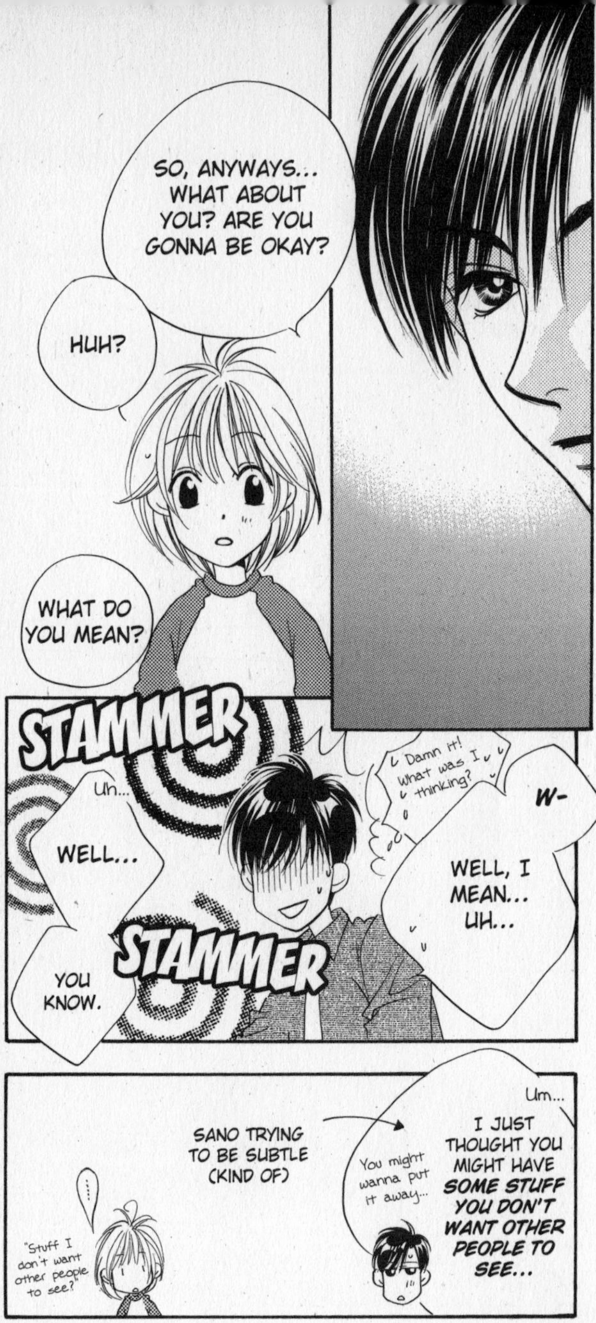
SO, ANYWAYS... WHAT ABOUT YOU? ARE YOU GONNA BE OKAY?
HUH?
WHAT DO YOU MEAN?
W-
Damn it! What was I thinking?
WELL, I MEAN... UH...
STAMMER
Uh...
WELL...
STAMMER
YOU KNOW.
Um...
I JUST THOUGHT YOU MIGHT HAVE **SOME STUFF YOU DON'T WANT OTHER PEOPLE TO SEE...**
You might wanna put it away...
SANO TRYING TO BE SUBTLE (KIND OF)
......
"Stuff I don't want other people to see?"

14

It's the new millennium! The 21st century! And the first Hana-Kimi book of the millennium is book 14! Umeda is on the cover... Did everyone guess that he'd be on it? Unfortunately, I haven't had time to draw many of the covers by myself lately. (I drew the covers for books 12 and 13, though.) I wonder who's going to be on the next cover. Will I get to draw the cover myself next time? I hope you're looking forward to book 15!

14

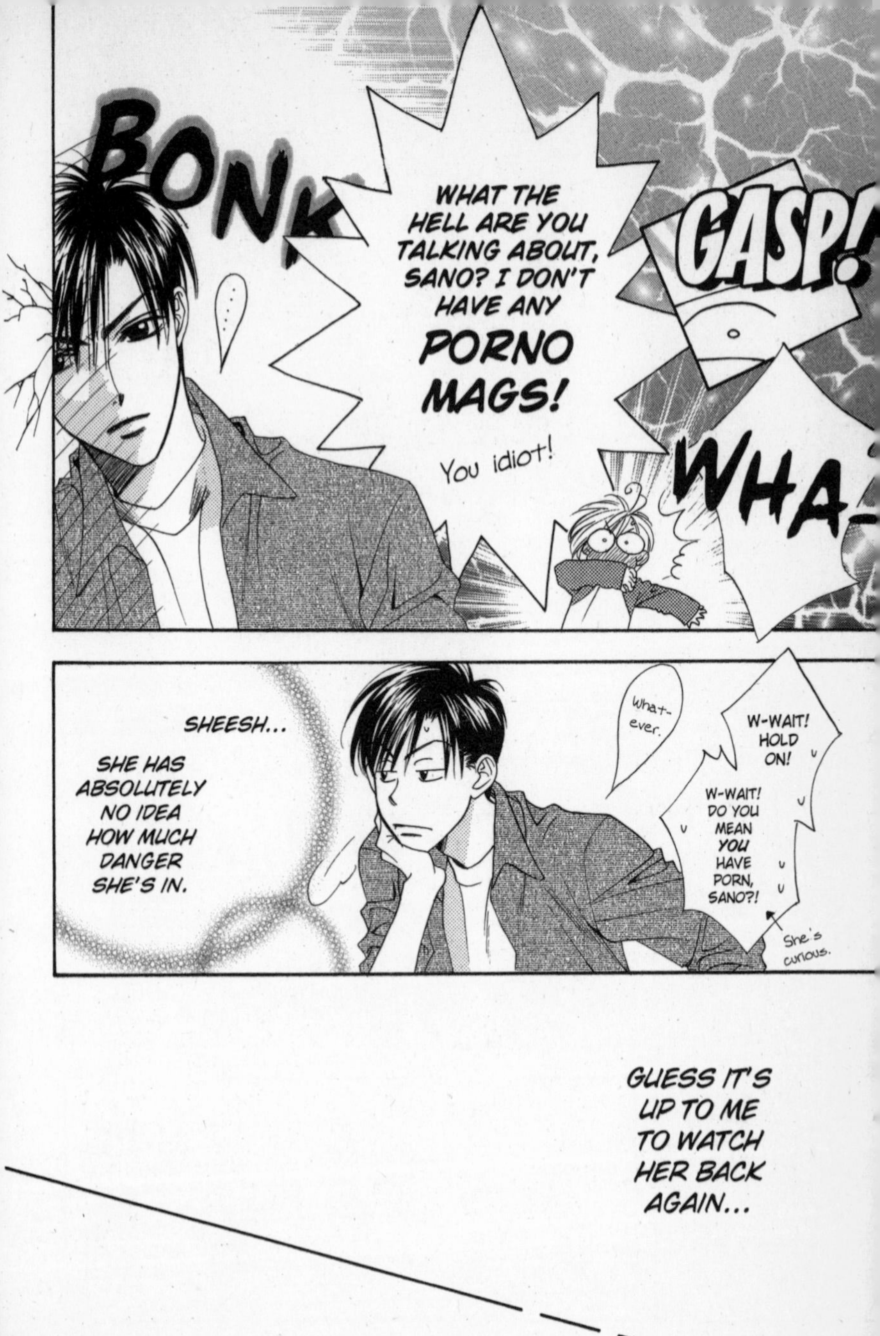
GASP!
WHAT THE HELL ARE YOU TALKING ABOUT, SANO? I DON'T HAVE ANY PORNO MAGS!
You idiot!
BONK
WHA-
W-WAIT! HOLD ON!
W-WAIT! DO YOU MEAN YOU HAVE PORN, SANO?!
She's curious.
What-ever.
SHEESH...
SHE HAS ABSOLUTELY NO IDEA HOW MUCH DANGER SHE'S IN.
GUESS IT'S UP TO ME TO WATCH HER BACK AGAIN...

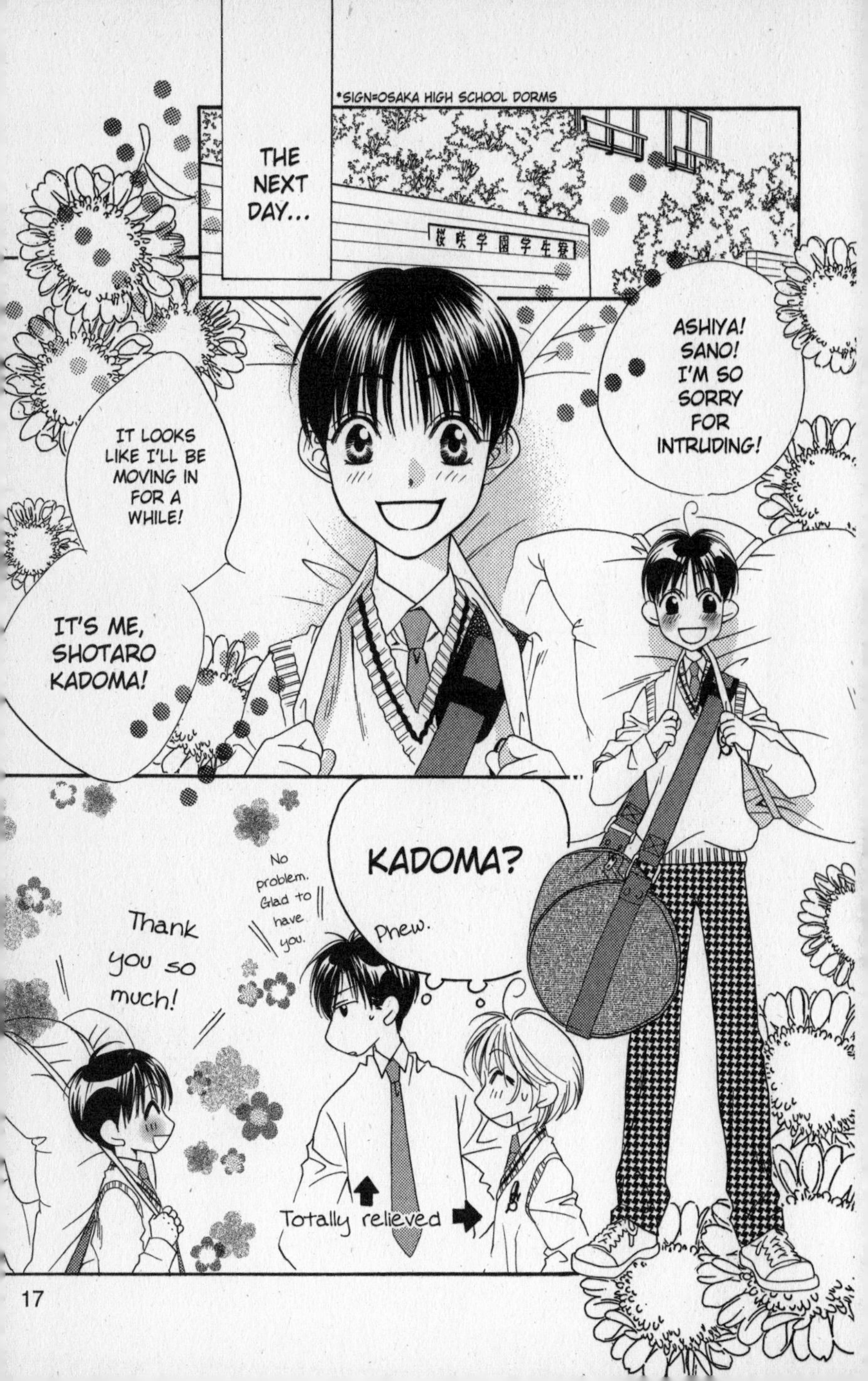
*SIGN=OSAKA HIGH SCHOOL DORMS
THE NEXT DAY...
桜咲学園学生寮
ASHIYA! SANO! I'M SO SORRY FOR INTRUDING!
IT LOOKS LIKE I'LL BE MOVING IN FOR A WHILE!
IT'S ME, SHOTARO KADOMA!
KADOMA?
Phew.
No problem. Glad to have you.
Thank you so much!
Totally relieved

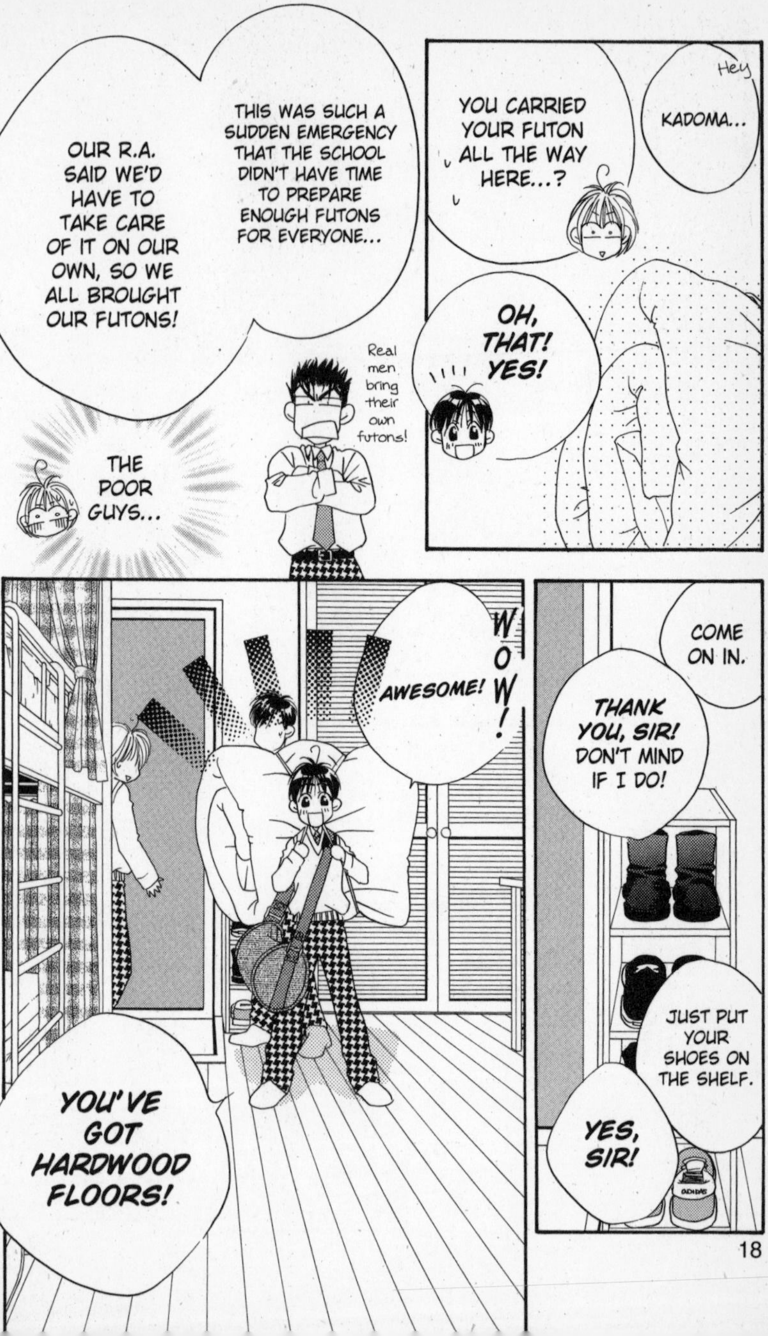
Hey
KADOMA...
YOU CARRIED YOUR FUTON ALL THE WAY HERE...?
OH, THAT! YES!
THIS WAS SUCH A SUDDEN EMERGENCY THAT THE SCHOOL DIDN'T HAVE TIME TO PREPARE ENOUGH FUTONS FOR EVERYONE...
OUR R.A. SAID WE'D HAVE TO TAKE CARE OF IT ON OUR OWN, SO WE ALL BROUGHT OUR FUTONS!
Real men bring their own futons!
THE POOR GUYS...
COME ON IN.
THANK YOU, SIR! DON'T MIND IF I DO!
JUST PUT YOUR SHOES ON THE SHELF.
YES, SIR!
AWESOME!
WOW!
YOU'VE GOT HARDWOOD FLOORS!

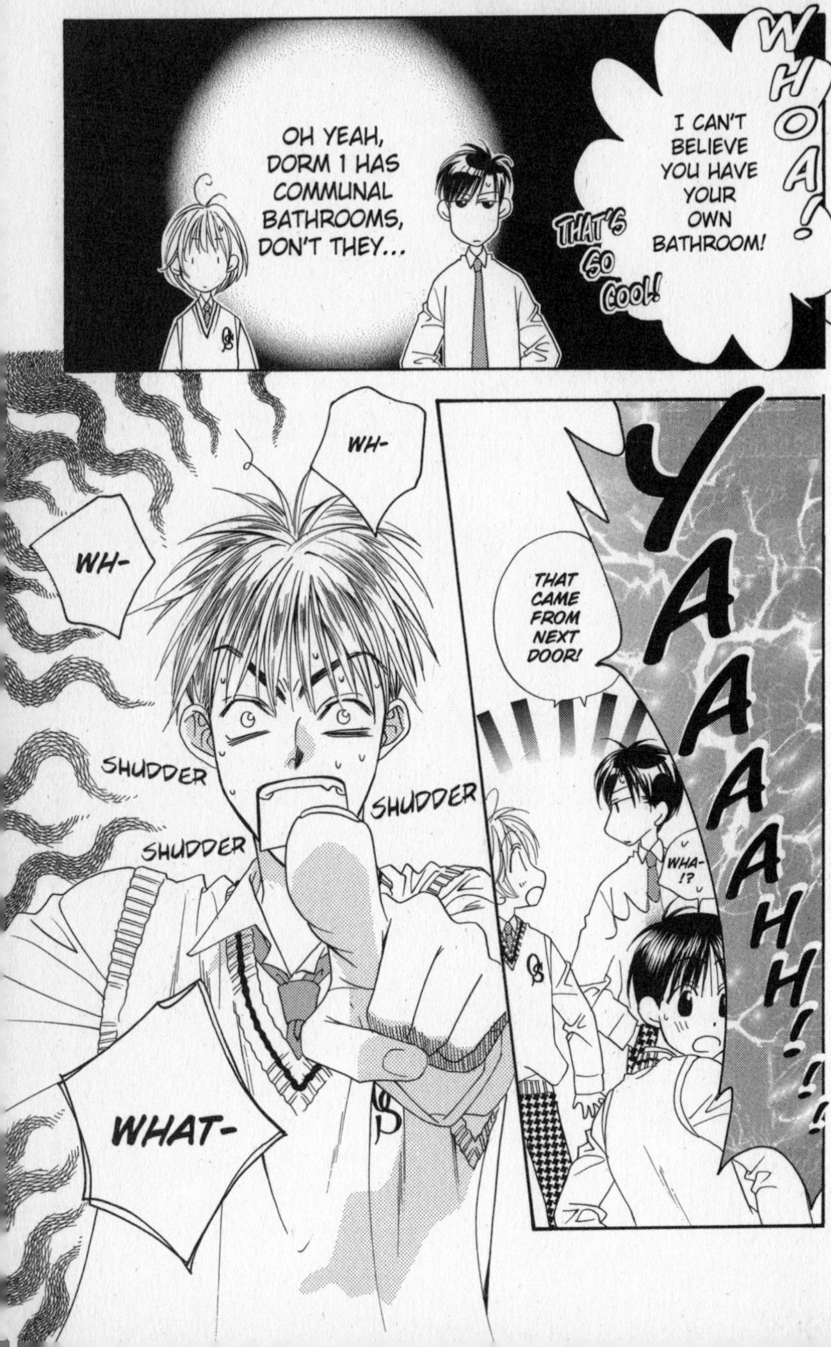
WHOA!
I CAN'T BELIEVE YOU HAVE YOUR OWN BATHROOM!
THAT'S SO COOL!
OH YEAH, DORM 1 HAS COMMUNAL BATHROOMS, DON'T THEY...
YAAAAAHH!!!
THAT CAME FROM NEXT DOOR!
WHA-!?
WH-
WH-
SHUDDER
SHUDDER
SHUDDER
WHAT-

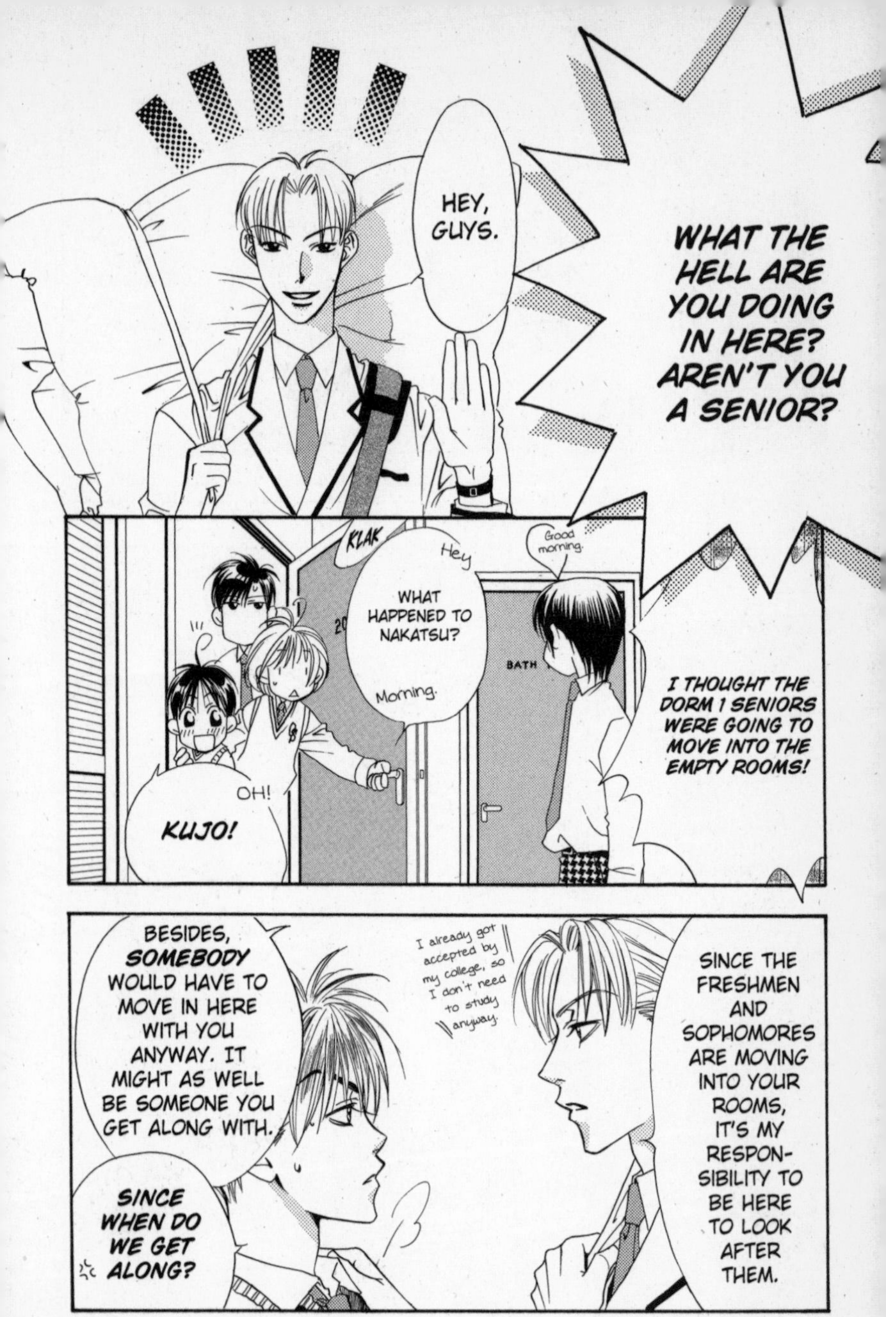
HEY, GUYS.
WHAT THE HELL ARE YOU DOING IN HERE? AREN'T YOU A SENIOR?
I THOUGHT THE DORM 1 SENIORS WERE GOING TO MOVE INTO THE EMPTY ROOMS!
Good morning.
KLAK
Hey
WHAT HAPPENED TO NAKATSU?
Morning.
BATH
OH!
KUJO!
SINCE THE FRESHMEN AND SOPHOMORES ARE MOVING INTO YOUR ROOMS, IT'S MY RESPONSIBILITY TO BE HERE TO LOOK AFTER THEM.
I already got accepted by my college, so I don't need to study anyway.
BESIDES, SOMEBODY WOULD HAVE TO MOVE IN HERE WITH YOU ANYWAY. IT MIGHT AS WELL BE SOMEONE YOU GET ALONG WITH.
SINCE WHEN DO WE GET ALONG?

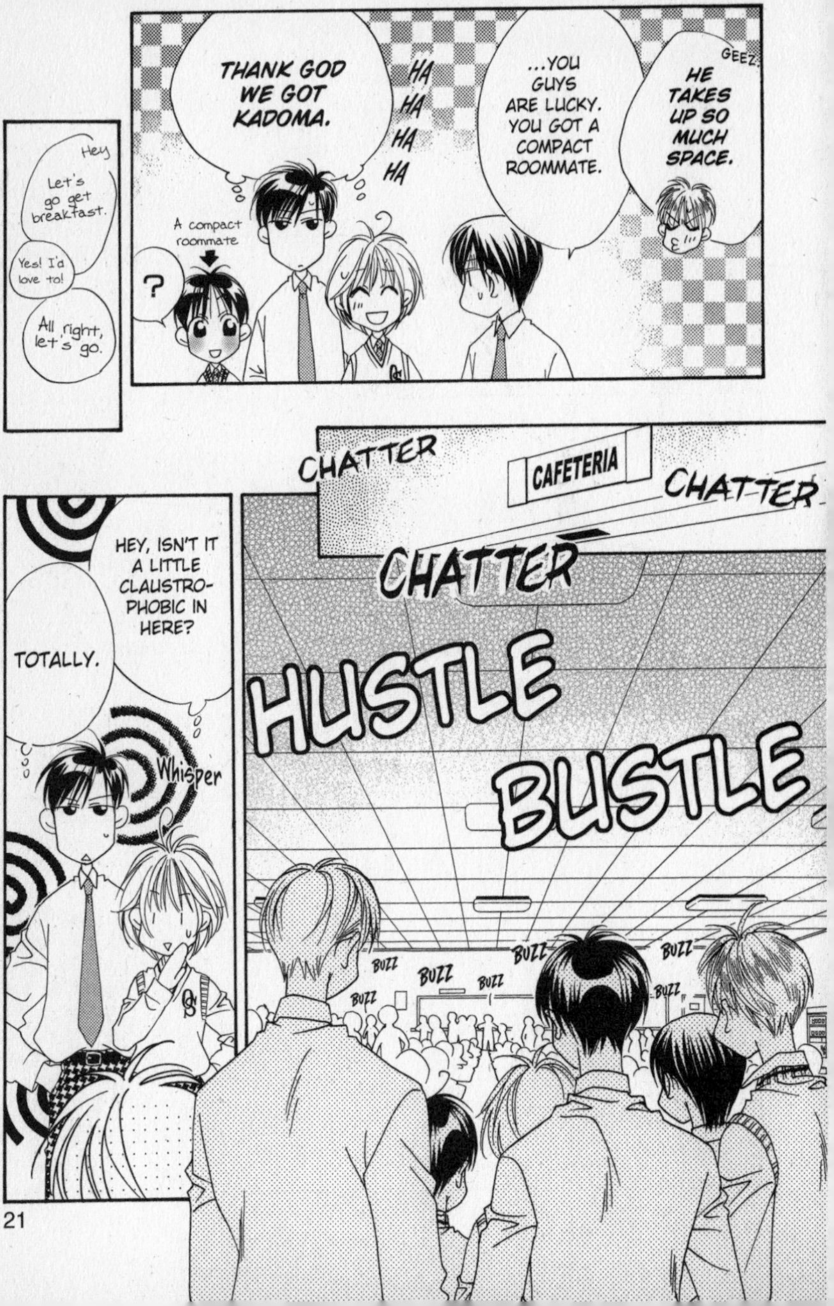

GEEZ
HE TAKES UP SO MUCH SPACE.
...YOU GUYS ARE LUCKY. YOU GOT A COMPACT ROOMMATE.
HA HA HA HA
THANK GOD WE GOT KADOMA.
A compact roommate
?
Hey
Let's go get breakfast.
Yes! I'd love to!
All right, let's go.
CHATTER
CAFETERIA
CHATTER
CHATTER
HUSTLE
BUSTLE
BUZZ
BUZZ
BUZZ
BUZZ
BUZZ
BUZZ
BUZZ
HEY, ISN'T IT A LITTLE CLAUSTRO-PHOBIC IN HERE?
TOTALLY.
Whisper

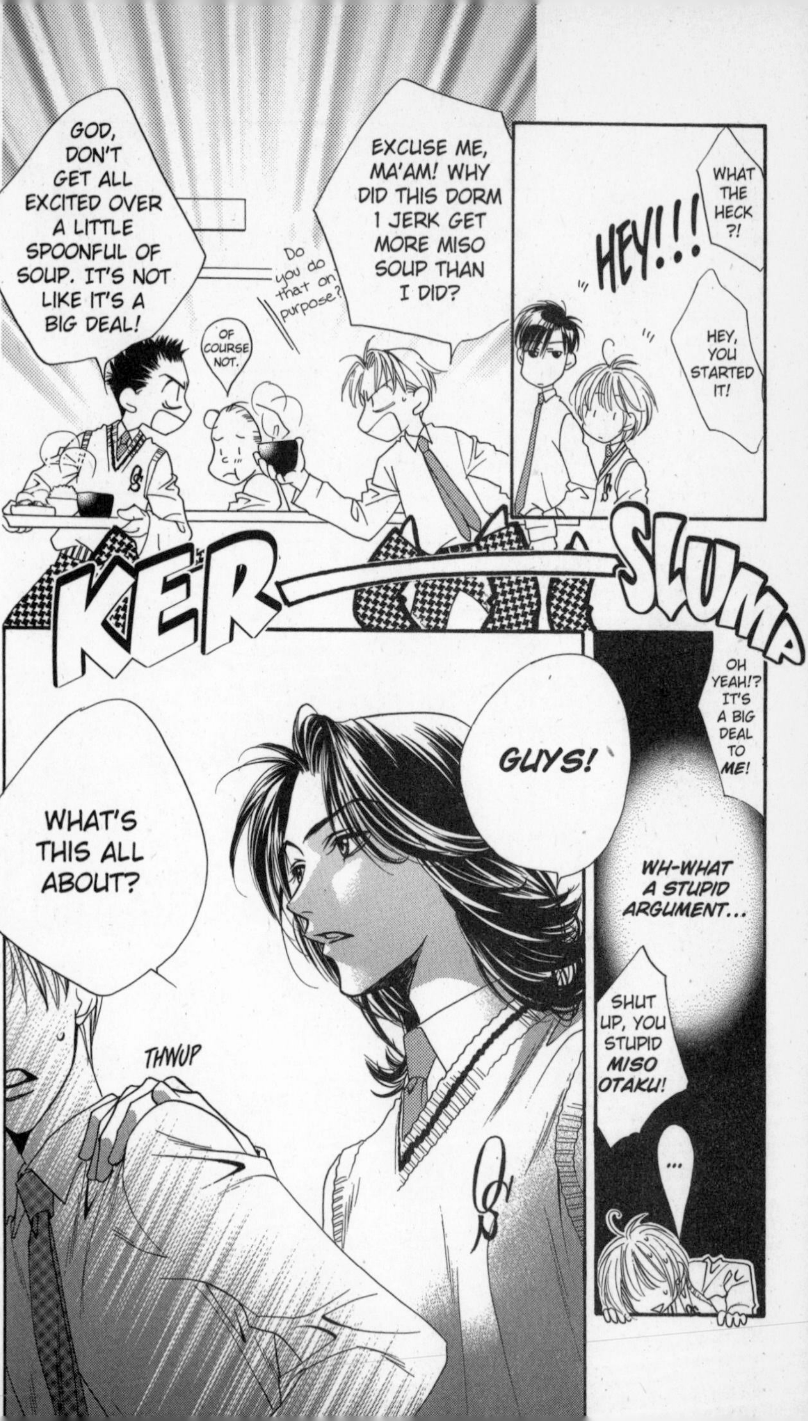
HEY!!!
WHAT THE HECK?!
HEY, YOU STARTED IT!
EXCUSE ME, MA'AM! WHY DID THIS DORM 1 JERK GET MORE MISO SOUP THAN I DID?
Do you do that on purpose?
OF COURSE NOT.
GOD, DON'T GET ALL EXCITED OVER A LITTLE SPOONFUL OF SOUP. IT'S NOT LIKE IT'S A BIG DEAL!
KER—SLUMP
OH YEAH!? IT'S A BIG DEAL TO ME!
WH-WHAT A STUPID ARGUMENT...
SHUT UP, YOU STUPID MISO OTAKU!
...
GUYS!
WHAT'S THIS ALL ABOUT?
THWUP

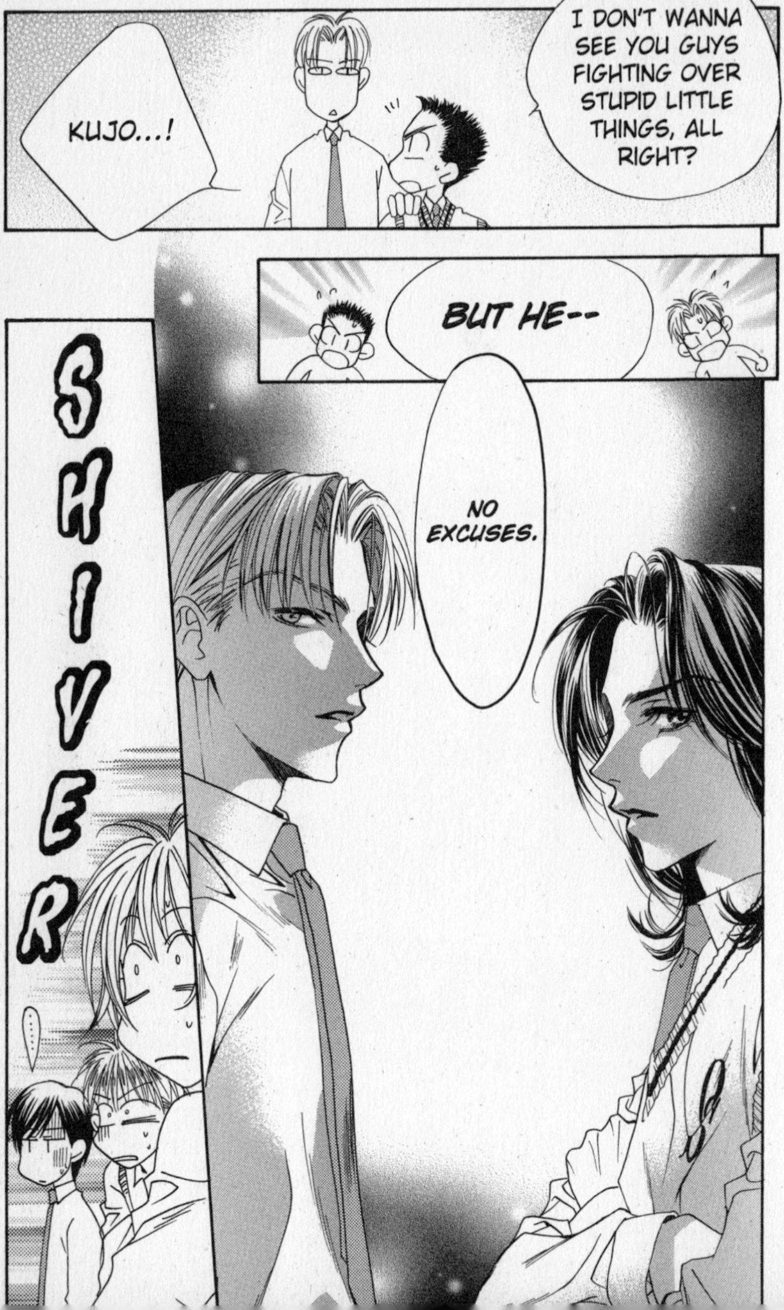
I DON'T WANNA SEE YOU GUYS FIGHTING OVER STUPID LITTLE THINGS, ALL RIGHT?
KUJO...!
BUT HE--
NO EXCUSES.
SHIVER
...!

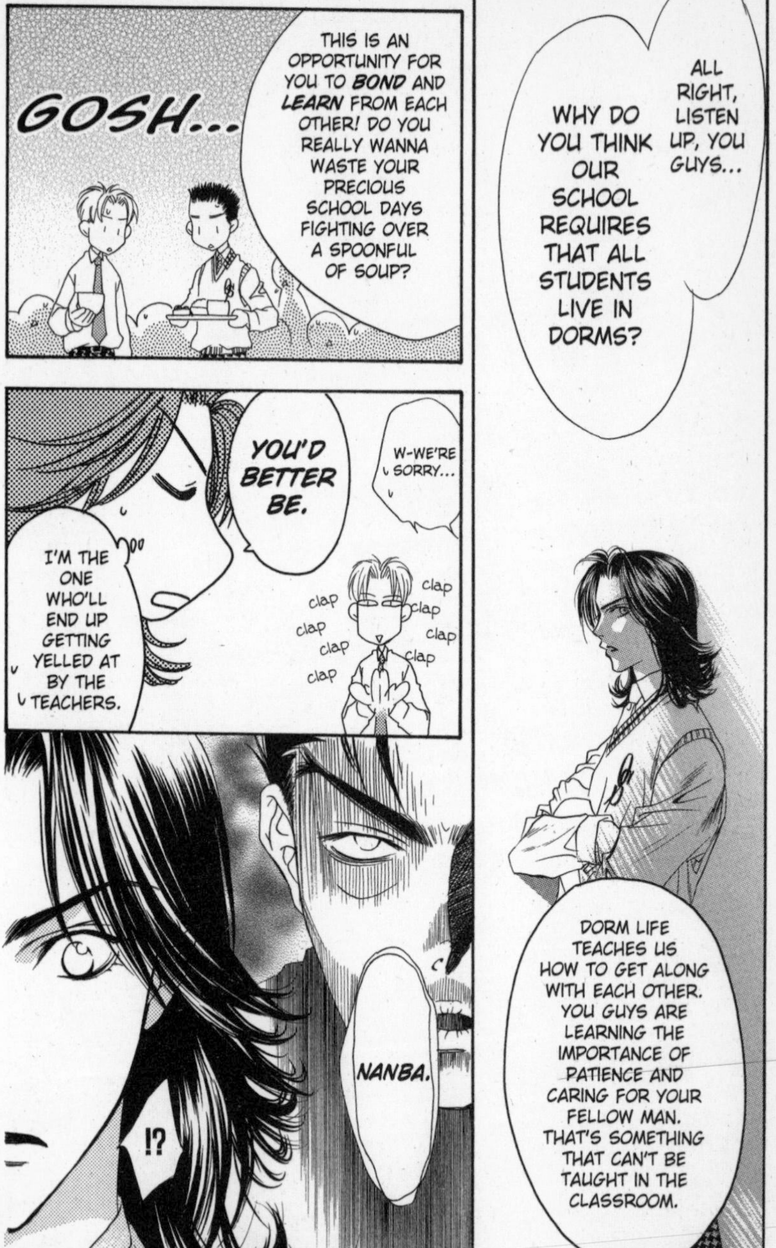
ALL RIGHT, LISTEN UP, YOU GUYS...
WHY DO YOU THINK OUR SCHOOL REQUIRES THAT ALL STUDENTS LIVE IN DORMS?
DORM LIFE TEACHES US HOW TO GET ALONG WITH EACH OTHER. YOU GUYS ARE LEARNING THE IMPORTANCE OF PATIENCE AND CARING FOR YOUR FELLOW MAN. THAT'S SOMETHING THAT CAN'T BE TAUGHT IN THE CLASSROOM.
THIS IS AN OPPORTUNITY FOR YOU TO BOND AND LEARN FROM EACH OTHER! DO YOU REALLY WANNA WASTE YOUR PRECIOUS SCHOOL DAYS FIGHTING OVER A SPOONFUL OF SOUP?
GOSH...
W-WE'RE SORRY...
YOU'D BETTER BE.
I'M THE ONE WHO'LL END UP GETTING YELLED AT BY THE TEACHERS.
clap clap clap clap clap clap clap clap clap
NANBA.
!?

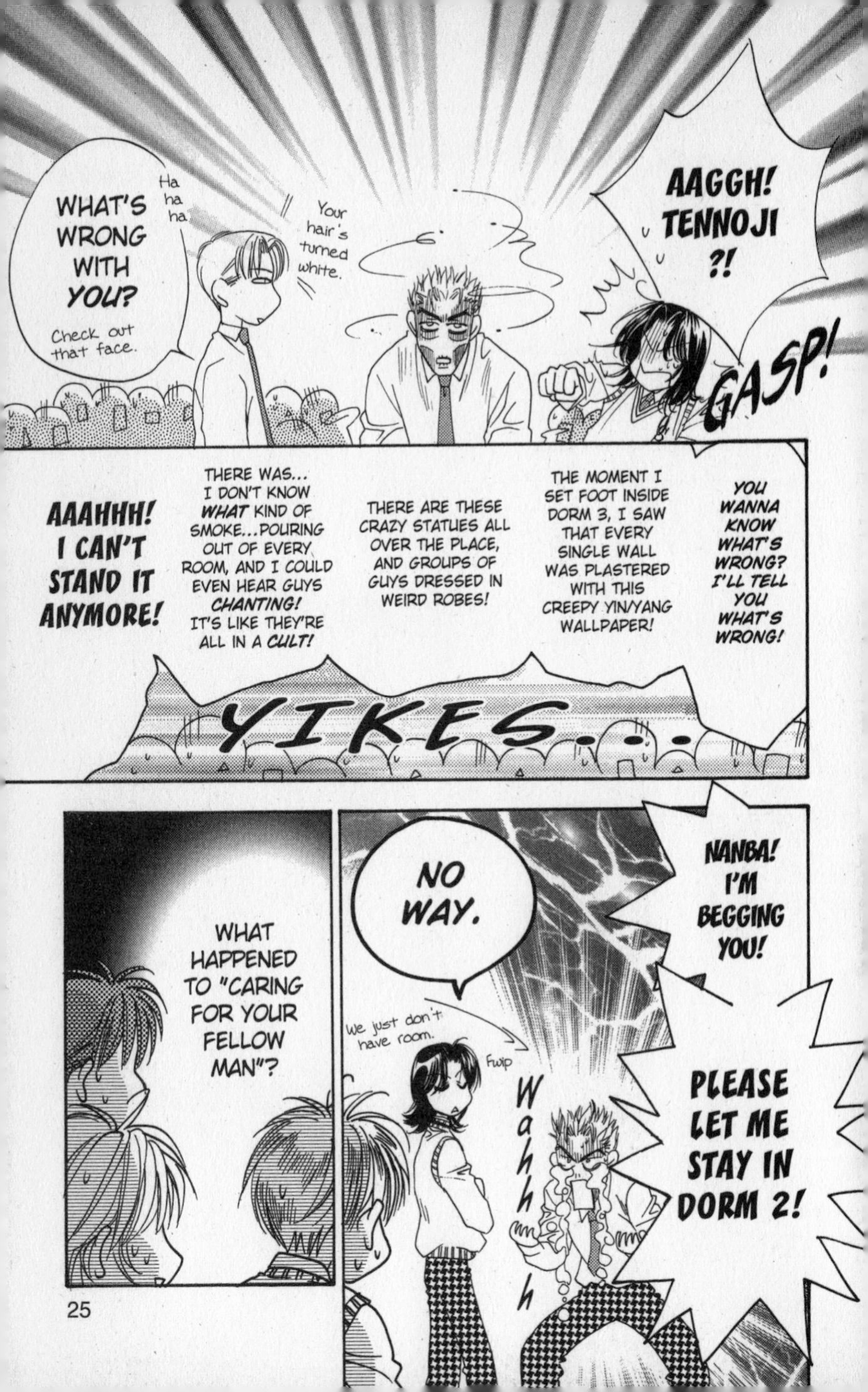
AAGGH! TENNOJI ?!
GASP!
Your hair's turned white.
Ha ha ha
WHAT'S WRONG WITH YOU?
Check out that face.
YOU WANNA KNOW WHAT'S WRONG? I'LL TELL YOU WHAT'S WRONG!
THE MOMENT I SET FOOT INSIDE DORM 3, I SAW THAT EVERY SINGLE WALL WAS PLASTERED WITH THIS CREEPY YIN/YANG WALLPAPER!
THERE ARE THESE CRAZY STATUES ALL OVER THE PLACE, AND GROUPS OF GUYS DRESSED IN WEIRD ROBES!
THERE WAS... I DON'T KNOW WHAT KIND OF SMOKE...POURING OUT OF EVERY ROOM, AND I COULD EVEN HEAR GUYS CHANTING! IT'S LIKE THEY'RE ALL IN A CULT!
AAAHHH! I CAN'T STAND IT ANYMORE!
YIKES...
NANBA! I'M BEGGING YOU!
NO WAY.
PLEASE LET ME STAY IN DORM 2!
Wahhh
Fwip
We just don't have room.
WHAT HAPPENED TO "CARING FOR YOUR FELLOW MAN"?

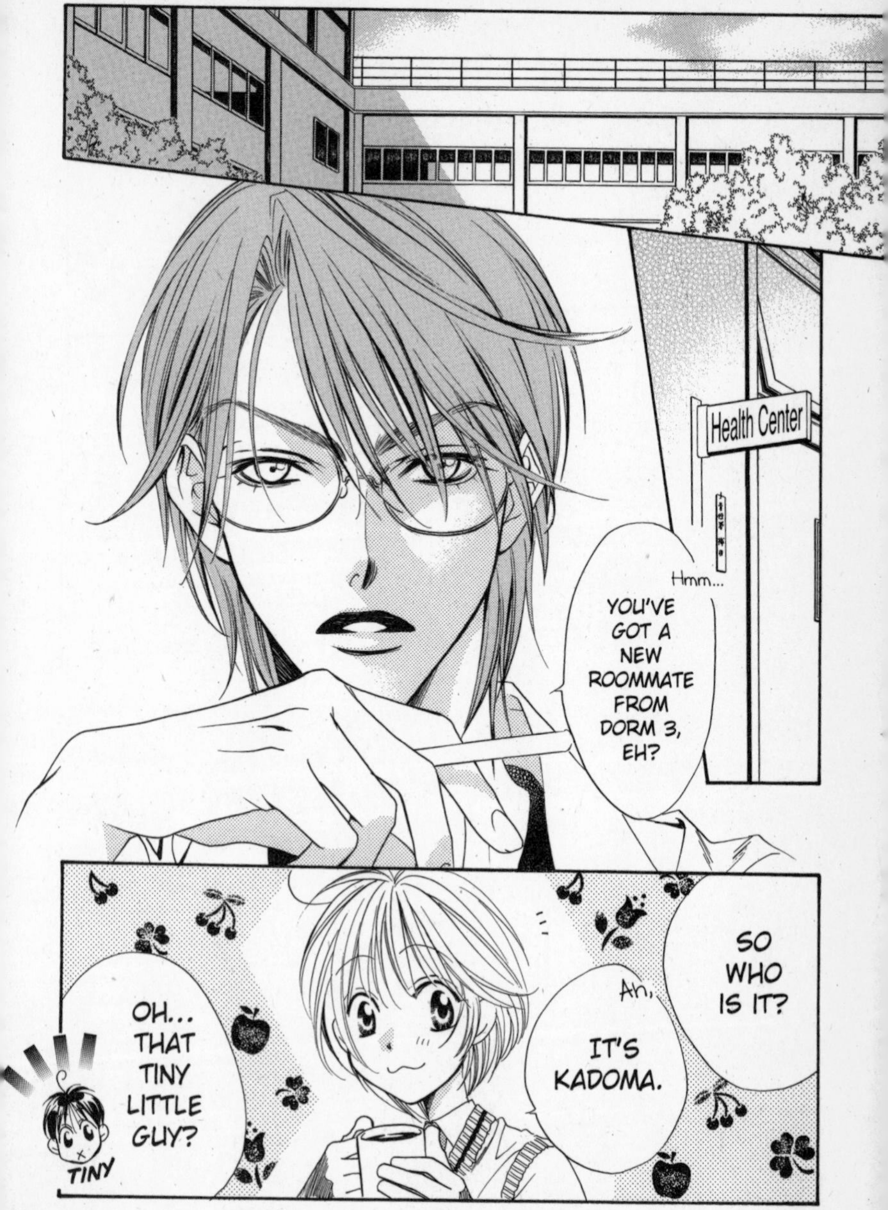
Health Center
Hmm...
YOU'VE GOT A NEW ROOMMATE FROM DORM 3, EH?
SO WHO IS IT?
Ah,
IT'S KADOMA.
OH... THAT TINY LITTLE GUY?
TINY

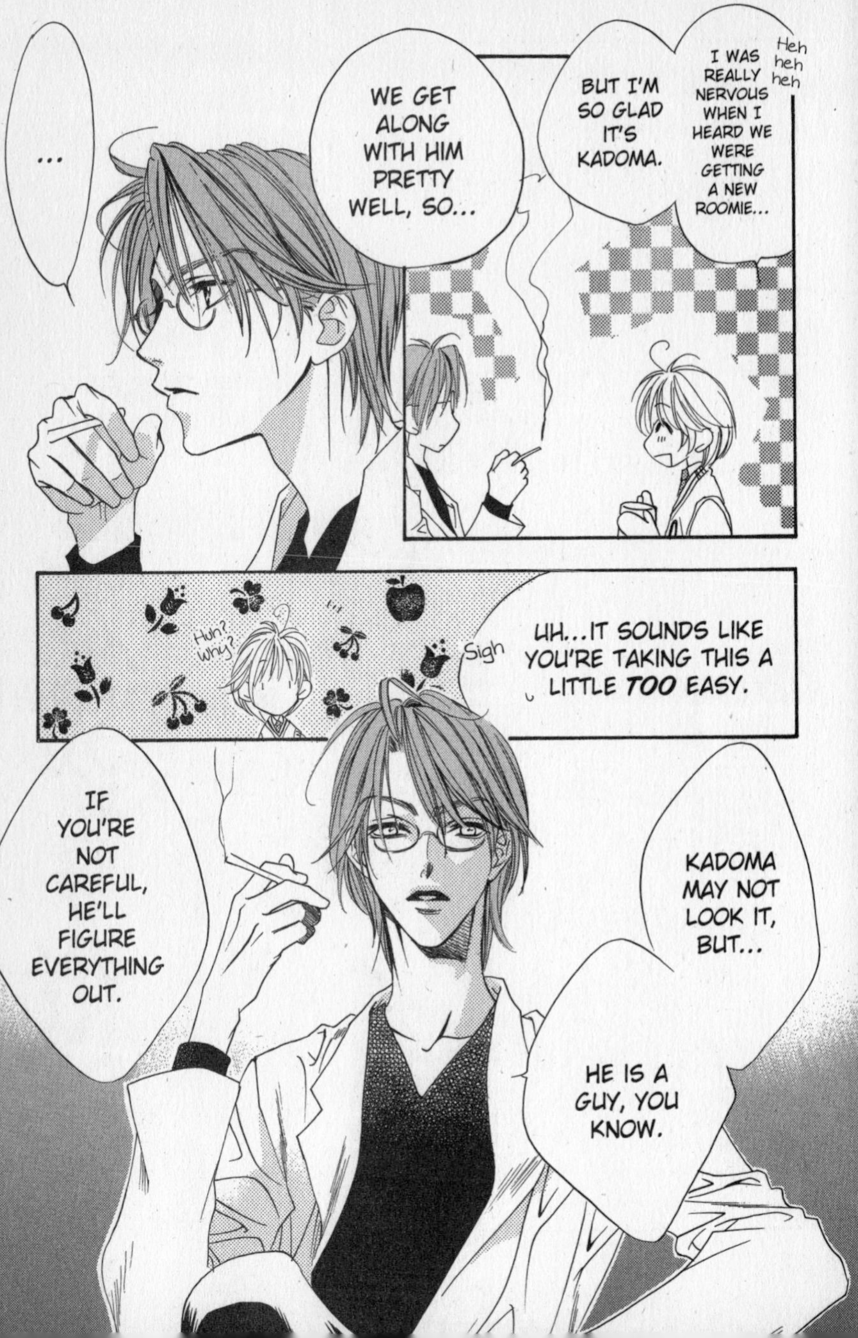
I WAS REALLY NERVOUS WHEN I HEARD WE WERE GETTING A NEW ROOMIE...
Heh heh heh
BUT I'M SO GLAD IT'S KADOMA.
WE GET ALONG WITH HIM PRETTY WELL, SO...
...
UH...IT SOUNDS LIKE YOU'RE TAKING THIS A LITTLE TOO EASY.
Sigh
Huh? Why?
KADOMA MAY NOT LOOK IT, BUT...
HE IS A GUY, YOU KNOW.
IF YOU'RE NOT CAREFUL, HE'LL FIGURE EVERYTHING OUT.

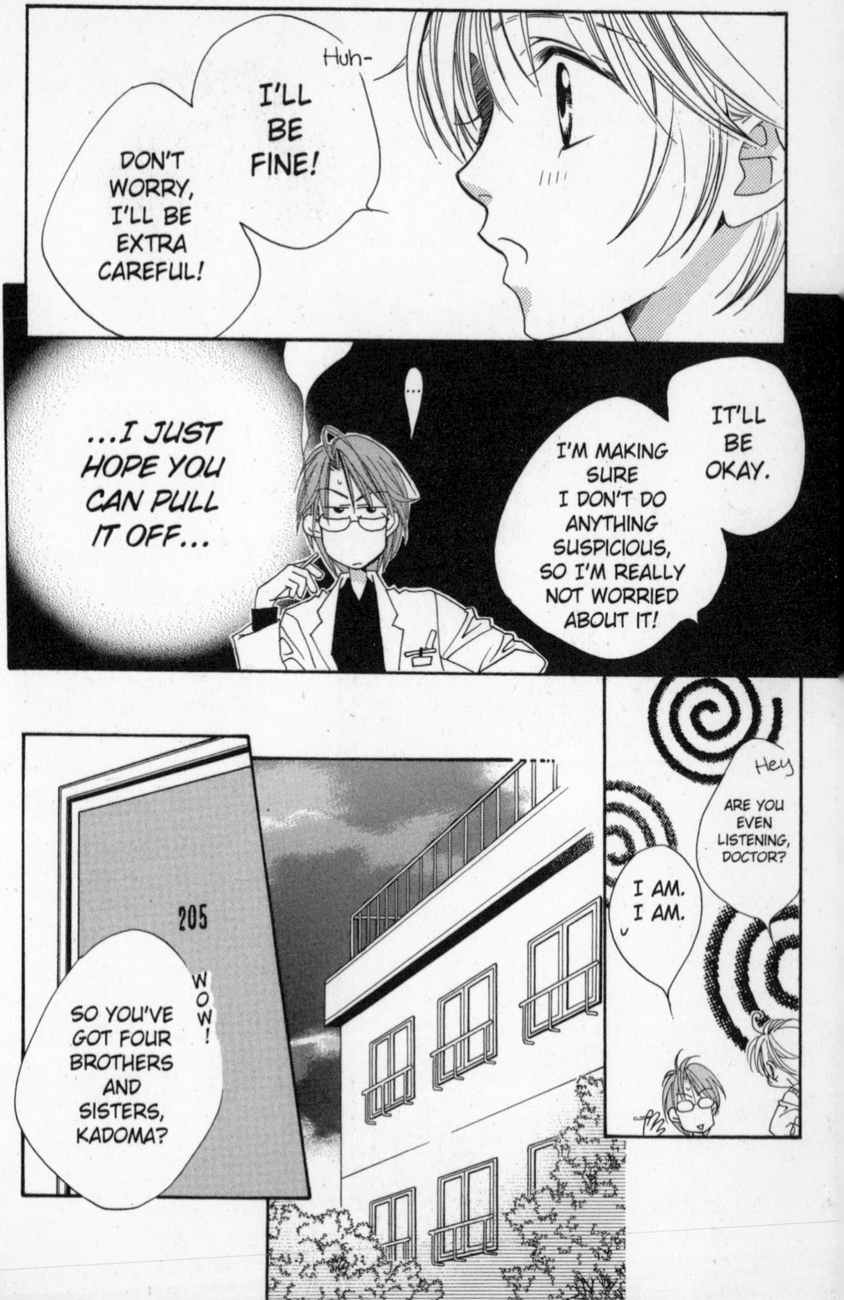
Huh-
I'LL BE FINE!
DON'T WORRY, I'LL BE EXTRA CAREFUL!
IT'LL BE OKAY.
I'M MAKING SURE I DON'T DO ANYTHING SUSPICIOUS, SO I'M REALLY NOT WORRIED ABOUT IT!
...
...I JUST HOPE YOU CAN PULL IT OFF...
Hey
ARE YOU EVEN LISTENING, DOCTOR?
I AM. I AM.
205
WOW!
SO YOU'VE GOT FOUR BROTHERS AND SISTERS, KADOMA?

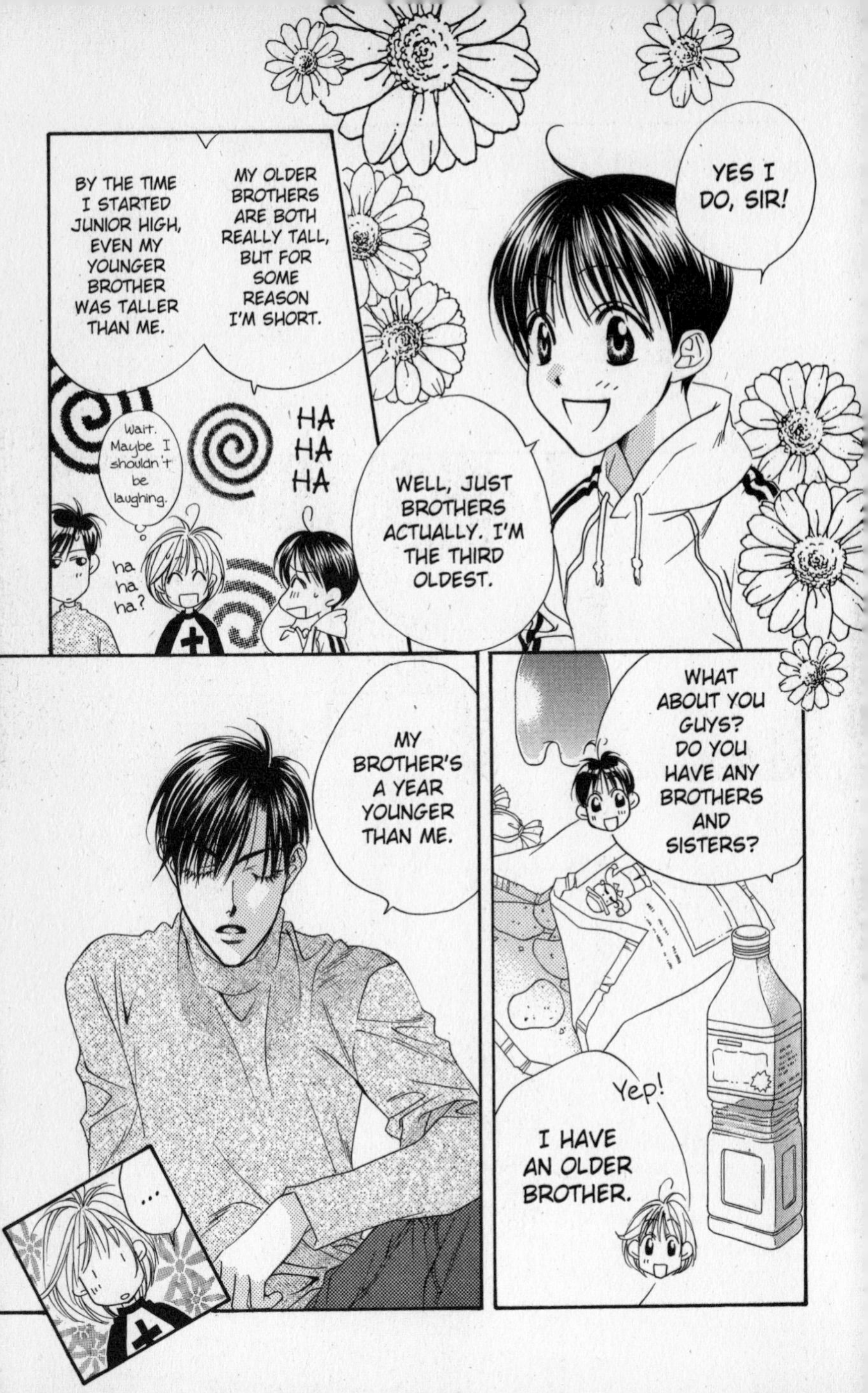
YES I DO, SIR!
WELL, JUST BROTHERS ACTUALLY. I'M THE THIRD OLDEST.
MY OLDER BROTHERS ARE BOTH REALLY TALL, BUT FOR SOME REASON I'M SHORT.
BY THE TIME I STARTED JUNIOR HIGH, EVEN MY YOUNGER BROTHER WAS TALLER THAN ME.
HA HA HA
Wait. Maybe I shouldn't be laughing.
ha ha ha?
WHAT ABOUT YOU GUYS? DO YOU HAVE ANY BROTHERS AND SISTERS?
Yep!
I HAVE AN OLDER BROTHER.
MY BROTHER'S A YEAR YOUNGER THAN ME.
...

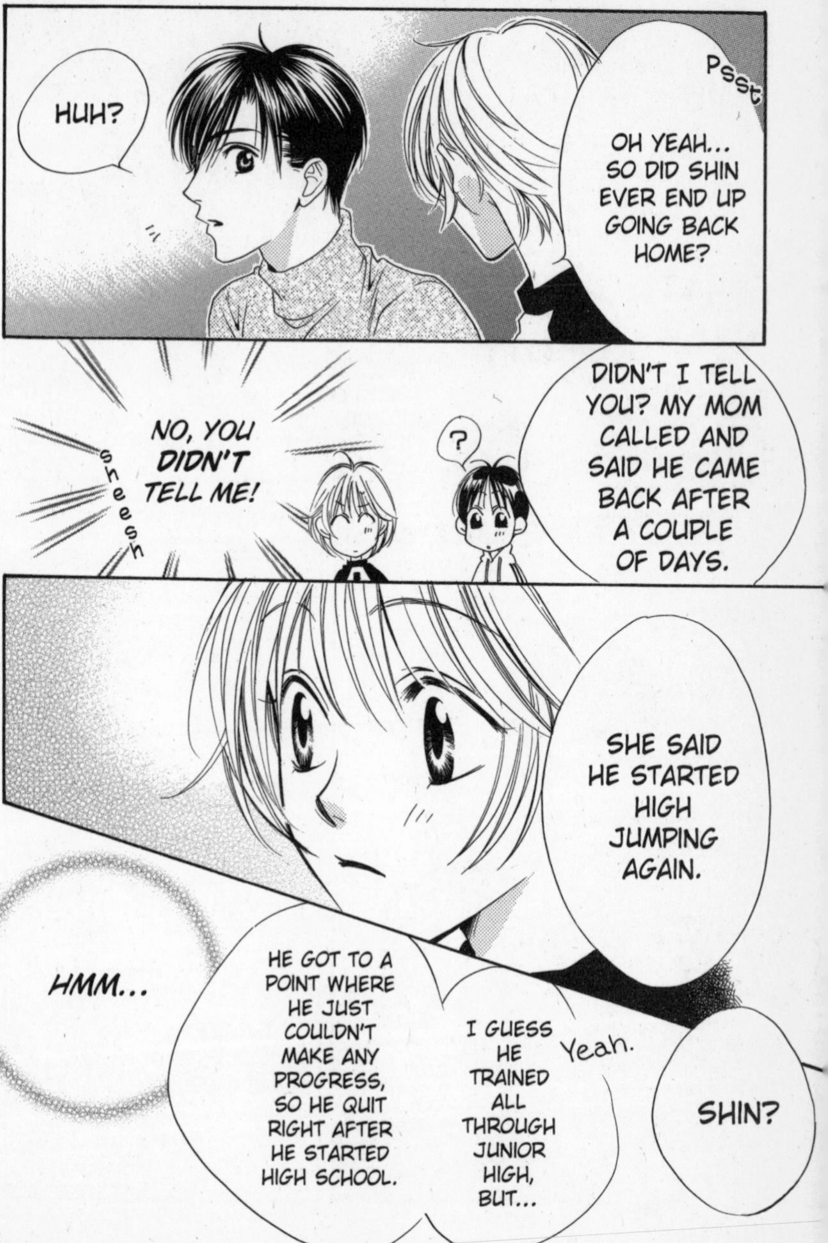
Pssst
OH YEAH... SO DID SHIN EVER END UP GOING BACK HOME?
HUH?
DIDN'T I TELL YOU? MY MOM CALLED AND SAID HE CAME BACK AFTER A COUPLE OF DAYS.
?
NO, YOU DIDN'T TELL ME!
sheesh
SHE SAID HE STARTED HIGH JUMPING AGAIN.
SHIN?
Yeah.
I GUESS HE TRAINED ALL THROUGH JUNIOR HIGH, BUT...
HE GOT TO A POINT WHERE HE JUST COULDN'T MAKE ANY PROGRESS, SO HE QUIT RIGHT AFTER HE STARTED HIGH SCHOOL.
HMM...

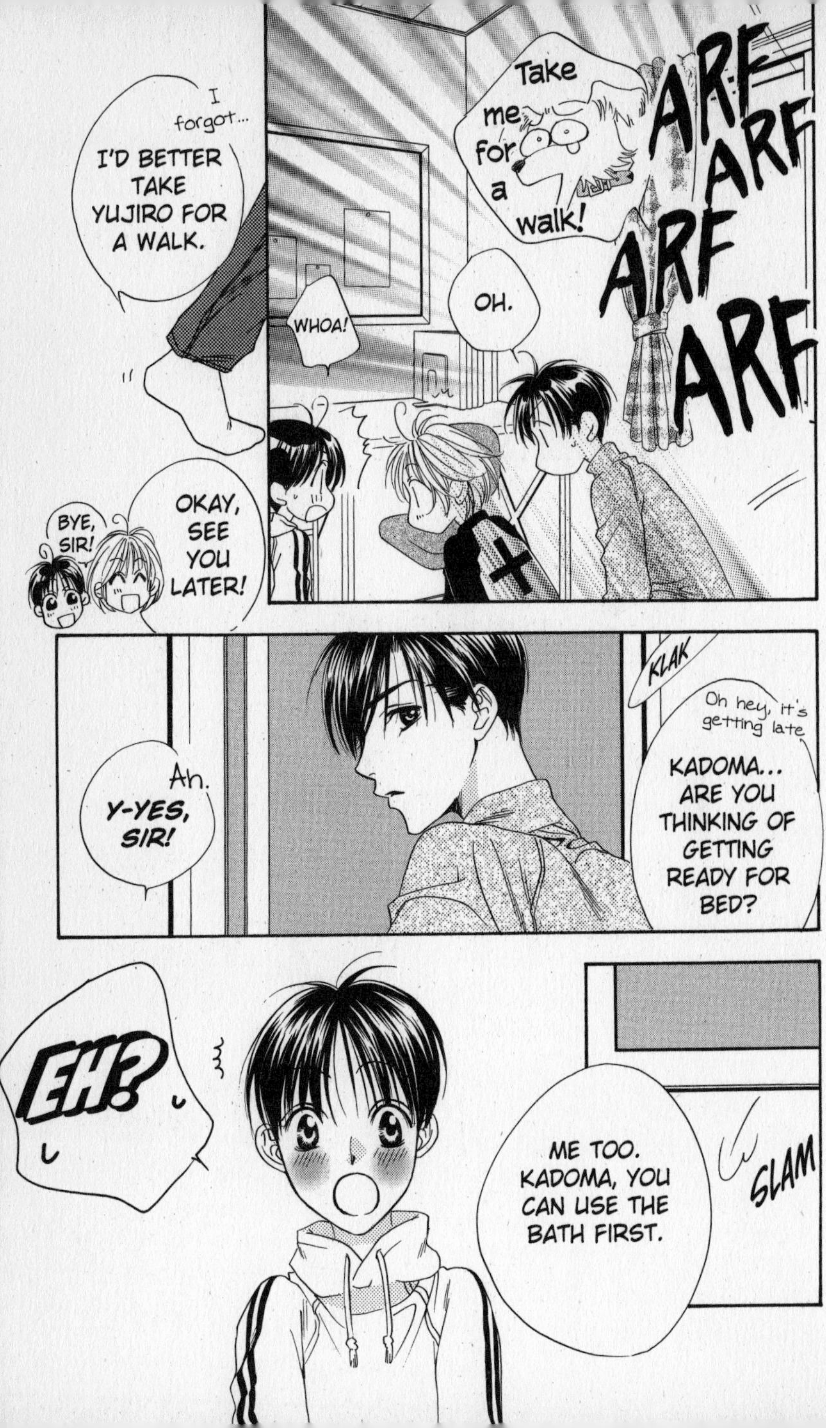
ARF ARF ARF ARF ARF
Take me for a walk!
OH.
WHOA!
I forgot...
I'D BETTER TAKE YUJIRO FOR A WALK.
OKAY, SEE YOU LATER!
BYE, SIR!
KLAK
Oh hey, it's getting late
KADOMA... ARE YOU THINKING OF GETTING READY FOR BED?
Ah.
Y-YES, SIR!
SLAM
ME TOO. KADOMA, YOU CAN USE THE BATH FIRST.
EH?

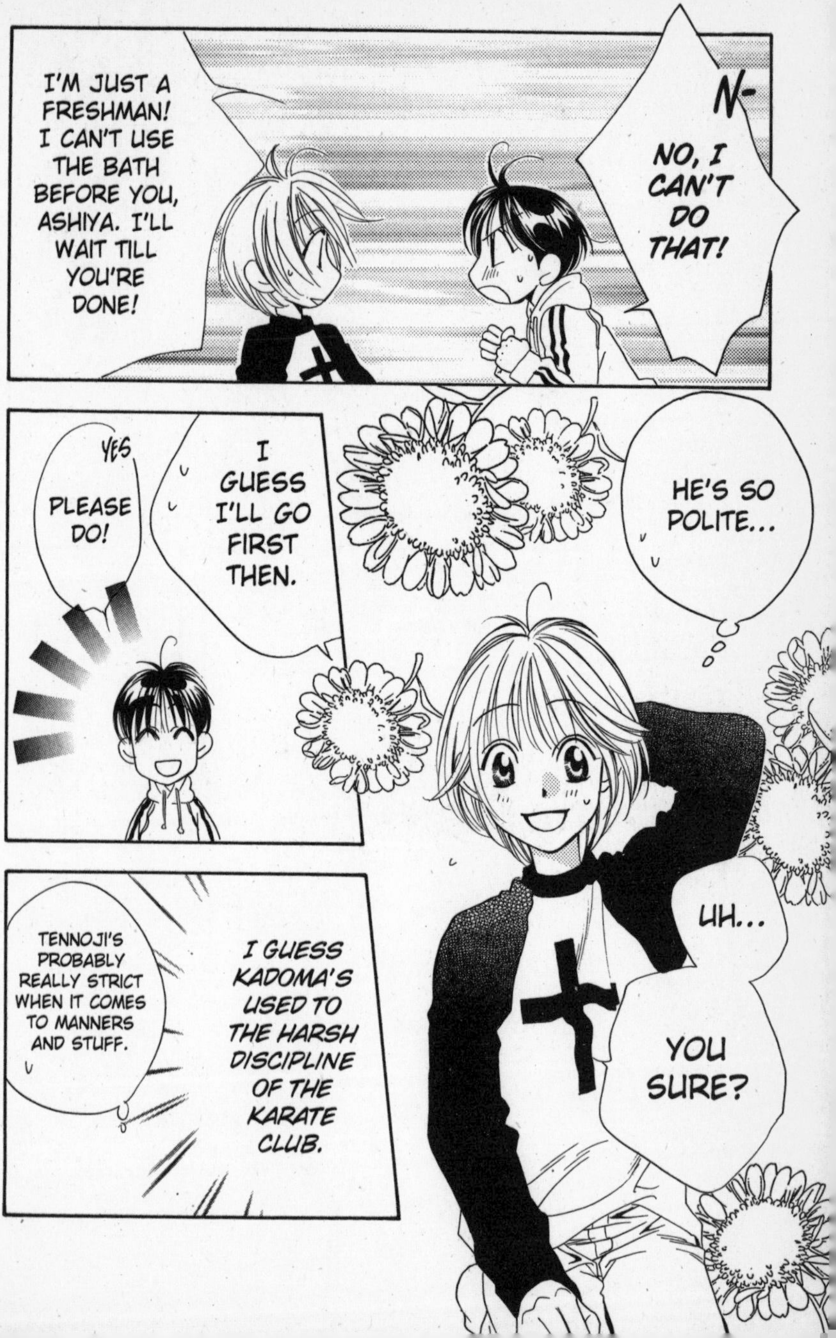
N-
NO, I CAN'T DO THAT!
I'M JUST A FRESHMAN! I CAN'T USE THE BATH BEFORE YOU, ASHIYA. I'LL WAIT TILL YOU'RE DONE!
HE'S SO POLITE...
UH...
YOU SURE?
I GUESS I'LL GO FIRST THEN.
YES
PLEASE DO!
I GUESS KADOMA'S USED TO THE HARSH DISCIPLINE OF THE KARATE CLUB.
TENNOJI'S PROBABLY REALLY STRICT WHEN IT COMES TO MANNERS AND STUFF.

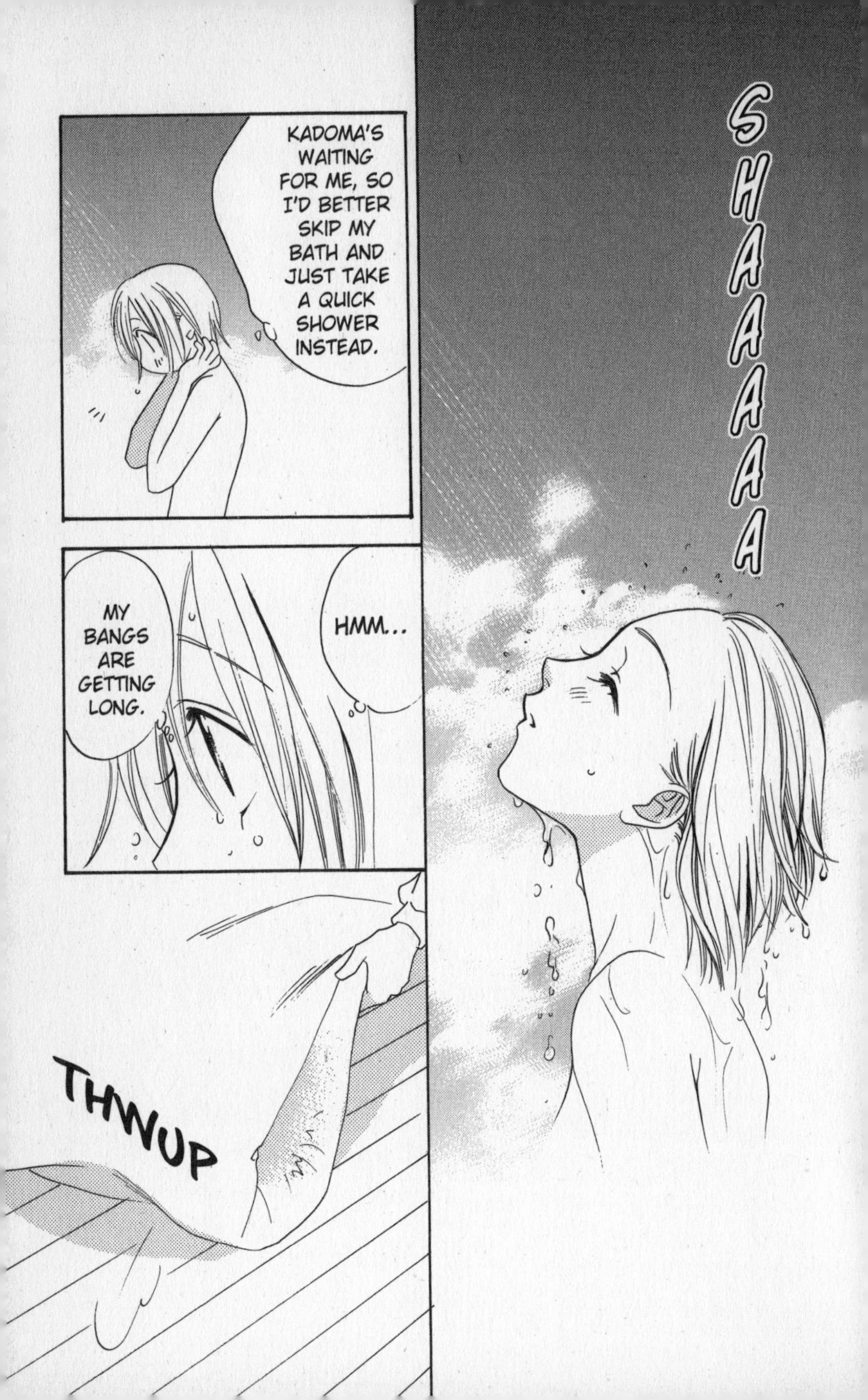
SHAAAAAA
KADOMA'S WAITING FOR ME, SO I'D BETTER SKIP MY BATH AND JUST TAKE A QUICK SHOWER INSTEAD.
HMM...
MY BANGS ARE GETTING LONG.
THWUP

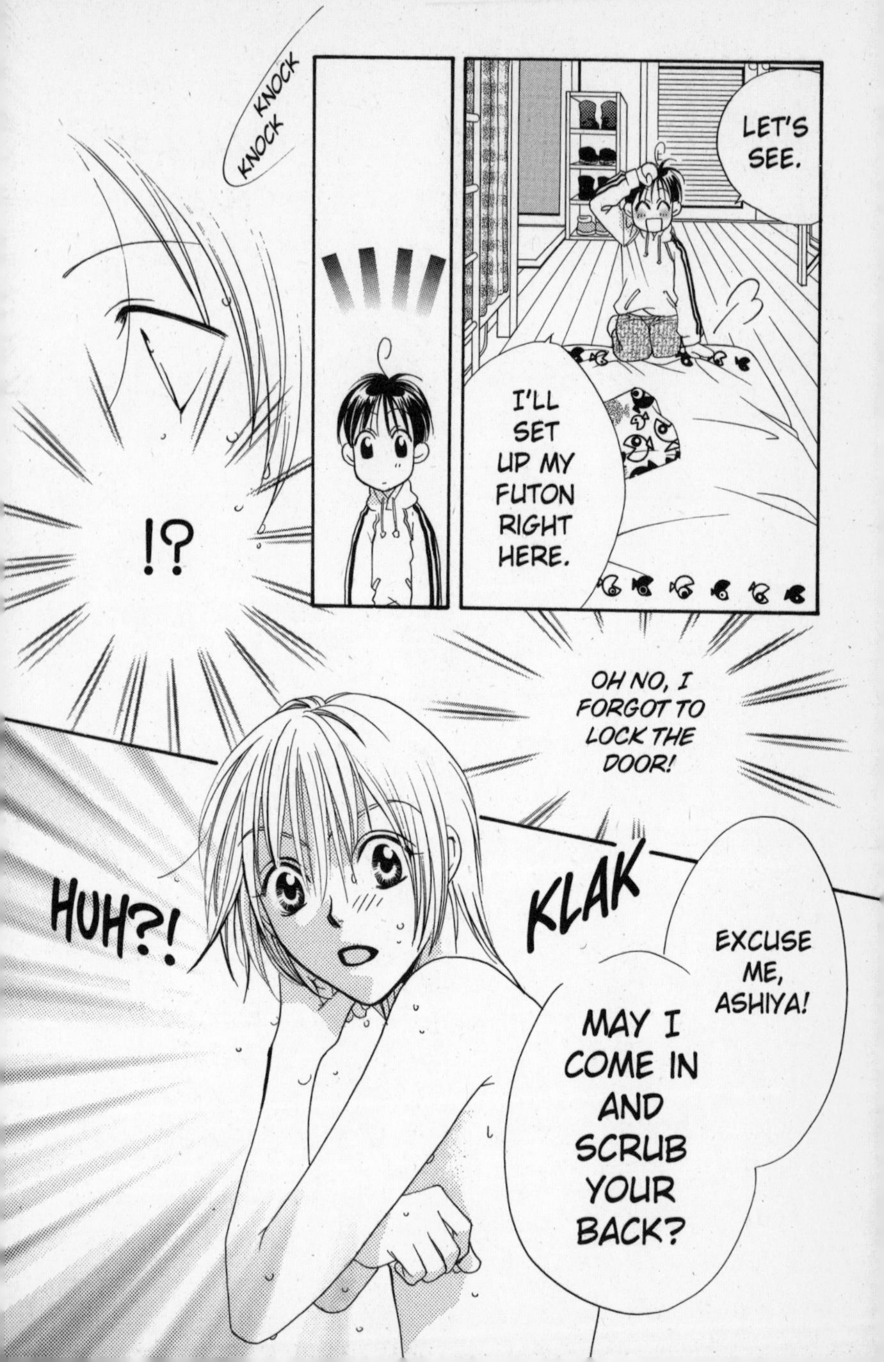
LET'S SEE.
I'LL SET UP MY FUTON RIGHT HERE.
KNOCK KNOCK
!?
OH NO, I FORGOT TO LOCK THE DOOR!
EXCUSE ME, ASHIYA!
MAY I COME IN AND SCRUB YOUR BACK?
KLAK
HUH?!

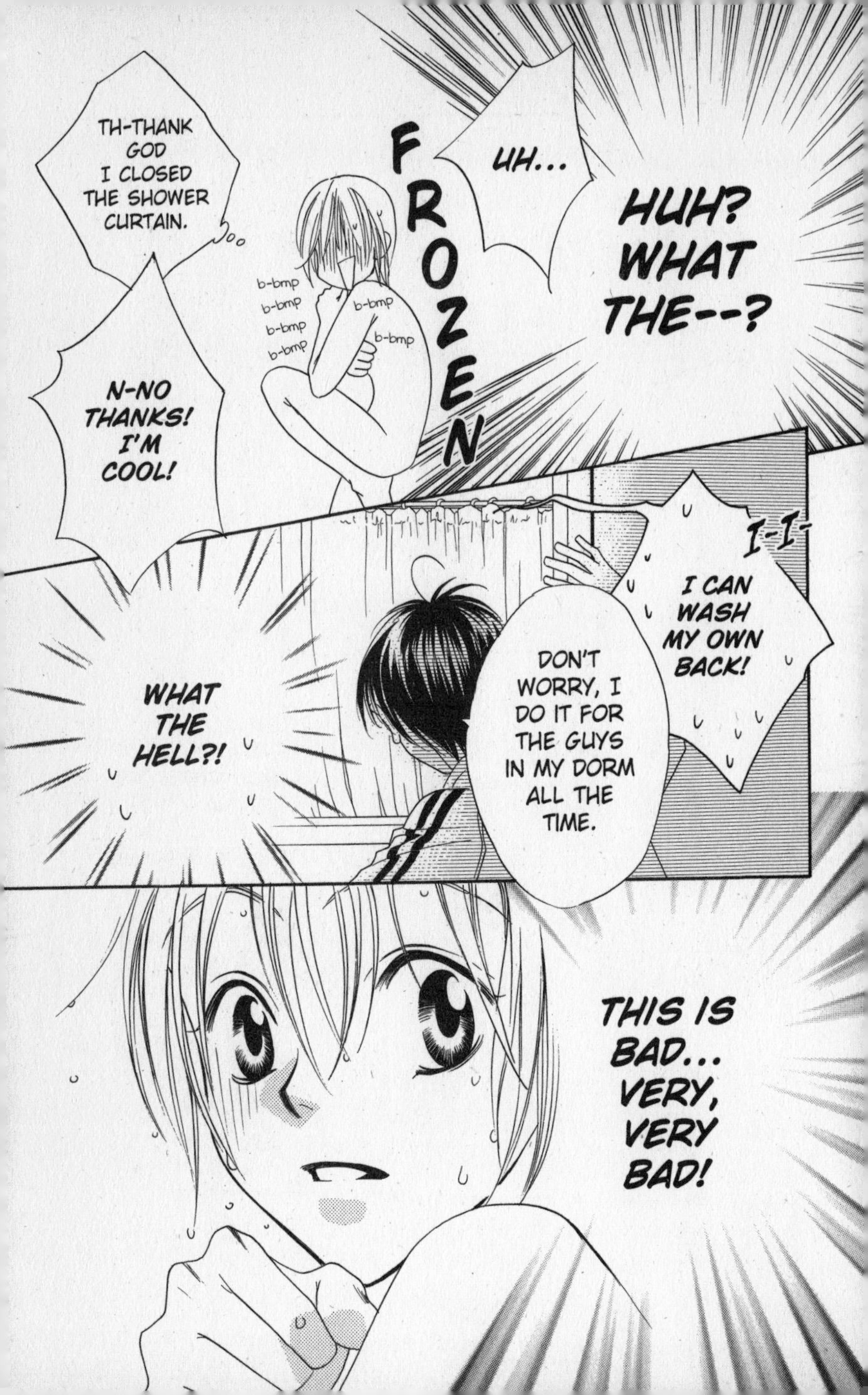
HUH? WHAT THE--?
UH...
FROZEN
b-bmp b-bmp b-bmp b-bmp b-bmp b-bmp
TH-THANK GOD I CLOSED THE SHOWER CURTAIN.
N-NO THANKS! I'M COOL!
I-I-
I CAN WASH MY OWN BACK!
DON'T WORRY, I DO IT FOR THE GUYS IN MY DORM ALL THE TIME.
WHAT THE HELL?!
THIS IS BAD... VERY, VERY BAD!

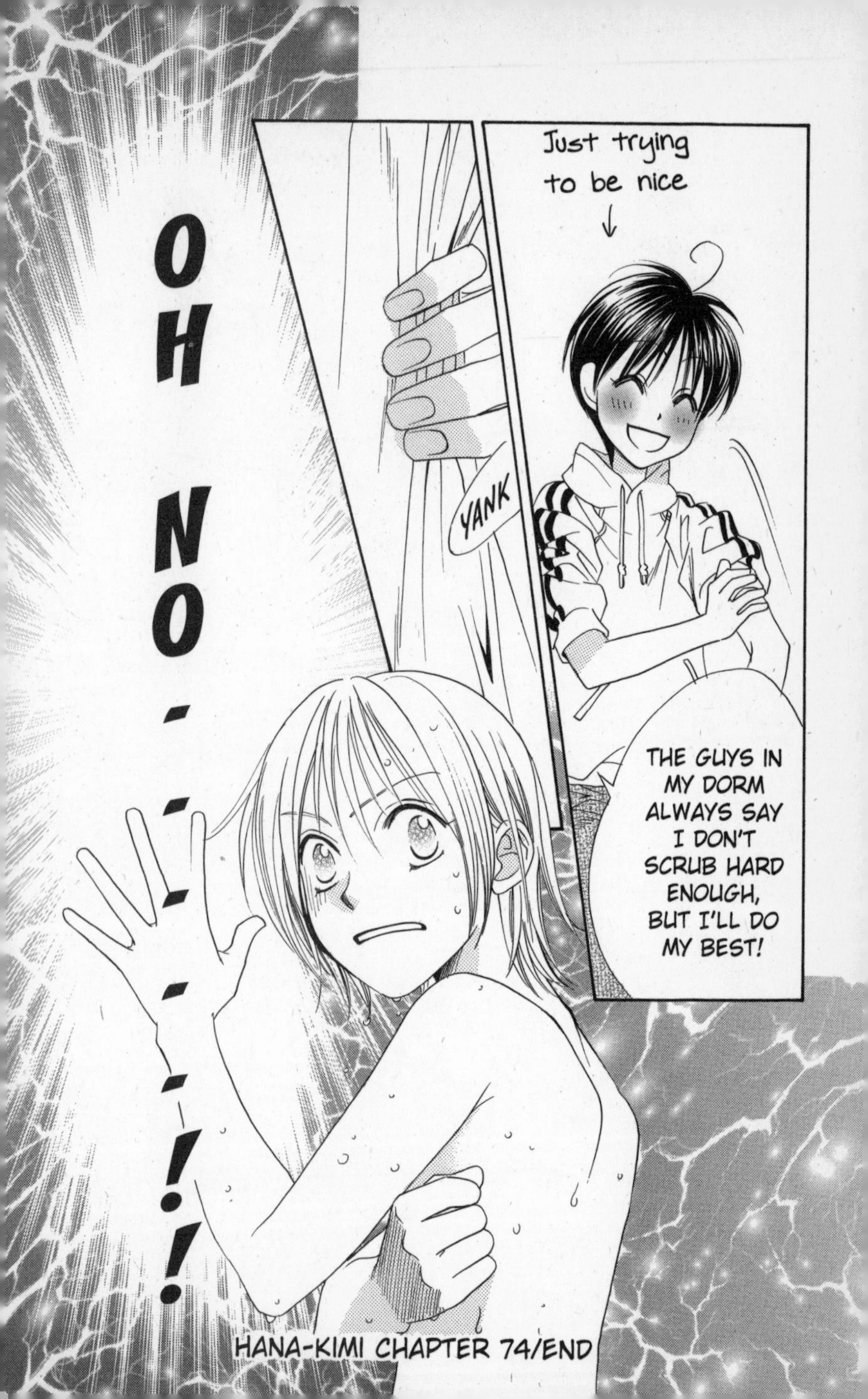
Just trying to be nice
THE GUYS IN MY DORM ALWAYS SAY I DON'T SCRUB HARD ENOUGH, BUT I'LL DO MY BEST!
YANK
OH NO------!!
HANA-KIMI CHAPTER 74/END

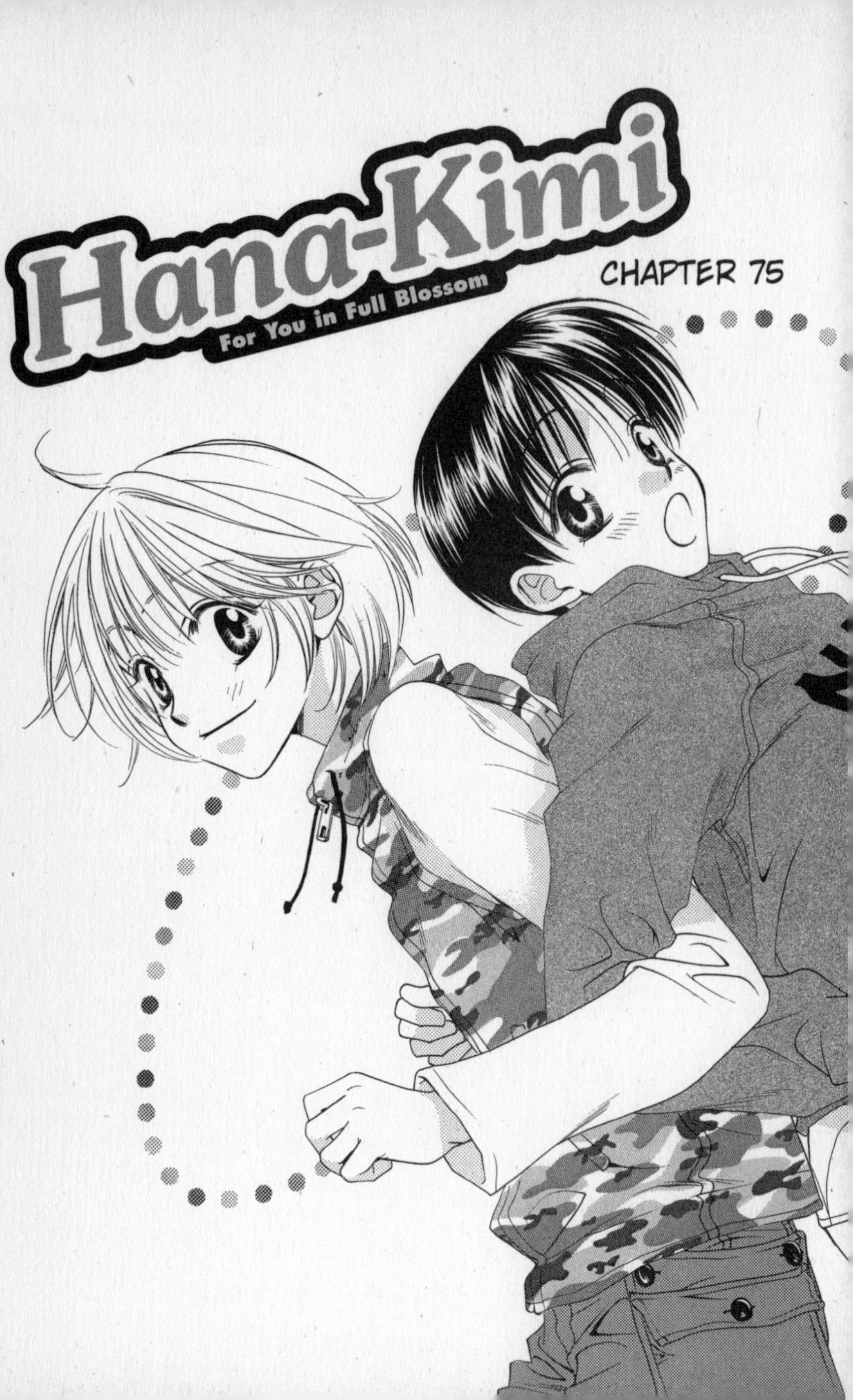
Hana-Kimi
For You in Full Blossom
CHAPTER 75

NO WAY!
Don't worry!
I'M ACTUALLY PRETTY GOOD AT WASHING PEOPLE'S BACKS!
I do it in my dorm all the time.
SOMEBODY PLEASE TELL ME THIS IS NOT HAPPENING!
...!
AGH
AGH
AGH
AGH
THE GUYS IN MY DORM ALWAYS SAY I DON'T SCRUB HARD ENOUGH, BUT...
I'LL DO MY BEST!

DVD

Lately, I've been addicted to DVDs. [laughs] I just love DVDs! Bravo! The resolution is much better than VHS, and when you watch foreign movies you can choose between subtitles or dubbing. And they're cheap! Well, maybe not that cheap, but they're cheap compared to videotapes. And they're so compact. I usually watch DVDs when I'm working. I've watched so many DVDs that I actually broke my DVD player. Sniff...

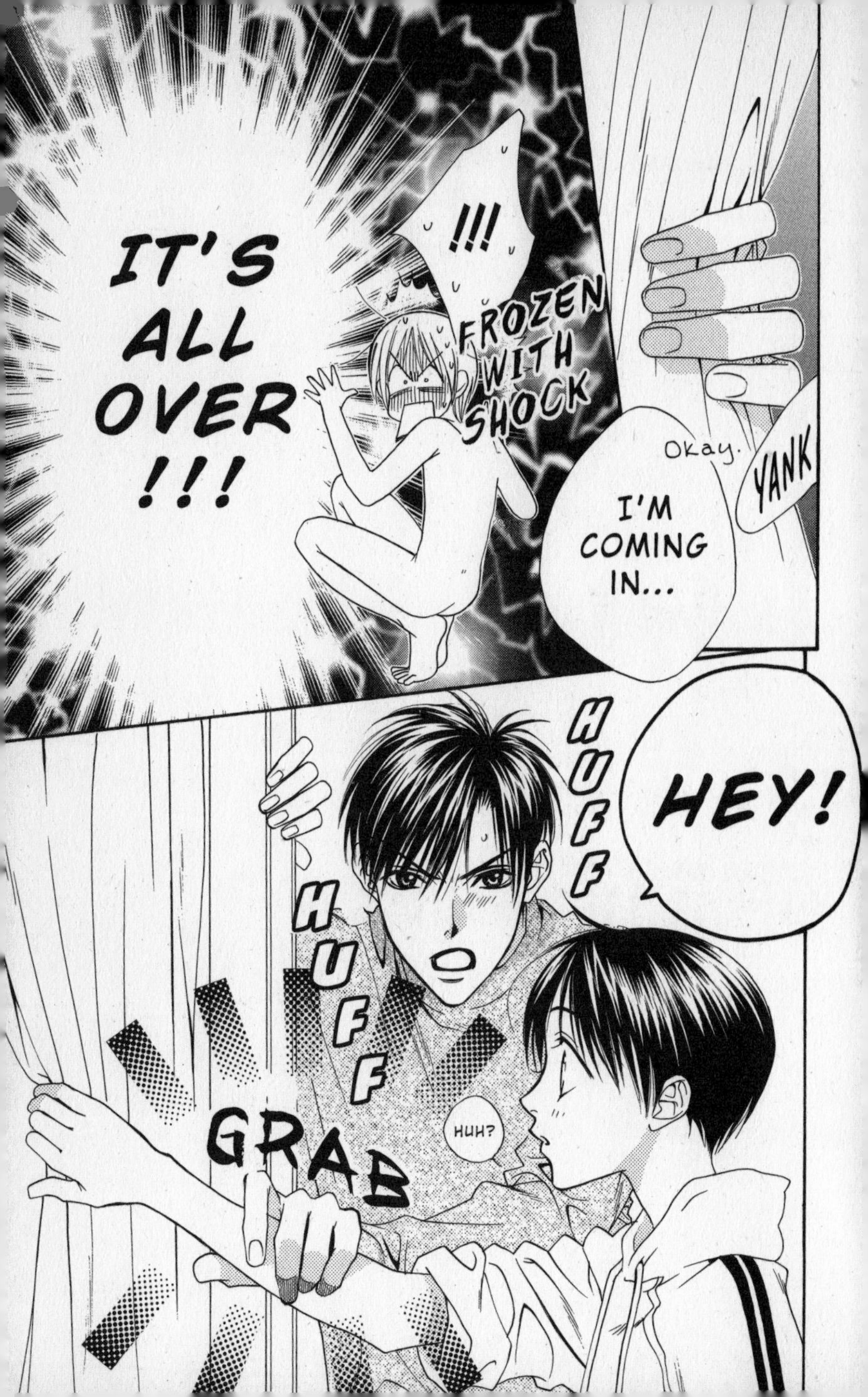

Okay.
I'M COMING IN...
YANK
IT'S ALL OVER!!!
!!!
FROZEN WITH SHOCK
HEY!
HUFF HUFF
HUFF HUFF
HUH?
GRAB

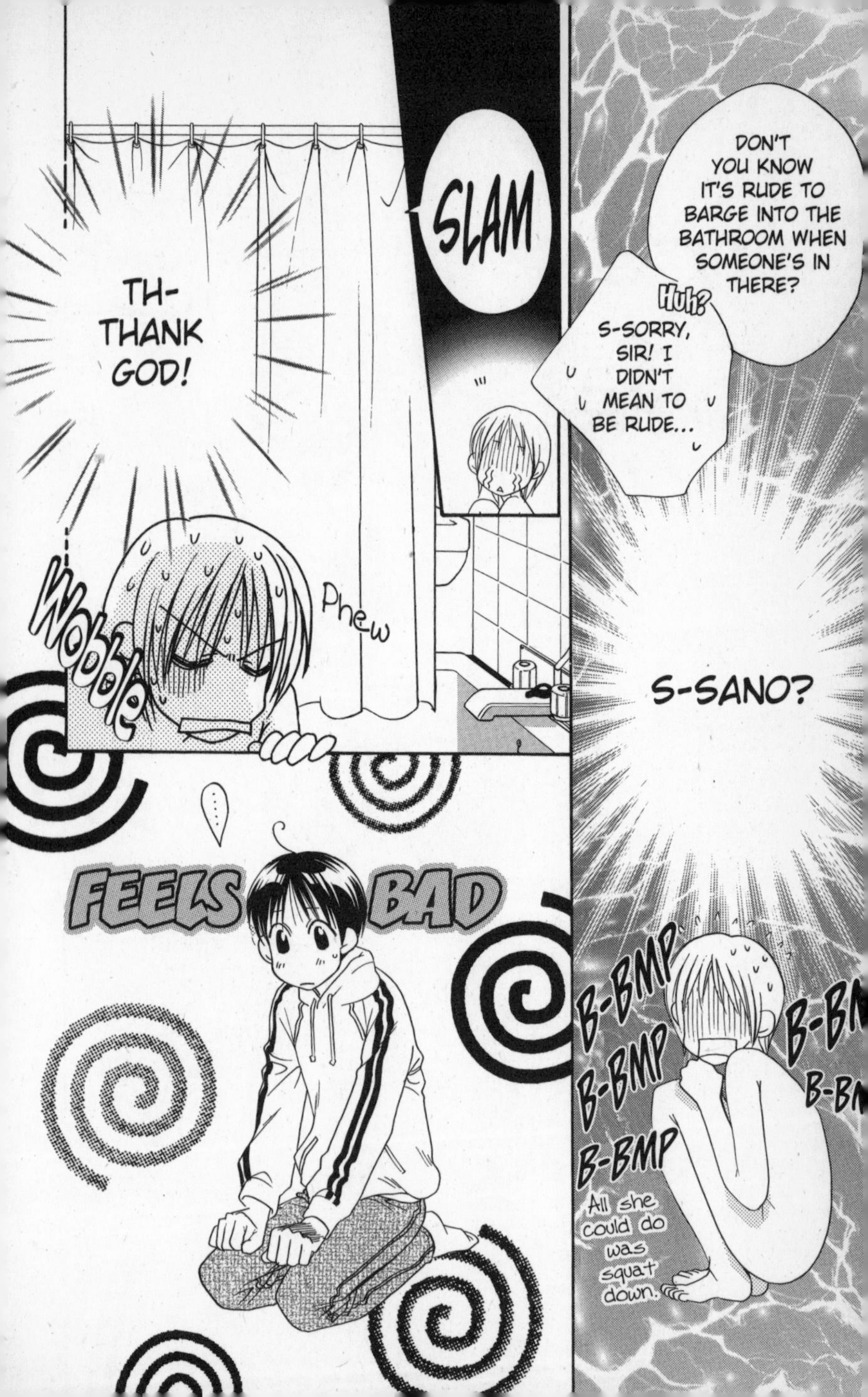
DON'T YOU KNOW IT'S RUDE TO BARGE INTO THE BATHROOM WHEN SOMEONE'S IN THERE?
Huh?
S-SORRY, SIR! I DIDN'T MEAN TO BE RUDE...
S-SANO?
B-BMP
B-BMP
B-BMP
B-BMP
B-BMP
All she could do was squat down.
SLAM
TH-THANK GOD!
Wobble
Phew
...
FEELS BAD

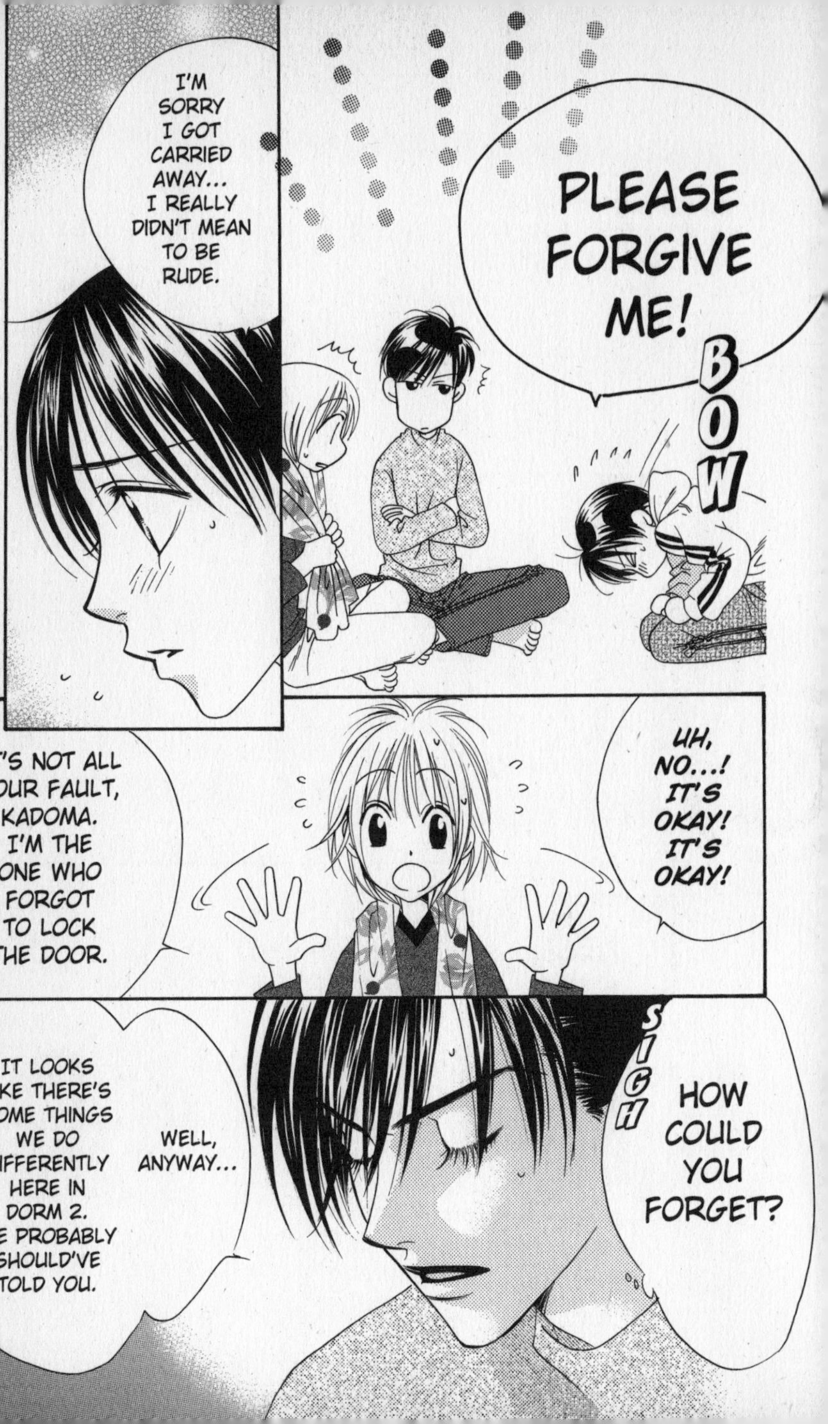
PLEASE FORGIVE ME!
BOW
I'M SORRY I GOT CARRIED AWAY... I REALLY DIDN'T MEAN TO BE RUDE.
UH, NO...! IT'S OKAY! IT'S OKAY!
IT'S NOT ALL YOUR FAULT, KADOMA. I'M THE ONE WHO FORGOT TO LOCK THE DOOR.
SIGH
HOW COULD YOU FORGET?
WELL, ANYWAY...
IT LOOKS LIKE THERE'S SOME THINGS WE DO DIFFERENTLY HERE IN DORM 2. WE PROBABLY SHOULD'VE TOLD YOU.

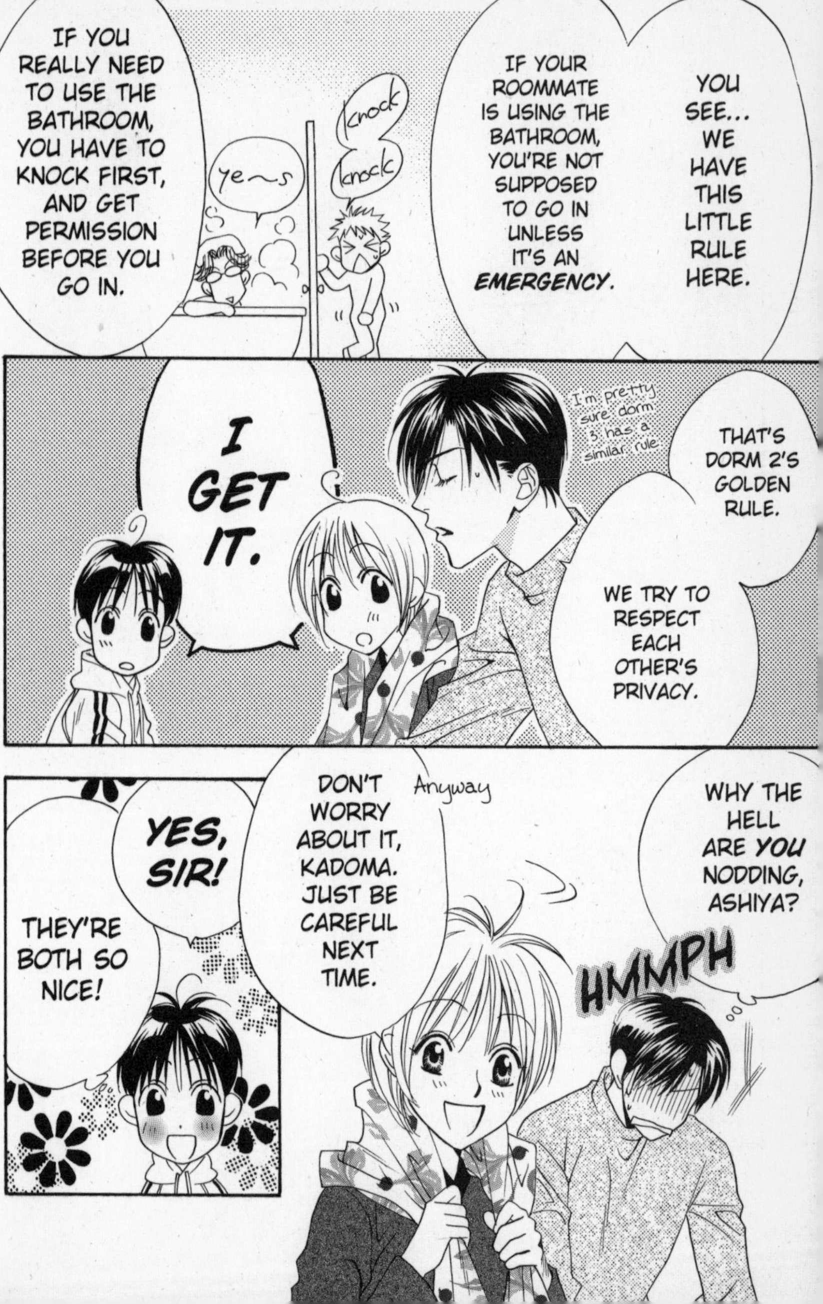
YOU SEE... WE HAVE THIS LITTLE RULE HERE.
IF YOUR ROOMMATE IS USING THE BATHROOM, YOU'RE NOT SUPPOSED TO GO IN UNLESS IT'S AN *EMERGENCY*.
Knock
Knock
ye~s
IF YOU REALLY NEED TO USE THE BATHROOM, YOU HAVE TO KNOCK FIRST, AND GET PERMISSION BEFORE YOU GO IN.
THAT'S DORM 2'S GOLDEN RULE.
I'm pretty sure dorm 3 has a similar rule
WE TRY TO RESPECT EACH OTHER'S PRIVACY.
I GET IT.
WHY THE HELL ARE *YOU* NODDING, ASHIYA?
HMMPH
Anyway
DON'T WORRY ABOUT IT, KADOMA. JUST BE CAREFUL NEXT TIME.
YES, SIR!
THEY'RE BOTH SO NICE!

"YOU'RE WRONG, NAKAJO!"

I often use the character "wa" in sentences like "~shite wa damesa". (You can't do ---) or "Konnichi wa" (Hello) or "Omae wa" (You). But I recently got a letter from a reader saying, "You're using it wrong." That's correct. I am using it wrong! I'm supposed to use the character "ha" instead of "wa." But actually, I use "wa" on purpose because when I use "ha", it looks too literal and serious when it's printed. So please, don't look at my work and think "Oh, so it's okay to use "wa" in a sentence like that." I don't want you to fail any grammar tests because of me.

Sometimes I also write words half in katakana and half in hiragana, like writing the "masu" in "shiteimasu" in katakana.

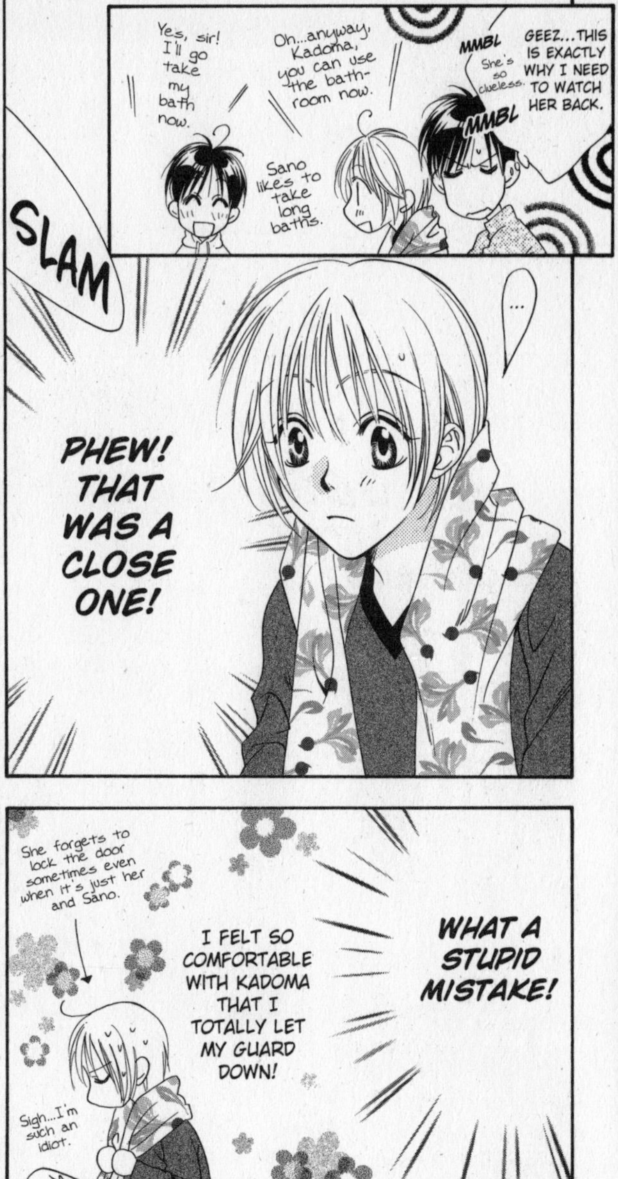

GEEZ...THIS IS EXACTLY WHY I NEED TO WATCH HER BACK.
MMBL
She's so clueless.
MMBL
Oh...anyway, Kadoma, you can use the bathroom now.
Sano likes to take long baths.
Yes, sir! I'll go take my bath now.
SLAM
...
PHEW! THAT WAS A CLOSE ONE!
WHAT A STUPID MISTAKE!
I FELT SO COMFORTABLE WITH KADOMA THAT I TOTALLY LET MY GUARD DOWN!
She forgets to lock the door sometimes even when it's just her and Sano.
Sigh...I'm such an idiot.

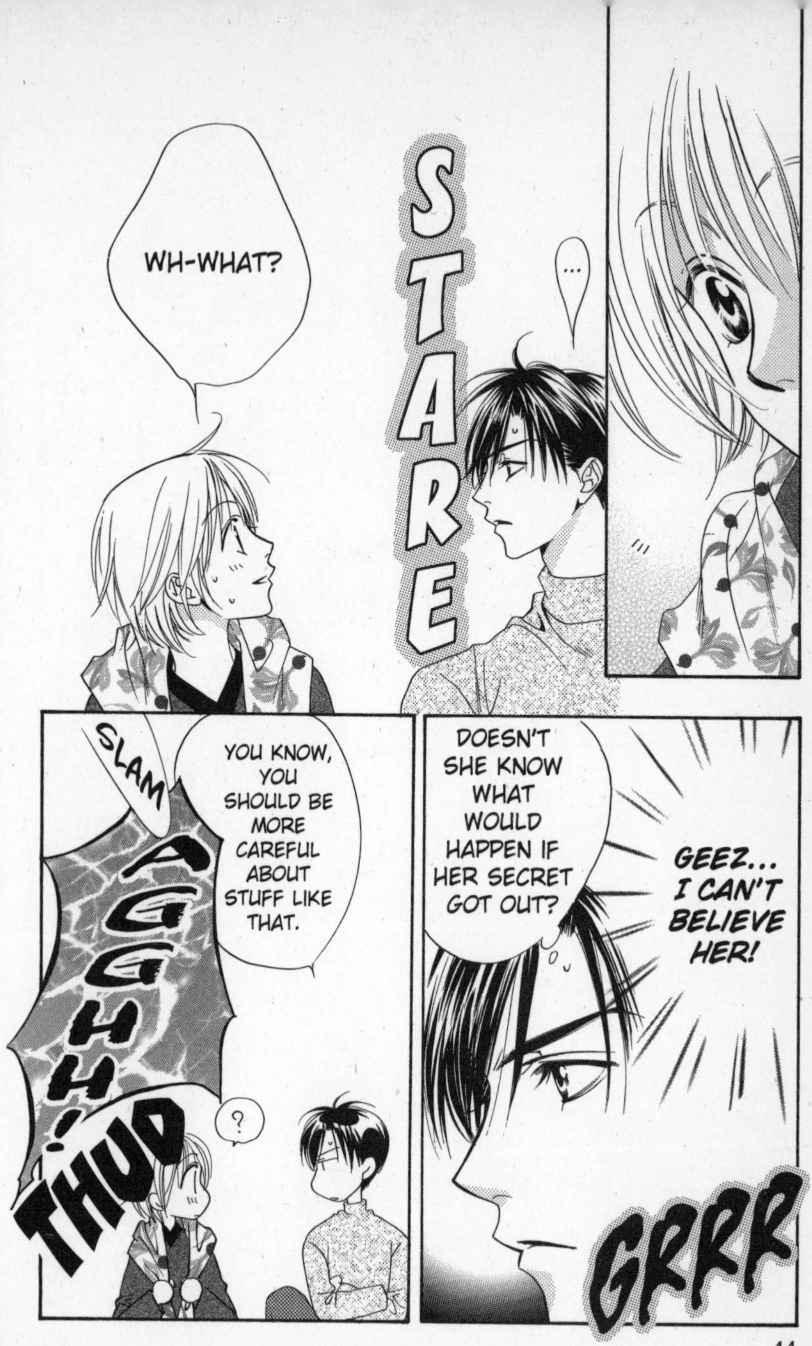
STARE
...
WH-WHAT?
DOESN'T SHE KNOW WHAT WOULD HAPPEN IF HER SECRET GOT OUT?
GEEZ... I CAN'T BELIEVE HER!
GRRR
YOU KNOW, YOU SHOULD BE MORE CAREFUL ABOUT STUFF LIKE THAT.
SLAM
AGGHH!
THUD
?

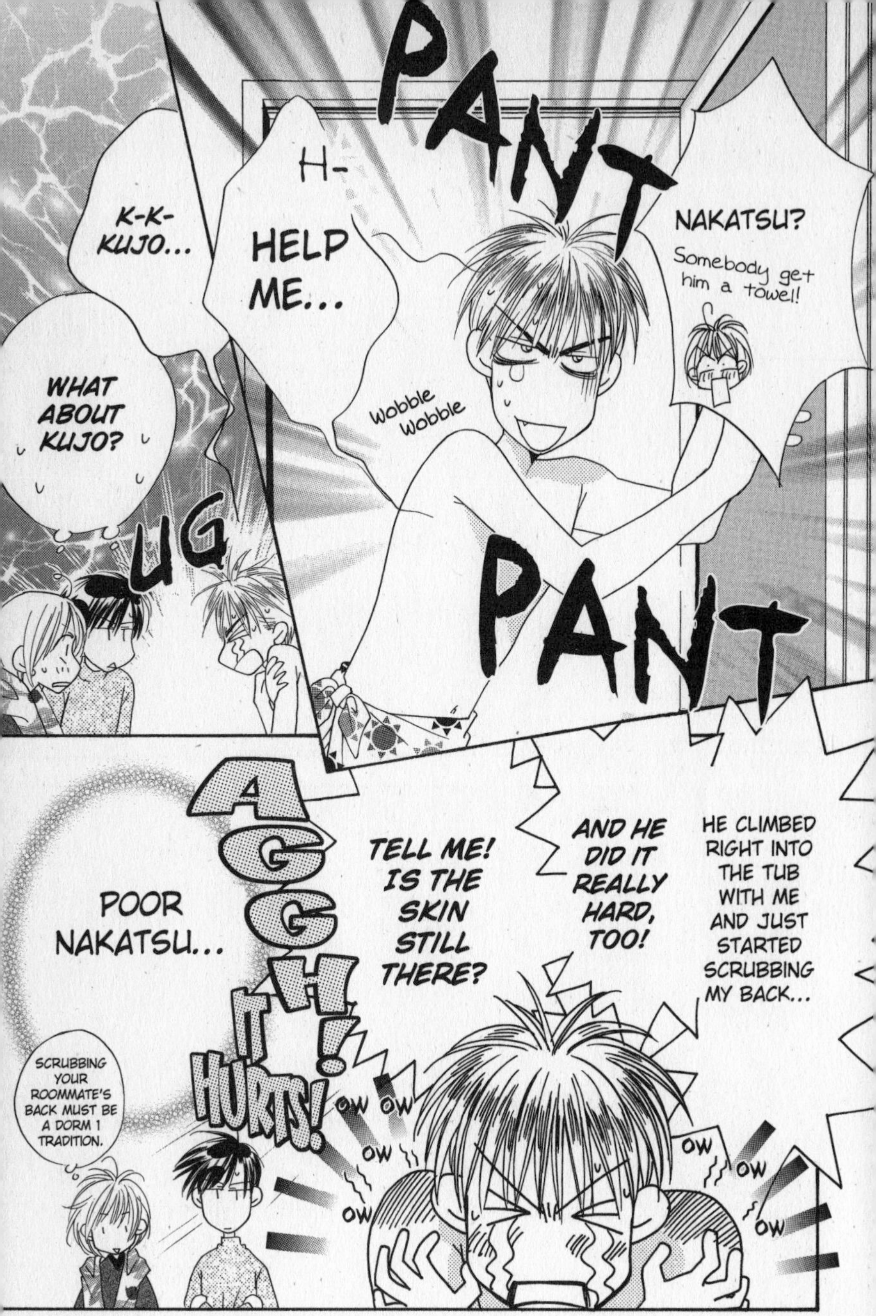
NAKATSU?
Somebody get him a towel!
PANT
H-
HELP ME...
Wobble Wobble
PANT
K-K-KUJO...
WHAT ABOUT KUJO?
UG
HE CLIMBED RIGHT INTO THE TUB WITH ME AND JUST STARTED SCRUBBING MY BACK...
AND HE DID IT REALLY HARD, TOO!
TELL ME! IS THE SKIN STILL THERE?
AGGH! IT HURTS!
OW OW
OW
OW
OW
OW
OW
POOR NAKATSU...
SCRUBBING YOUR ROOMMATE'S BACK MUST BE A DORM 1 TRADITION.

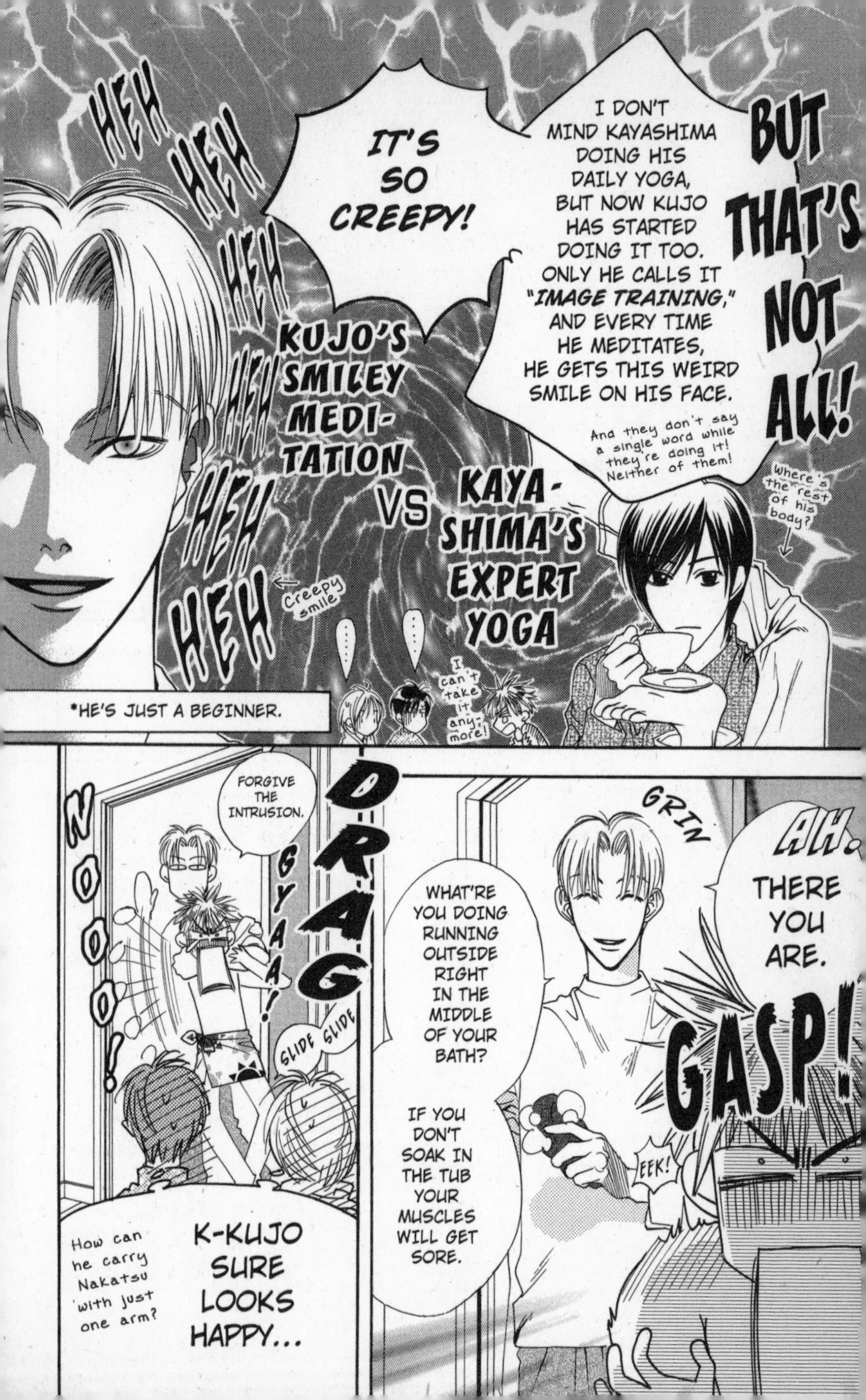
BUT THAT'S NOT ALL!
I DON'T MIND KAYASHIMA DOING HIS DAILY YOGA, BUT NOW KUJO HAS STARTED DOING IT TOO. ONLY HE CALLS IT "IMAGE TRAINING," AND EVERY TIME HE MEDITATES, HE GETS THIS WEIRD SMILE ON HIS FACE.
IT'S SO CREEPY!
HEH HEH HEH HEH HEH HEH
And they don't say a single word while they're doing it! Neither of them!
Where's the rest of his body?
KAYA-SHIMA'S EXPERT YOGA
VS
KUJO'S SMILEY MEDI-TATION
Creepy smile
I can't take it any-more!
*HE'S JUST A BEGINNER.
AH. THERE YOU ARE.
GASP!
GRIN
WHAT'RE YOU DOING RUNNING OUTSIDE RIGHT IN THE MIDDLE OF YOUR BATH?
IF YOU DON'T SOAK IN THE TUB YOUR MUSCLES WILL GET SORE.
EEK!
DRAG
FORGIVE THE INTRUSION.
GYAAA!
NOOOO!
SLIDE SLIDE
K-KUJO SURE LOOKS HAPPY...
How can he carry Nakatsu with just one arm?

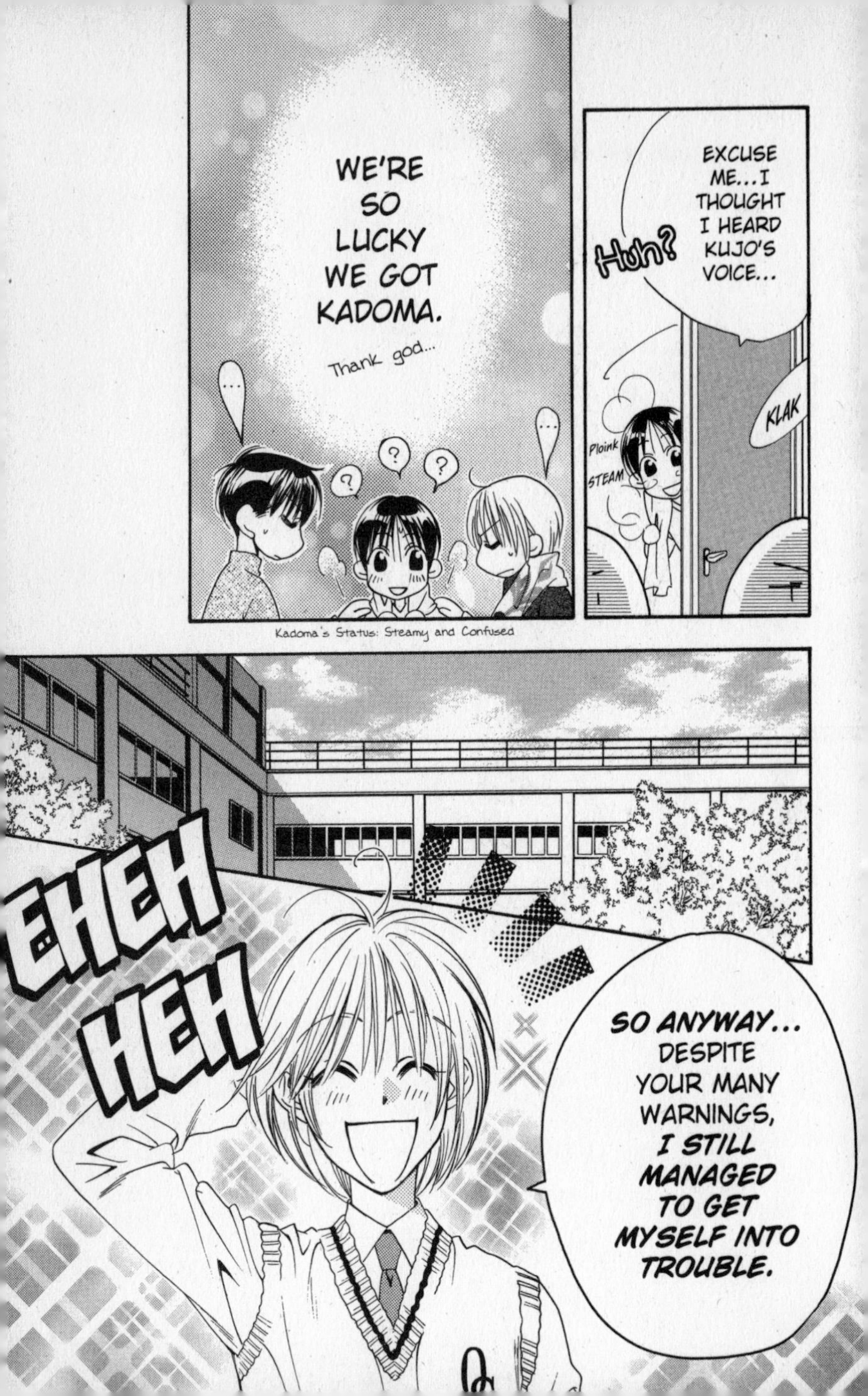
EXCUSE ME...I THOUGHT I HEARD KUJO'S VOICE...
Huh?
KLAK
Ploink
STEAM
WE'RE SO LUCKY WE GOT KADOMA.
Thank god...
...
?
?
?
...
Kadoma's Status: Steamy and Confused
EHEH HEH
SO ANYWAY... DESPITE YOUR MANY WARNINGS, I STILL MANAGED TO GET MYSELF INTO TROUBLE.

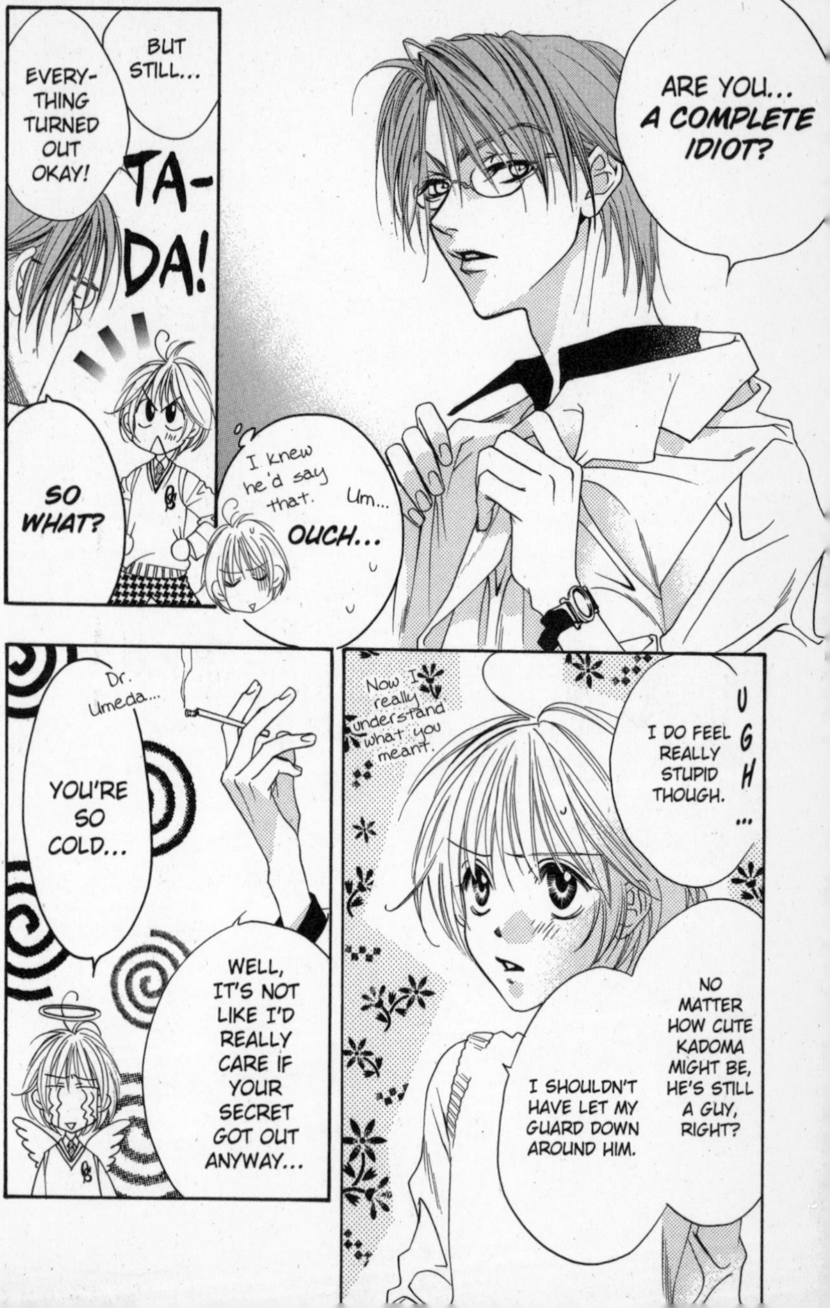
ARE YOU... A COMPLETE IDIOT?
I knew he'd say that.
Um...
OUCH...
BUT STILL...
EVERY-THING TURNED OUT OKAY!
TA-DA!
SO WHAT?
Now I really understand what you meant.
I DO FEEL REALLY STUPID THOUGH.
UGH...
NO MATTER HOW CUTE KADOMA MIGHT BE, HE'S STILL A GUY, RIGHT?
I SHOULDN'T HAVE LET MY GUARD DOWN AROUND HIM.
Dr. Umeda...
YOU'RE SO COLD...
WELL, IT'S NOT LIKE I'D REALLY CARE IF YOUR SECRET GOT OUT ANYWAY...

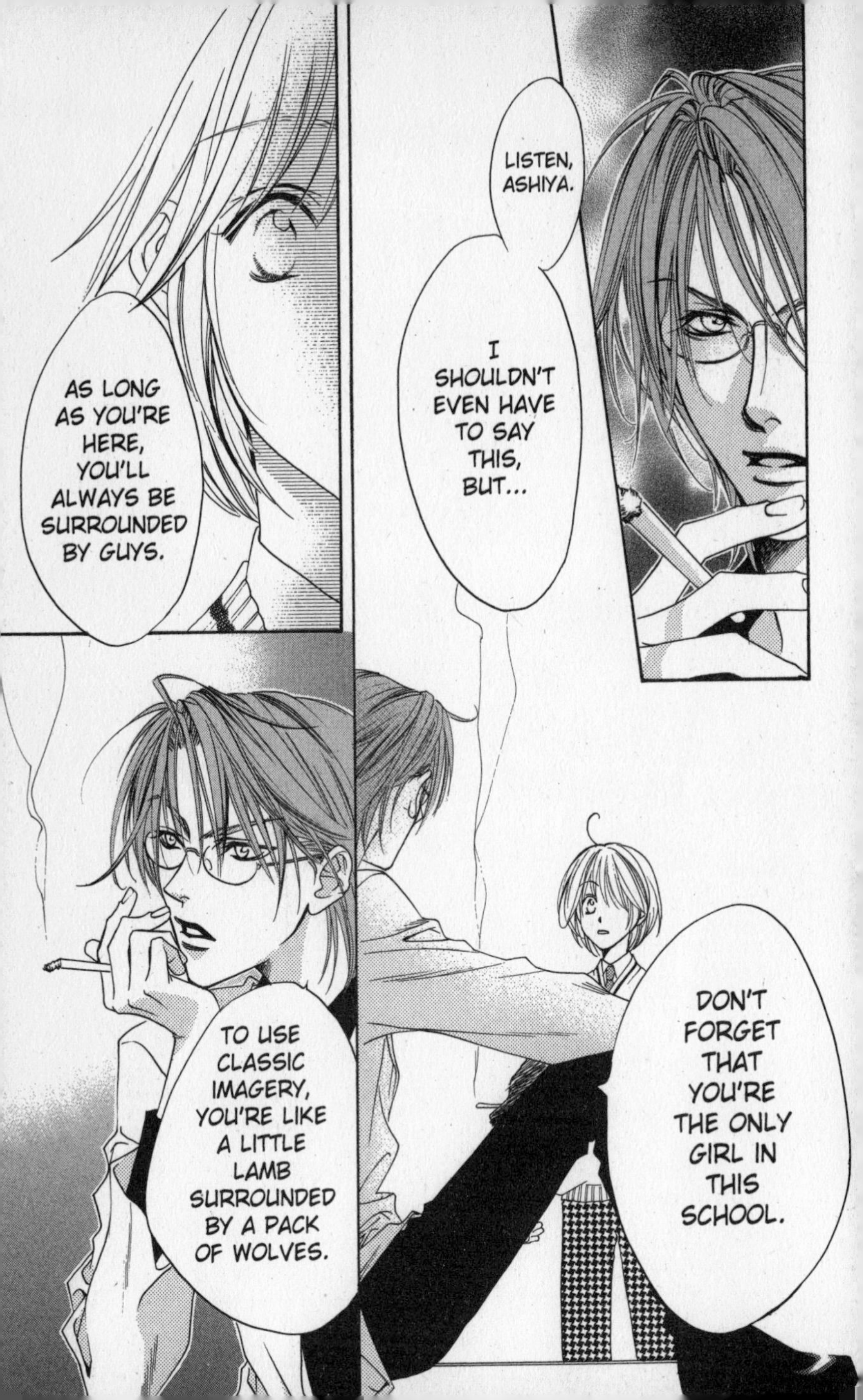
LISTEN, ASHIYA.
I SHOULDN'T EVEN HAVE TO SAY THIS, BUT...
AS LONG AS YOU'RE HERE, YOU'LL ALWAYS BE SURROUNDED BY GUYS.
DON'T FORGET THAT YOU'RE THE ONLY GIRL IN THIS SCHOOL.
TO USE CLASSIC IMAGERY, YOU'RE LIKE A LITTLE LAMB SURROUNDED BY A PACK OF WOLVES.

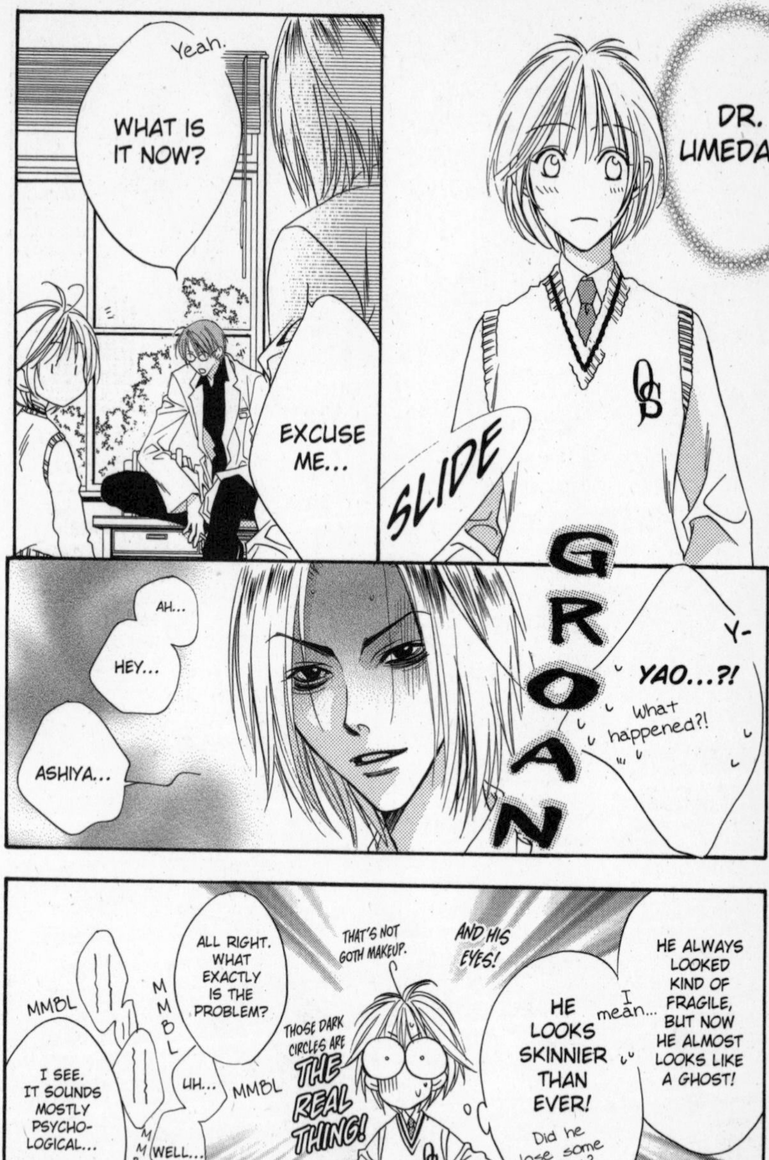
DR. UMEDA...
SLIDE
EXCUSE ME...
WHAT IS IT NOW?
Yeah.
Y-YAO...?!
What happened?!
GROAN
AH...
HEY...
ASHIYA...
HE ALWAYS LOOKED KIND OF FRAGILE, BUT NOW HE ALMOST LOOKS LIKE A GHOST!
I mean...
HE LOOKS SKINNIER THAN EVER!
Did he lose some weight?
AND HIS EYES!
THAT'S NOT GOTH MAKEUP.
THOSE DARK CIRCLES ARE THE REAL THING!
ALL RIGHT. WHAT EXACTLY IS THE PROBLEM?
MMBL
UH...
MMBL
WELL...
MMBL
MMBL
I SEE. IT SOUNDS MOSTLY PSYCHOLOGICAL...
Hmm...

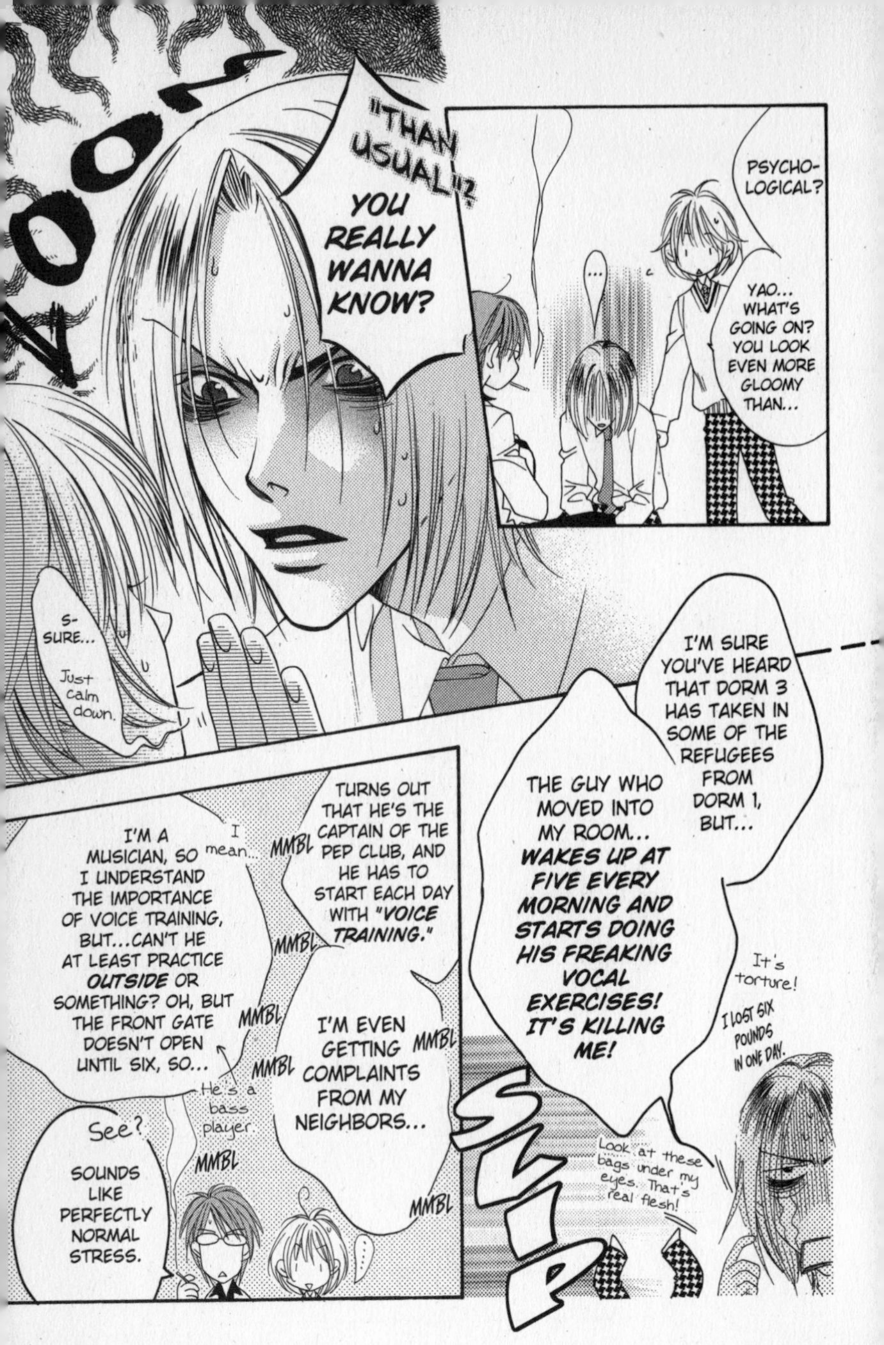
PSYCHO-LOGICAL?
YAO... WHAT'S GOING ON? YOU LOOK EVEN MORE GLOOMY THAN...
...
VOOO
"THAN USUAL"!? YOU REALLY WANNA KNOW?
S-SURE...
Just calm down.
I'M SURE YOU'VE HEARD THAT DORM 3 HAS TAKEN IN SOME OF THE REFUGEES FROM DORM 1, BUT...
THE GUY WHO MOVED INTO MY ROOM... WAKES UP AT FIVE EVERY MORNING AND STARTS DOING HIS FREAKING VOCAL EXERCISES! IT'S KILLING ME!
It's torture!
I LOST SIX POUNDS IN ONE DAY.
Look at these bags under my eyes. That's real flesh!
SLIP
TURNS OUT THAT HE'S THE CAPTAIN OF THE PEP CLUB, AND HE HAS TO START EACH DAY WITH "VOICE TRAINING."
I mean...
I'M A MUSICIAN, SO I UNDERSTAND THE IMPORTANCE OF VOICE TRAINING, BUT...CAN'T HE AT LEAST PRACTICE OUTSIDE OR SOMETHING? OH, BUT THE FRONT GATE DOESN'T OPEN UNTIL SIX, SO...
MMBL
MMBL
MMBL
I'M EVEN GETTING COMPLAINTS FROM MY NEIGHBORS...
MMBL
MMBL
He's a bass player.
MMBL
MMBL
See?
SOUNDS LIKE PERFECTLY NORMAL STRESS.

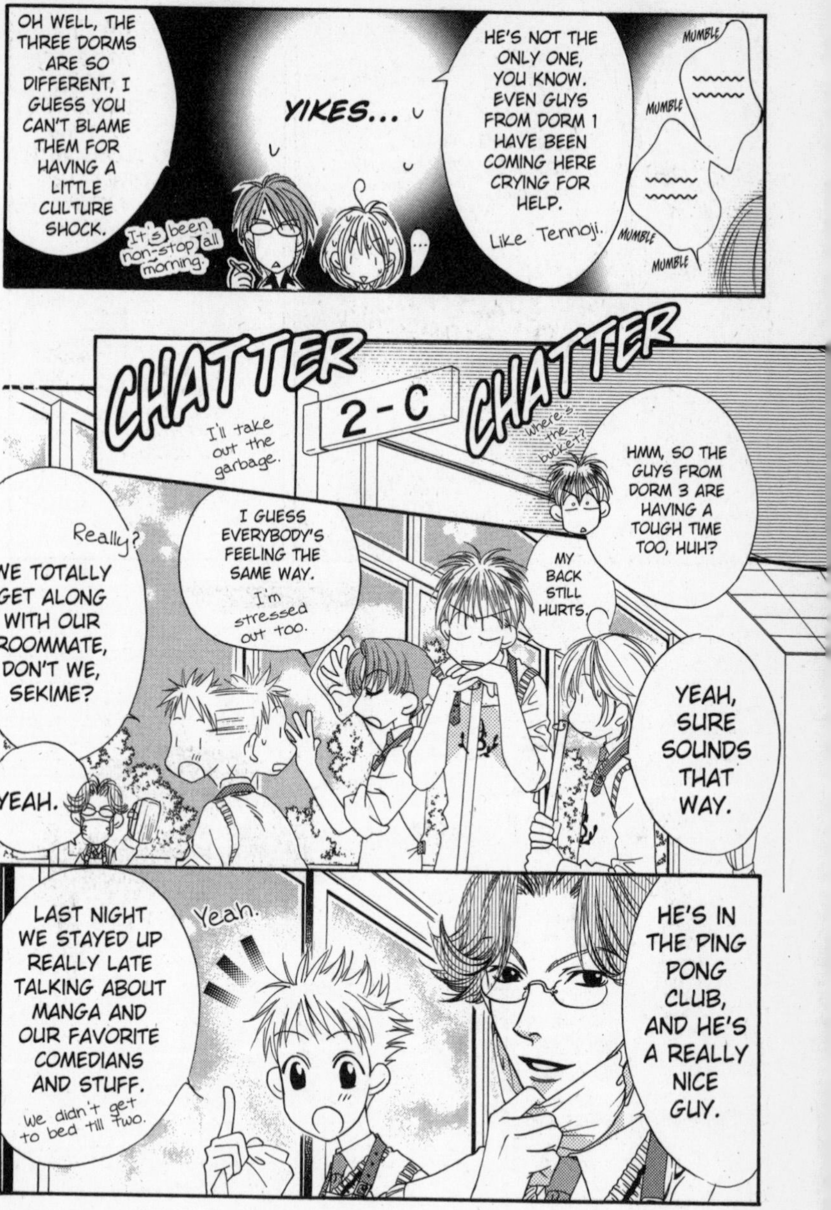
MUMBLE
MUMBLE
HE'S NOT THE ONLY ONE, YOU KNOW. EVEN GUYS FROM DORM 1 HAVE BEEN COMING HERE CRYING FOR HELP.
Like Tennoji.
MUMBLE
MUMBLE
YIKES...
OH WELL, THE THREE DORMS ARE SO DIFFERENT, I GUESS YOU CAN'T BLAME THEM FOR HAVING A LITTLE CULTURE SHOCK.
...
It's been non-stop all morning.
CHATTER
CHATTER
2-C
Where's the bucket?
HMM, SO THE GUYS FROM DORM 3 ARE HAVING A TOUGH TIME TOO, HUH?
I'll take out the garbage.
MY BACK STILL HURTS.
I GUESS EVERYBODY'S FEELING THE SAME WAY.
I'm stressed out too.
Really?
WE TOTALLY GET ALONG WITH OUR ROOMMATE, DON'T WE, SEKIME?
YEAH, SURE SOUNDS THAT WAY.
YEAH.
HE'S IN THE PING PONG CLUB, AND HE'S A REALLY NICE GUY.
Yeah.
LAST NIGHT WE STAYED UP REALLY LATE TALKING ABOUT MANGA AND OUR FAVORITE COMEDIANS AND STUFF.
We didn't get to bed till two.

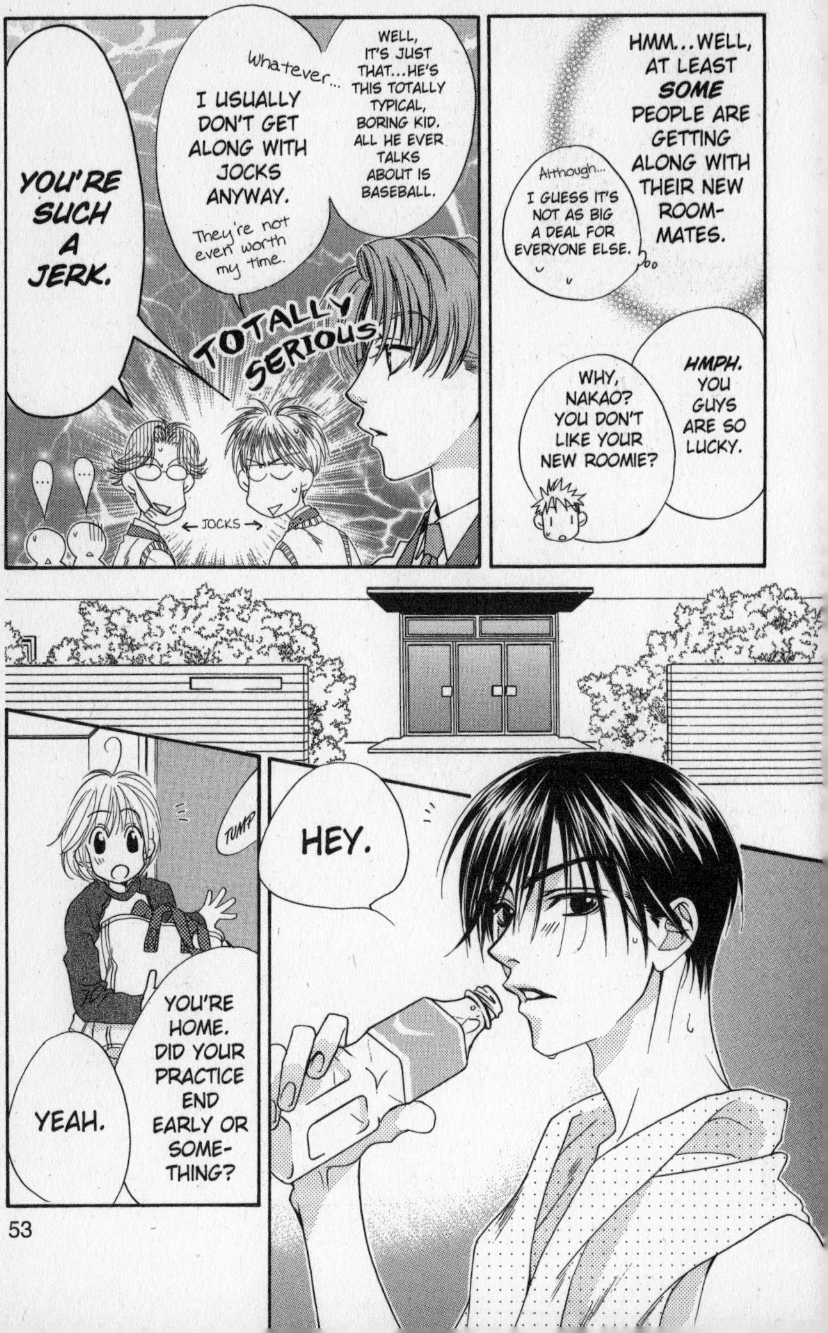

HMM...WELL, AT LEAST **SOME** PEOPLE ARE GETTING ALONG WITH THEIR NEW ROOM-MATES.
Although...
I GUESS IT'S NOT AS BIG A DEAL FOR EVERYONE ELSE.
HMPH. YOU GUYS ARE SO LUCKY.
WHY, NAKAO? YOU DON'T LIKE YOUR NEW ROOMIE?
WELL, IT'S JUST THAT...HE'S THIS TOTALLY TYPICAL, BORING KID. ALL HE EVER TALKS ABOUT IS BASEBALL.
Whatever...
I USUALLY DON'T GET ALONG WITH JOCKS ANYWAY.
They're not even worth my time.
TOTALLY SERIOUS
YOU'RE SUCH A JERK.
← JOCKS →
HEY.
TUMP
YOU'RE HOME. DID YOUR PRACTICE END EARLY OR SOME-THING?
YEAH.

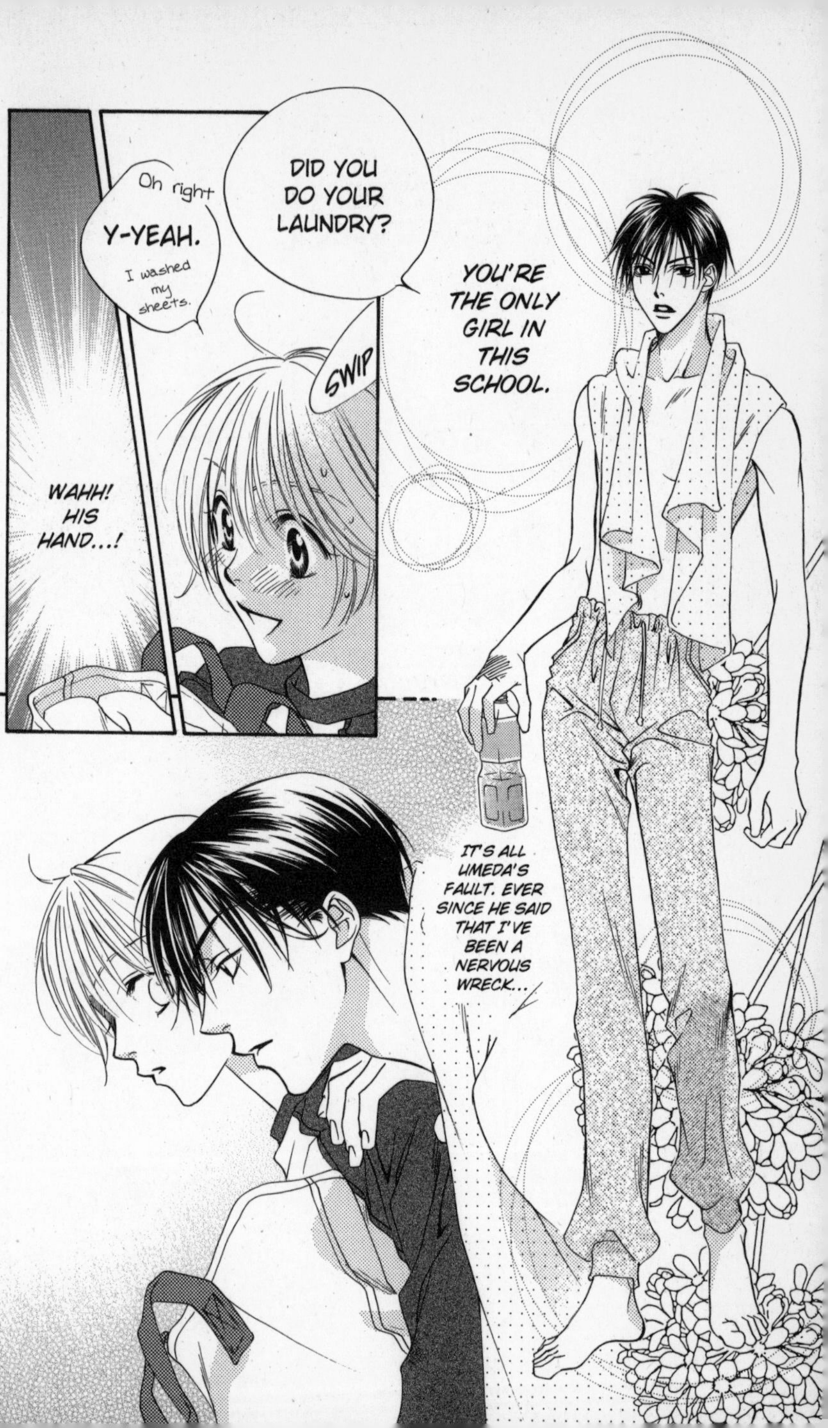
YOU'RE THE ONLY GIRL IN THIS SCHOOL.
IT'S ALL UMEDA'S FAULT. EVER SINCE HE SAID THAT I'VE BEEN A NERVOUS WRECK...
DID YOU DO YOUR LAUNDRY?
SWIP
Oh right
Y-YEAH.
I washed my sheets.
WAHH! HIS HAND...!

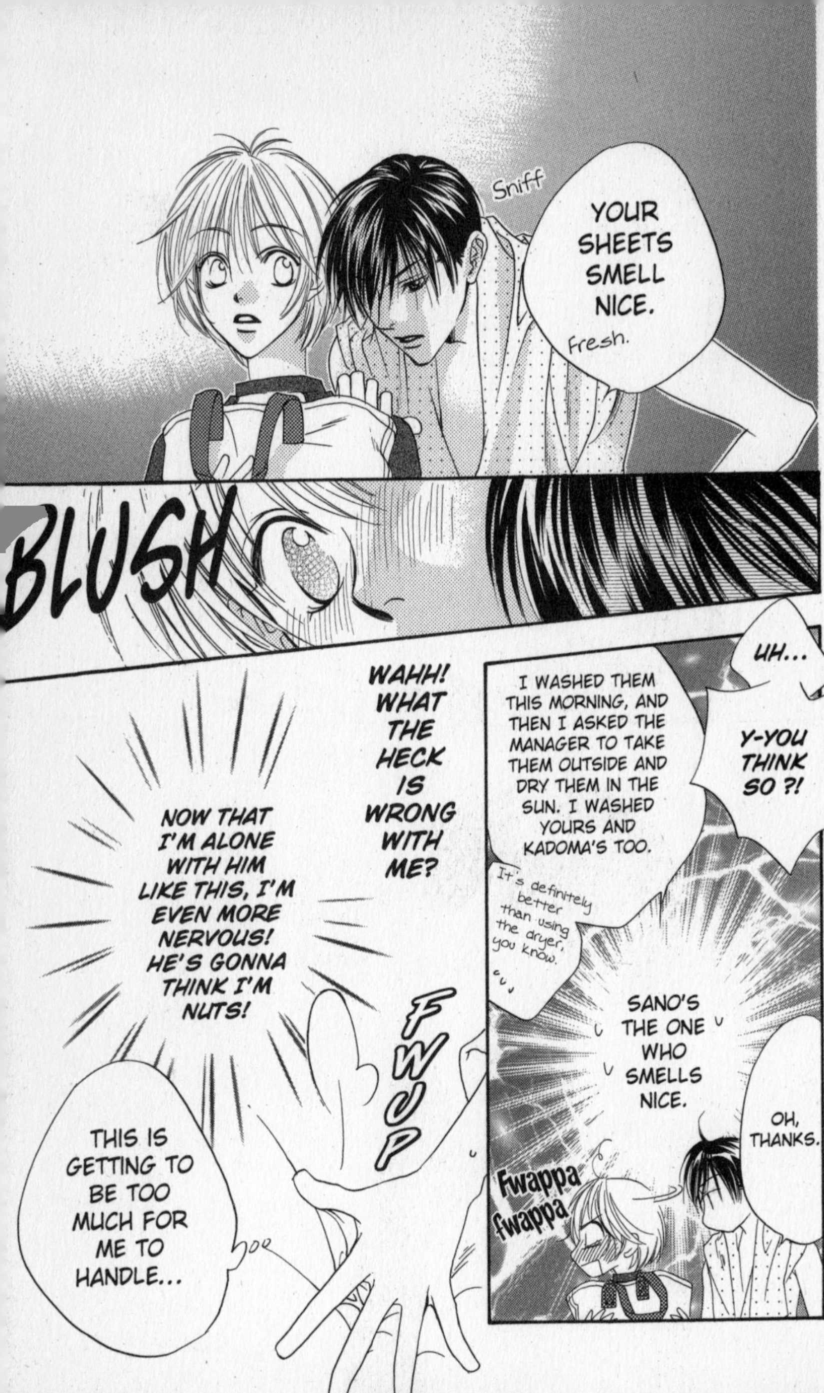

Sniff
YOUR SHEETS SMELL NICE.
Fresh.
BLUSH
UH...
Y-YOU THINK SO ?!
I WASHED THEM THIS MORNING, AND THEN I ASKED THE MANAGER TO TAKE THEM OUTSIDE AND DRY THEM IN THE SUN. I WASHED YOURS AND KADOMA'S TOO.
It's definitely better than using the dryer, you know.
SANO'S THE ONE WHO SMELLS NICE.
OH, THANKS.
Fwappa fwappa
WAHH! WHAT THE HECK IS WRONG WITH ME?
NOW THAT I'M ALONE WITH HIM LIKE THIS, I'M EVEN MORE NERVOUS! HE'S GONNA THINK I'M NUTS!
FWUP
THIS IS GETTING TO BE TOO MUCH FOR ME TO HANDLE...

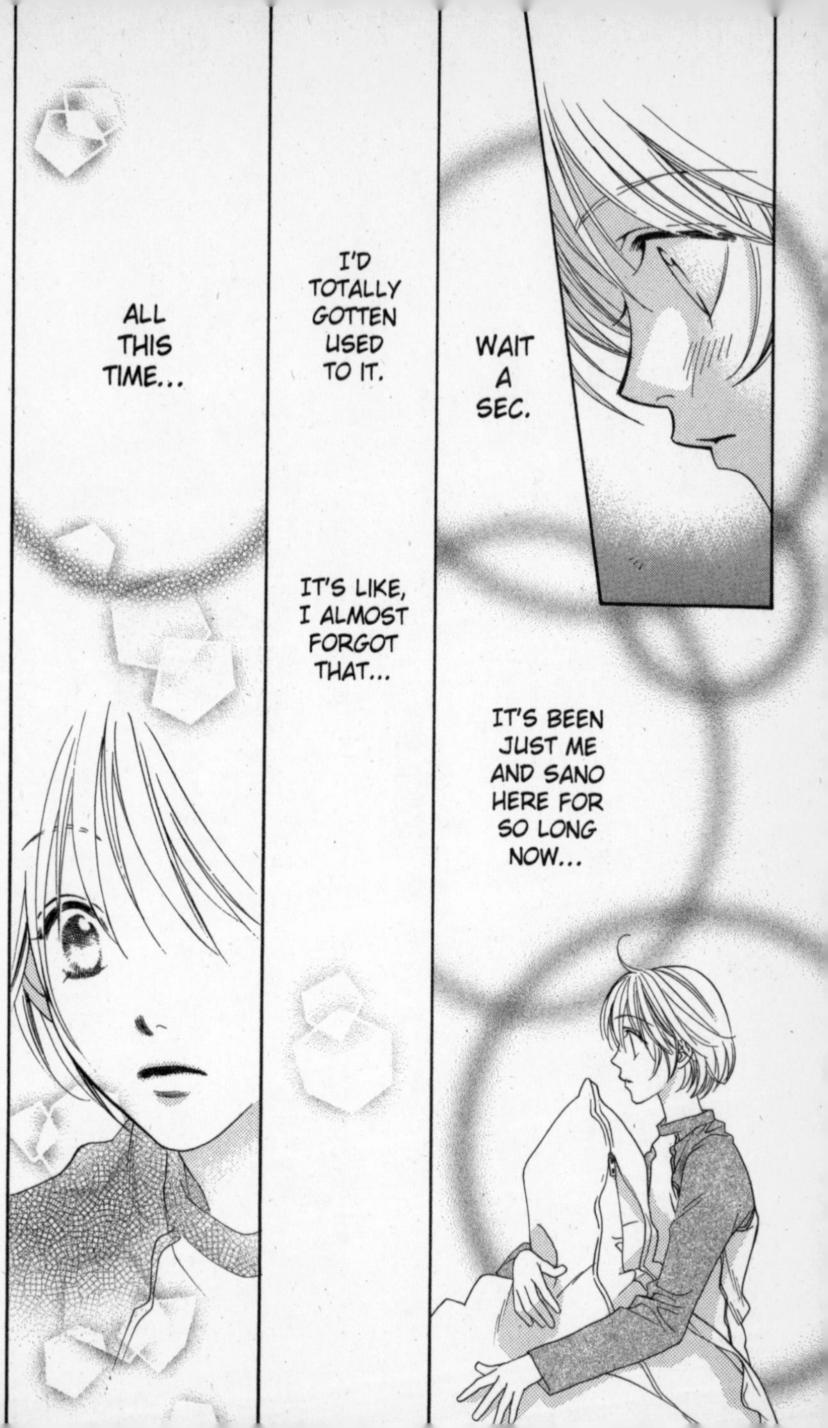
WAIT A SEC.
IT'S BEEN JUST ME AND SANO HERE FOR SO LONG NOW...
I'D TOTALLY GOTTEN USED TO IT.
IT'S LIKE, I ALMOST FORGOT THAT...
ALL THIS TIME...

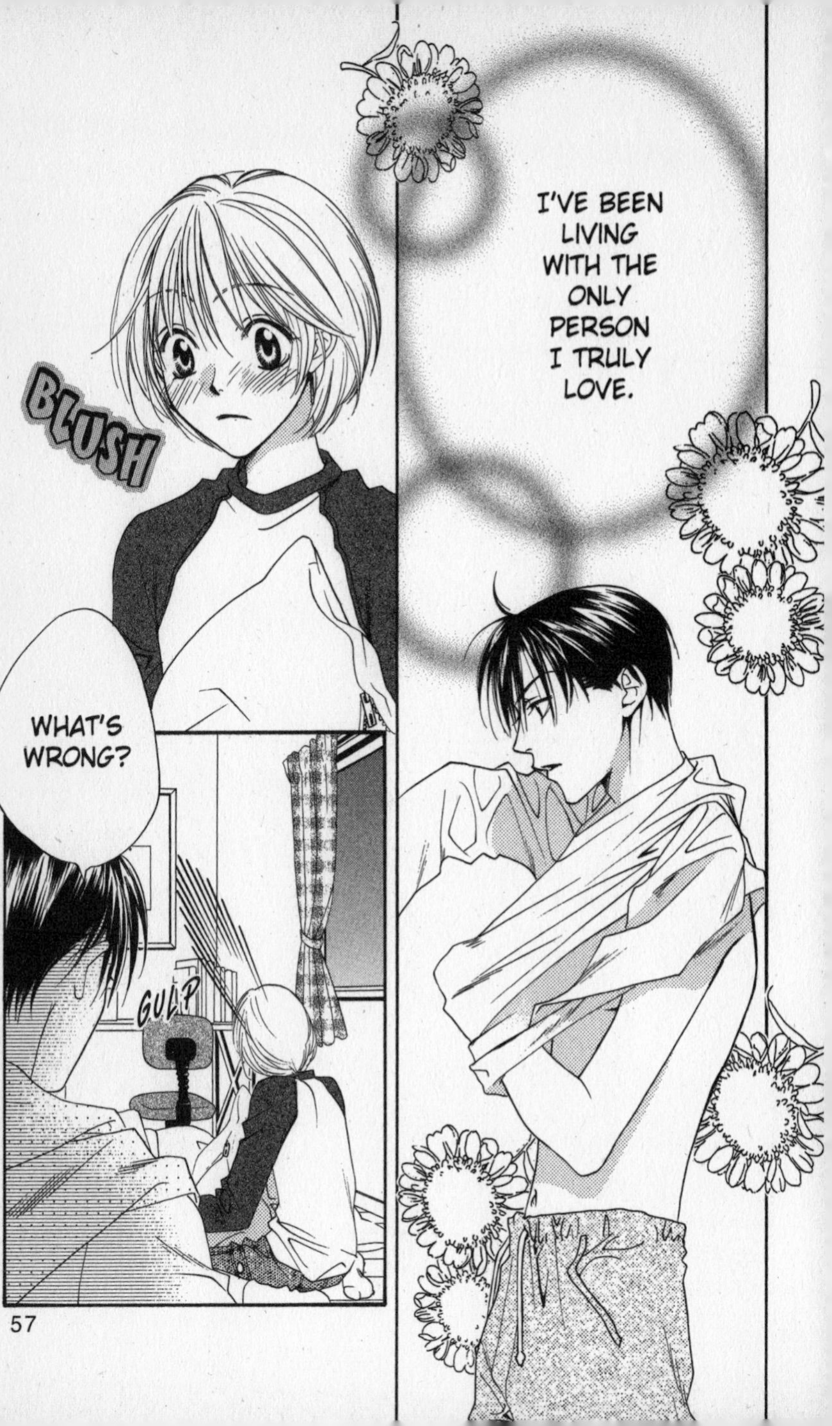
I'VE BEEN LIVING WITH THE ONLY PERSON I TRULY LOVE.
BLUSH
WHAT'S WRONG?
GULP

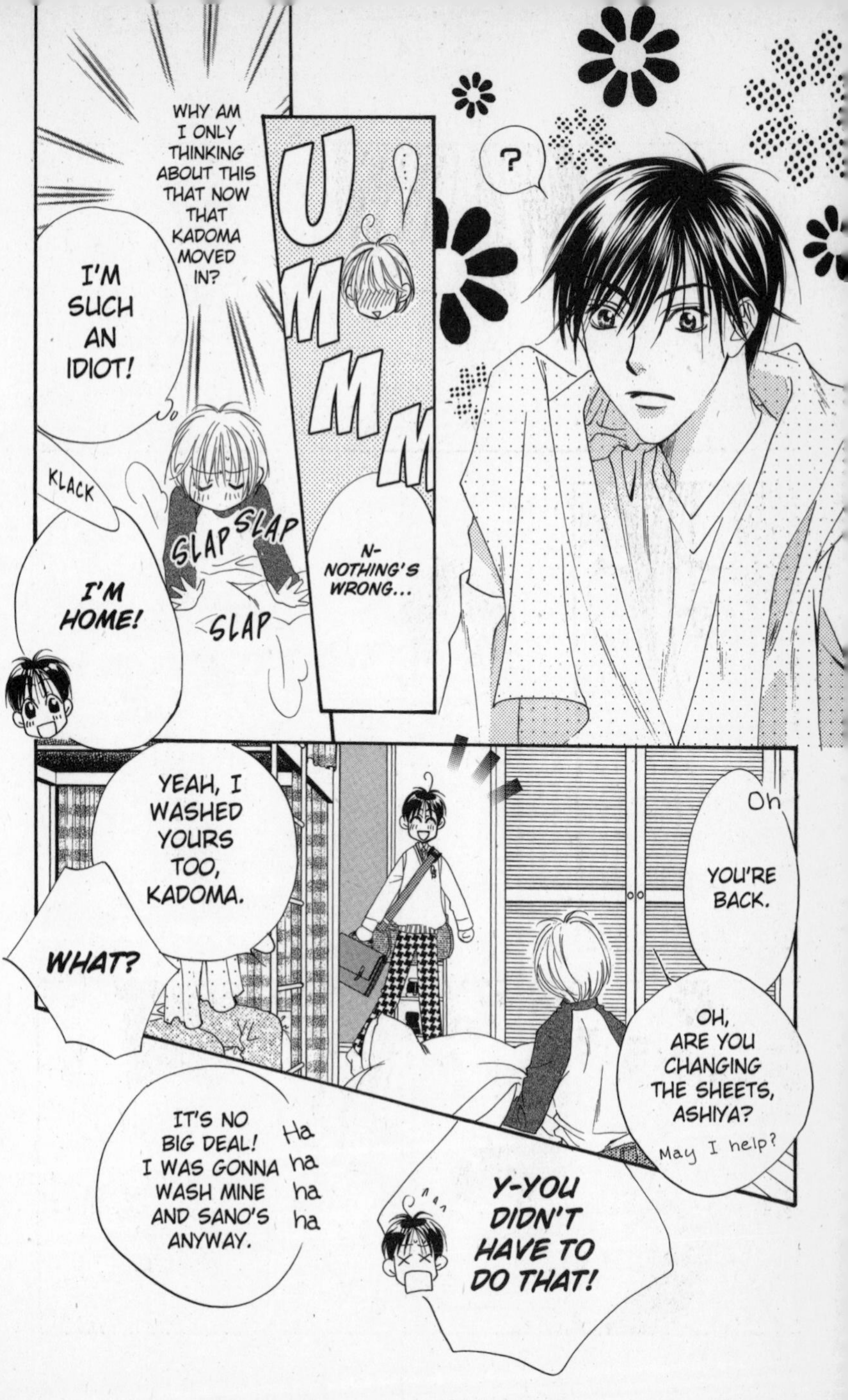
?
UMMM
!
N-NOTHING'S WRONG...
WHY AM I ONLY THINKING ABOUT THIS THAT NOW THAT KADOMA MOVED IN?
I'M SUCH AN IDIOT!
SLAP SLAP
SLAP
KLACK
I'M HOME!
Oh
YOU'RE BACK.
OH, ARE YOU CHANGING THE SHEETS, ASHIYA?
May I help?
YEAH, I WASHED YOURS TOO, KADOMA.
WHAT?
Y-YOU DIDN'T HAVE TO DO THAT!
IT'S NO BIG DEAL! I WAS GONNA WASH MINE AND SANO'S ANYWAY.
Ha ha ha ha

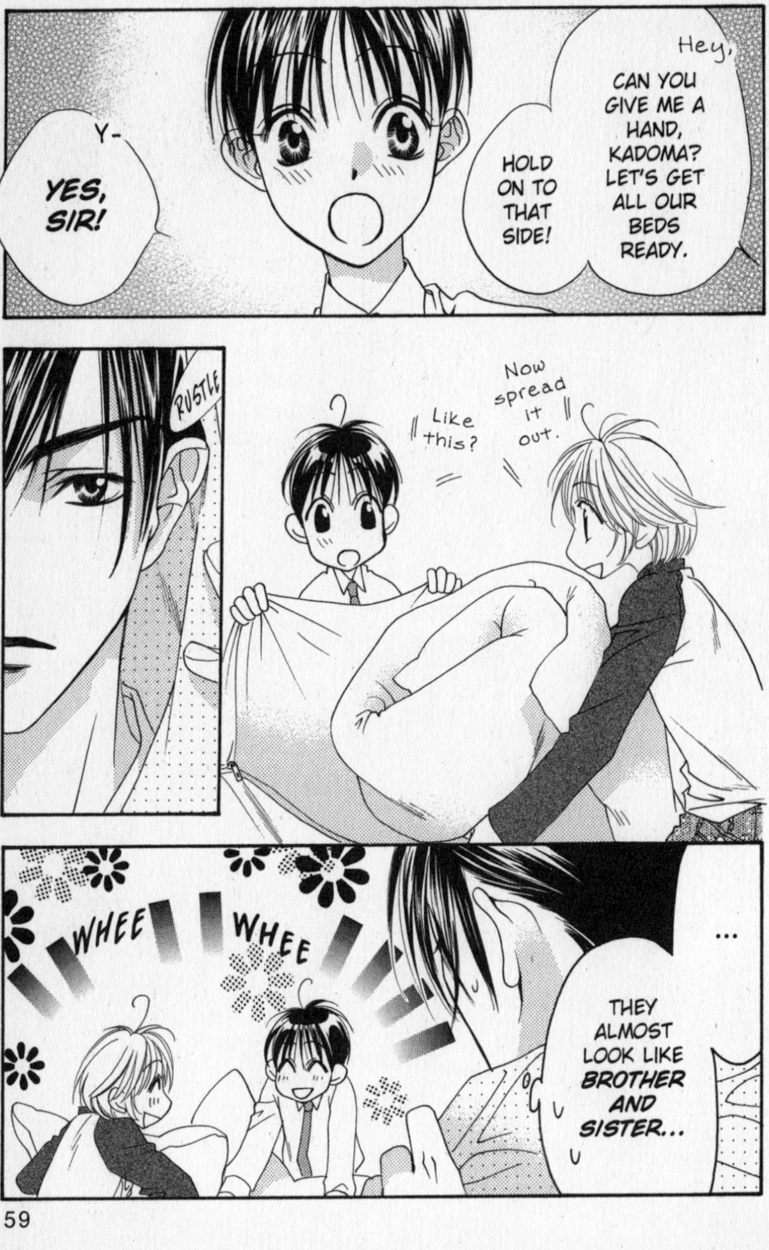
Hey,
CAN YOU GIVE ME A HAND, KADOMA? LET'S GET ALL OUR BEDS READY.
HOLD ON TO THAT SIDE!
Y-
YES, SIR!
Now spread it out.
Like this?
RUSTLE
...
THEY ALMOST LOOK LIKE BROTHER AND SISTER...
WHEE
WHEE

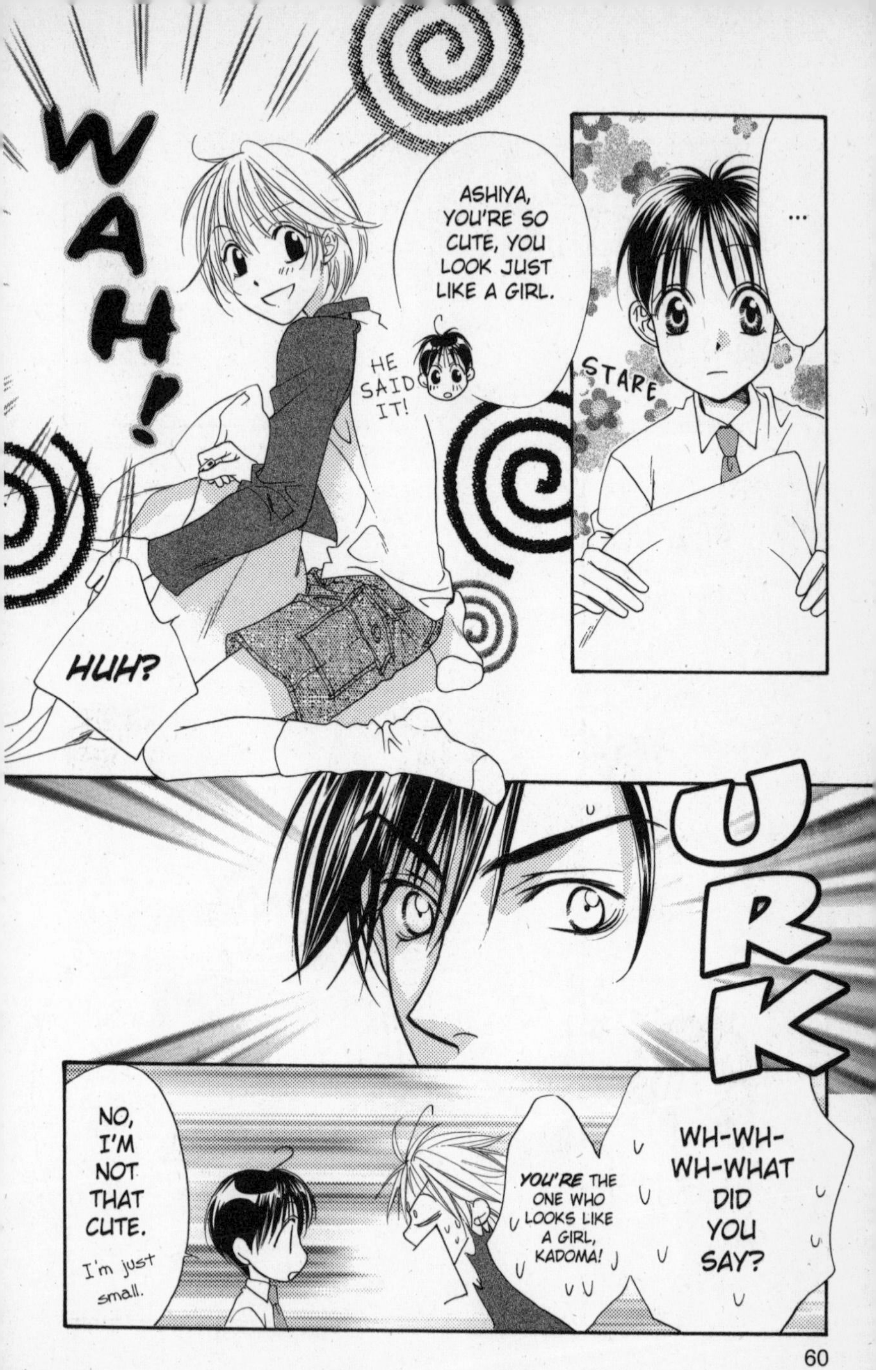
...
STARE
WAH!
ASHIYA, YOU'RE SO CUTE, YOU LOOK JUST LIKE A GIRL.
HE SAID IT!
HUH?
URK
WH-WH-WH-WHAT DID YOU SAY?
YOU'RE THE ONE WHO LOOKS LIKE A GIRL, KADOMA!
NO, I'M NOT THAT CUTE.
I'm just small.

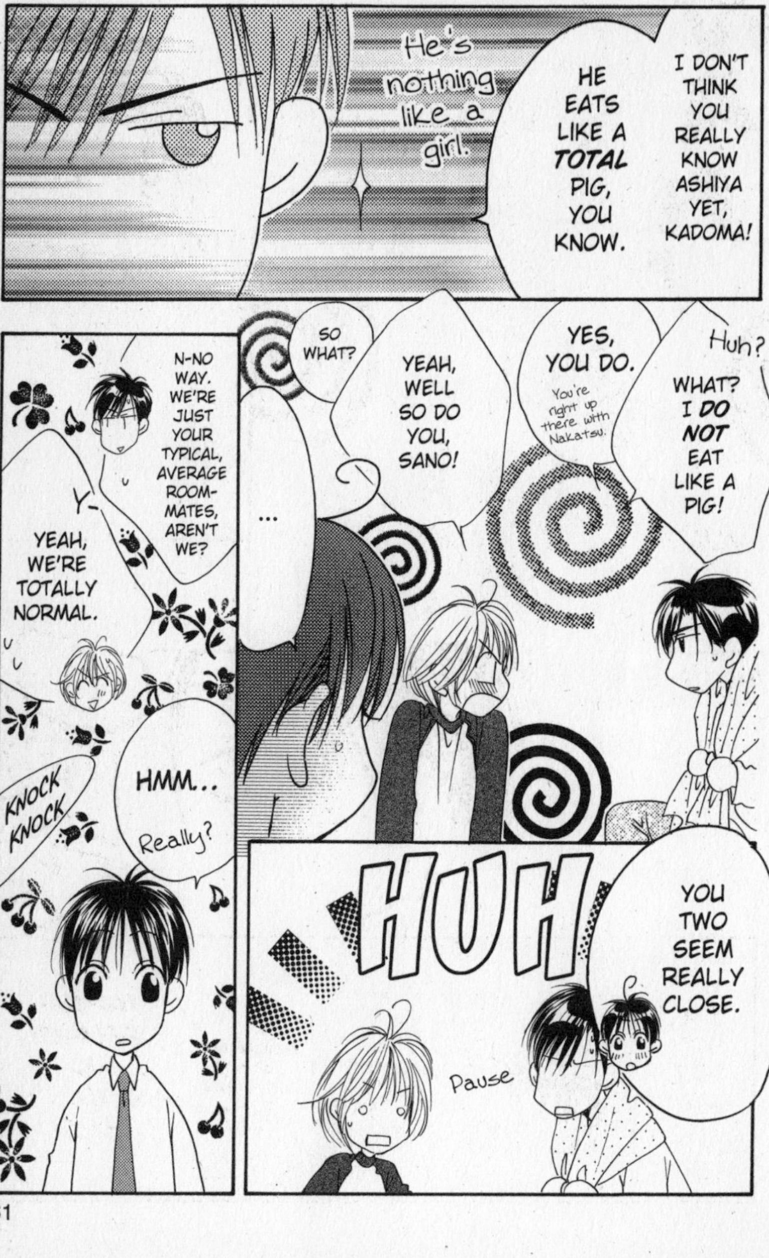
I DON'T THINK YOU REALLY KNOW ASHIYA YET, KADOMA!
HE EATS LIKE A *TOTAL* PIG, YOU KNOW.
He's nothing like a girl.
Huh?
WHAT? I *DO NOT* EAT LIKE A PIG!
YES, YOU DO.
You're right up there with Nakatsu.
YEAH, WELL SO DO YOU, SANO!
SO WHAT?
...
YOU TWO SEEM REALLY CLOSE.
HUH
Pause
N-NO WAY. WE'RE JUST YOUR TYPICAL, AVERAGE ROOMMATES, AREN'T WE?
Y-
YEAH, WE'RE TOTALLY NORMAL.
HMM..
Really?
KNOCK KNOCK

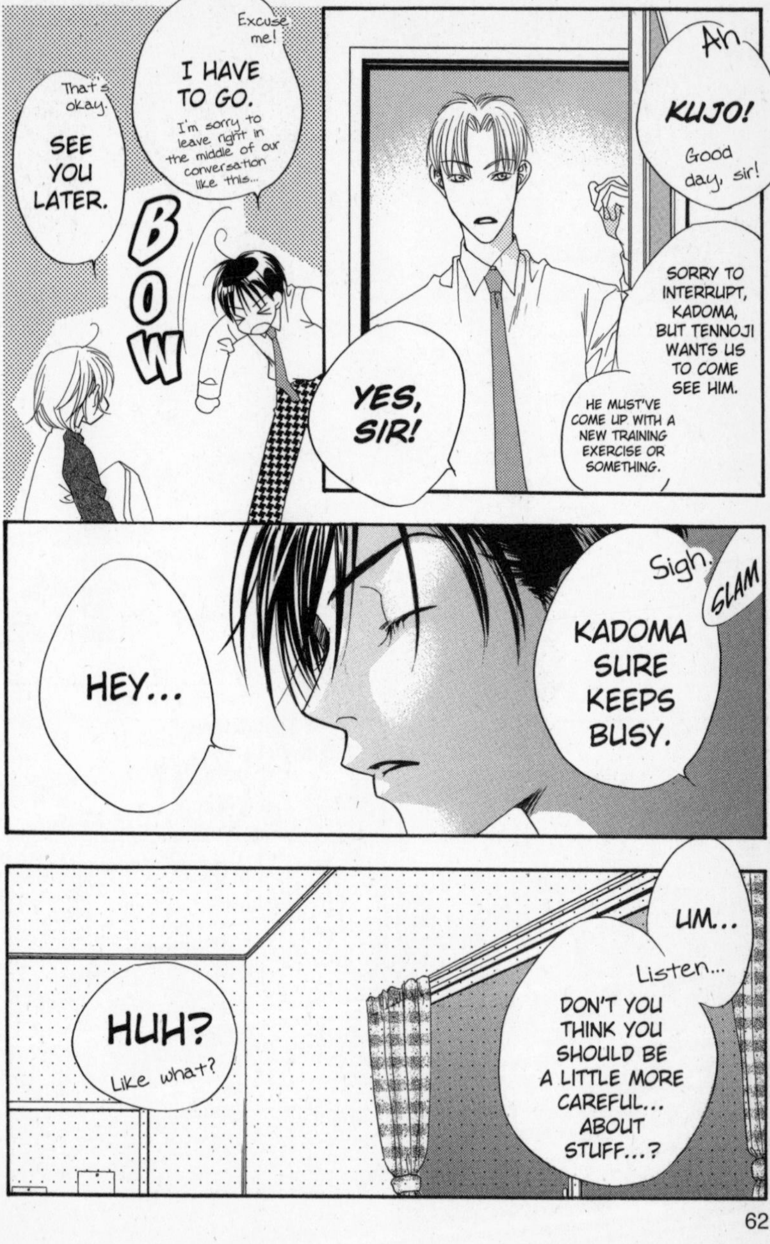
Ah
KUJO! Good day, sir!
SORRY TO INTERRUPT, KADOMA, BUT TENNOJI WANTS US TO COME SEE HIM.
HE MUST'VE COME UP WITH A NEW TRAINING EXERCISE OR SOMETHING.
YES, SIR!
Excuse me!
I HAVE TO GO. I'm sorry to leave right in the middle of our conversation like this...
BOW
That's okay. SEE YOU LATER.
SLAM
Sigh. KADOMA SURE KEEPS BUSY.
HEY...
UM...
Listen... DON'T YOU THINK YOU SHOULD BE A LITTLE MORE CAREFUL... ABOUT STUFF...?
HUH? Like what?

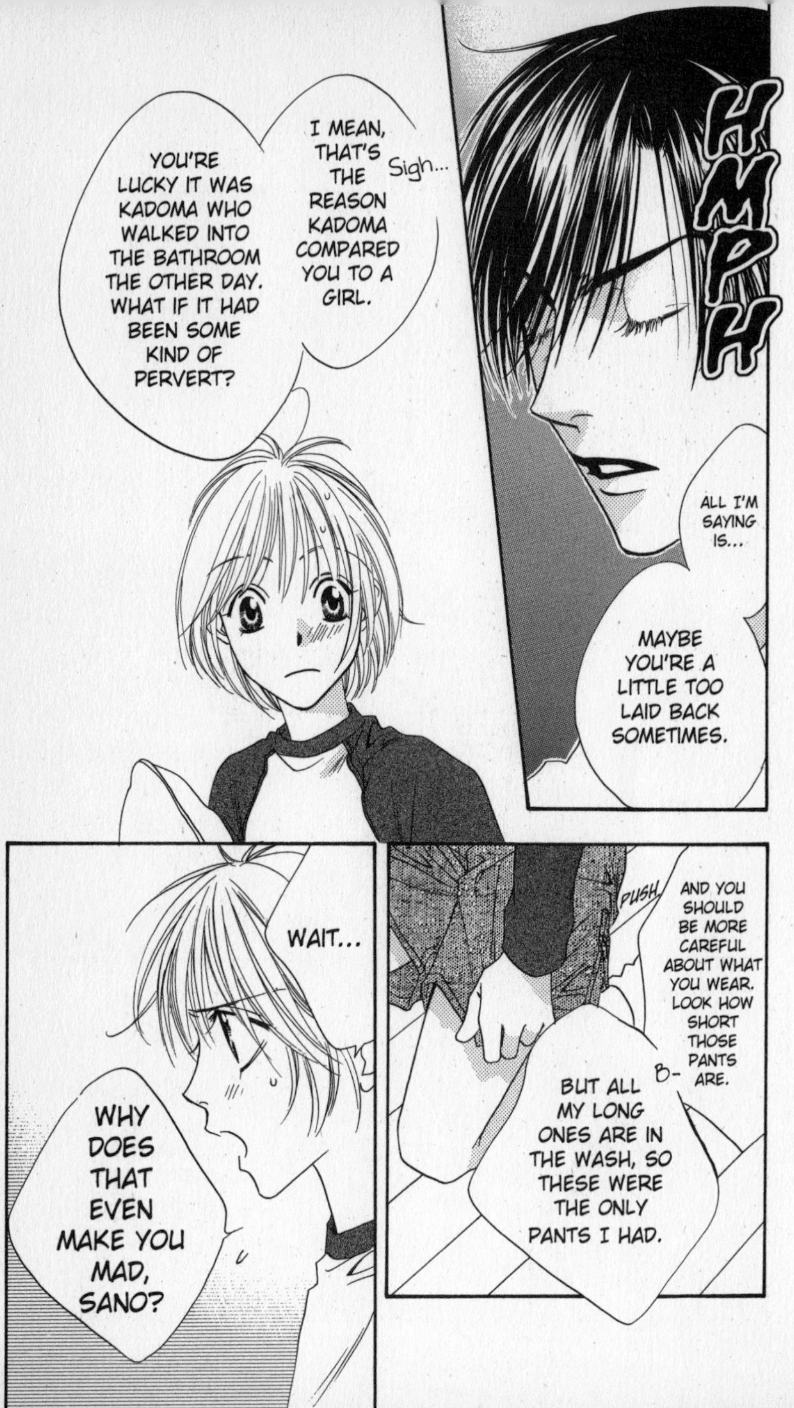
HMPH
ALL I'M SAYING IS...
MAYBE YOU'RE A LITTLE TOO LAID BACK SOMETIMES.
I MEAN, THAT'S THE REASON KADOMA COMPARED YOU TO A GIRL.
Sigh...
YOU'RE LUCKY IT WAS KADOMA WHO WALKED INTO THE BATHROOM THE OTHER DAY. WHAT IF IT HAD BEEN SOME KIND OF PERVERT?
AND YOU SHOULD BE MORE CAREFUL ABOUT WHAT YOU WEAR. LOOK HOW SHORT THOSE PANTS ARE.
PUSH
B-
BUT ALL MY LONG ONES ARE IN THE WASH, SO THESE WERE THE ONLY PANTS I HAD.
WAIT...
WHY DOES THAT EVEN MAKE YOU MAD, SANO?

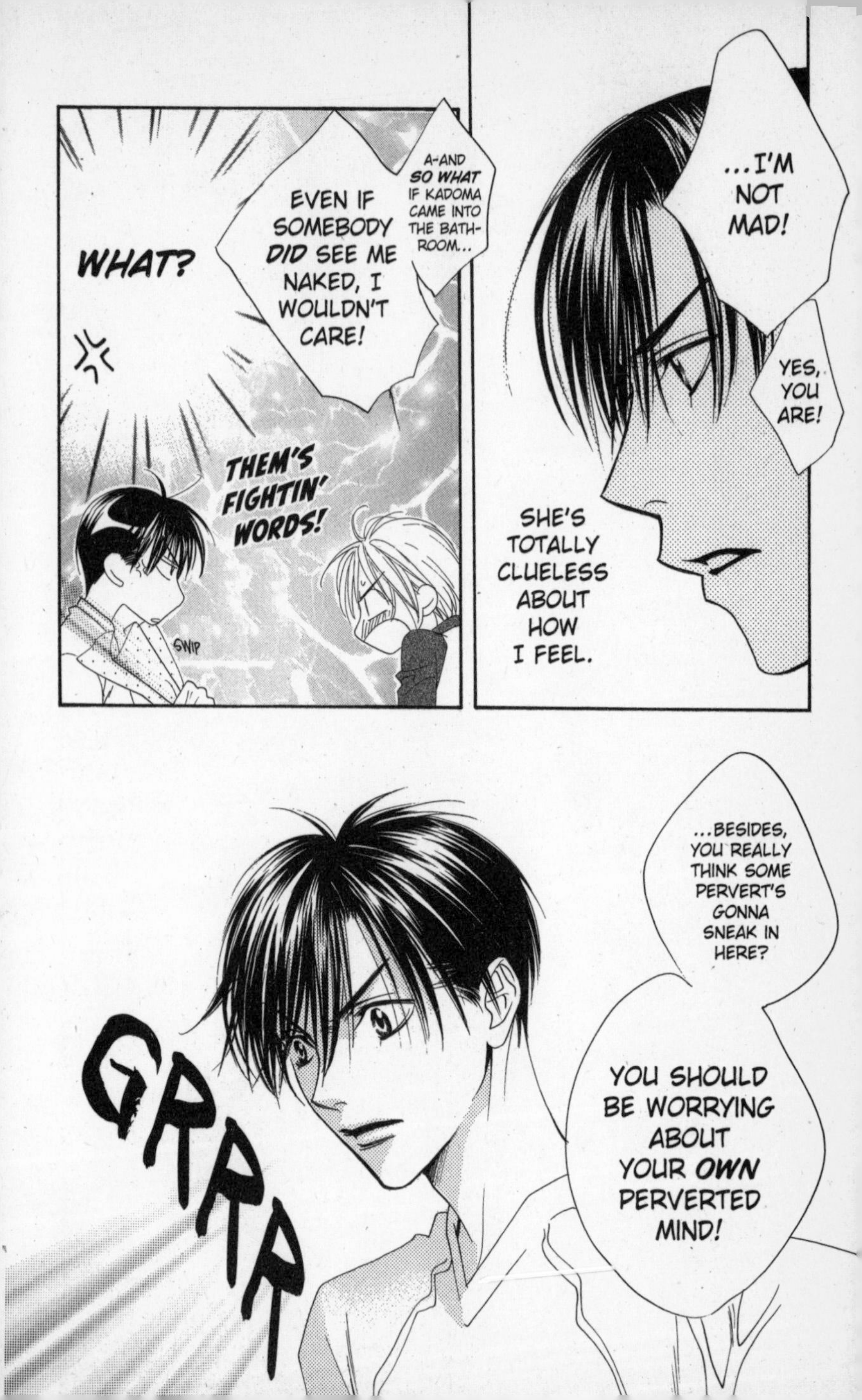
...I'M NOT MAD!
YES, YOU ARE!
SHE'S TOTALLY CLUELESS ABOUT HOW I FEEL.
A-AND *SO WHAT* IF KADOMA CAME INTO THE BATH-ROOM...
EVEN IF SOMEBODY *DID* SEE ME NAKED, I WOULDN'T CARE!
WHAT?
THEM'S FIGHTIN' WORDS!
SWIP
...BESIDES, YOU REALLY THINK SOME PERVERT'S GONNA SNEAK IN HERE?
YOU SHOULD BE WORRYING ABOUT YOUR *OWN* PERVERTED MIND!
GRRR

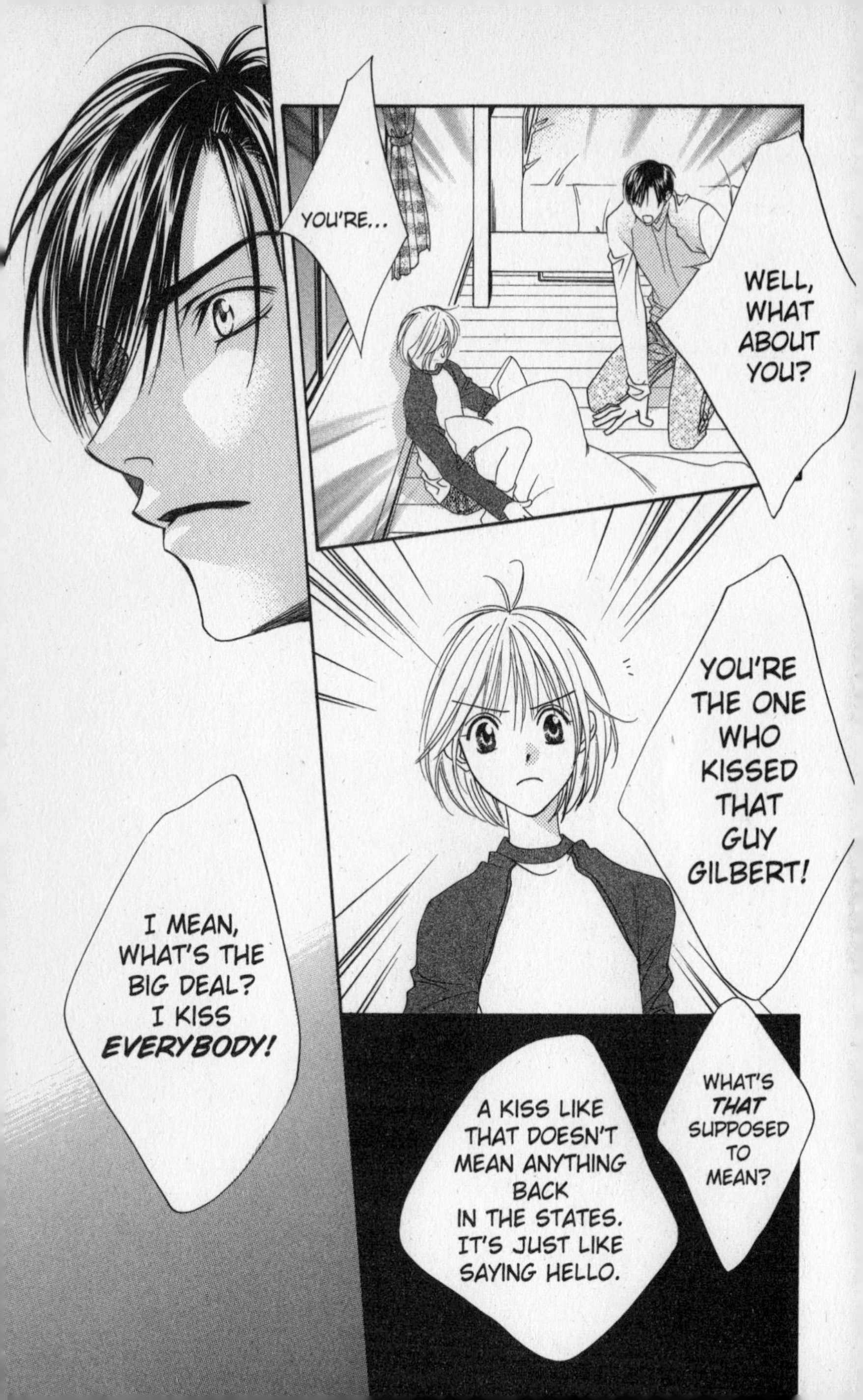
WELL, WHAT ABOUT YOU?
YOU'RE...
YOU'RE THE ONE WHO KISSED THAT GUY GILBERT!
WHAT'S *THAT* SUPPOSED TO MEAN?
A KISS LIKE THAT DOESN'T MEAN ANYTHING BACK IN THE STATES. IT'S JUST LIKE SAYING HELLO.
I MEAN, WHAT'S THE BIG DEAL? I KISS *EVERYBODY!*

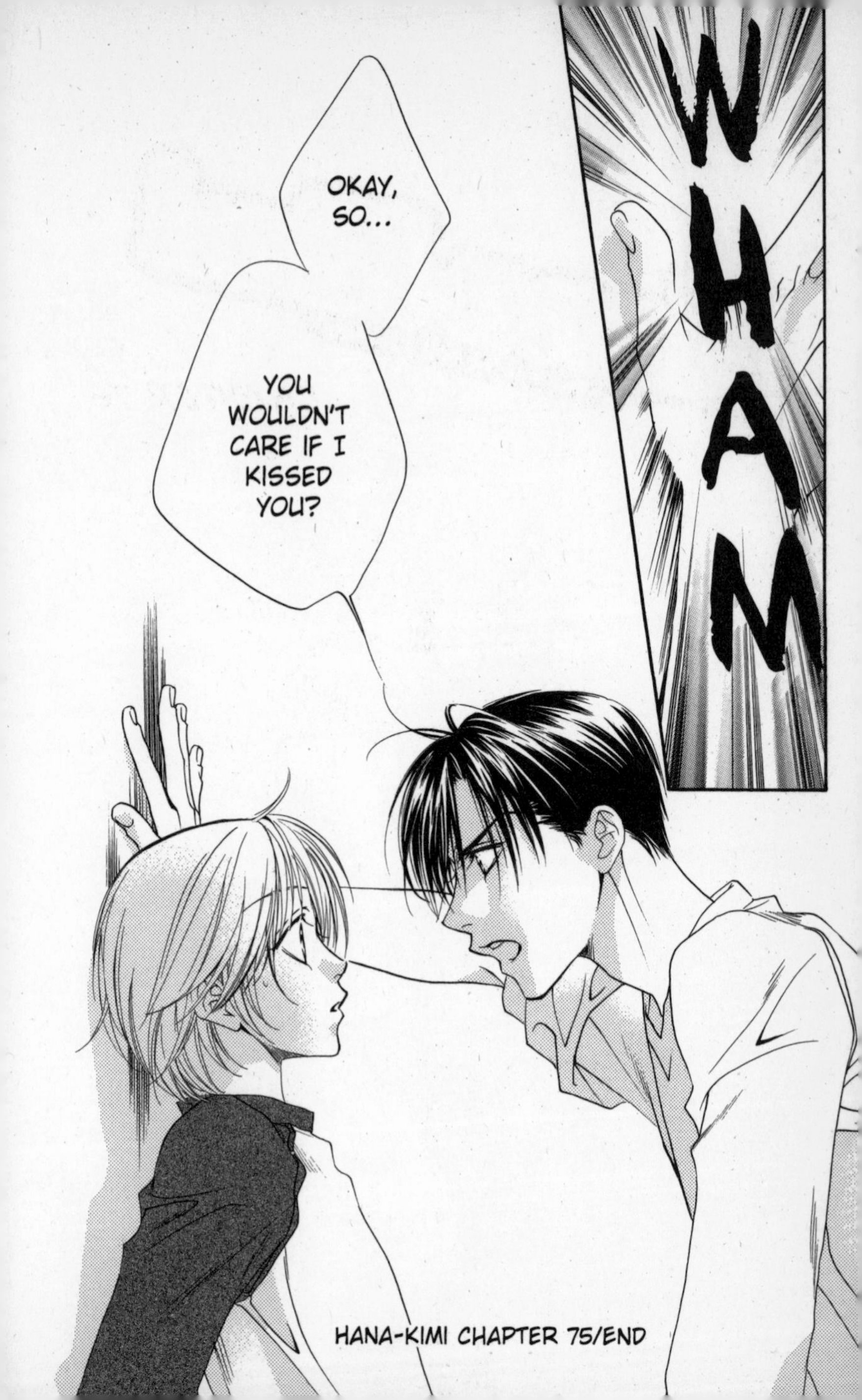
WHAM
OKAY, SO...
YOU WOULDN'T CARE IF I KISSED YOU?

HANA-KIMI CHAPTER 75/END

Hana-Kimi
For You in Full Blossom

CHAPTER 76

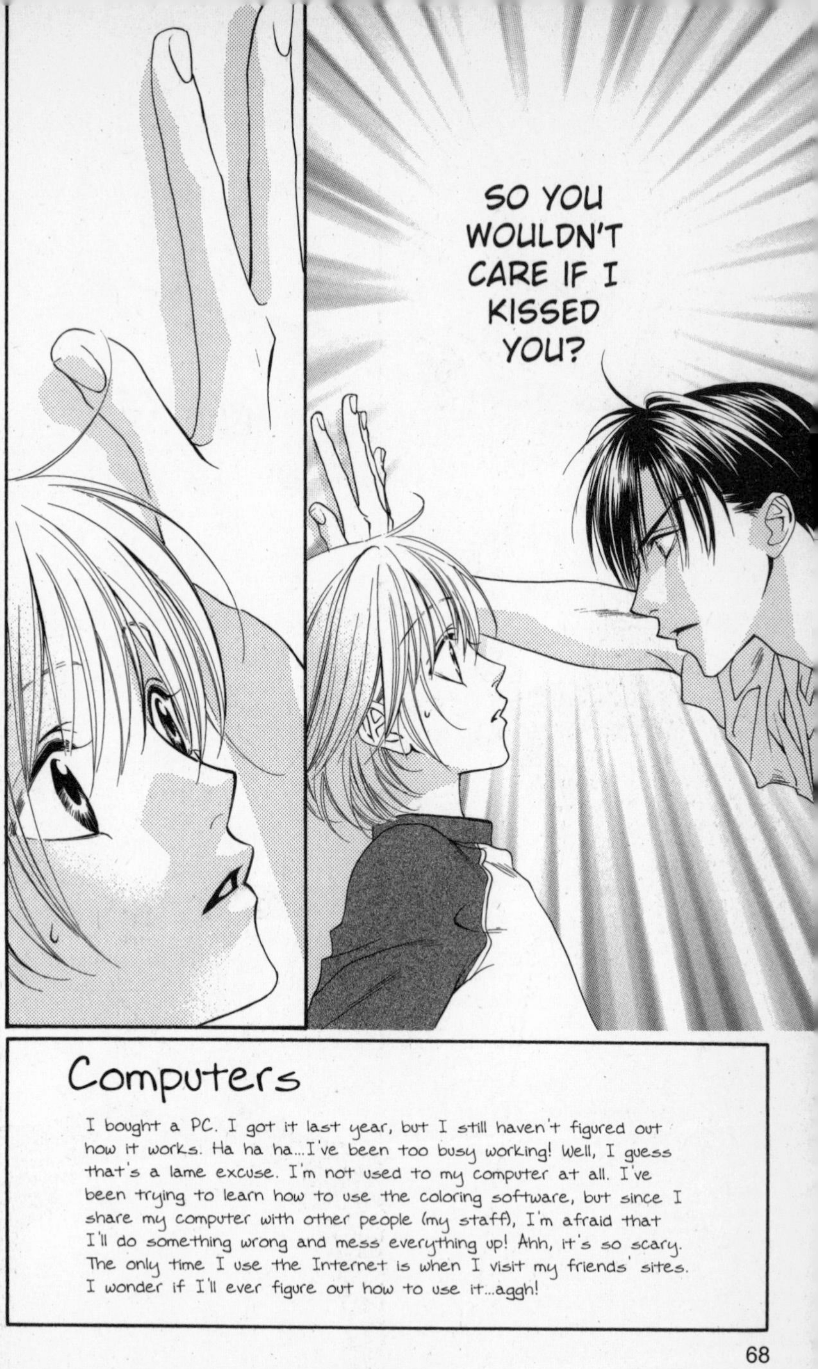
SO YOU WOULDN'T CARE IF I KISSED YOU?

Computers

I bought a PC. I got it last year, but I still haven't figured out how it works. Ha ha ha...I've been too busy working! Well, I guess that's a lame excuse. I'm not used to my computer at all. I've been trying to learn how to use the coloring software, but since I share my computer with other people (my staff), I'm afraid that I'll do something wrong and mess everything up! Ahh, it's so scary. The only time I use the Internet is when I visit my friends' sites. I wonder if I'll ever figure out how to use it...aggh!

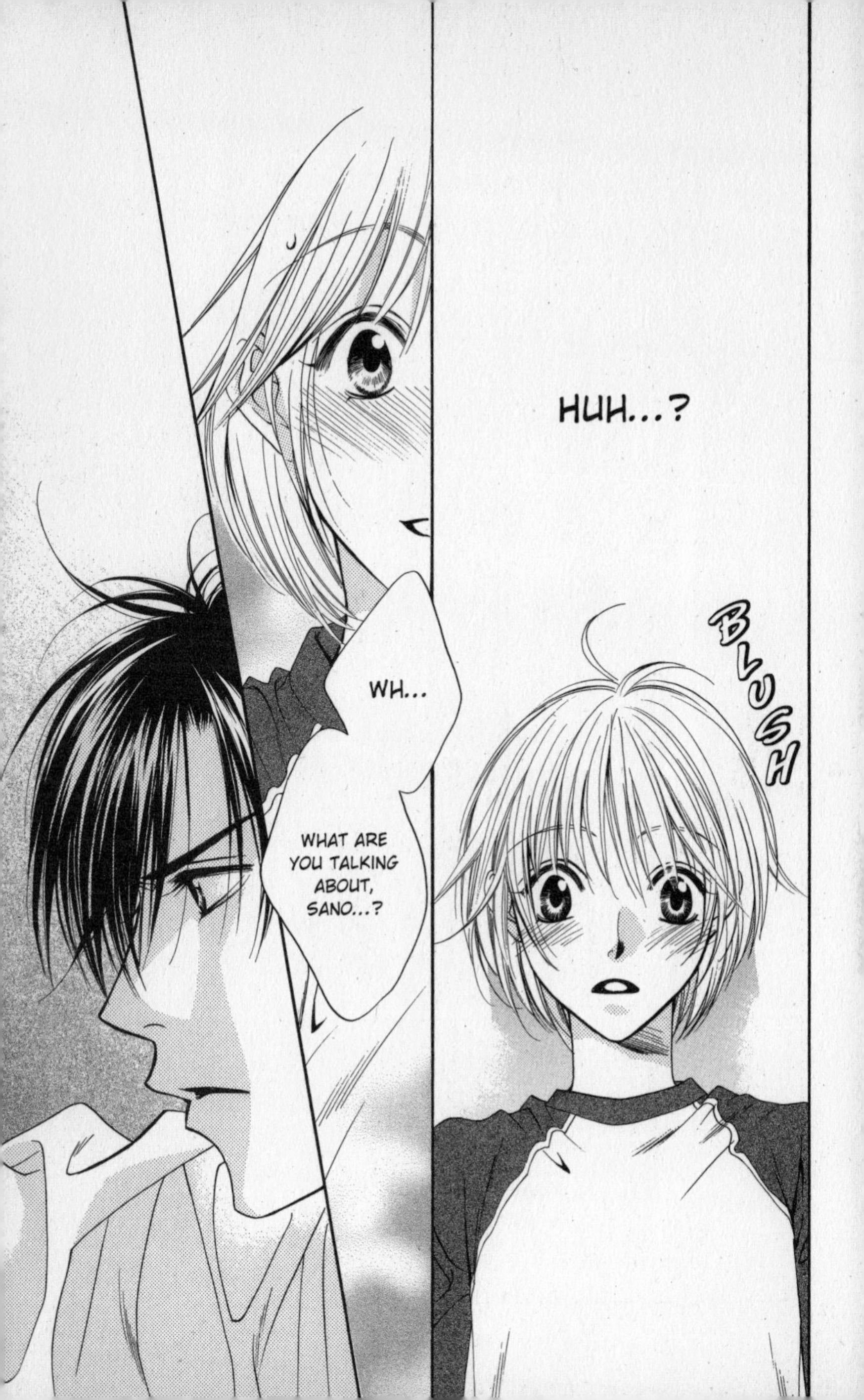
HUH...?
BLUSH
WH...
WHAT ARE YOU TALKING ABOUT, SANO...?

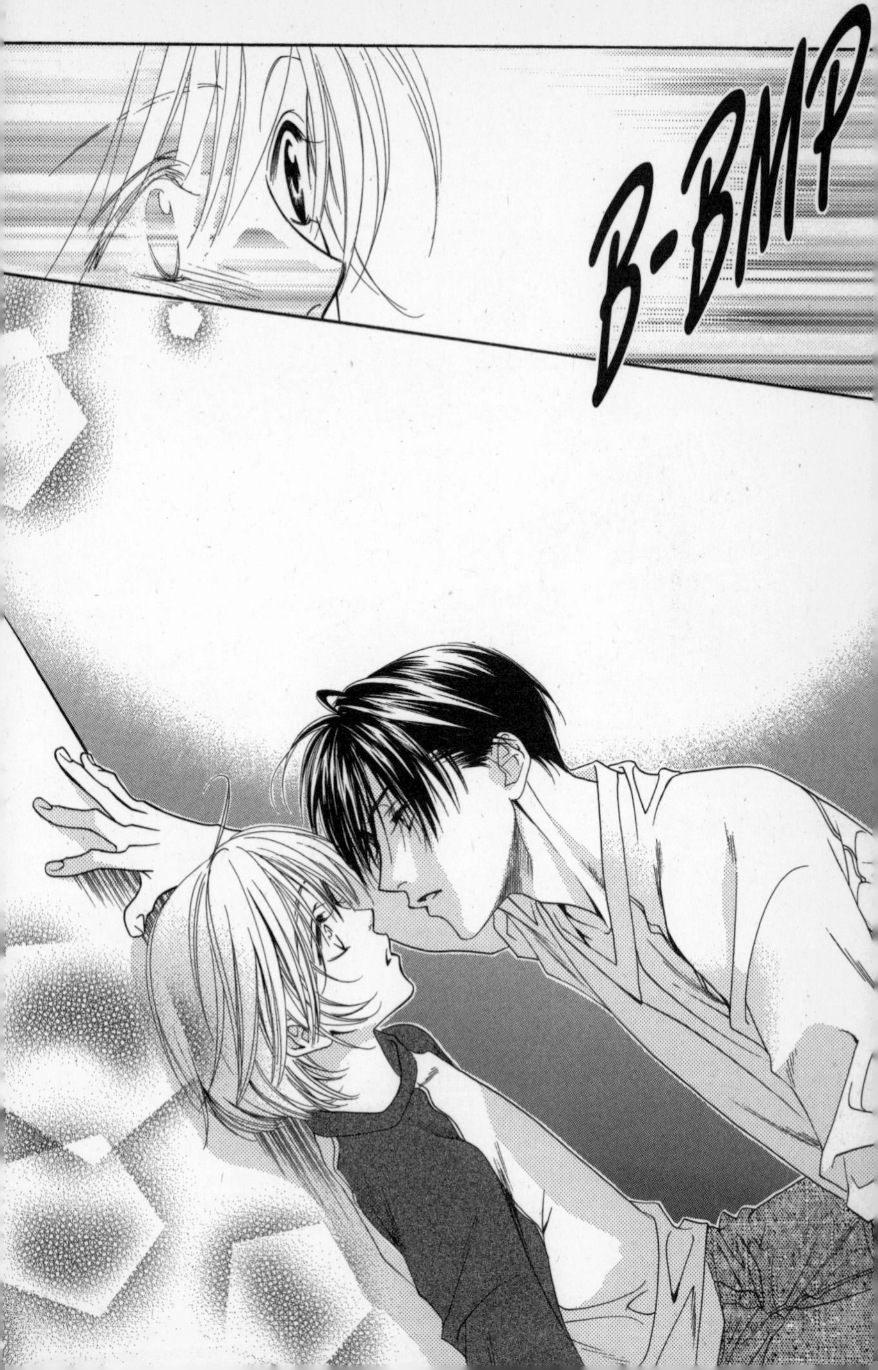
B-BMP

WH...
WHAT SHOULD I DO?
OH MY GOD... SANO'S GONNA...
OH NO... WHAT DO I DO?
I CAN...
...FEEL HIS BREATH...
...ON MY LIPS.

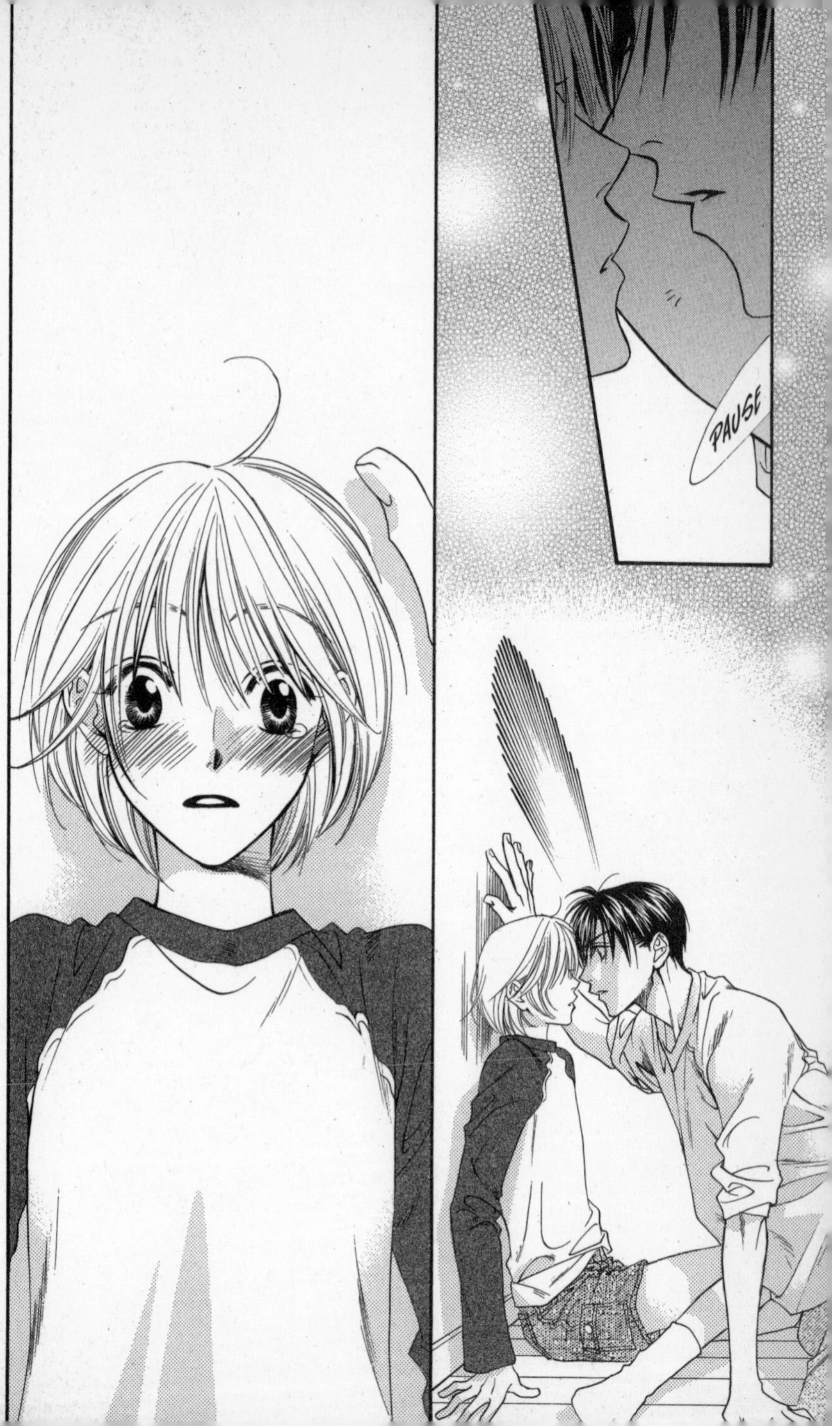
PAUSE

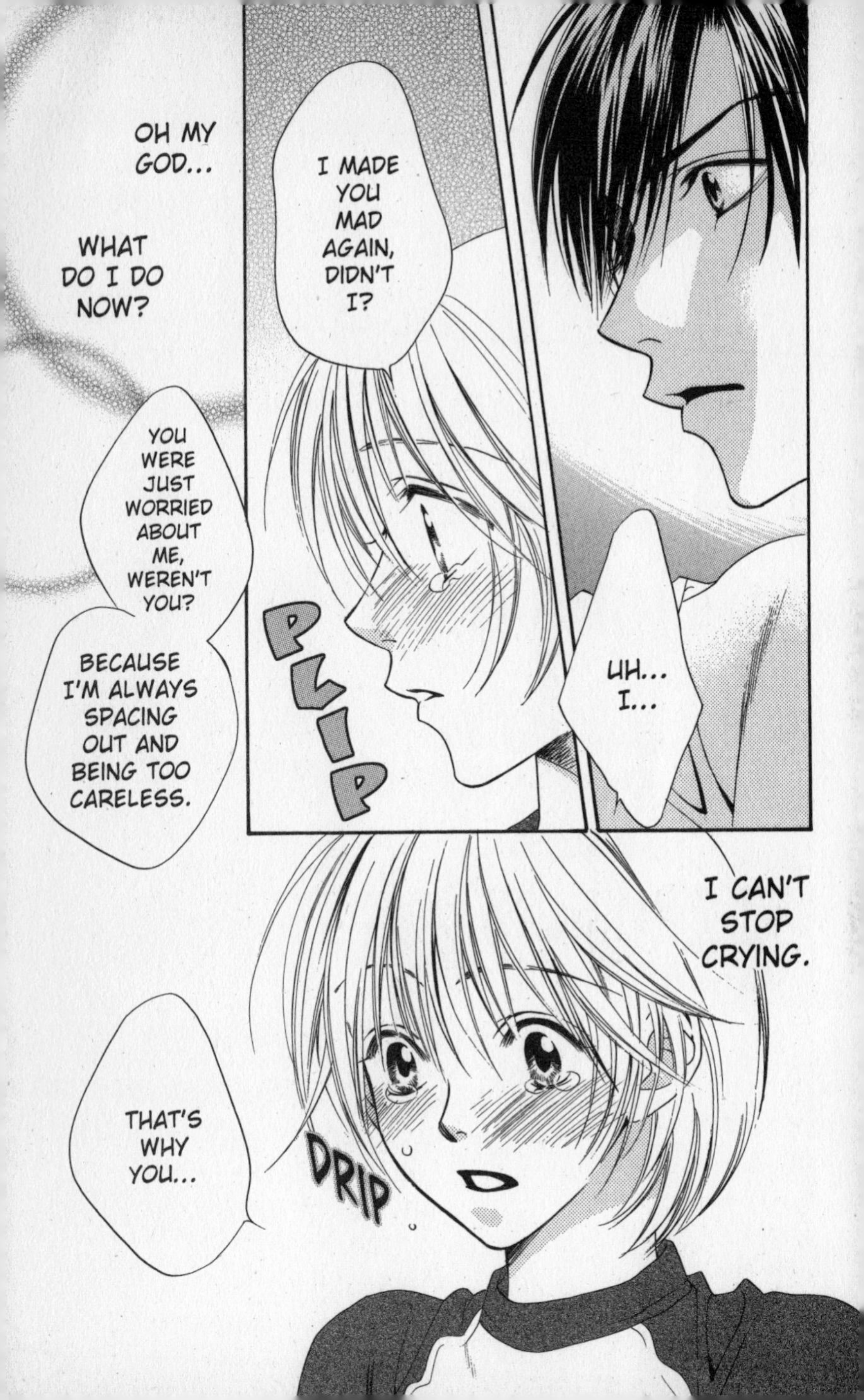
UH... I...
I MADE YOU MAD AGAIN, DIDN'T I?
PLIP
OH MY GOD...
WHAT DO I DO NOW?
YOU WERE JUST WORRIED ABOUT ME, WEREN'T YOU?
BECAUSE I'M ALWAYS SPACING OUT AND BEING TOO CARELESS.
I CAN'T STOP CRYING.
DRIP
THAT'S WHY YOU...

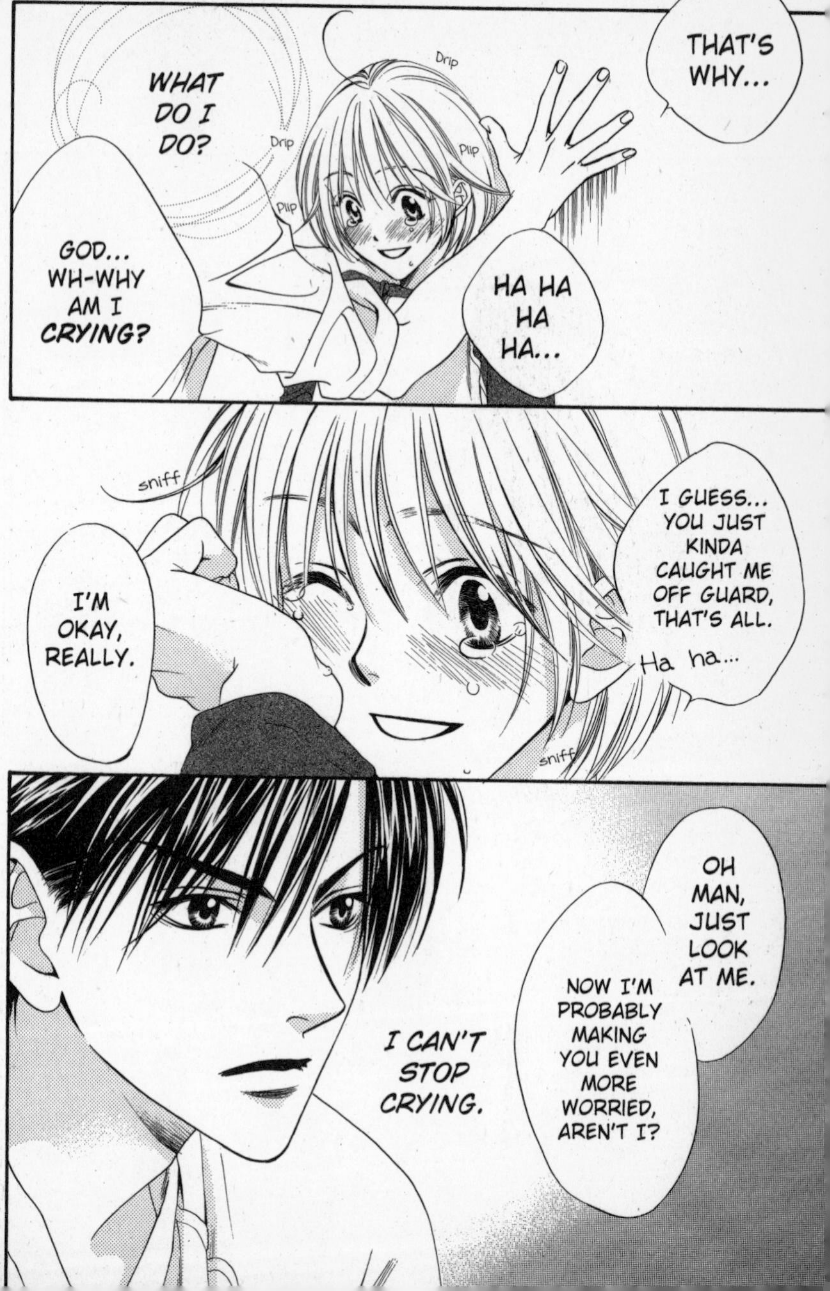
THAT'S WHY...
Drip
WHAT DO I DO?
Drip
Plip
Plip
HA HA HA HA...
GOD... WH-WHY AM I CRYING?
I GUESS... YOU JUST KINDA CAUGHT ME OFF GUARD, THAT'S ALL.
Ha ha...
sniff
I'M OKAY, REALLY.
sniff
OH MAN, JUST LOOK AT ME.
NOW I'M PROBABLY MAKING YOU EVEN MORE WORRIED, AREN'T I?
I CAN'T STOP CRYING.

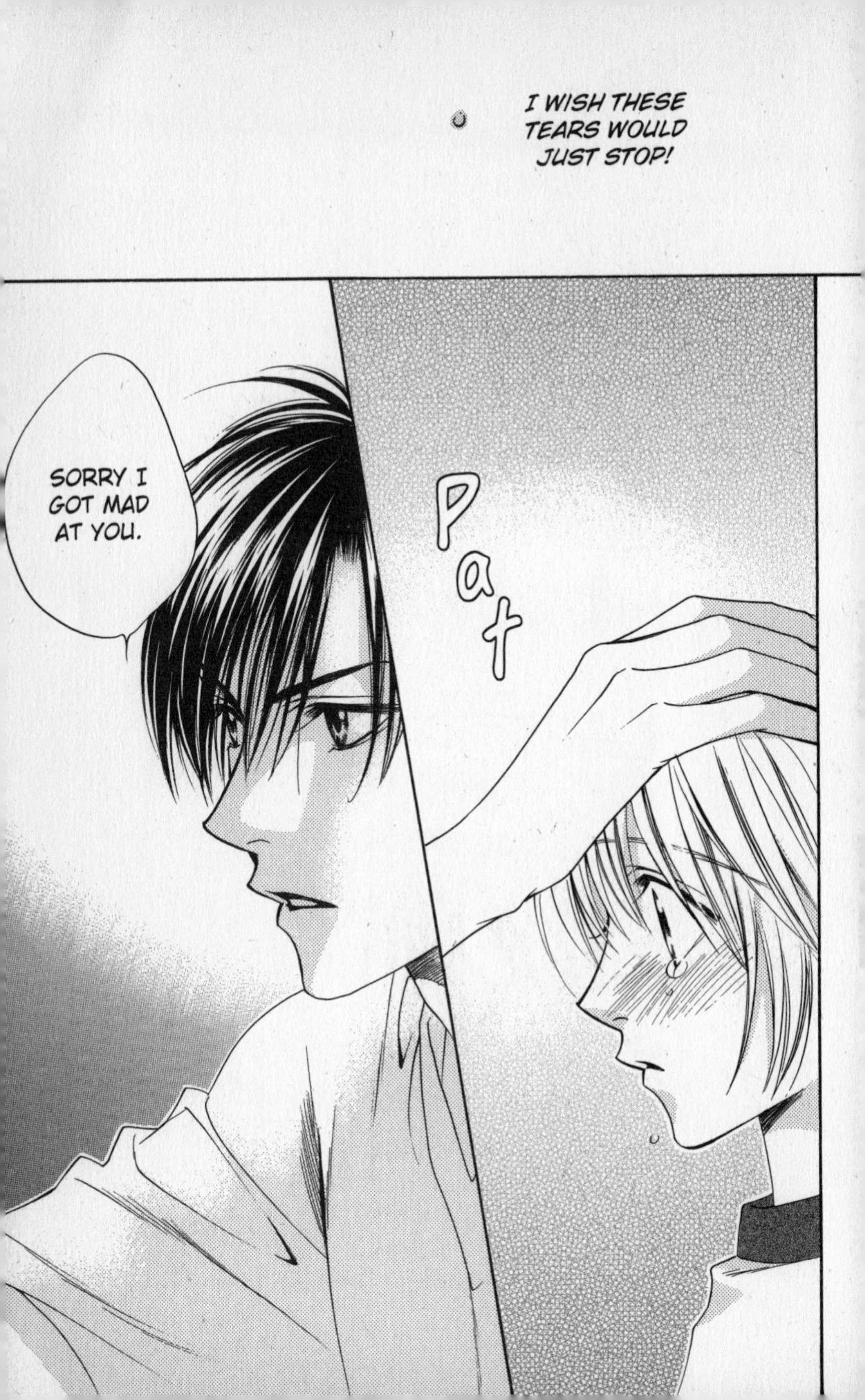
I WISH THESE TEARS WOULD JUST STOP!
Pat
SORRY I GOT MAD AT YOU.

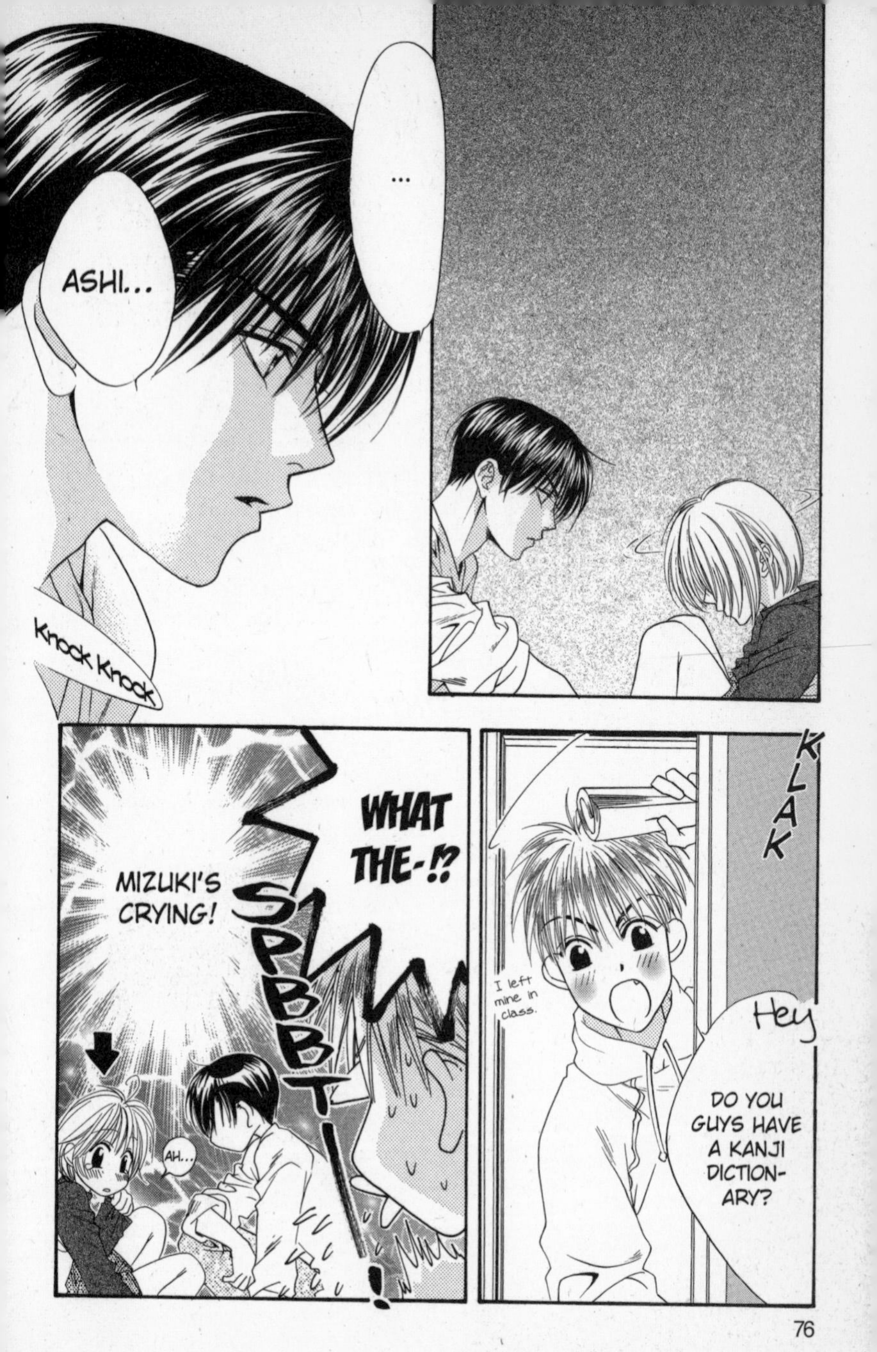
...
ASHI...
Knock Knock
KLAK
Hey
DO YOU GUYS HAVE A KANJI DICTION-ARY?
I left mine in class.
WHAT THE-!?
SPBBT!
MIZUKI'S CRYING!
AH...

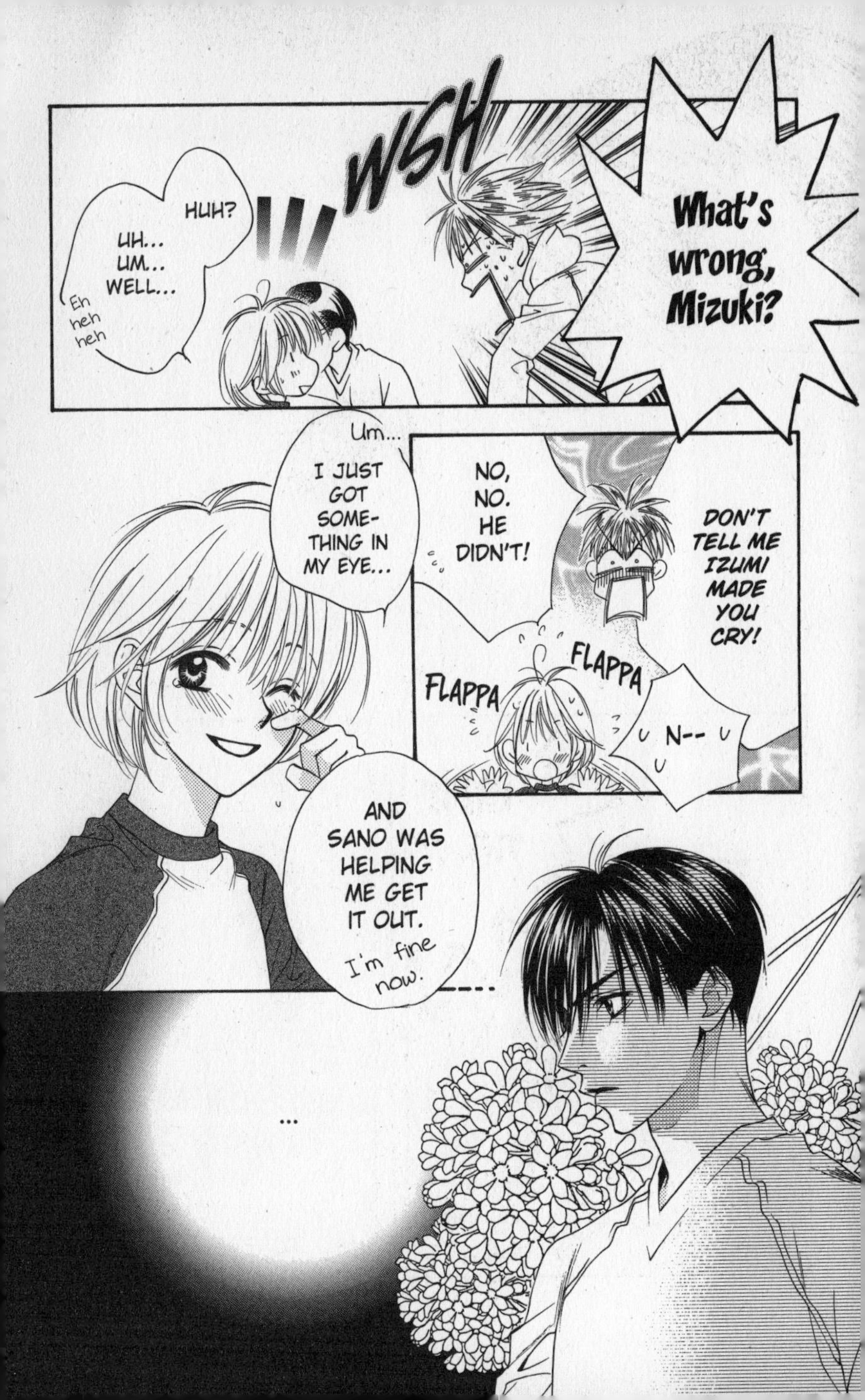
What's wrong, Mizuki?
WSH
HUH?
UH... UM... WELL...
Eh heh heh
DON'T TELL ME IZUMI MADE YOU CRY!
NO, NO. HE DIDN'T!
FLAPPA
FLAPPA
N--
Um...
I JUST GOT SOMETHING IN MY EYE...
AND SANO WAS HELPING ME GET IT OUT.
I'm fine now.
...

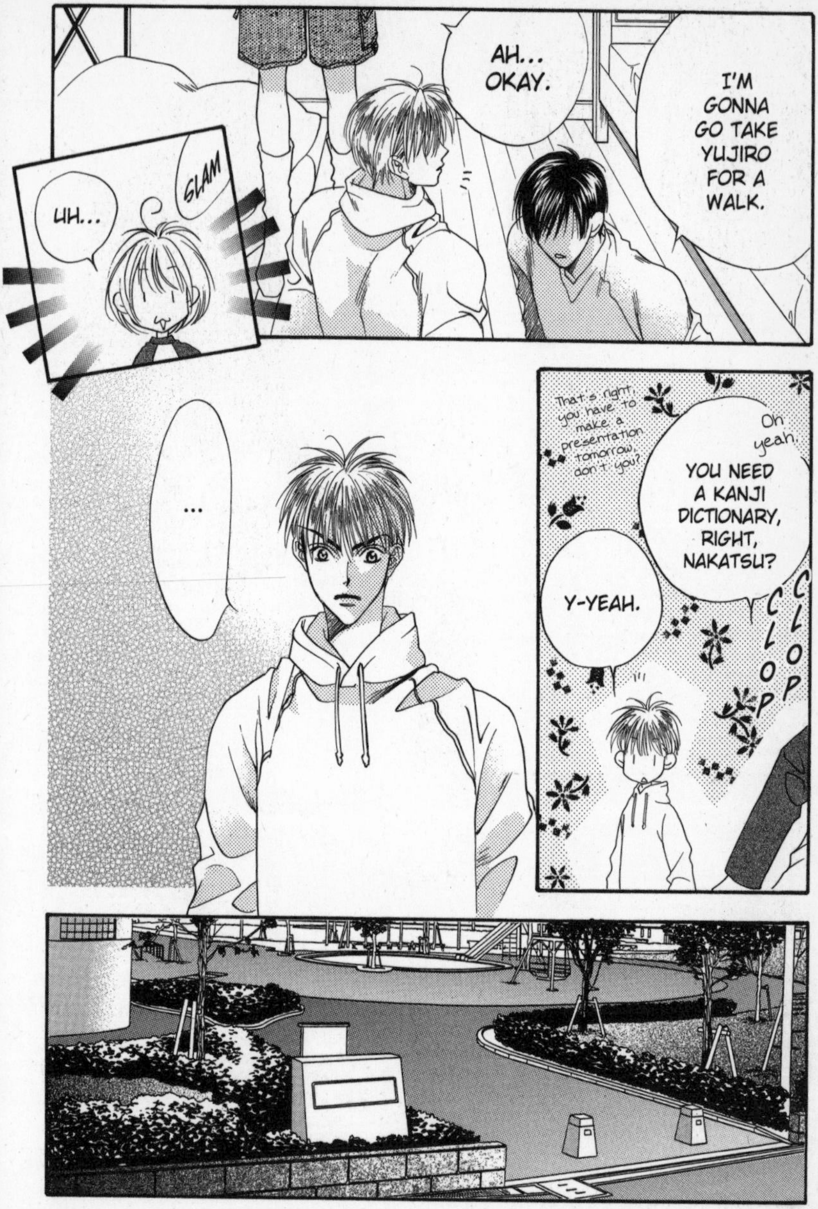
I'M GONNA GO TAKE YUJIRO FOR A WALK.
AH... OKAY.
SLAM
UH...
Oh yeah.
YOU NEED A KANJI DICTIONARY, RIGHT, NAKATSU?
That's right, you have to make a presentation tomorrow, don't you?
Y-YEAH.
CLOP CLOP
...

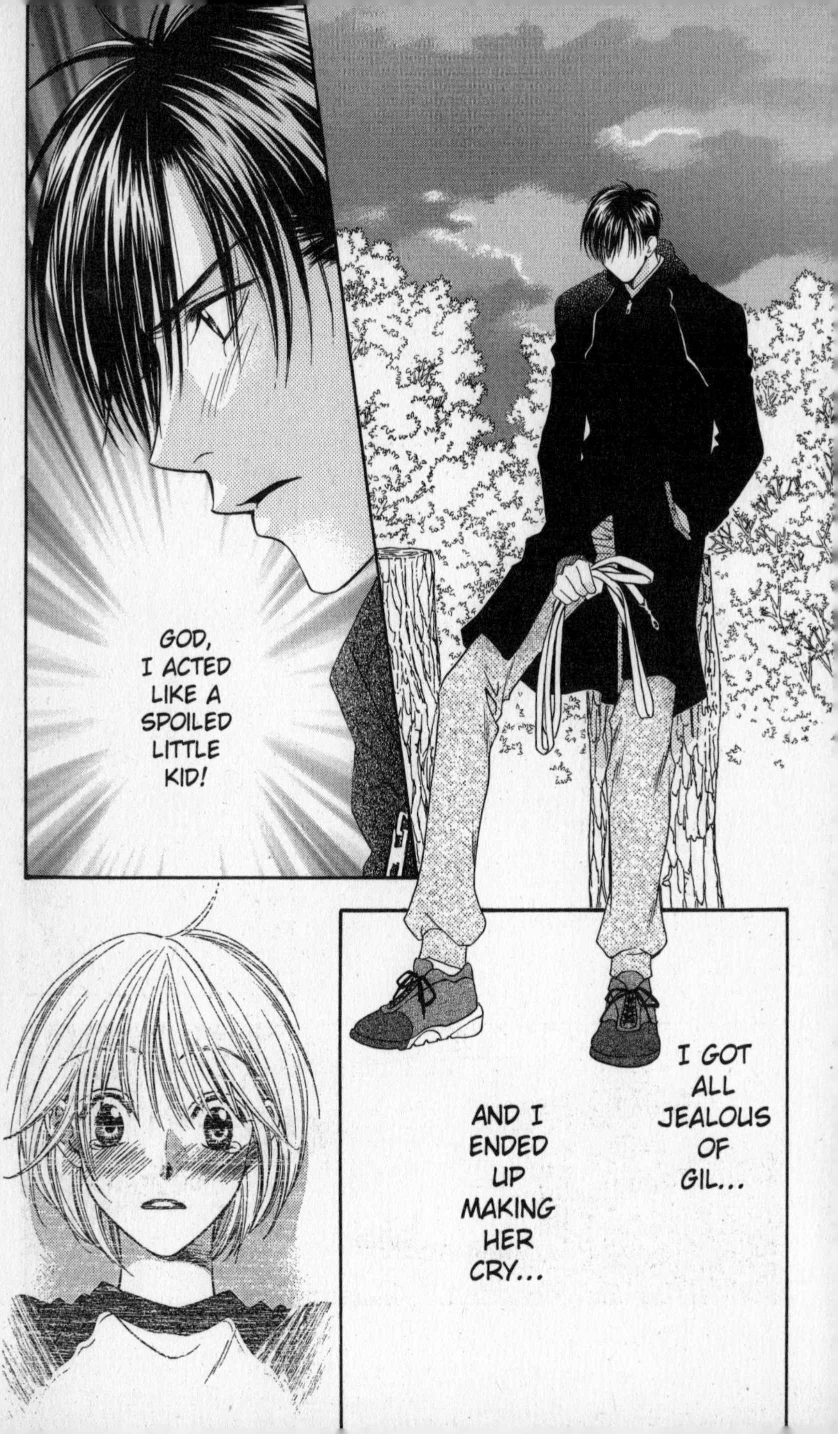
GOD, I ACTED LIKE A SPOILED LITTLE KID!
I GOT ALL JEALOUS OF GIL...
AND I ENDED UP MAKING HER CRY...

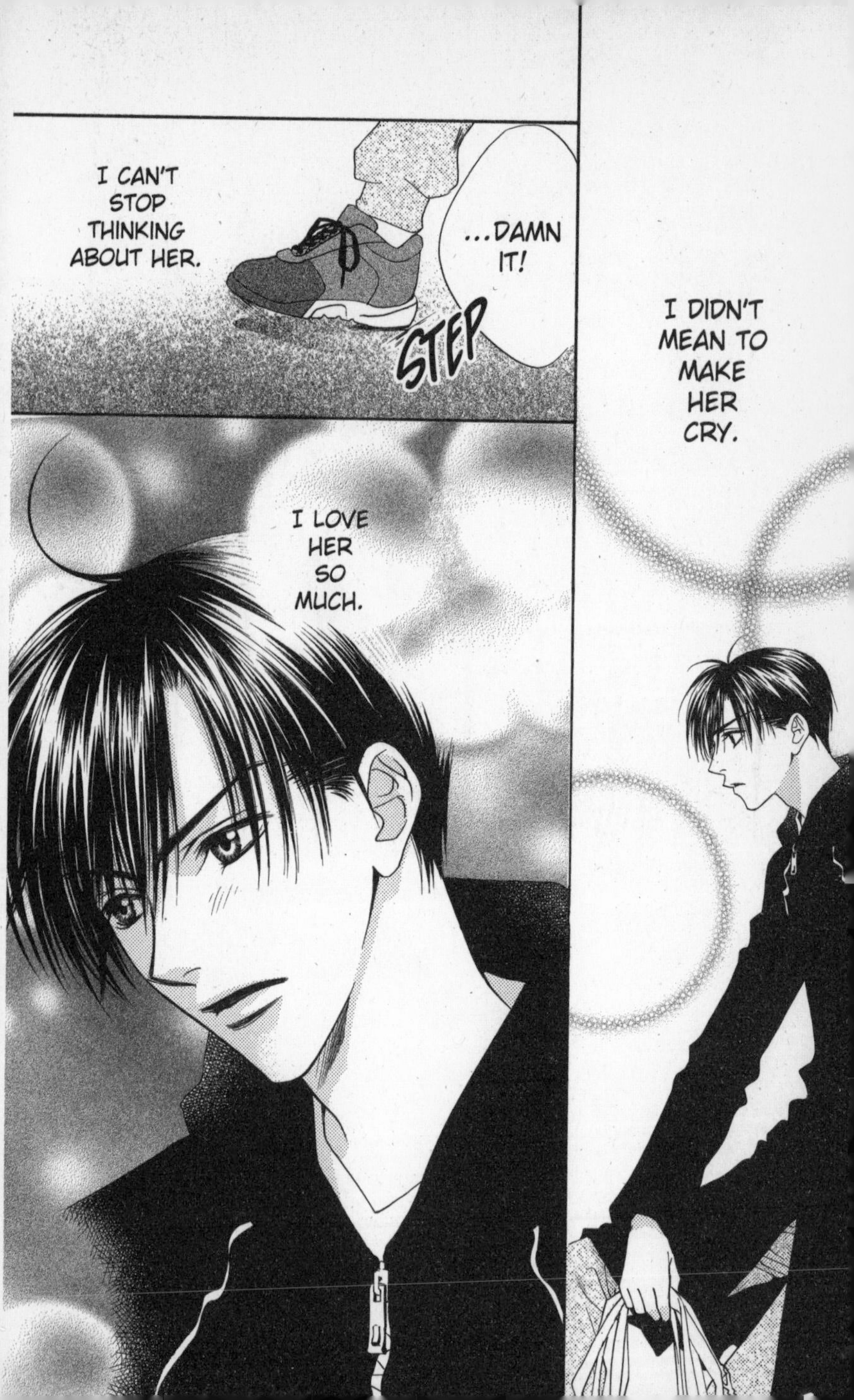
I DIDN'T MEAN TO MAKE HER CRY.
...DAMN IT!
STEP
I CAN'T STOP THINKING ABOUT HER.
I LOVE HER SO MUCH.

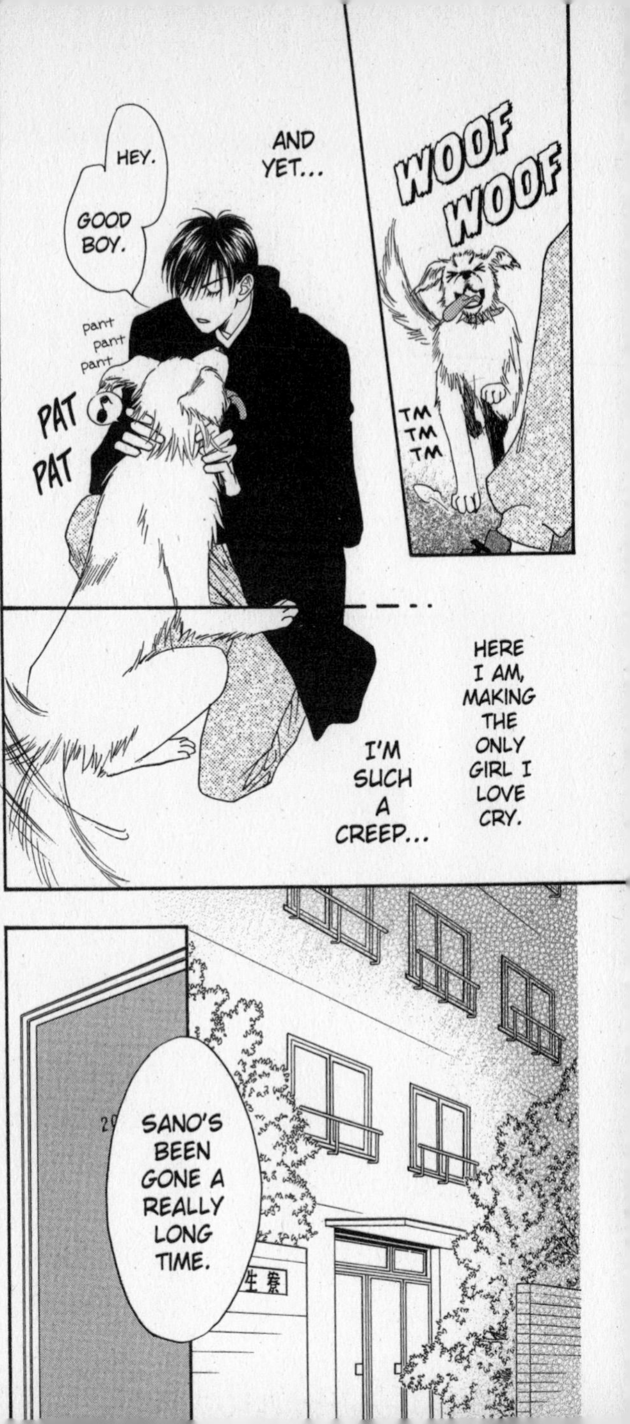
WOOF WOOF
TM TM TM
AND YET...
HEY.
GOOD BOY.
pant pant pant
PAT PAT
HERE I AM, MAKING THE ONLY GIRL I LOVE CRY.
I'M SUCH A CREEP...
SANO'S BEEN GONE A REALLY LONG TIME.

"You're wrong, Nakajo! Part 2"

Thank you all for sending in comments about my character book [currently only available in Japan... sorry! -The Editor] Actually, one of the readers found a typo! I was so shocked. I proofread that thing so many times, darn it. Kayashima's name was printed as "DAIKI", but it should've been "TAIKI" instead. Oh no! To be precise, his name is "TAIKI (Big Tree)." I'd like to apologize to everybody. Also, I know it's too late to say anything now that the book has already been published, but I realized after I read the final copy, that I came off as sounding totally arrogant. (Ha ha...ha) I know I can be a little clueless and kind of stupid sometimes, but I guess that's just me. I've changed a bit since then, so it was kind of interesting to look back and see how much progress I've made.

It was kind of embarrassing actually.

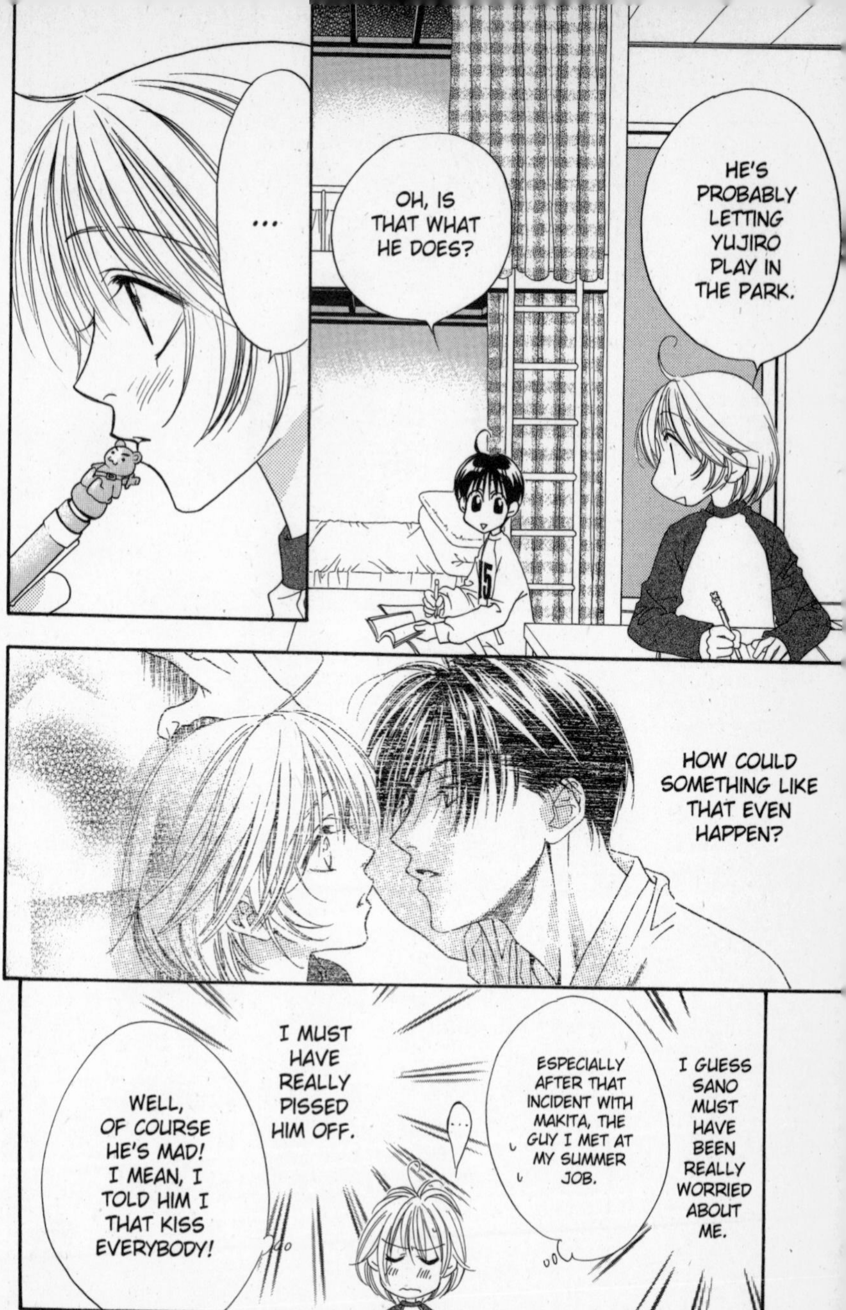
HE'S PROBABLY LETTING YUJIRO PLAY IN THE PARK.
OH, IS THAT WHAT HE DOES?
...
HOW COULD SOMETHING LIKE THAT EVEN HAPPEN?
I GUESS SANO MUST HAVE BEEN REALLY WORRIED ABOUT ME.
ESPECIALLY AFTER THAT INCIDENT WITH MAKITA, THE GUY I MET AT MY SUMMER JOB.
...
I MUST HAVE REALLY PISSED HIM OFF.
WELL, OF COURSE HE'S MAD! I MEAN, I TOLD HIM I THAT KISS EVERYBODY!

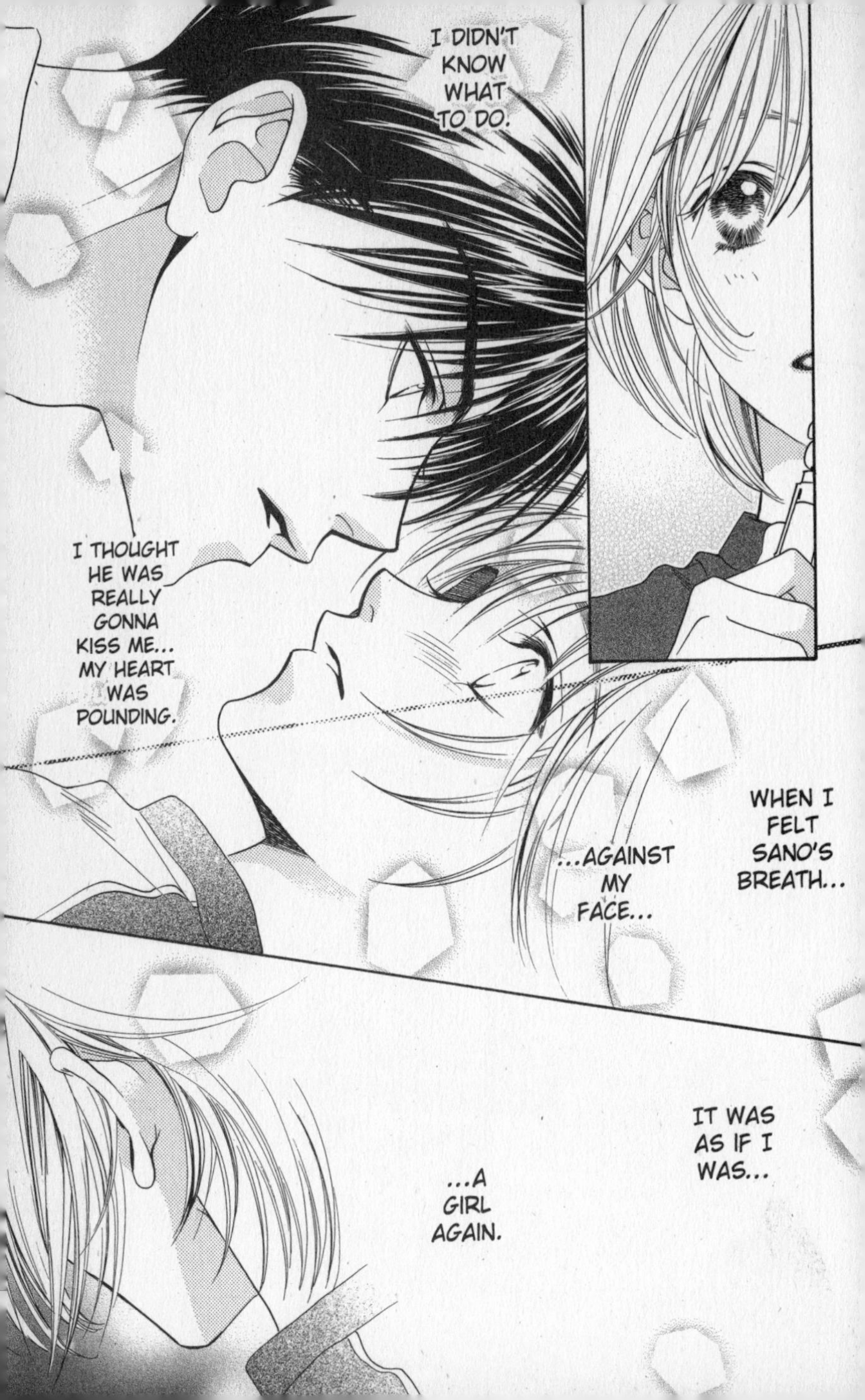
I DIDN'T KNOW WHAT TO DO.
I THOUGHT HE WAS REALLY GONNA KISS ME... MY HEART WAS POUNDING.
WHEN I FELT SANO'S BREATH...
...AGAINST MY FACE...
IT WAS AS IF I WAS...
...A GIRL AGAIN.

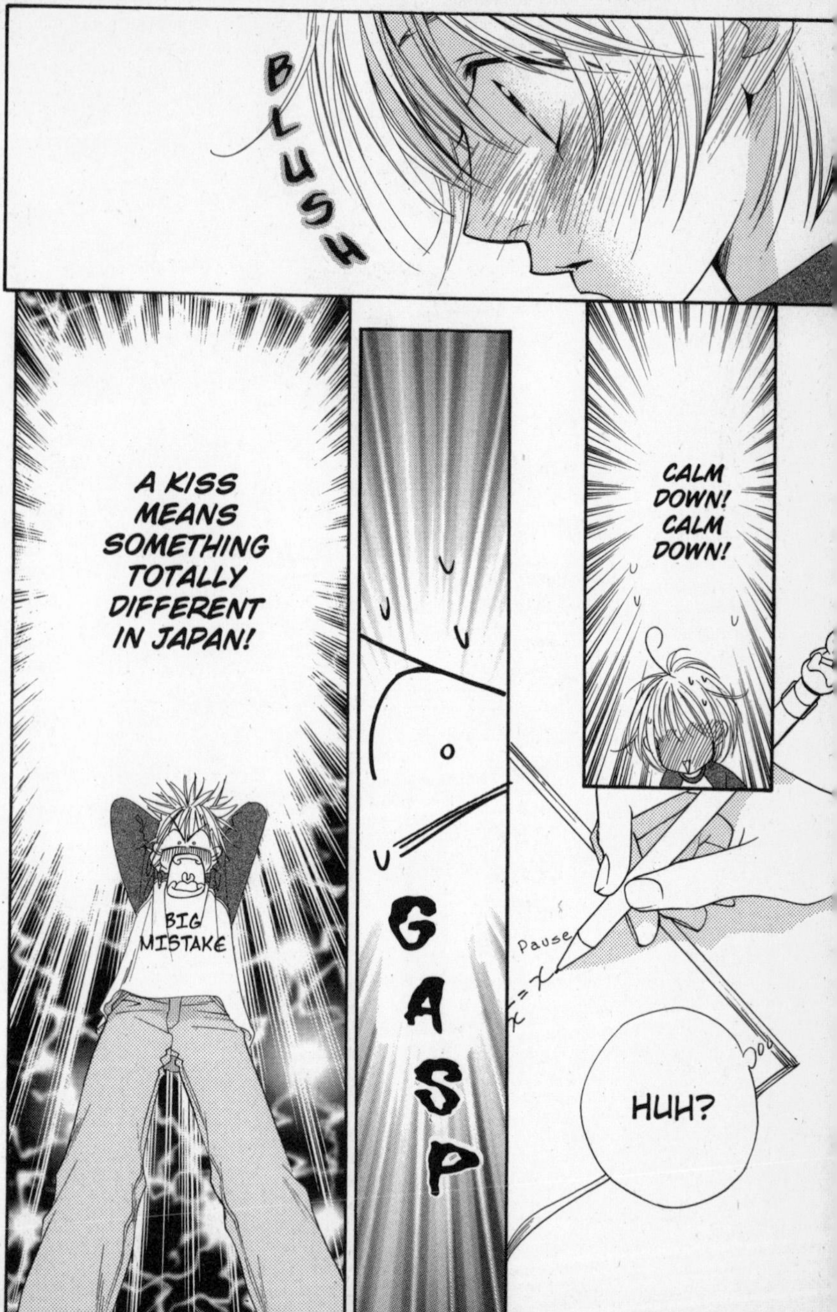
BLUSH
CALM DOWN! CALM DOWN!
Pause
HUH?
GASP
A KISS MEANS SOMETHING TOTALLY DIFFERENT IN JAPAN!
BIG MISTAKE

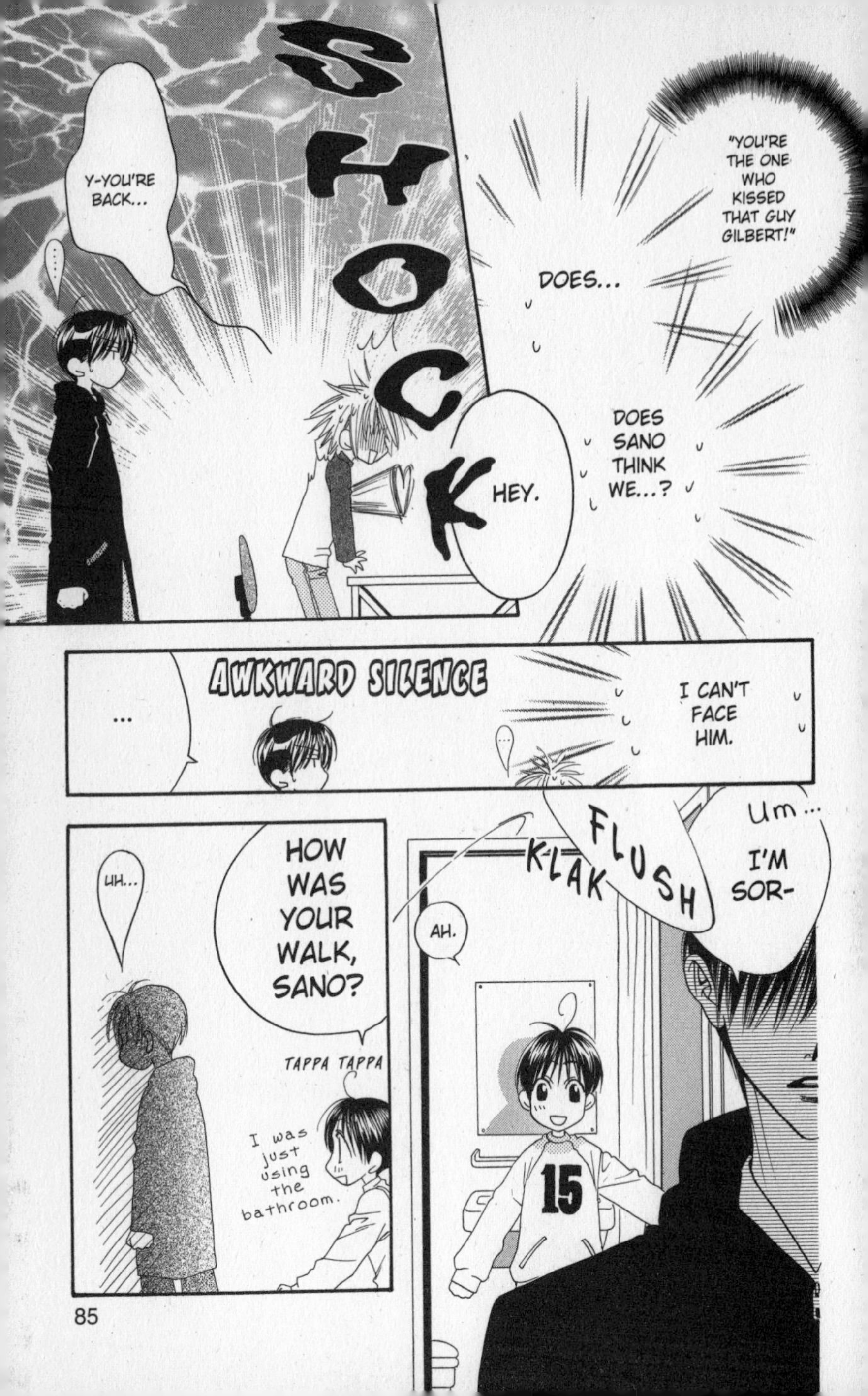
"YOU'RE THE ONE WHO KISSED THAT GUY GILBERT!"
DOES...
DOES SANO THINK WE...?
SHOCK
HEY.
Y-YOU'RE BACK...
...
I CAN'T FACE HIM.
...
AWKWARD SILENCE
...
Um... I'M SOR-
FLUSH
KLAK
AH.
HOW WAS YOUR WALK, SANO?
TAPPA TAPPA
I was just using the bathroom.
UH...

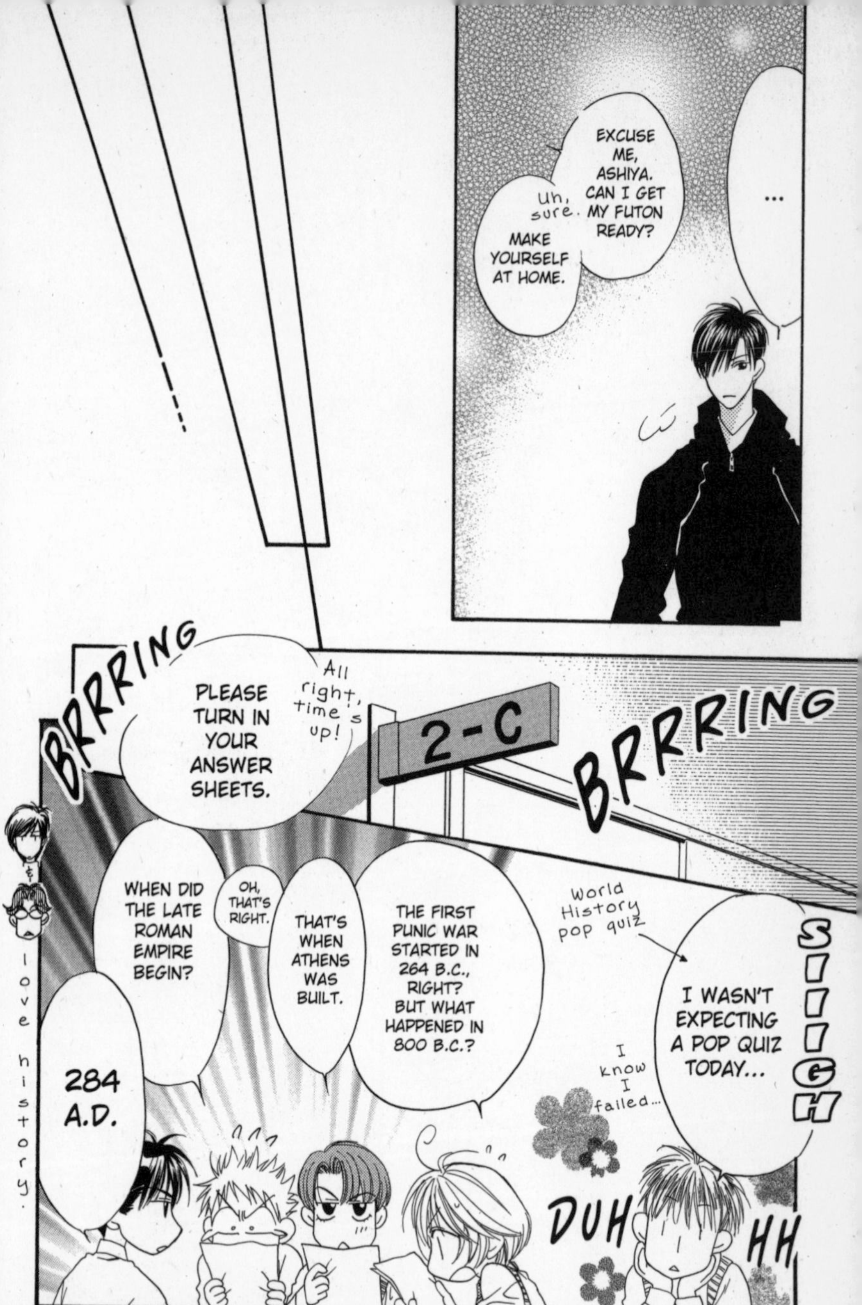
...
EXCUSE ME, ASHIYA. CAN I GET MY FUTON READY?
Uh, sure.
MAKE YOURSELF AT HOME.
BRRRING
2-C
BRRRING
All right, time's up!
PLEASE TURN IN YOUR ANSWER SHEETS.
SIIIGH
World History pop quiz
I WASN'T EXPECTING A POP QUIZ TODAY...
I know I failed...
THE FIRST PUNIC WAR STARTED IN 264 B.C., RIGHT? BUT WHAT HAPPENED IN 800 B.C.?
THAT'S WHEN ATHENS WAS BUILT.
OH, THAT'S RIGHT.
WHEN DID THE LATE ROMAN EMPIRE BEGIN?
284 A.D.
DUHHH
love history.

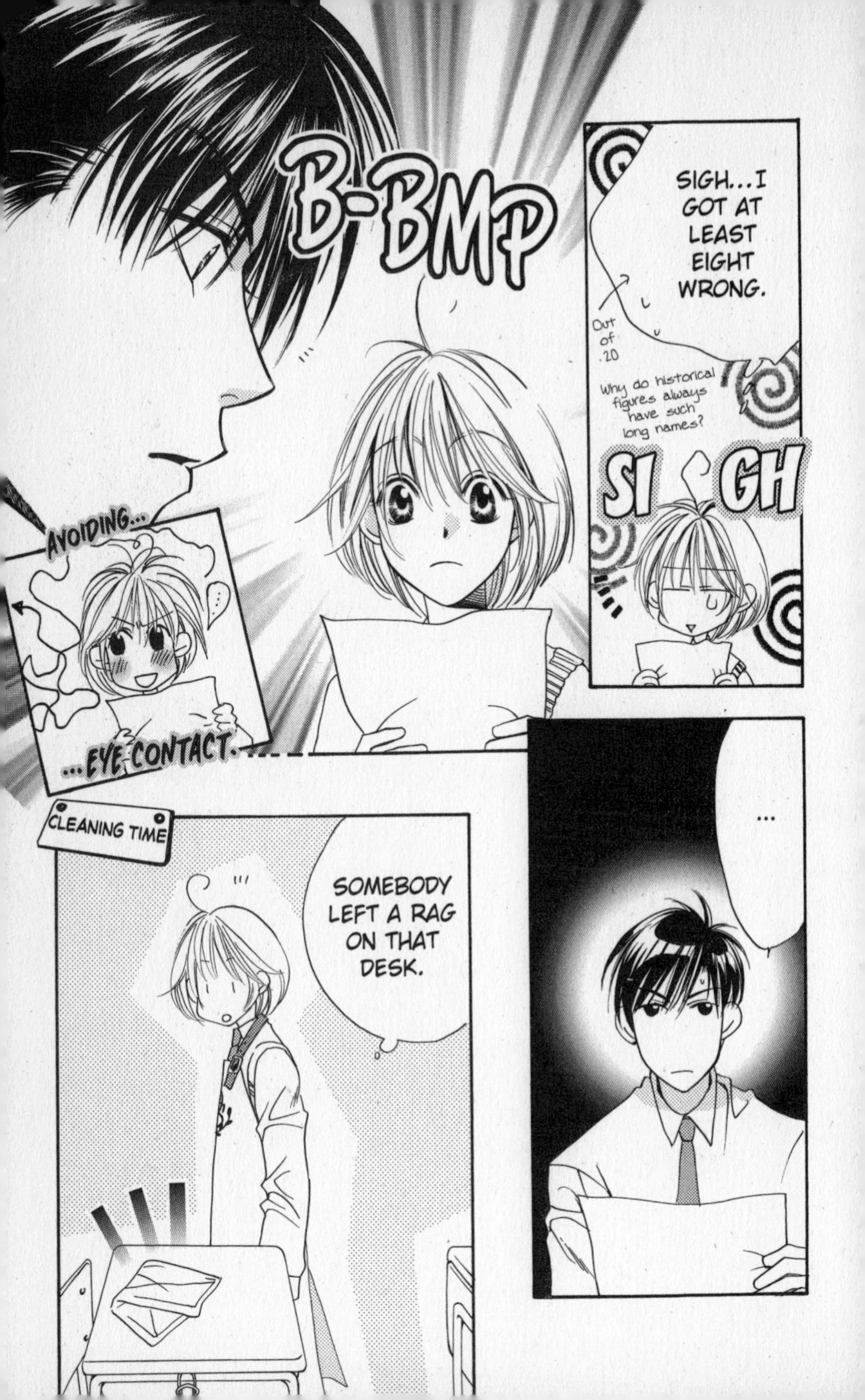

SIGH...I GOT AT LEAST EIGHT WRONG.
Out of 20
Why do historical figures always have such long names?
SIGH
B-BMP
AVOIDING...
...EYE CONTACT.
...
CLEANING TIME
SOMEBODY LEFT A RAG ON THAT DESK.

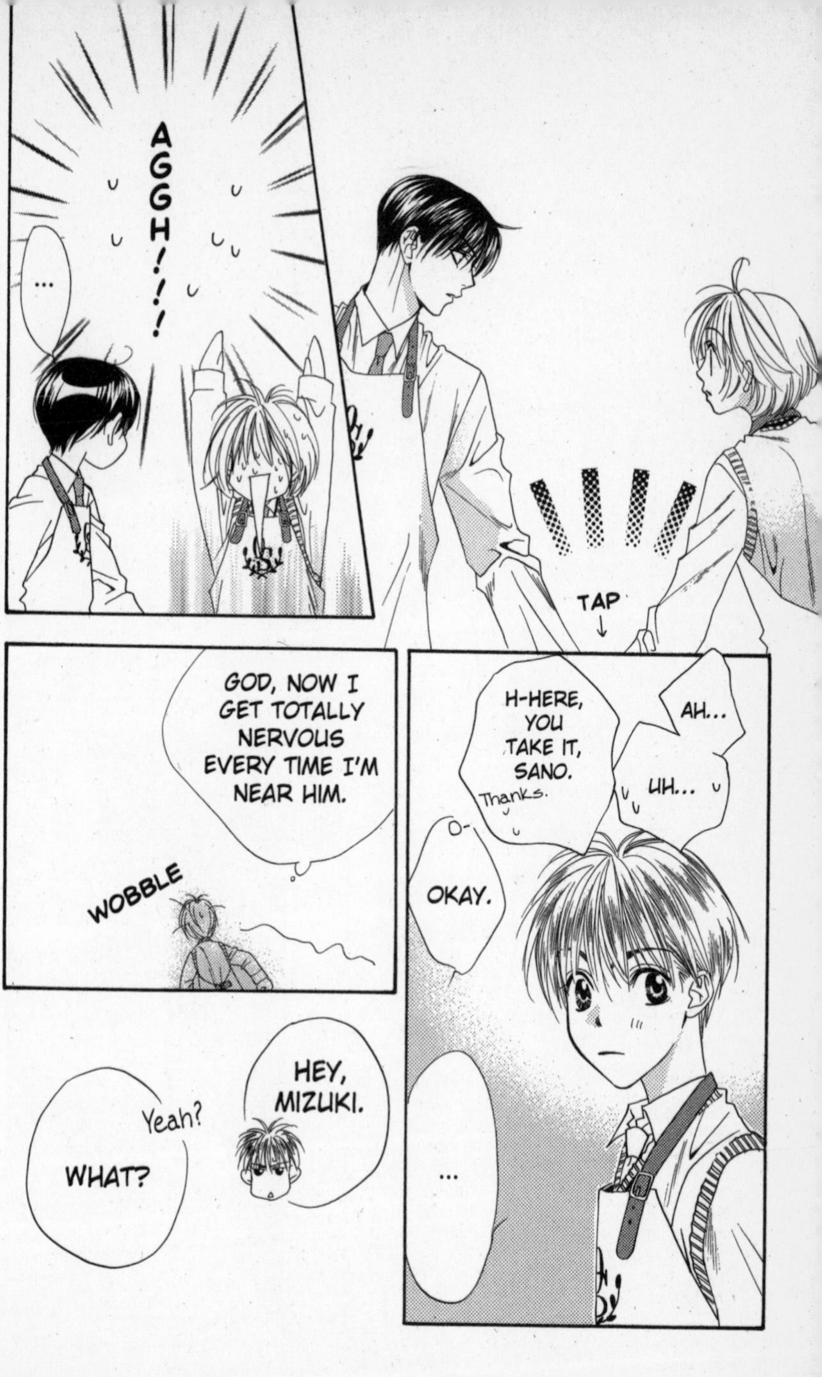
TAP
AGGH!!!
...
AH...
UH...
H-HERE, YOU TAKE IT, SANO.
Thanks.
O-
OKAY.
...
GOD, NOW I GET TOTALLY NERVOUS EVERY TIME I'M NEAR HIM.
WOBBLE
HEY, MIZUKI.
WHAT?
Yeah?

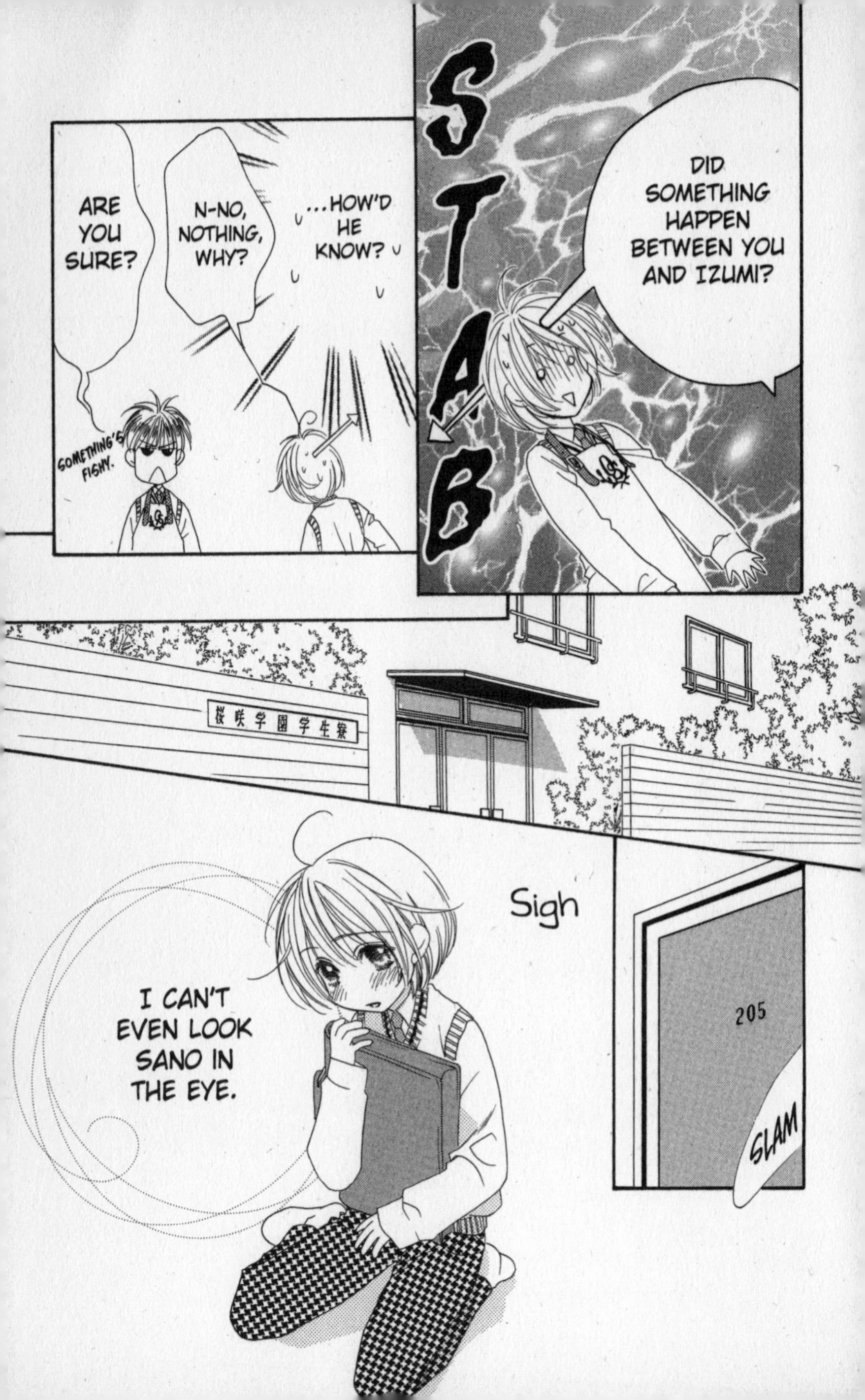
STAB
DID SOMETHING HAPPEN BETWEEN YOU AND IZUMI?
...HOW'D HE KNOW?
N-NO, NOTHING, WHY?
ARE YOU SURE?
SOMETHING'S FISHY.
桜咲学園学生寮
205
SLAM
Sigh
I CAN'T EVEN LOOK SANO IN THE EYE.

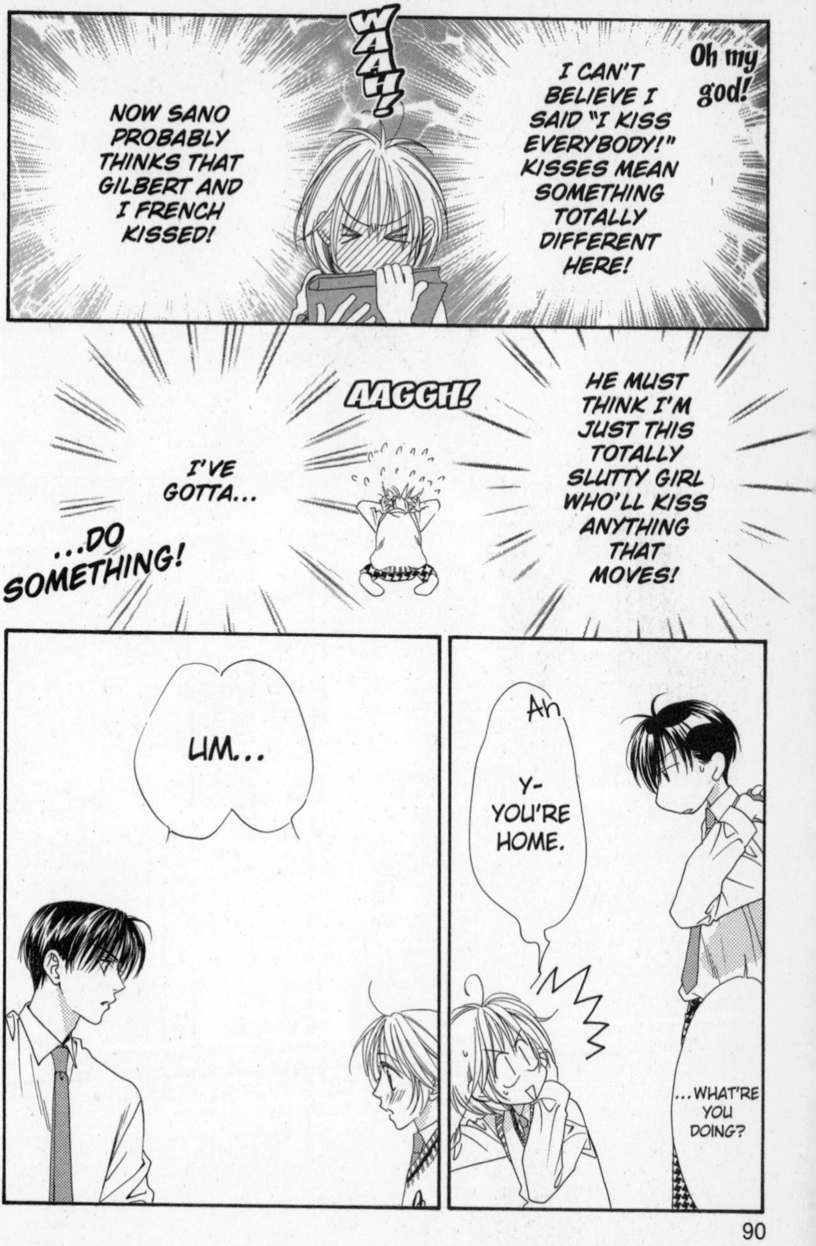
Oh my god!
I CAN'T BELIEVE I SAID "I KISS EVERYBODY!" KISSES MEAN SOMETHING TOTALLY DIFFERENT HERE!
WAAH!
NOW SANO PROBABLY THINKS THAT GILBERT AND I FRENCH KISSED!
HE MUST THINK I'M JUST THIS TOTALLY SLUTTY GIRL WHO'LL KISS ANYTHING THAT MOVES!
AAGGH!
I'VE GOTTA...
...DO SOMETHING!
Ah
Y- YOU'RE HOME.
...WHAT'RE YOU DOING?
UM...

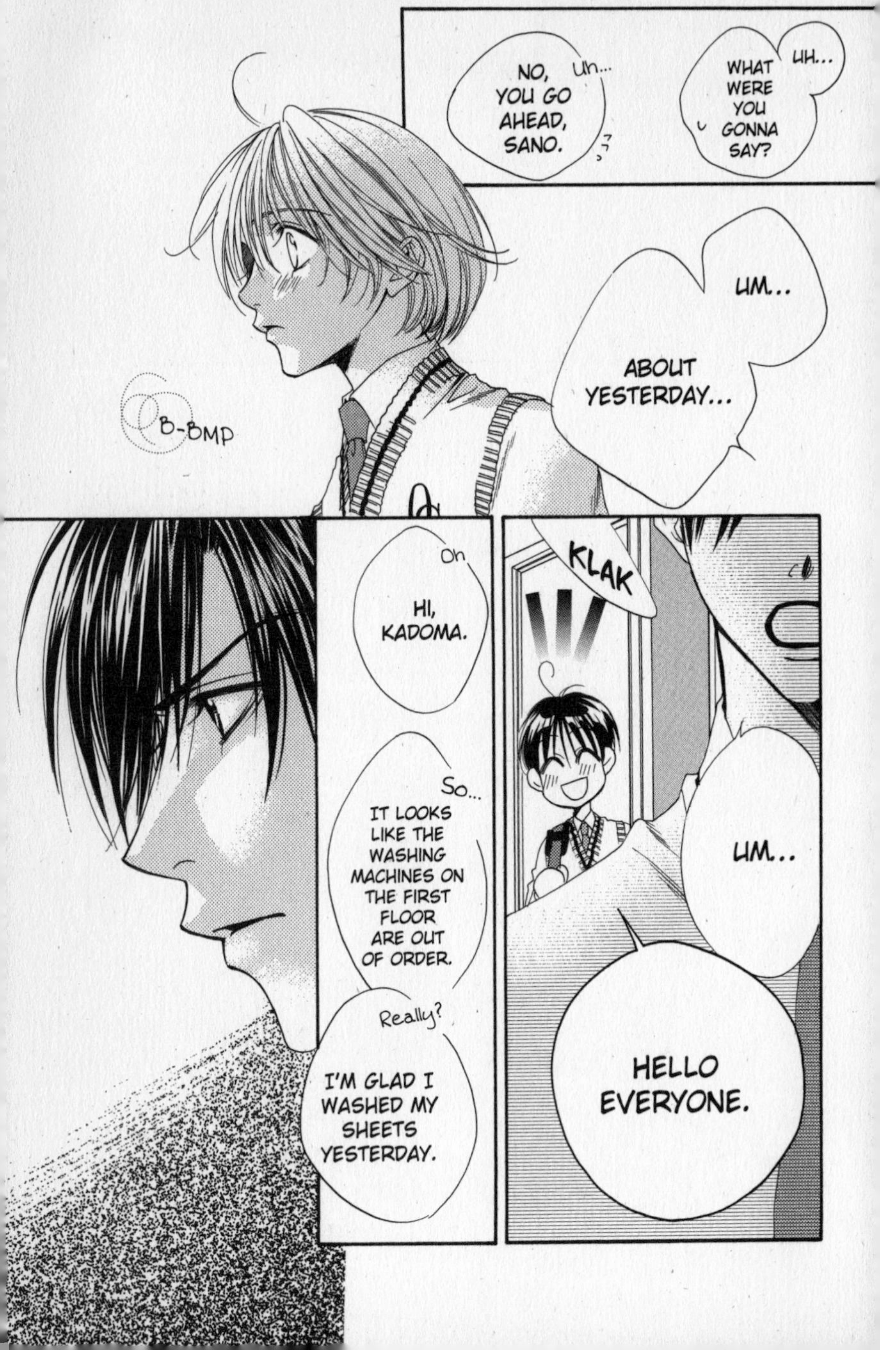
uh...
WHAT WERE YOU GONNA SAY?
Uh...
NO, YOU GO AHEAD, SANO.
UM...
ABOUT YESTERDAY...
B-BMP
KLAK
UM...
HELLO EVERYONE.
Oh
HI, KADOMA.
So...
IT LOOKS LIKE THE WASHING MACHINES ON THE FIRST FLOOR ARE OUT OF ORDER.
Really?
I'M GLAD I WASHED MY SHEETS YESTERDAY.

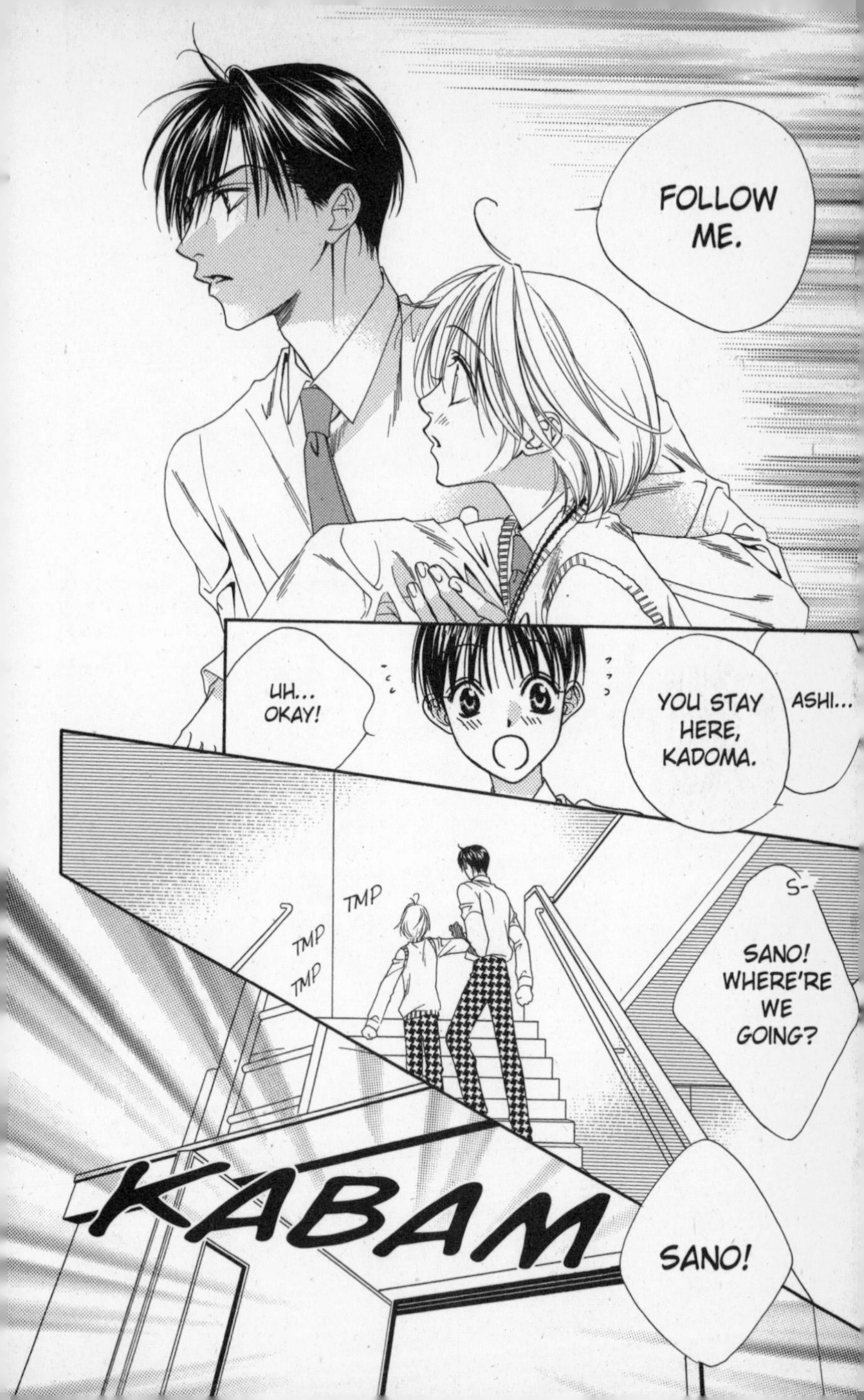
FOLLOW ME.
ASHI...
YOU STAY HERE, KADOMA.
UH... OKAY!
S-
SANO! WHERE'RE WE GOING?
TMP
TMP
TMP
SANO!
KABAM

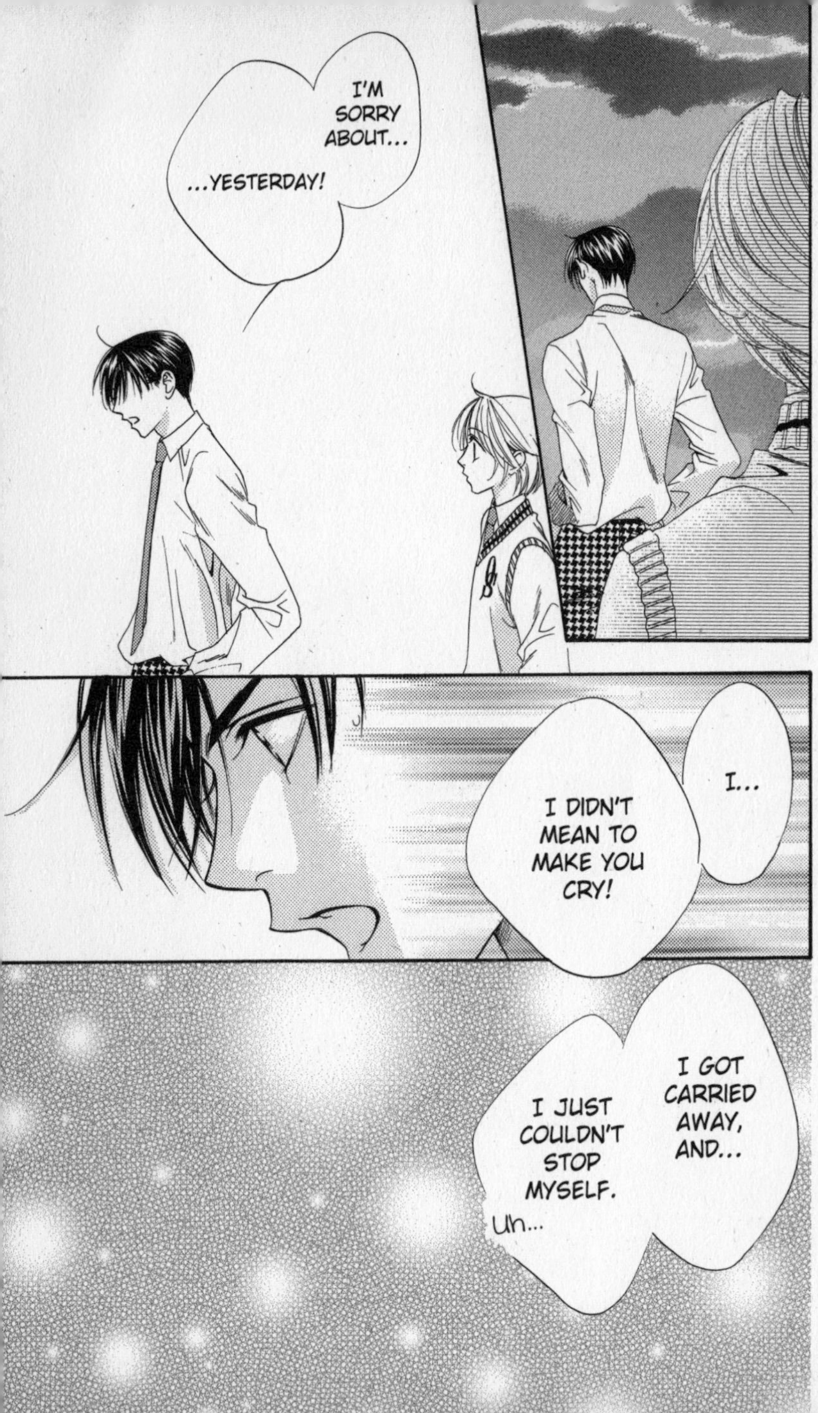
I'M SORRY ABOUT...
...YESTERDAY!
I...
I DIDN'T MEAN TO MAKE YOU CRY!
I GOT CARRIED AWAY, AND...
I JUST COULDN'T STOP MYSELF.
Uh...

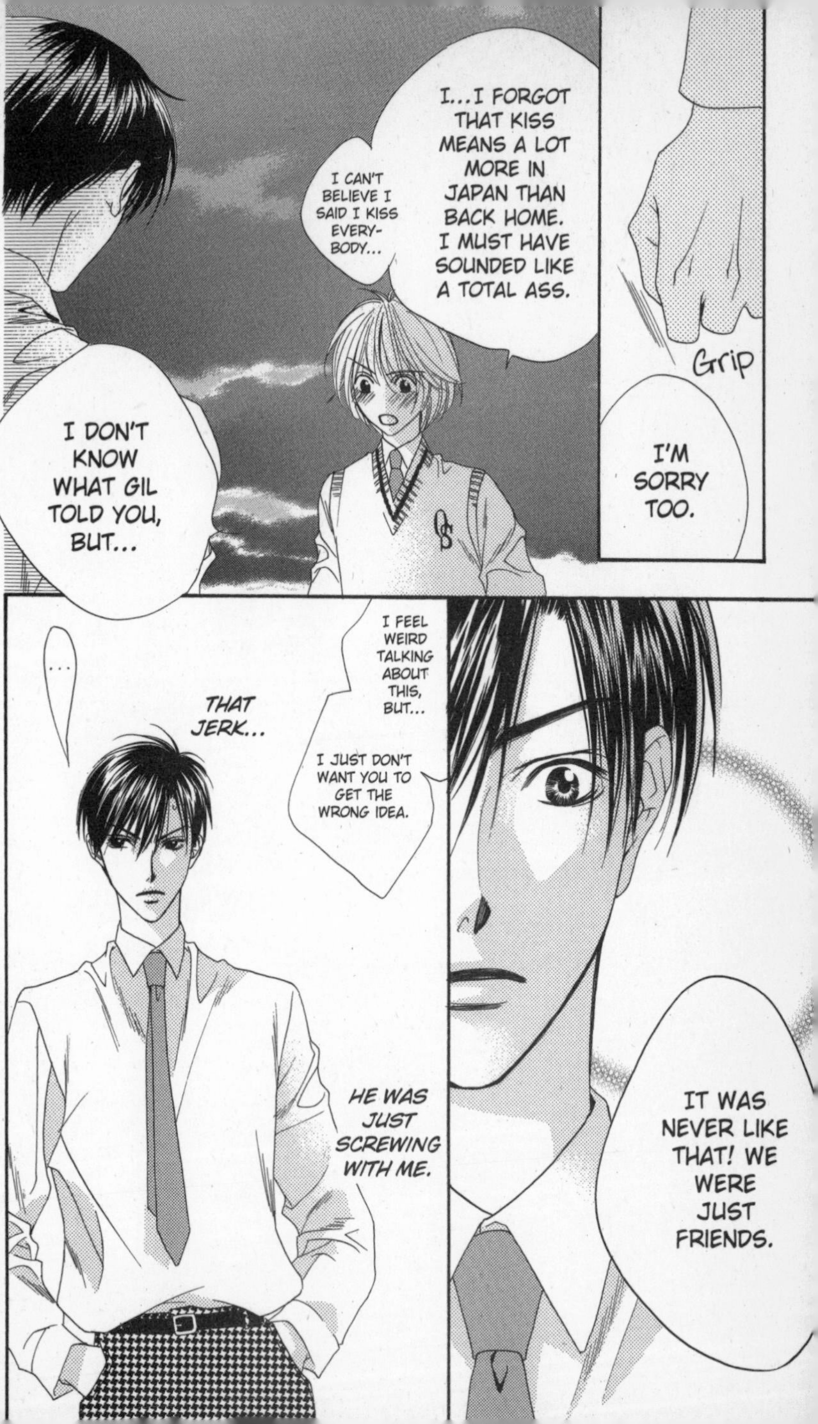
Grip
I'M SORRY TOO.
I...I FORGOT THAT KISS MEANS A LOT MORE IN JAPAN THAN BACK HOME. I MUST HAVE SOUNDED LIKE A TOTAL ASS.
I CAN'T BELIEVE I SAID I KISS EVERY-BODY...
I DON'T KNOW WHAT GIL TOLD YOU, BUT...
IT WAS NEVER LIKE THAT! WE WERE JUST FRIENDS.
I FEEL WEIRD TALKING ABOUT THIS, BUT...
I JUST DON'T WANT YOU TO GET THE WRONG IDEA.
THAT JERK...
...
HE WAS JUST SCREWING WITH ME.

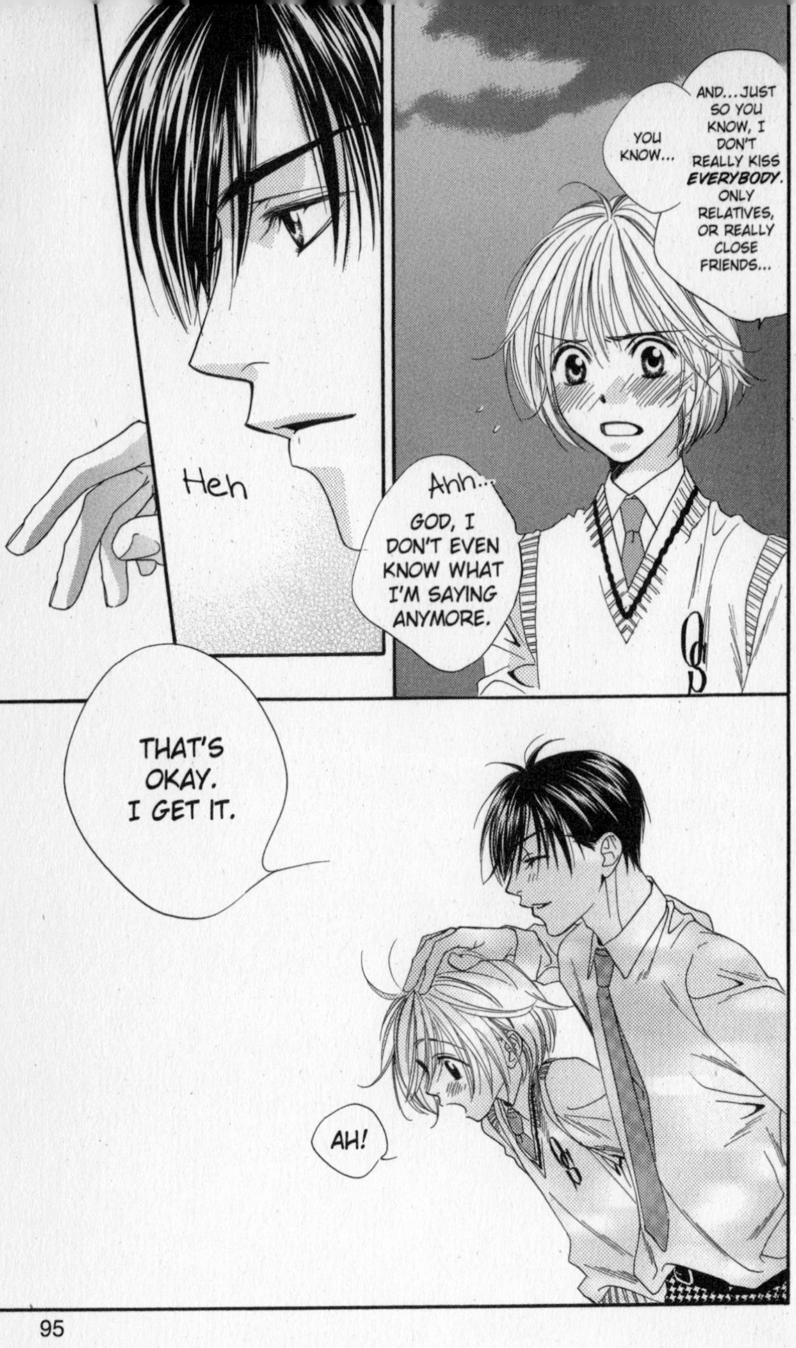
AND...JUST SO YOU KNOW, I DON'T REALLY KISS **EVERYBODY**. ONLY RELATIVES, OR REALLY CLOSE FRIENDS...
YOU KNOW...
Anh...
GOD, I DON'T EVEN KNOW WHAT I'M SAYING ANYMORE.
Heh
THAT'S OKAY. I GET IT.
AH!

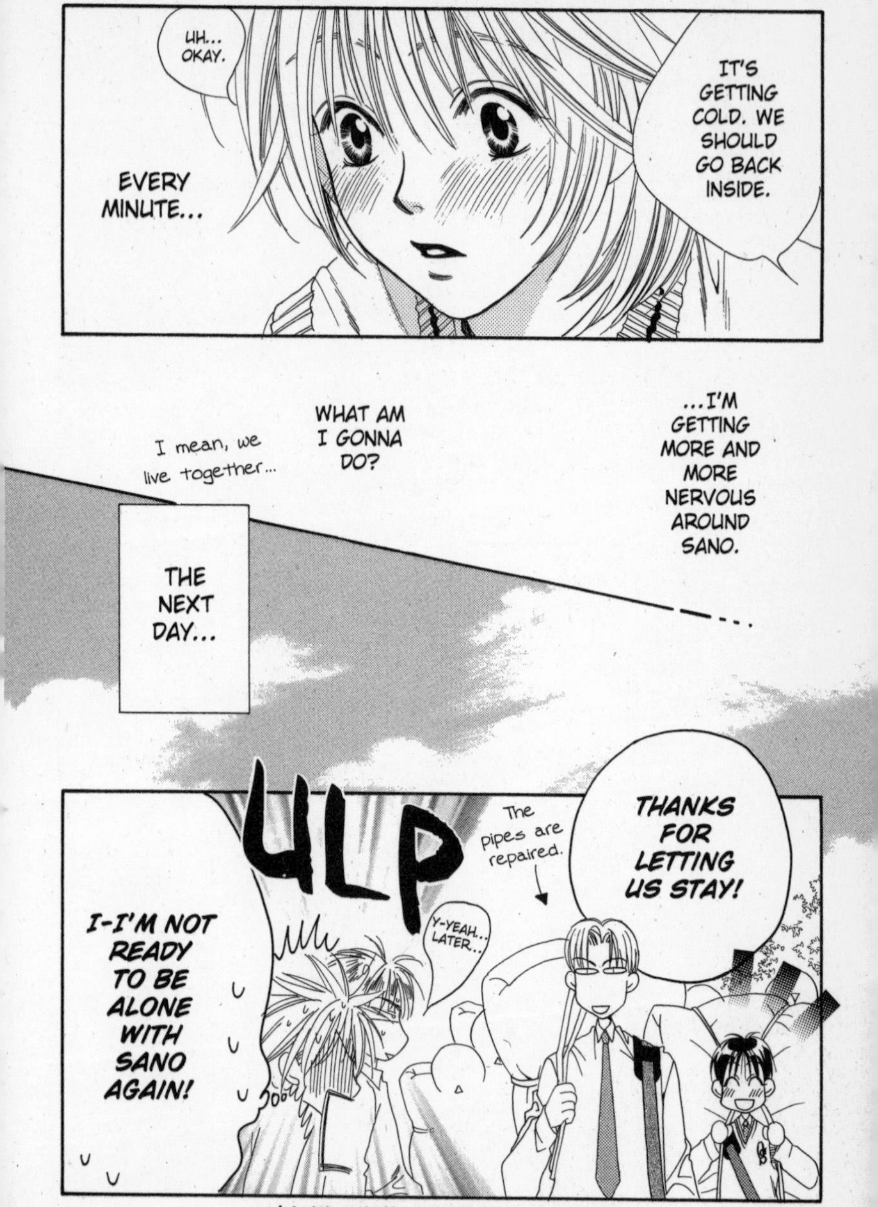
IT'S GETTING COLD. WE SHOULD GO BACK INSIDE.
UH... OKAY.
EVERY MINUTE...
...I'M GETTING MORE AND MORE NERVOUS AROUND SANO.
WHAT AM I GONNA DO?
I mean, we live together...
THE NEXT DAY...
THANKS FOR LETTING US STAY!
The pipes are repaired.
ULP
Y-YEAH... LATER...
I-I'M NOT READY TO BE ALONE WITH SANO AGAIN!

✿ PROLOGUE ✿

The stories you're about to read are special episodes about Umeda's days as an Osaka High student. (They're really long!) I like to call them "Tales of Umeda's Osaka High Days!" He's one of the most popular characters among both male and female Hana-Kimi readers, and he has many passionate fans. Lots of readers have written in saying, "I want to know more about Umeda's relationship with Ryoichi Kijima (from Yumemiru Happa)!" So here you are! Hope you enjoy them!

While I was working on these stories, there was one thing I couldn't live without. I'm talking about music! (That's actually really rare for me) When I was writing episode one, I listened to Sting's "Desert Rose." I listened to Madonna's "Bedtime Story" and Akino Arai's "Goddess in the Morning" when I was writing episodes two and three. I listened to them over and over again. Without these albums, Umeda's stories could never have been written! (I'm exaggerating)

Akina as a high school freshman. He looks so young. (He's actually not even in these stories)

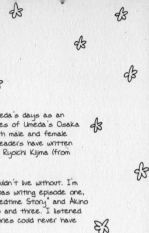

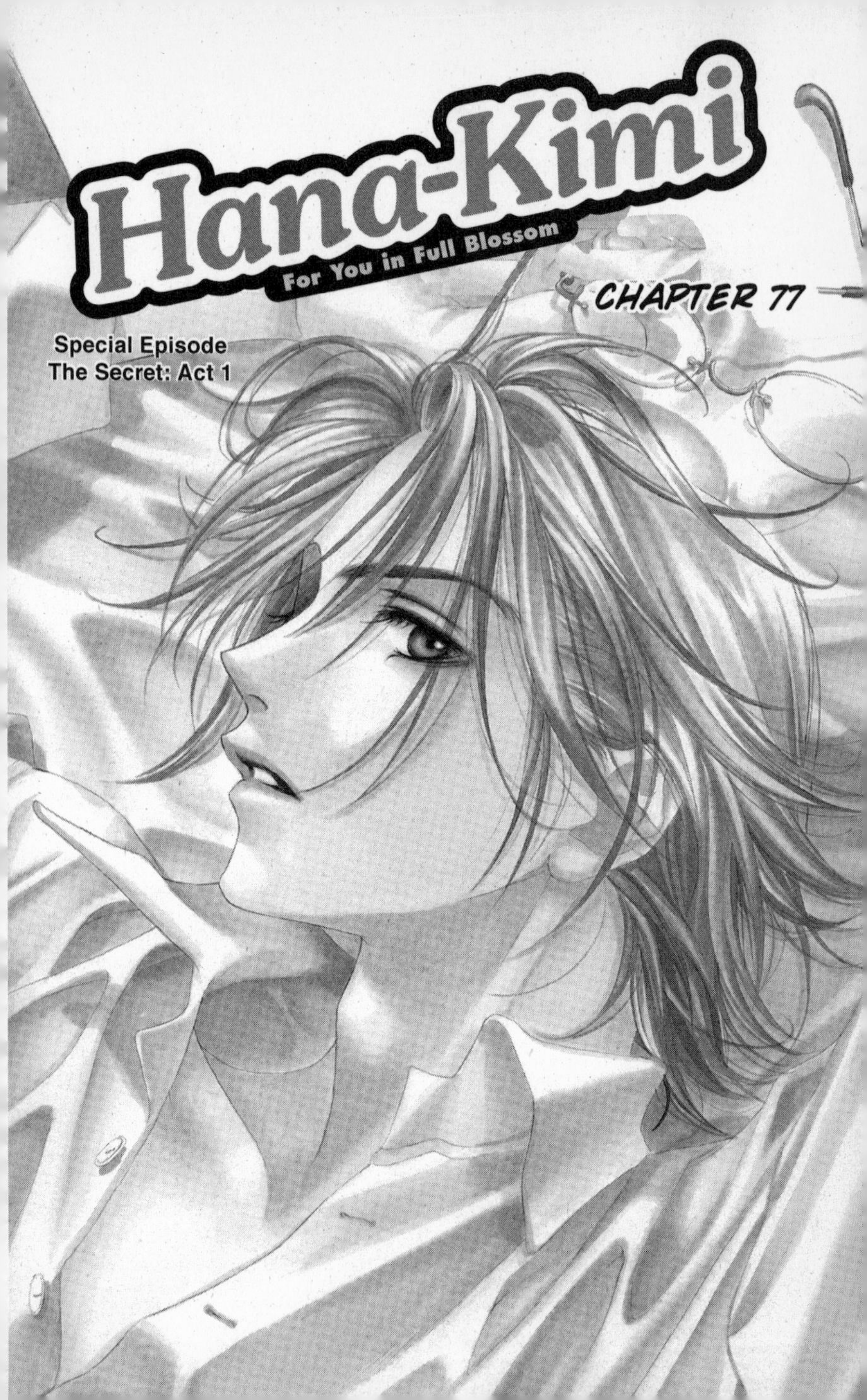
Hana-Kimi
For You in Full Blossom
CHAPTER 77
Special Episode
The Secret: Act 1

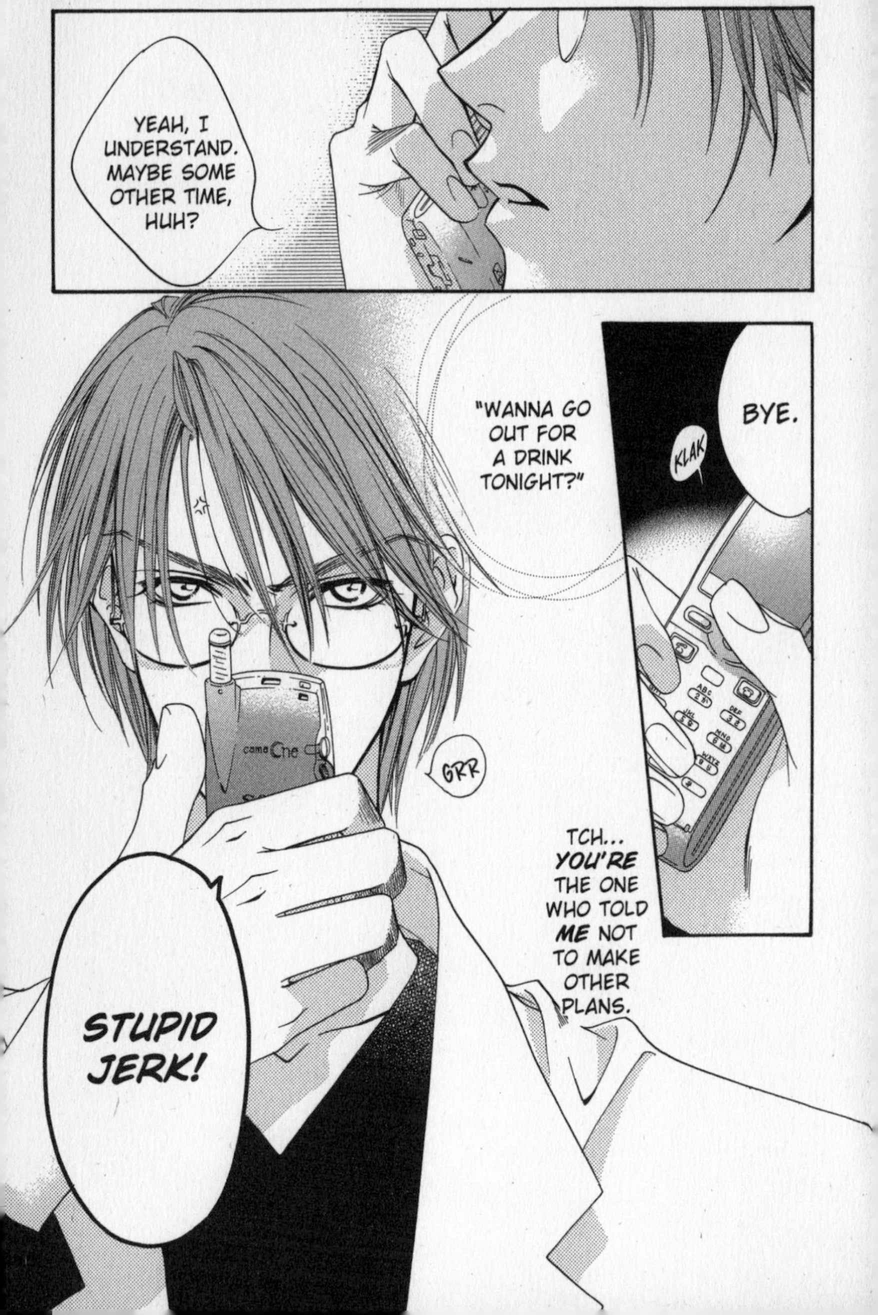
YEAH, I UNDERSTAND. MAYBE SOME OTHER TIME, HUH?
BYE.
KLAK
"WANNA GO OUT FOR A DRINK TONIGHT?"
TCH... YOU'RE THE ONE WHO TOLD ME NOT TO MAKE OTHER PLANS.
GRR
STUPID JERK!

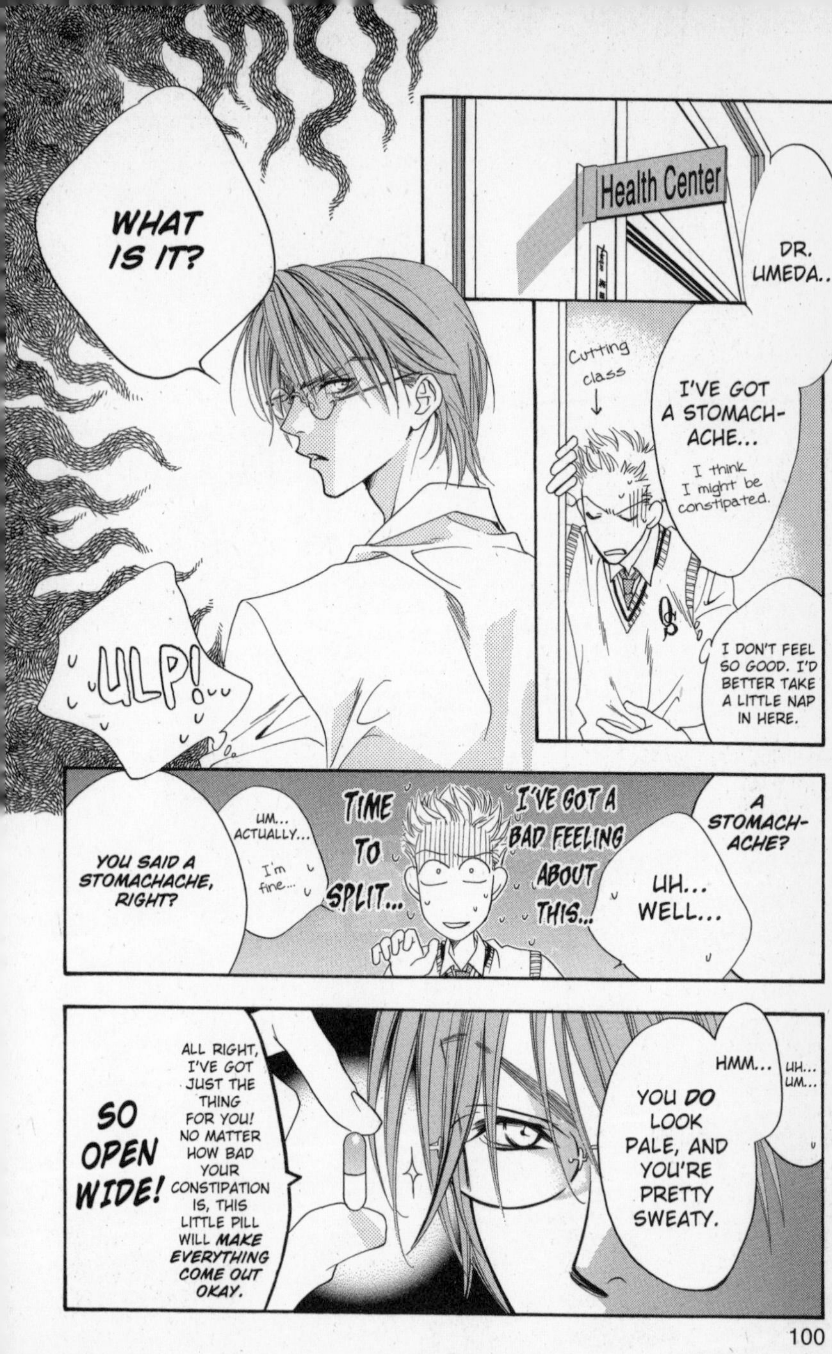
Health Center
DR. UMEDA...
Cutting class
I'VE GOT A STOMACHACHE...
I think I might be constipated.
I DON'T FEEL SO GOOD. I'D BETTER TAKE A LITTLE NAP IN HERE.
WHAT IS IT?
ULP!
A STOMACHACHE?
UH... WELL...
I'VE GOT A BAD FEELING ABOUT THIS...
TIME TO SPLIT...
UM... ACTUALLY...
I'm fine...
YOU SAID A STOMACHACHE, RIGHT?
HMM...
UH... UM...
YOU *DO* LOOK PALE, AND YOU'RE PRETTY SWEATY.
ALL RIGHT, I'VE GOT JUST THE THING FOR YOU! NO MATTER HOW BAD YOUR CONSTIPATION IS, THIS LITTLE PILL WILL ***MAKE EVERYTHING COME OUT OKAY.***
SO OPEN WIDE!

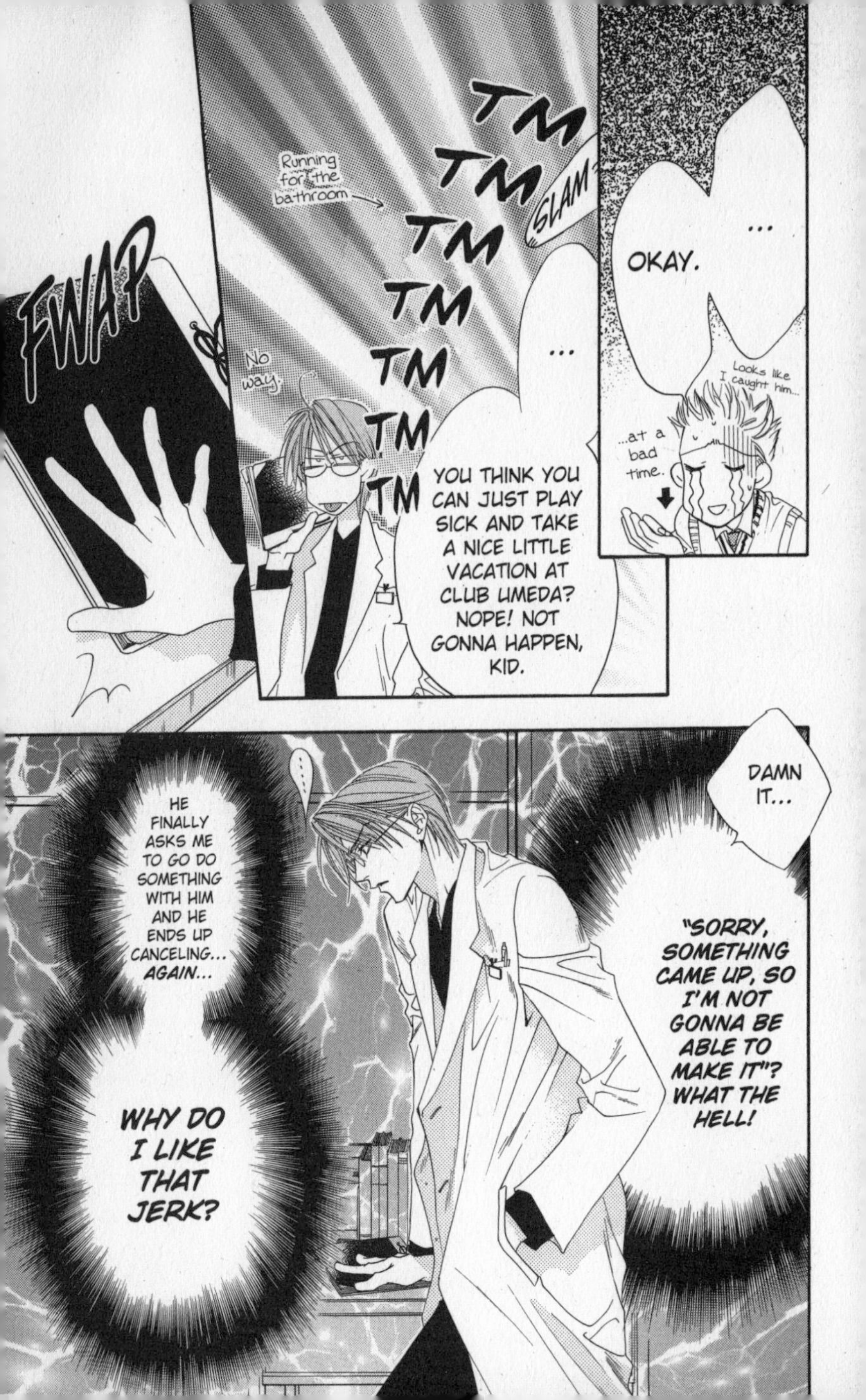
...
OKAY.
Looks like I caught him...
...at a bad time.
SLAM
TM TM TM TM TM TM TM
Running for the bathroom
...
YOU THINK YOU CAN JUST PLAY SICK AND TAKE A NICE LITTLE VACATION AT CLUB UMEDA? NOPE! NOT GONNA HAPPEN, KID.
No way.
FWAP
DAMN IT...
"SORRY, SOMETHING CAME UP, SO I'M NOT GONNA BE ABLE TO MAKE IT"? WHAT THE HELL!
...
HE FINALLY ASKS ME TO GO DO SOMETHING WITH HIM AND HE ENDS UP CANCELING... AGAIN...
WHY DO I LIKE THAT JERK?

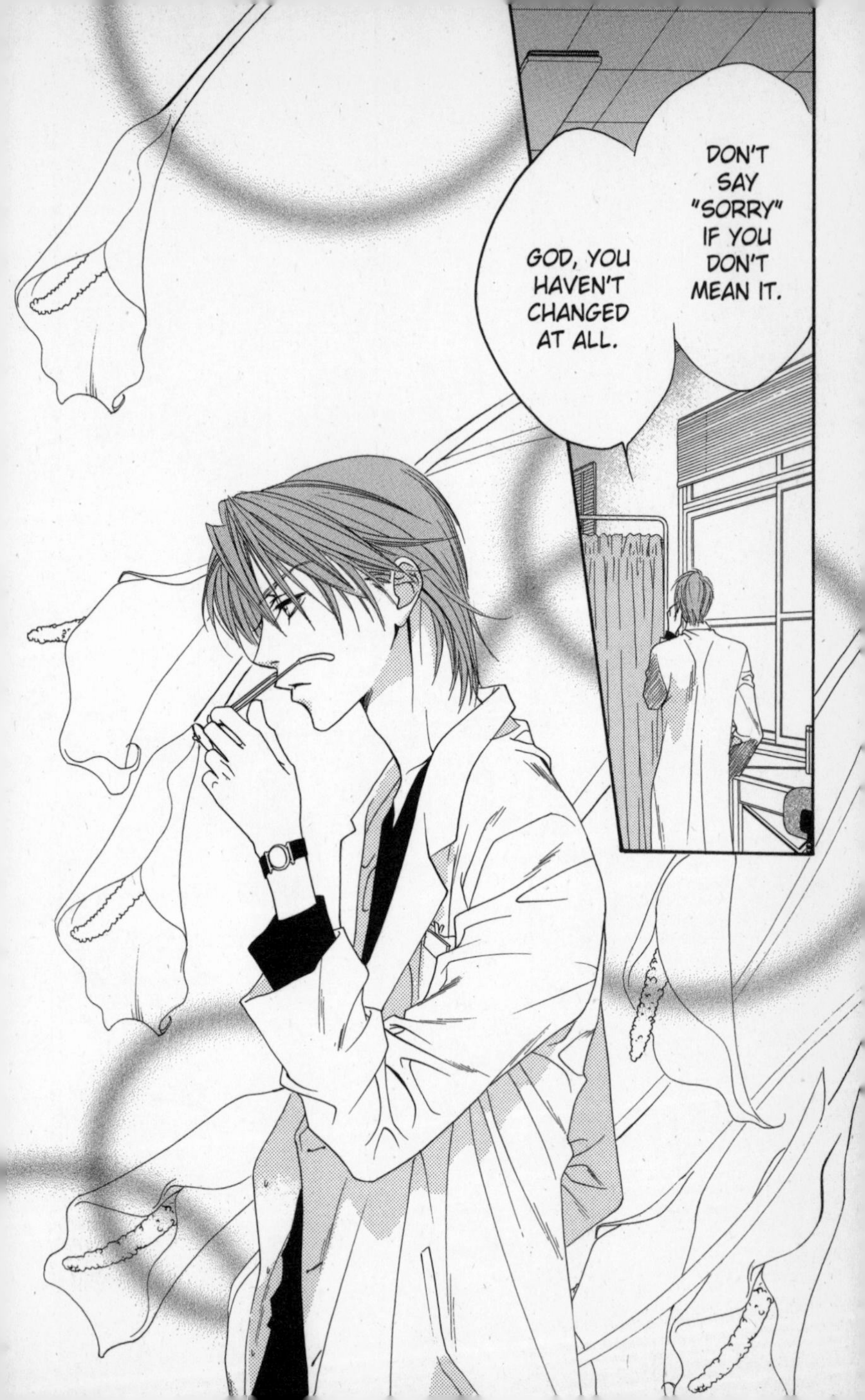
DON'T SAY "SORRY" IF YOU DON'T MEAN IT.
GOD, YOU HAVEN'T CHANGED AT ALL.

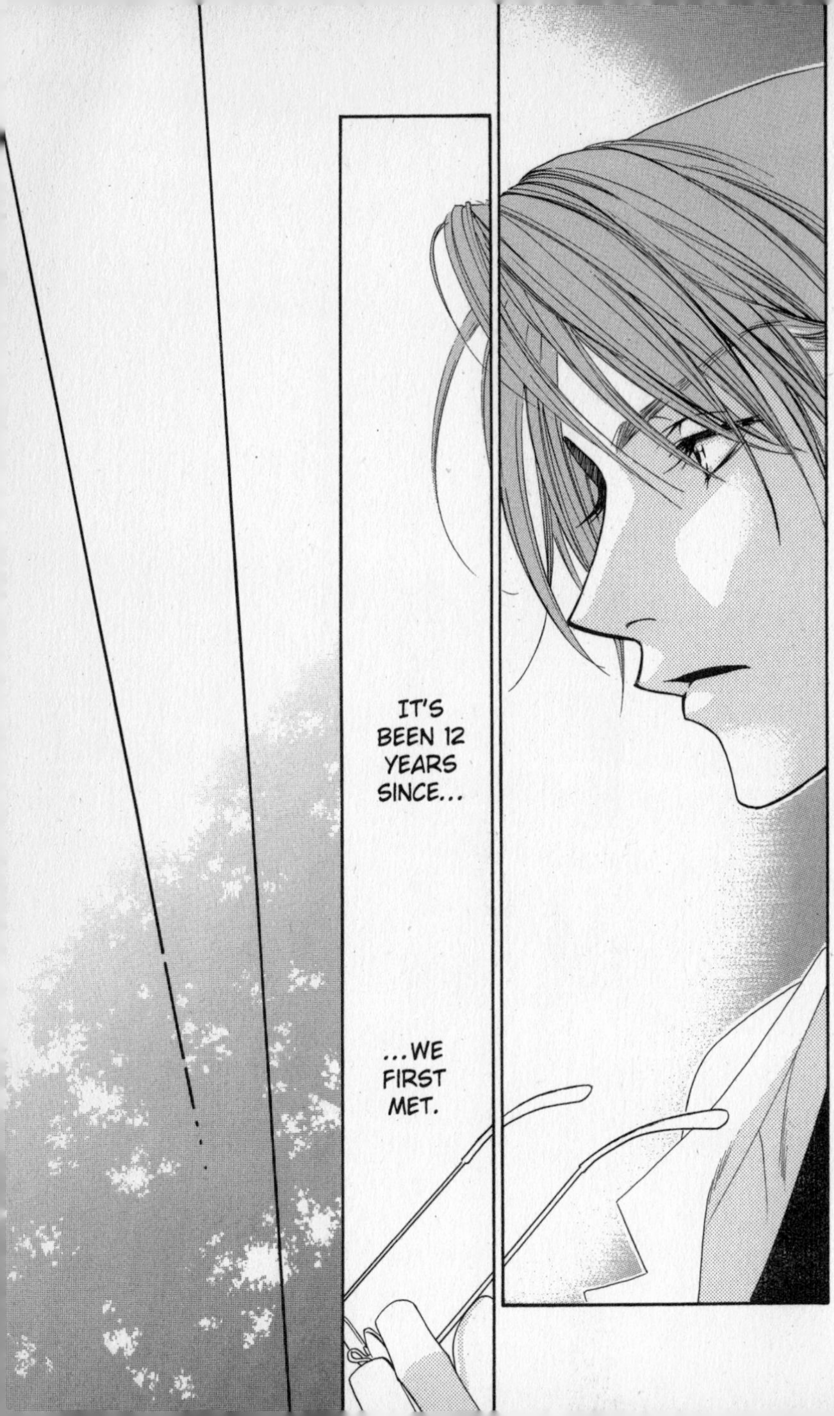
IT'S BEEN 12 YEARS SINCE...
...WE FIRST MET.

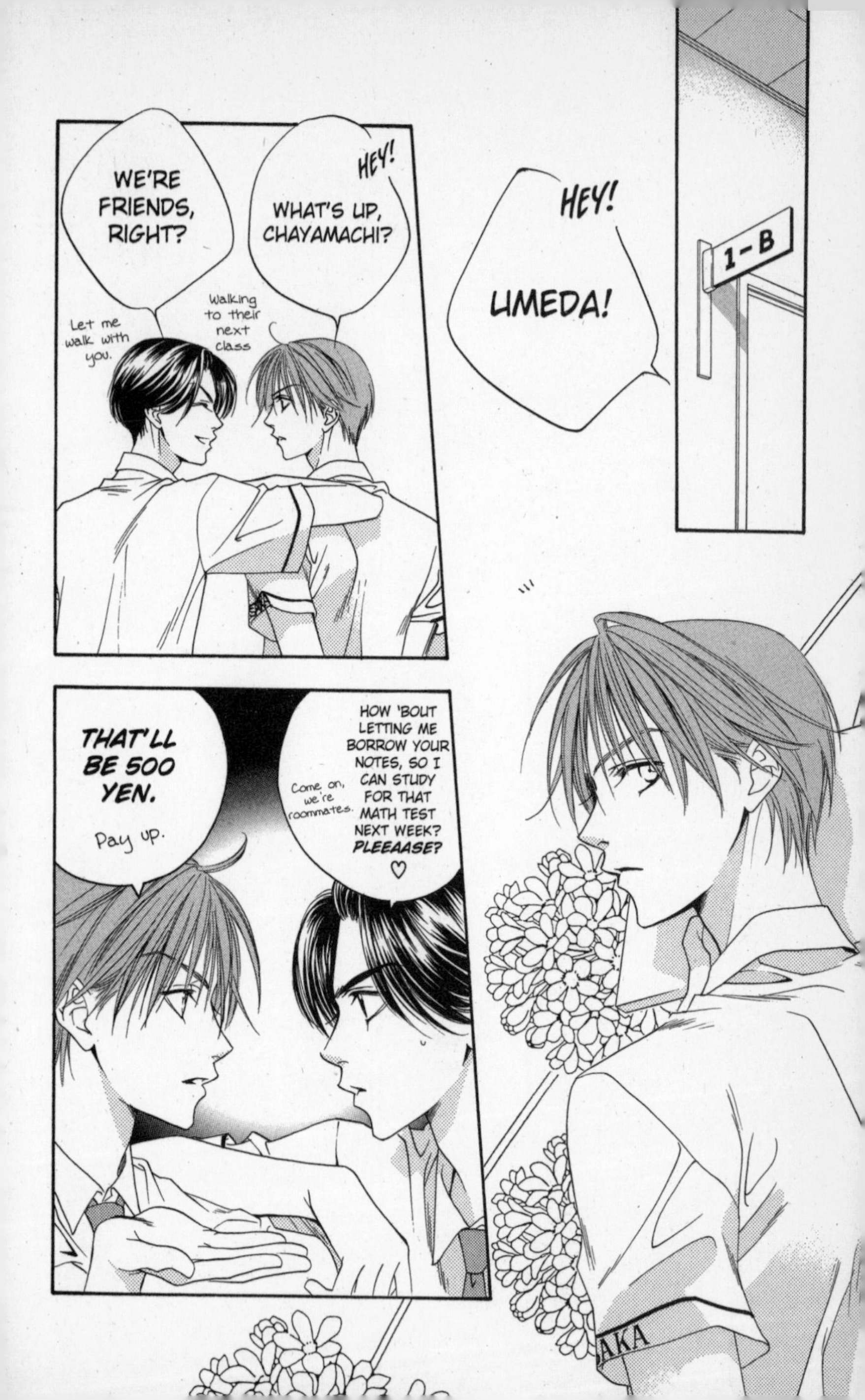
HEY!
UMEDA!
HEY!
WHAT'S UP, CHAYAMACHI?
Walking to their next class
WE'RE FRIENDS, RIGHT?
Let me walk with you.
HOW 'BOUT LETTING ME BORROW YOUR NOTES, SO I CAN STUDY FOR THAT MATH TEST NEXT WEEK? PLEEAASE? ♡
Come on, we're roommates.
THAT'LL BE 500 YEN.
Pay up.

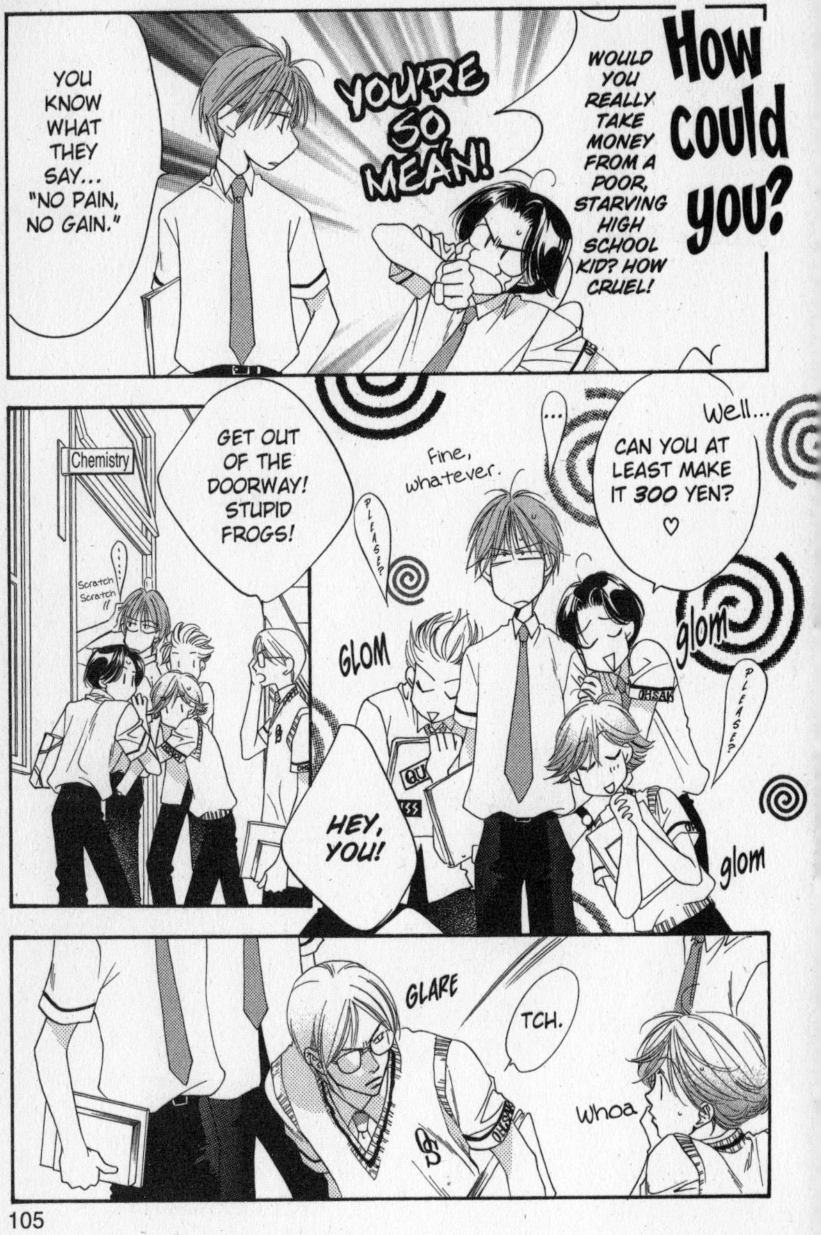
How could you?
WOULD YOU REALLY TAKE MONEY FROM A POOR, STARVING HIGH SCHOOL KID? HOW CRUEL!
YOU'RE SO MEAN!
YOU KNOW WHAT THEY SAY... "NO PAIN, NO GAIN."
Well...
CAN YOU AT LEAST MAKE IT 300 YEN? ♡
glom
PLEASE?
...
Fine, whatever.
PLEASE?
GLOM
glom
HEY, YOU!
GET OUT OF THE DOORWAY! STUPID FROGS!
Chemistry
...
Scratch Scratch
GLARE
TCH.
Whoa

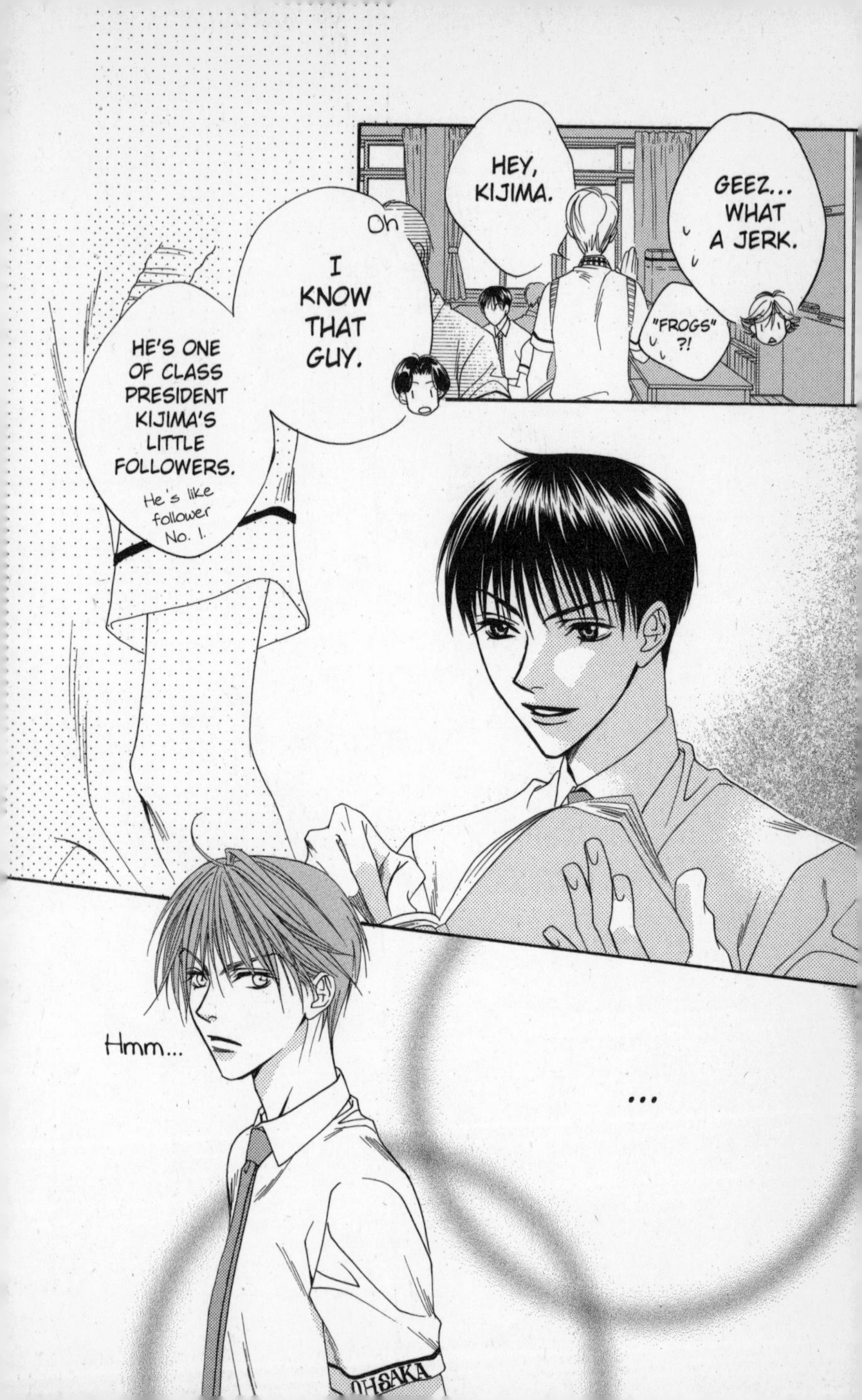
GEEZ... WHAT A JERK.
"FROGS" ?!
HEY, KIJIMA.
Oh
I KNOW THAT GUY.
HE'S ONE OF CLASS PRESIDENT KIJIMA'S LITTLE FOLLOWERS.
He's like follower No. 1.
...
Hmm...
OHSAKA

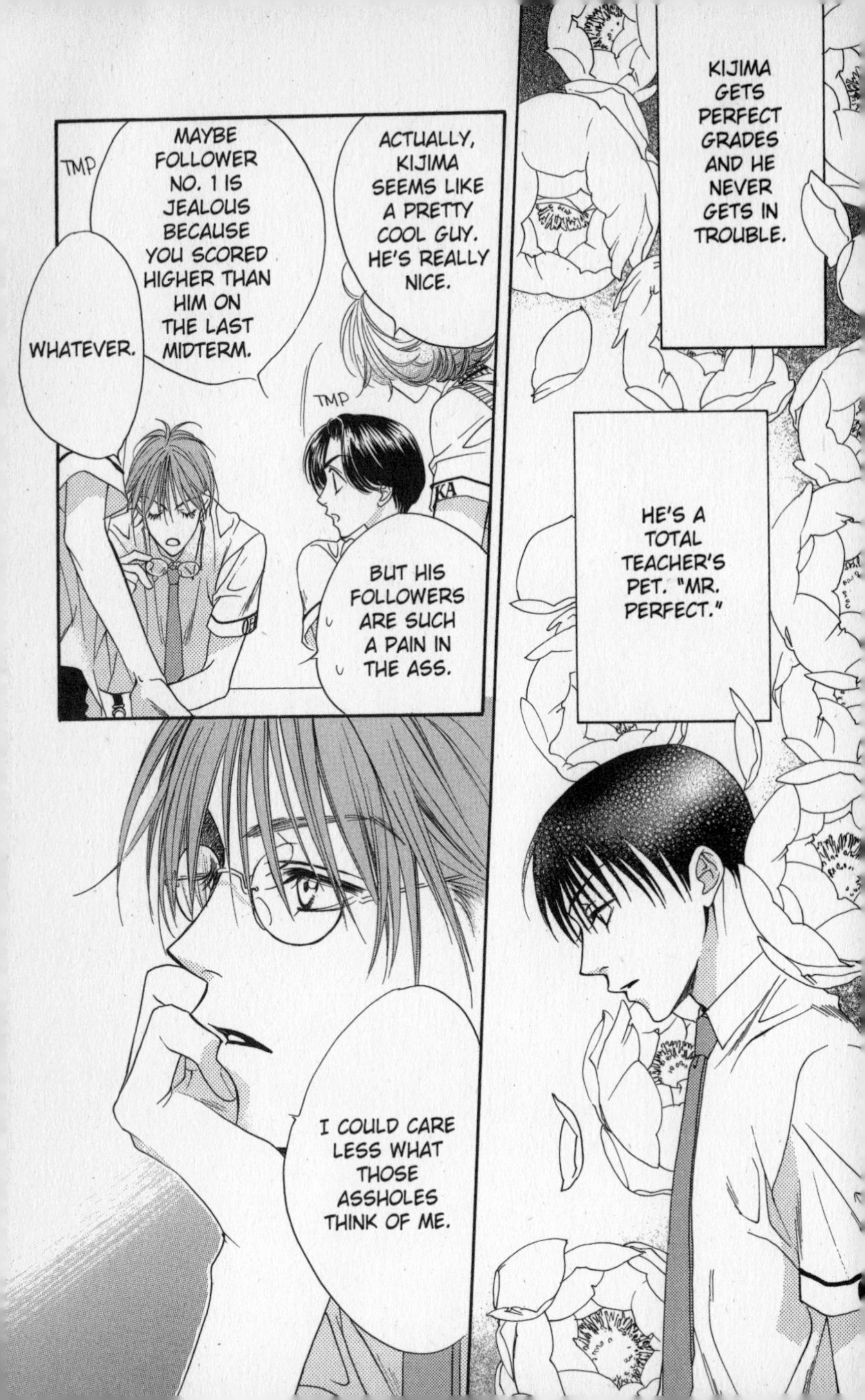
KIJIMA GETS PERFECT GRADES AND HE NEVER GETS IN TROUBLE.
HE'S A TOTAL TEACHER'S PET. "MR. PERFECT."
ACTUALLY, KIJIMA SEEMS LIKE A PRETTY COOL GUY. HE'S REALLY NICE.
BUT HIS FOLLOWERS ARE SUCH A PAIN IN THE ASS.
TMP
KA
MAYBE FOLLOWER NO. 1 IS JEALOUS BECAUSE YOU SCORED HIGHER THAN HIM ON THE LAST MIDTERM.
TMP
WHATEVER.
I COULD CARE LESS WHAT THOSE ASSHOLES THINK OF ME.

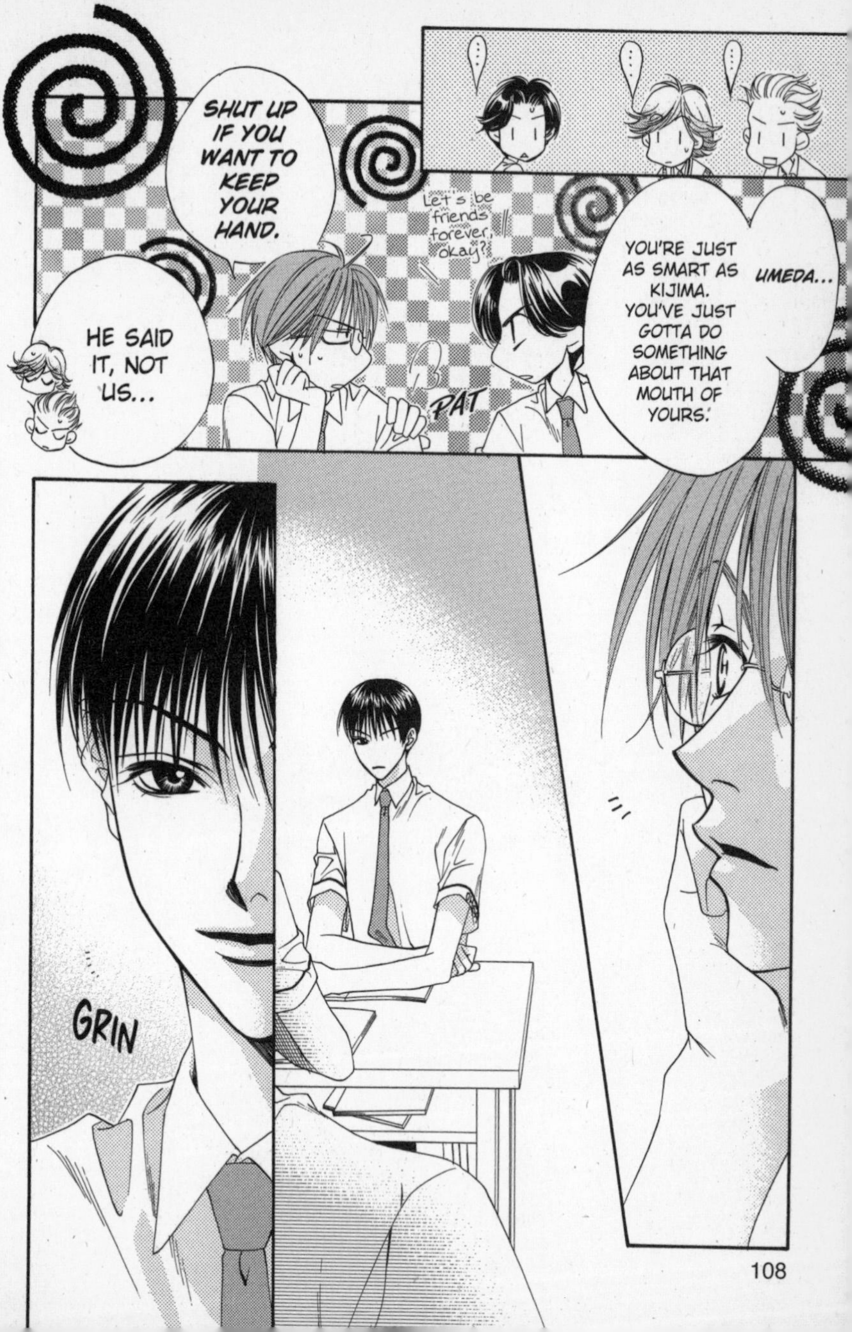
UMEDA...
YOU'RE JUST AS SMART AS KIJIMA. YOU'VE JUST GOTTA DO SOMETHING ABOUT THAT MOUTH OF YOURS.
Let's be friends forever, okay?
PAT
SHUT UP IF YOU WANT TO KEEP YOUR HAND.
HE SAID IT, NOT US...
GRIN

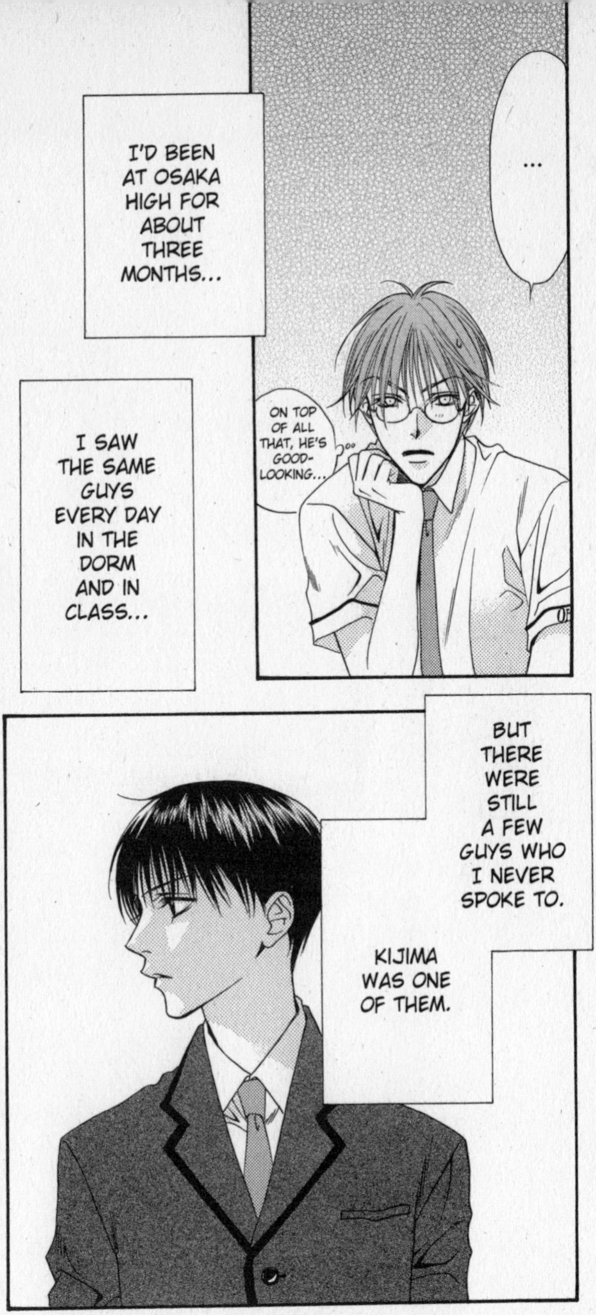
...
ON TOP OF ALL THAT, HE'S GOOD-LOOKING...
I'D BEEN AT OSAKA HIGH FOR ABOUT THREE MONTHS...
I SAW THE SAME GUYS EVERY DAY IN THE DORM AND IN CLASS...
BUT THERE WERE STILL A FEW GUYS WHO I NEVER SPOKE TO.
KIJIMA WAS ONE OF THEM.

「BGM」

While I was working on the Umeda episodes, I kept listening to Sting's "Desert Rose" over and over again. Oh my god! It's awesome! This song is so good ~ Sigh. I usually don't listen to music while I work because it's too distracting, but I had no problem this time. That's strange! I was totally enjoying the song while I was working. (Was I drunk?) I love Sting. ~ I managed to luck out and get tickets for Sting's Japan Tour, but the show happened to be on the same day as my deadline, so I couldn't make it...aggh. I got so bummed out that I haven't been able to listen to any of his songs since. I still haven't gotten over it...sniff.

After I finished the first chapter, I listened to other songs too.

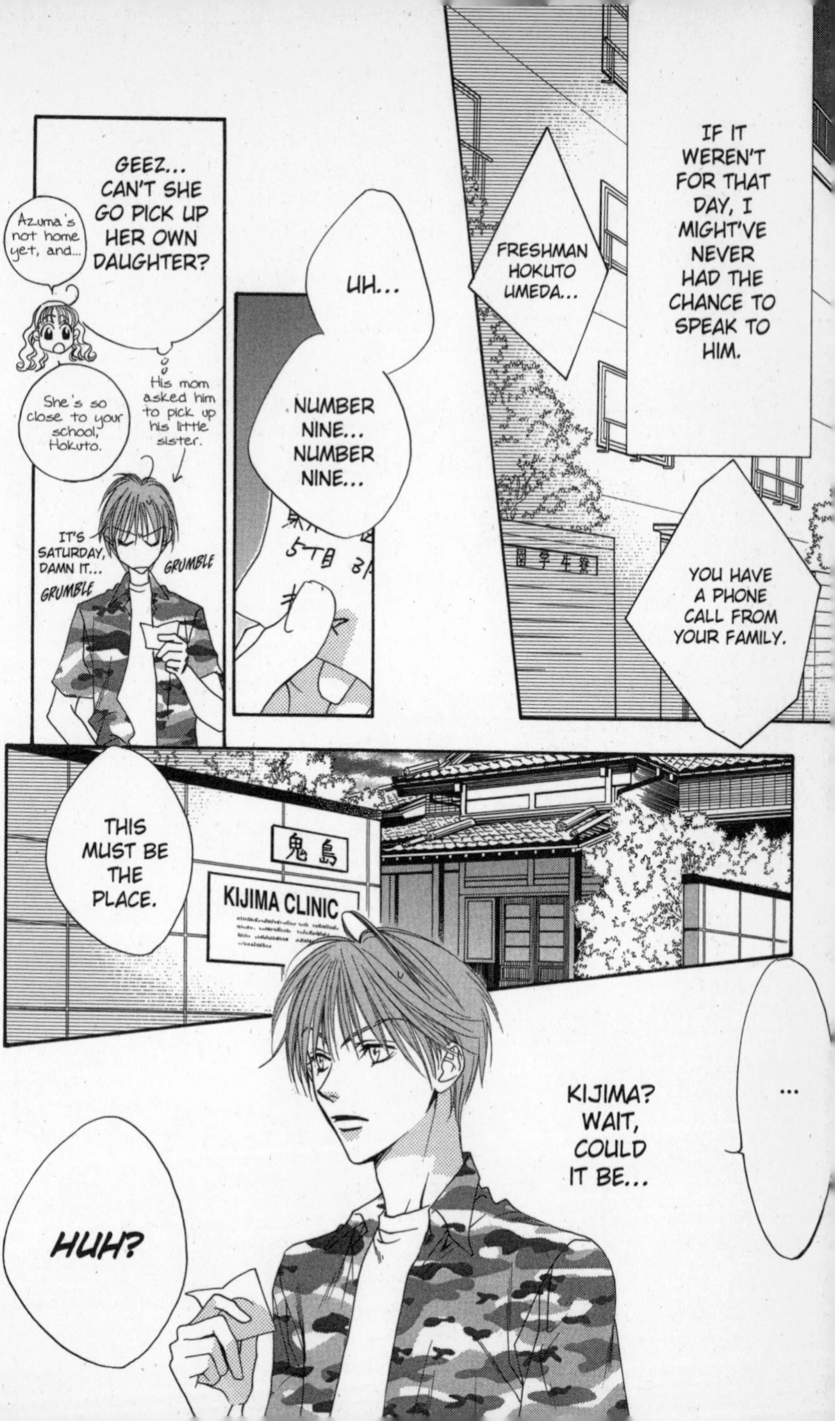
IF IT WEREN'T FOR THAT DAY, I MIGHT'VE NEVER HAD THE CHANCE TO SPEAK TO HIM.
FRESHMAN HOKUTO UMEDA...
YOU HAVE A PHONE CALL FROM YOUR FAMILY.
UH...
NUMBER NINE... NUMBER NINE...
GEEZ... CAN'T SHE GO PICK UP HER OWN DAUGHTER?
Azuma's not home yet, and...
She's so close to your school, Hokuto.
His mom asked him to pick up his little sister.
IT'S SATURDAY, DAMN IT...
GRUMBLE
GRUMBLE
THIS MUST BE THE PLACE.
鬼島
KIJIMA CLINIC
...
KIJIMA? WAIT, COULD IT BE...
HUH?

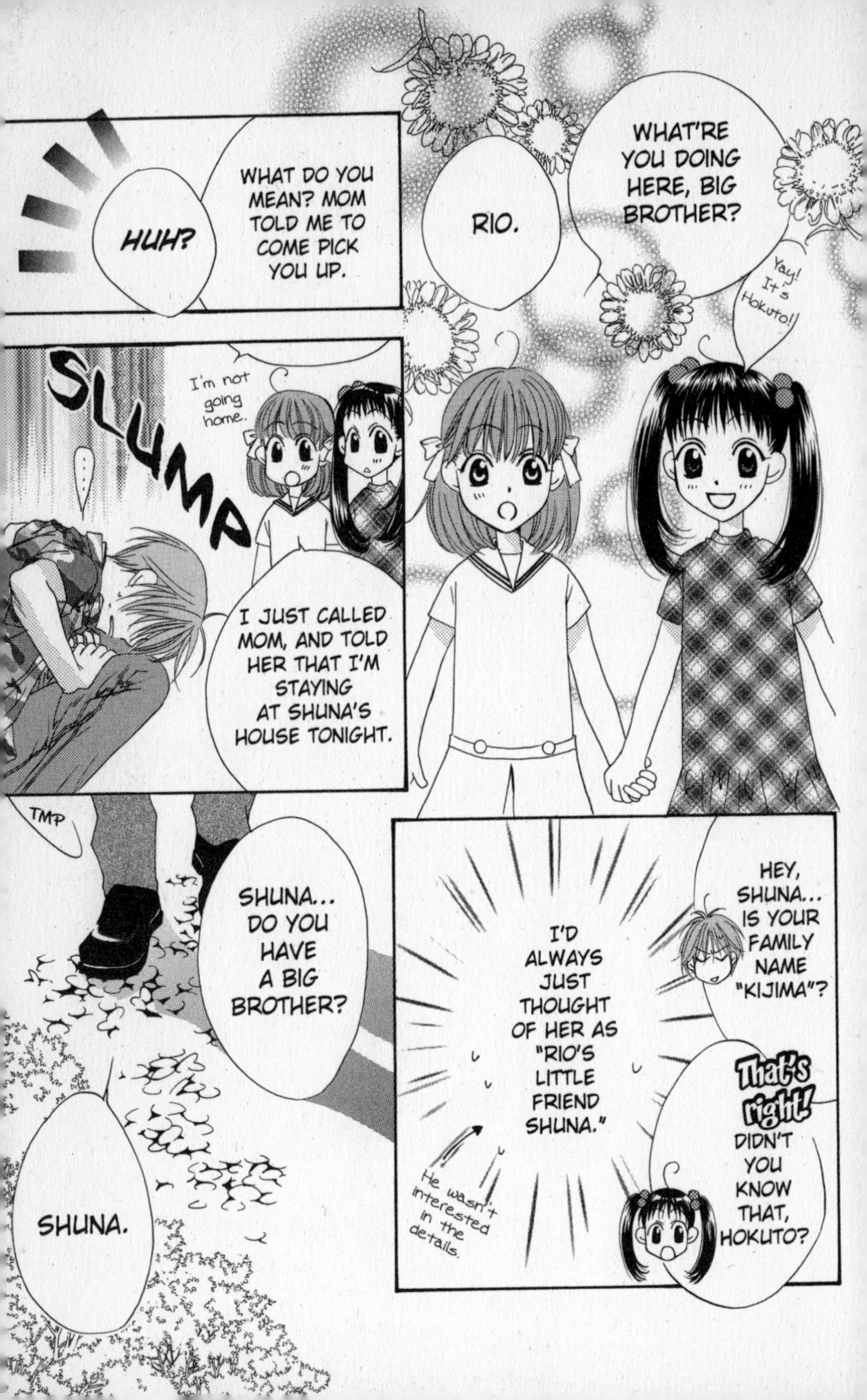
WHAT'RE YOU DOING HERE, BIG BROTHER?
Yay! It's Hokuto!!
RIO.
WHAT DO YOU MEAN? MOM TOLD ME TO COME PICK YOU UP.
HUH?
I'm not going home.
I JUST CALLED MOM, AND TOLD HER THAT I'M STAYING AT SHUNA'S HOUSE TONIGHT.
SLUMP
...
HEY, SHUNA... IS YOUR FAMILY NAME "KIJIMA"?
That's right! DIDN'T YOU KNOW THAT, HOKUTO?
I'D ALWAYS JUST THOUGHT OF HER AS "RIO'S LITTLE FRIEND SHUNA."
He wasn't interested in the details.
TMP
SHUNA... DO YOU HAVE A BIG BROTHER?
SHUNA.

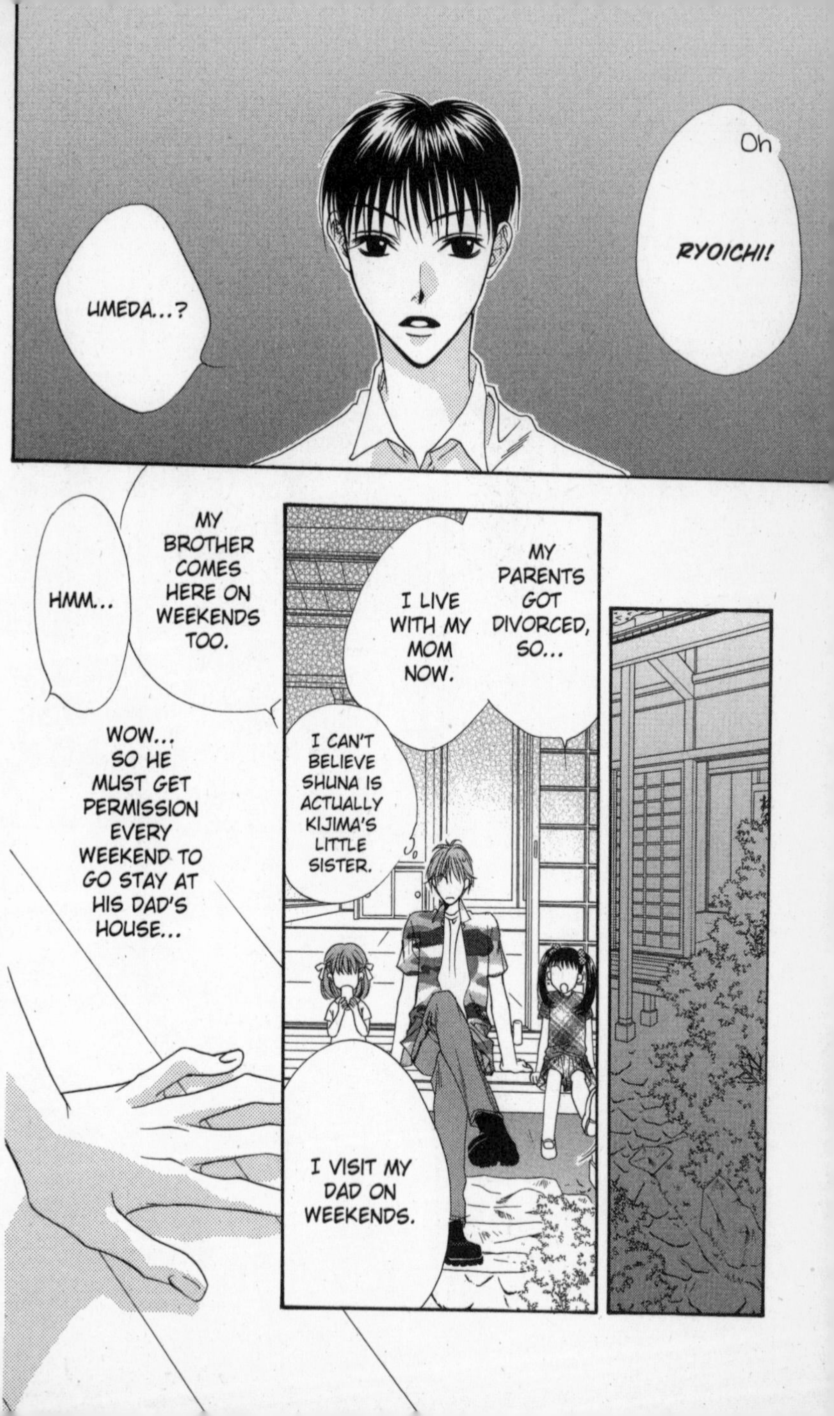
Oh
RYOICHI!
UMEDA...?
MY PARENTS GOT DIVORCED, SO...
I LIVE WITH MY MOM NOW.
I CAN'T BELIEVE SHUNA IS ACTUALLY KIJIMA'S LITTLE SISTER.
I VISIT MY DAD ON WEEKENDS.
MY BROTHER COMES HERE ON WEEKENDS TOO.
HMM...
WOW... SO HE MUST GET PERMISSION EVERY WEEKEND TO GO STAY AT HIS DAD'S HOUSE...

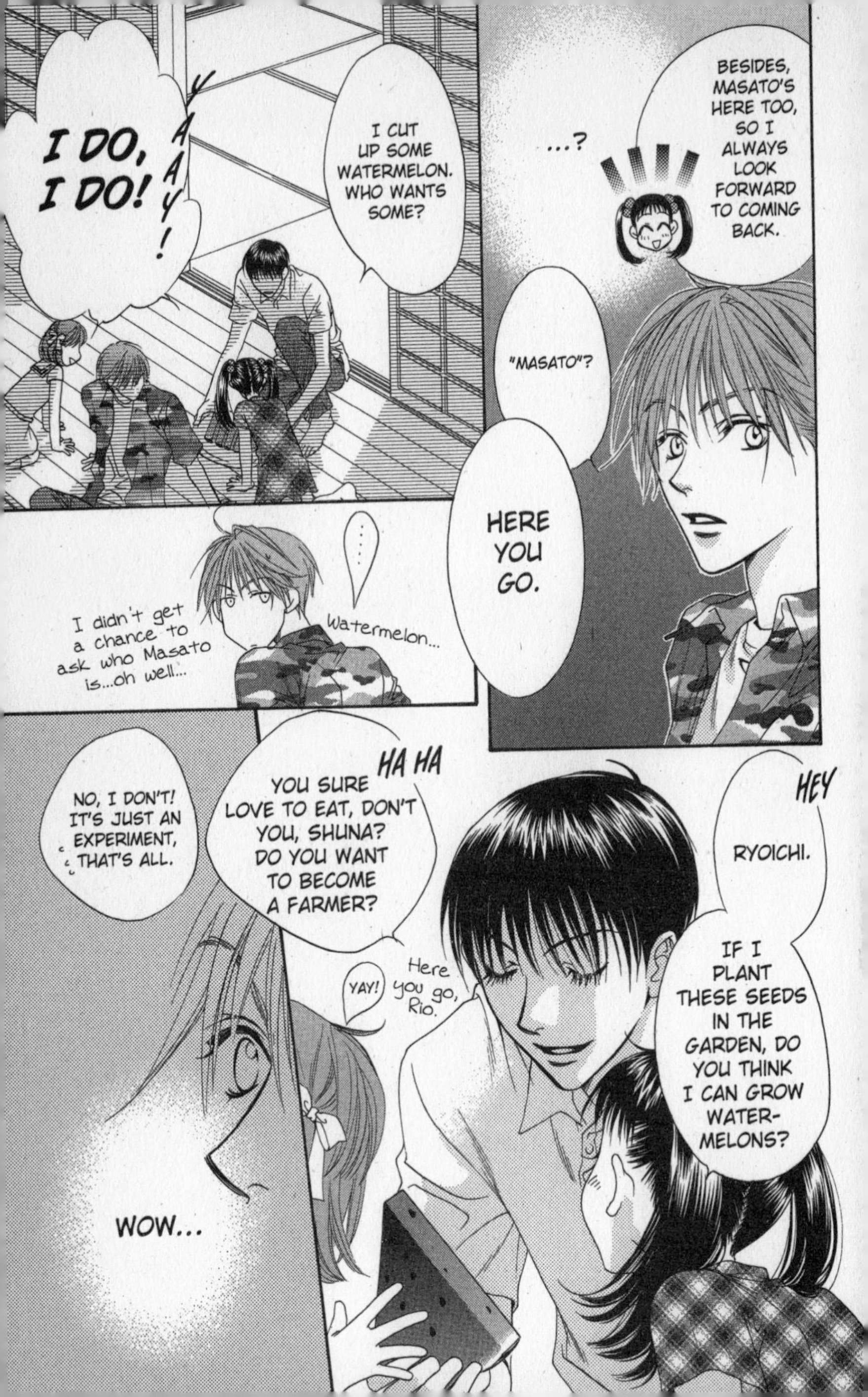
BESIDES, MASATO'S HERE TOO, SO I ALWAYS LOOK FORWARD TO COMING BACK.
...?
"MASATO"?
HERE YOU GO.
I CUT UP SOME WATERMELON. WHO WANTS SOME?
YAAAY!
I DO, I DO!
...
Watermelon...
I didn't get a chance to ask who Masato is...oh well...
HEY
RYOICHI.
IF I PLANT THESE SEEDS IN THE GARDEN, DO YOU THINK I CAN GROW WATER-MELONS?
HA HA
YOU SURE LOVE TO EAT, DON'T YOU, SHUNA? DO YOU WANT TO BECOME A FARMER?
NO, I DON'T! IT'S JUST AN EXPERIMENT, THAT'S ALL.
Here you go, Rio.
YAY!
WOW...

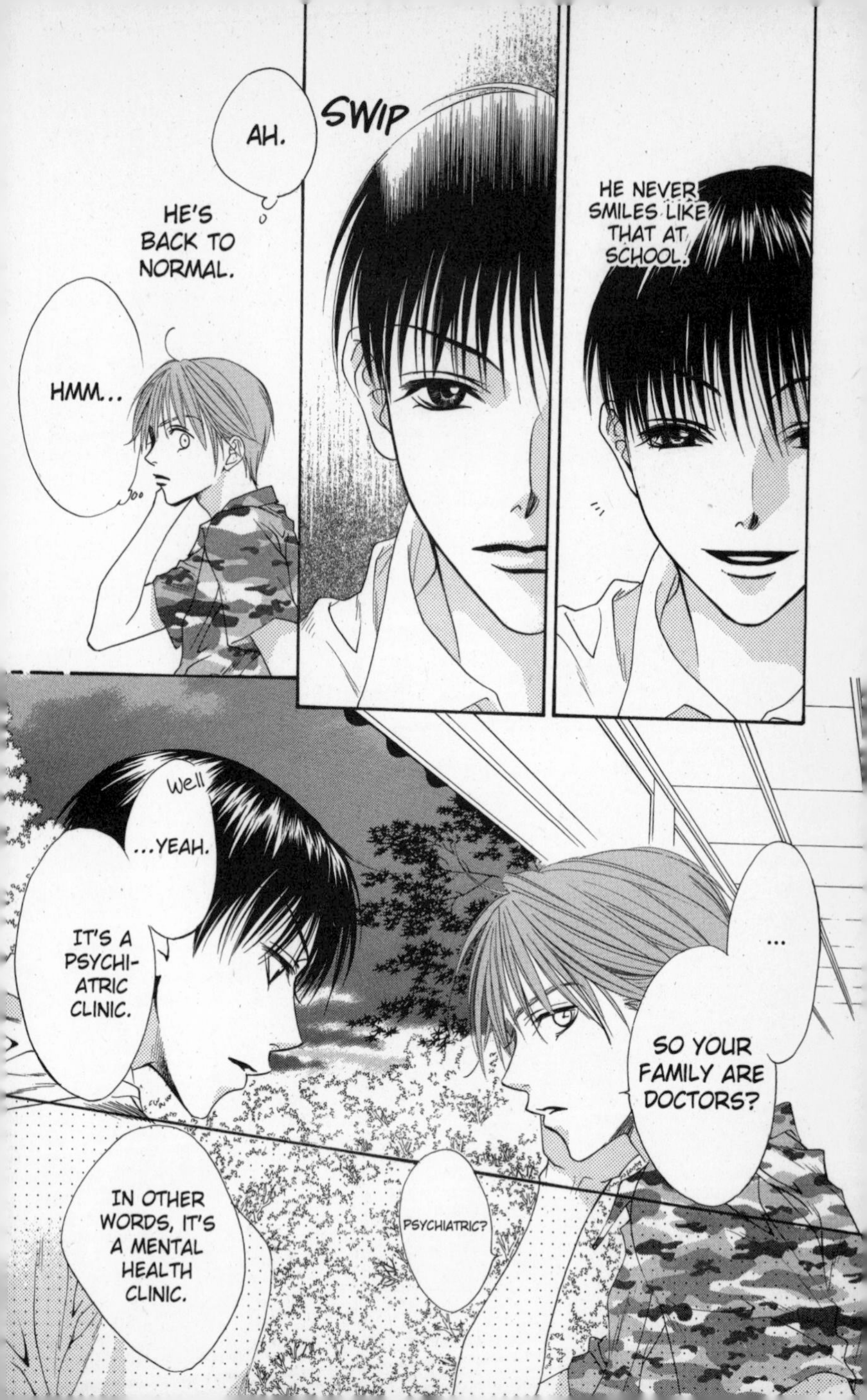
HE NEVER SMILES LIKE THAT AT SCHOOL.
SWIP
AH.
HE'S BACK TO NORMAL.
HMM...
...
SO YOUR FAMILY ARE DOCTORS?
Well ...YEAH.
IT'S A PSYCHIATRIC CLINIC.
PSYCHIATRIC?
IN OTHER WORDS, IT'S A MENTAL HEALTH CLINIC.

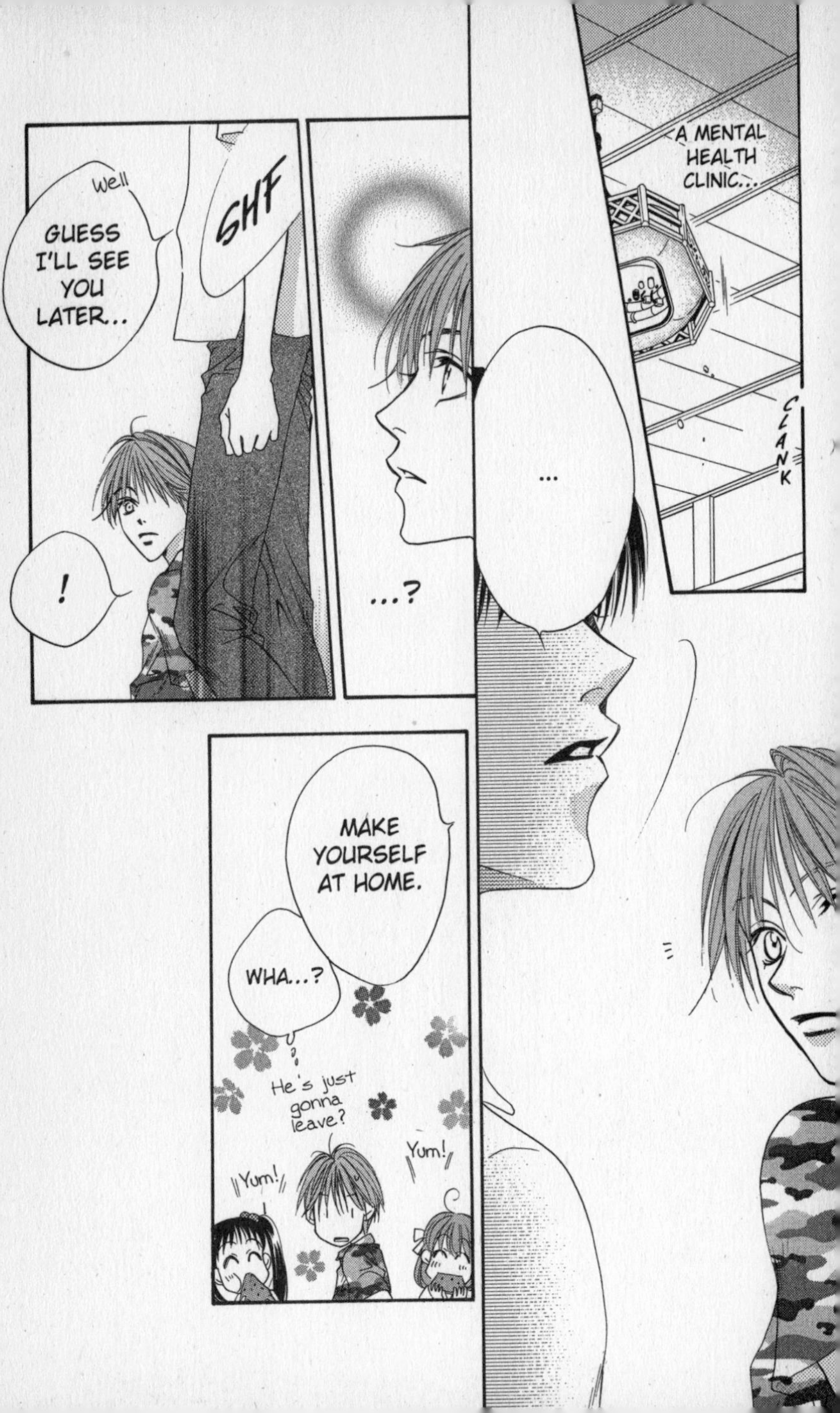
A MENTAL HEALTH CLINIC...
CLANK
...
...?
Well
GUESS I'LL SEE YOU LATER...
SHF
!
MAKE YOURSELF AT HOME.
WHA...?
He's just gonna leave?
Yum!
Yum!

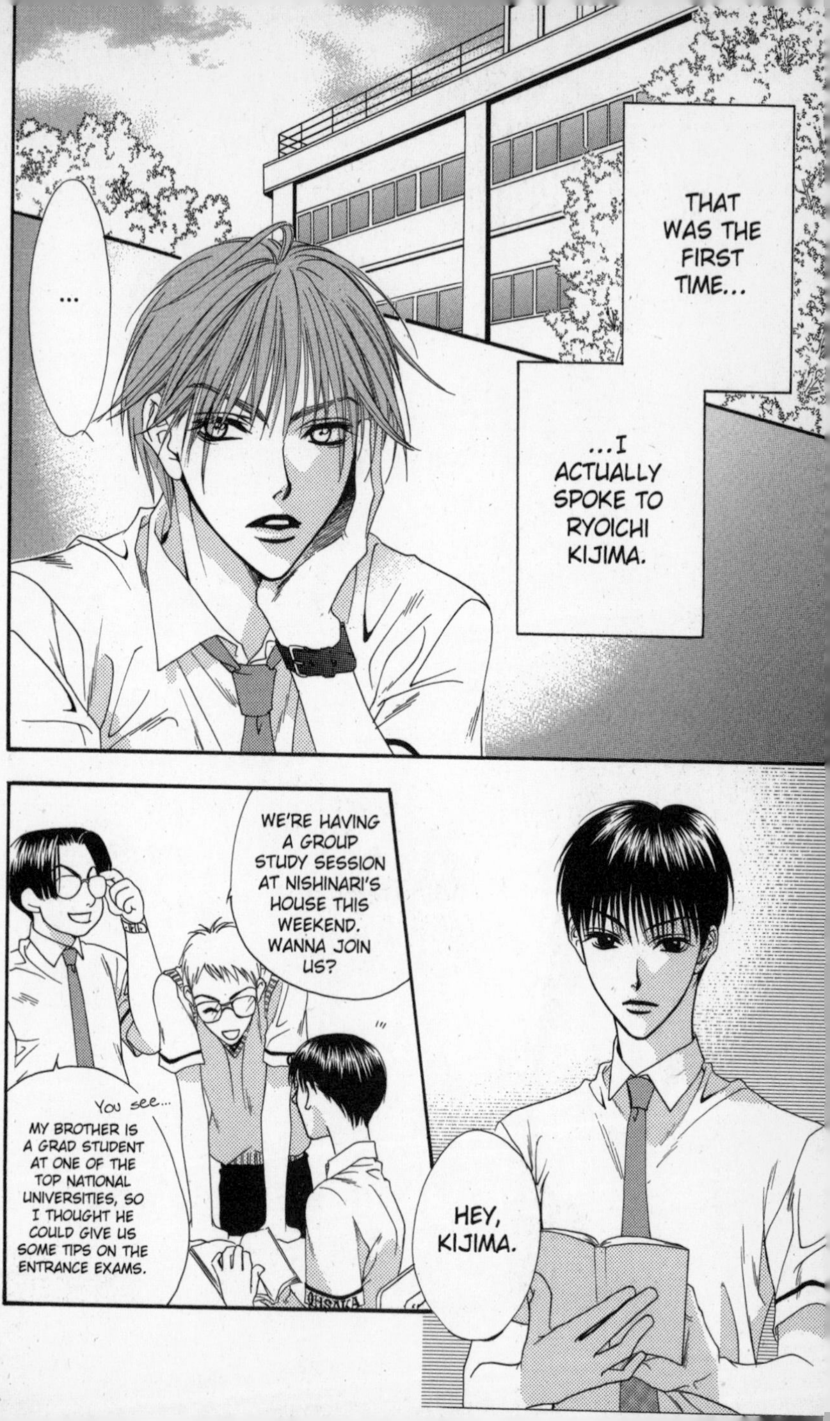
THAT WAS THE FIRST TIME...
...I ACTUALLY SPOKE TO RYOICHI KIJIMA.
...
HEY, KIJIMA.
WE'RE HAVING A GROUP STUDY SESSION AT NISHINARI'S HOUSE THIS WEEKEND. WANNA JOIN US?
You see...
MY BROTHER IS A GRAD STUDENT AT ONE OF THE TOP NATIONAL UNIVERSITIES, SO I THOUGHT HE COULD GIVE US SOME TIPS ON THE ENTRANCE EXAMS.

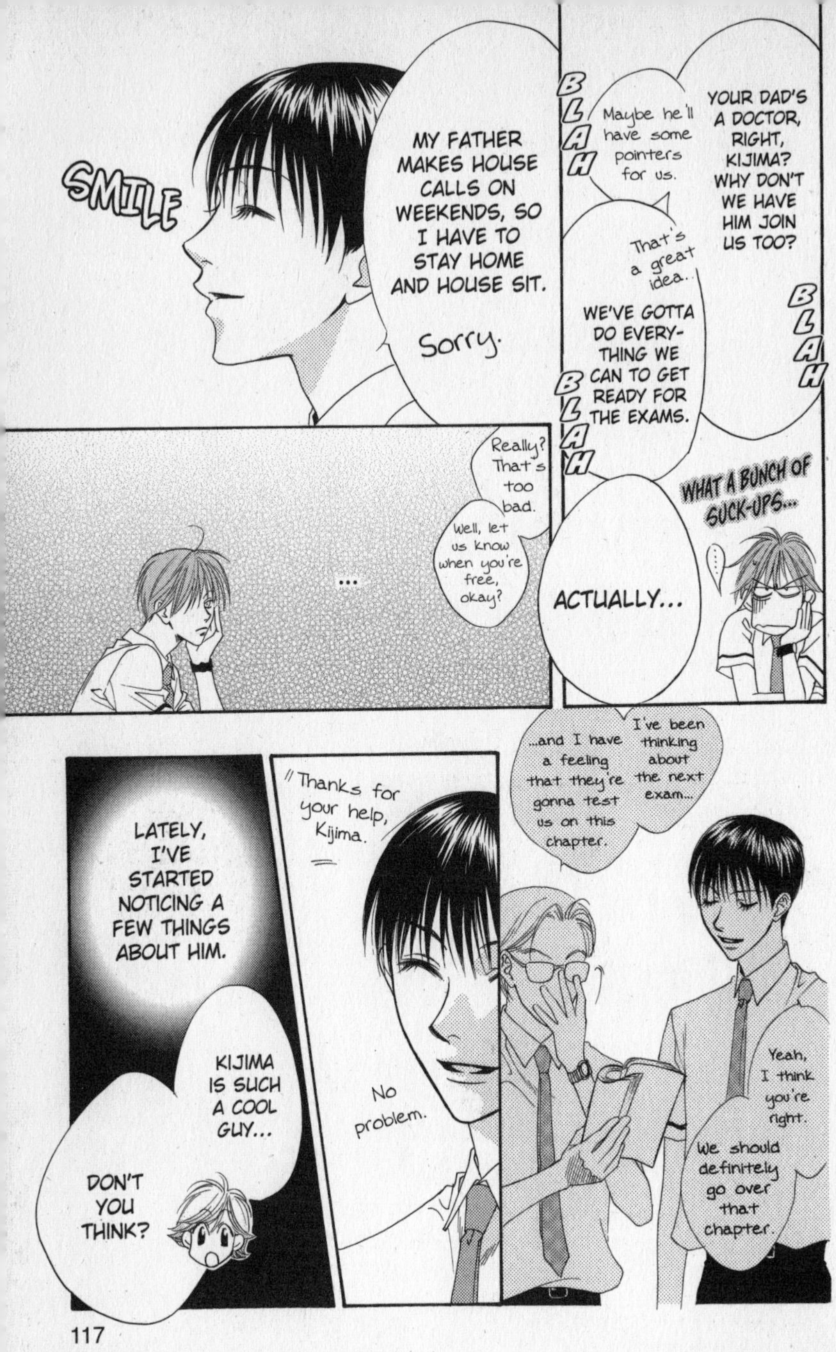
YOUR DAD'S A DOCTOR, RIGHT, KIJIMA? WHY DON'T WE HAVE HIM JOIN US TOO?
BLAH
Maybe he'll have some pointers for us.
BLAH
That's a great idea...
WE'VE GOTTA DO EVERY-THING WE CAN TO GET READY FOR THE EXAMS.
BLAH
WHAT A BUNCH OF SUCK-UPS...
...
ACTUALLY...
MY FATHER MAKES HOUSE CALLS ON WEEKENDS, SO I HAVE TO STAY HOME AND HOUSE SIT.
SMILE
Sorry.
Really? That's too bad.
Well, let us know when you're free, okay?
...
I've been thinking about the next exam...
...and I have a feeling that they're gonna test us on this chapter.
Yeah, I think you're right.
We should definitely go over that chapter.
Thanks for your help, Kijima.
No problem.
LATELY, I'VE STARTED NOTICING A FEW THINGS ABOUT HIM.
KIJIMA IS SUCH A COOL GUY...
DON'T YOU THINK?

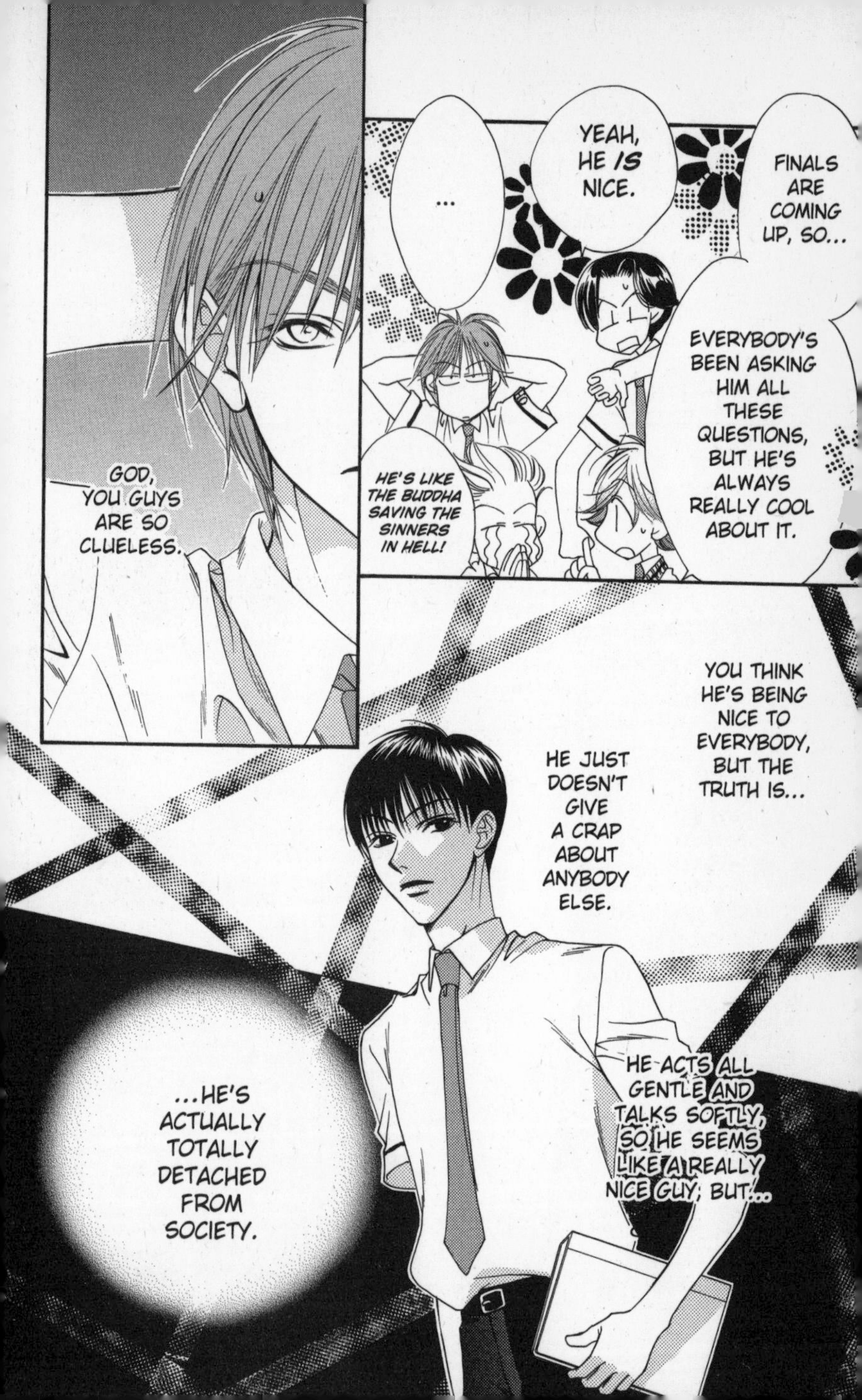
FINALS ARE COMING UP, SO...
EVERYBODY'S BEEN ASKING HIM ALL THESE QUESTIONS, BUT HE'S ALWAYS REALLY COOL ABOUT IT.
YEAH, HE *IS* NICE.
...
HE'S LIKE THE BUDDHA SAVING THE SINNERS IN HELL!
GOD, YOU GUYS ARE SO CLUELESS.
YOU THINK HE'S BEING NICE TO EVERYBODY, BUT THE TRUTH IS...
HE JUST DOESN'T GIVE A CRAP ABOUT ANYBODY ELSE.
HE ACTS ALL GENTLE AND TALKS SOFTLY, SO HE SEEMS LIKE A REALLY NICE GUY, BUT...
...HE'S ACTUALLY TOTALLY DETACHED FROM SOCIETY.

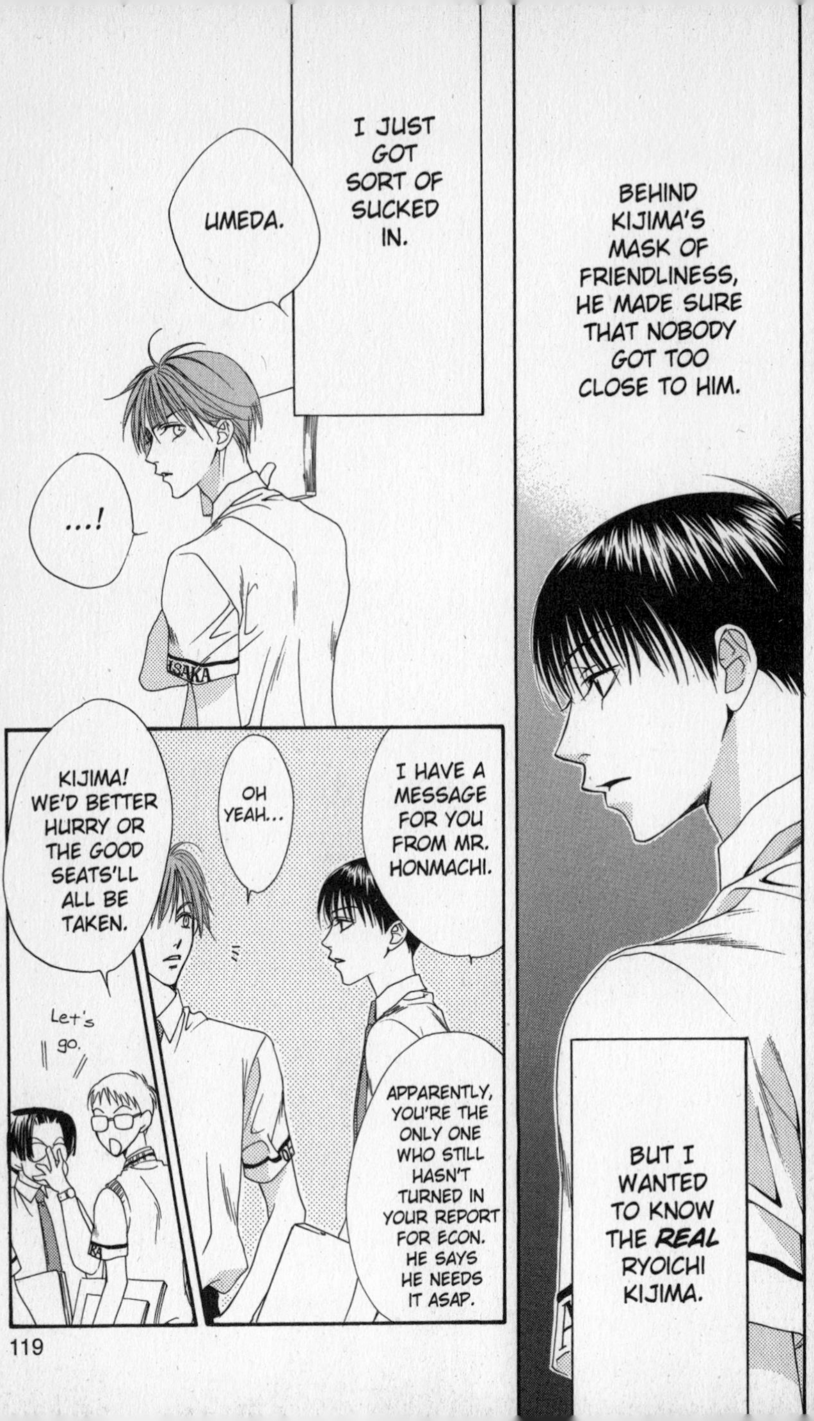
BEHIND KIJIMA'S MASK OF FRIENDLINESS, HE MADE SURE THAT NOBODY GOT TOO CLOSE TO HIM.
BUT I WANTED TO KNOW THE *REAL* RYOICHI KIJIMA.
I JUST GOT SORT OF SUCKED IN.
UMEDA.
...!
I HAVE A MESSAGE FOR YOU FROM MR. HONMACHI.
APPARENTLY, YOU'RE THE ONLY ONE WHO STILL HASN'T TURNED IN YOUR REPORT FOR ECON. HE SAYS HE NEEDS IT ASAP.
OH YEAH...
KIJIMA! WE'D BETTER HURRY OR THE GOOD SEATS'LL ALL BE TAKEN.
Let's go.

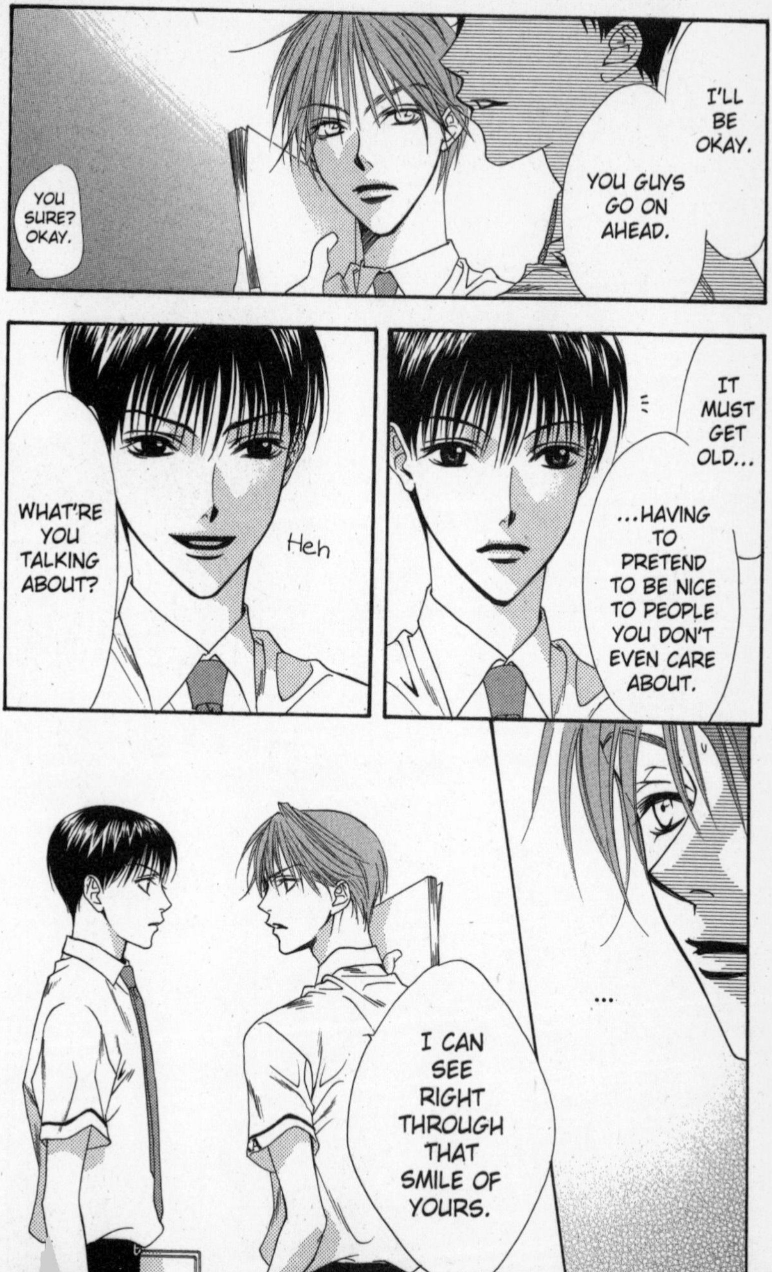
I'LL BE OKAY.
YOU GUYS GO ON AHEAD.
YOU SURE? OKAY.
IT MUST GET OLD...
...HAVING TO PRETEND TO BE NICE TO PEOPLE YOU DON'T EVEN CARE ABOUT.
WHAT'RE YOU TALKING ABOUT?
Heh
...
I CAN SEE RIGHT THROUGH THAT SMILE OF YOURS.

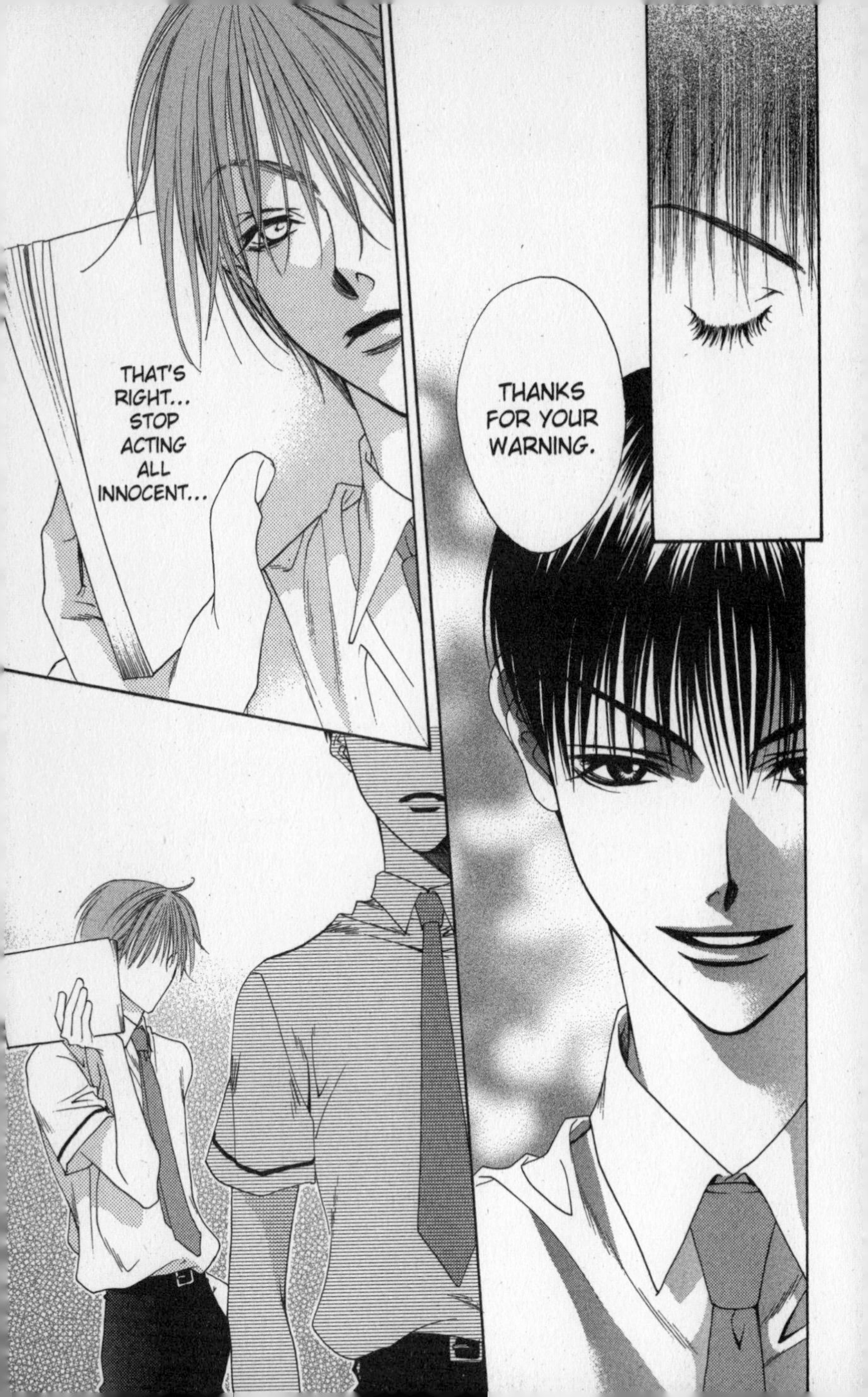
THANKS FOR YOUR WARNING.
THAT'S RIGHT... STOP ACTING ALL INNOCENT...

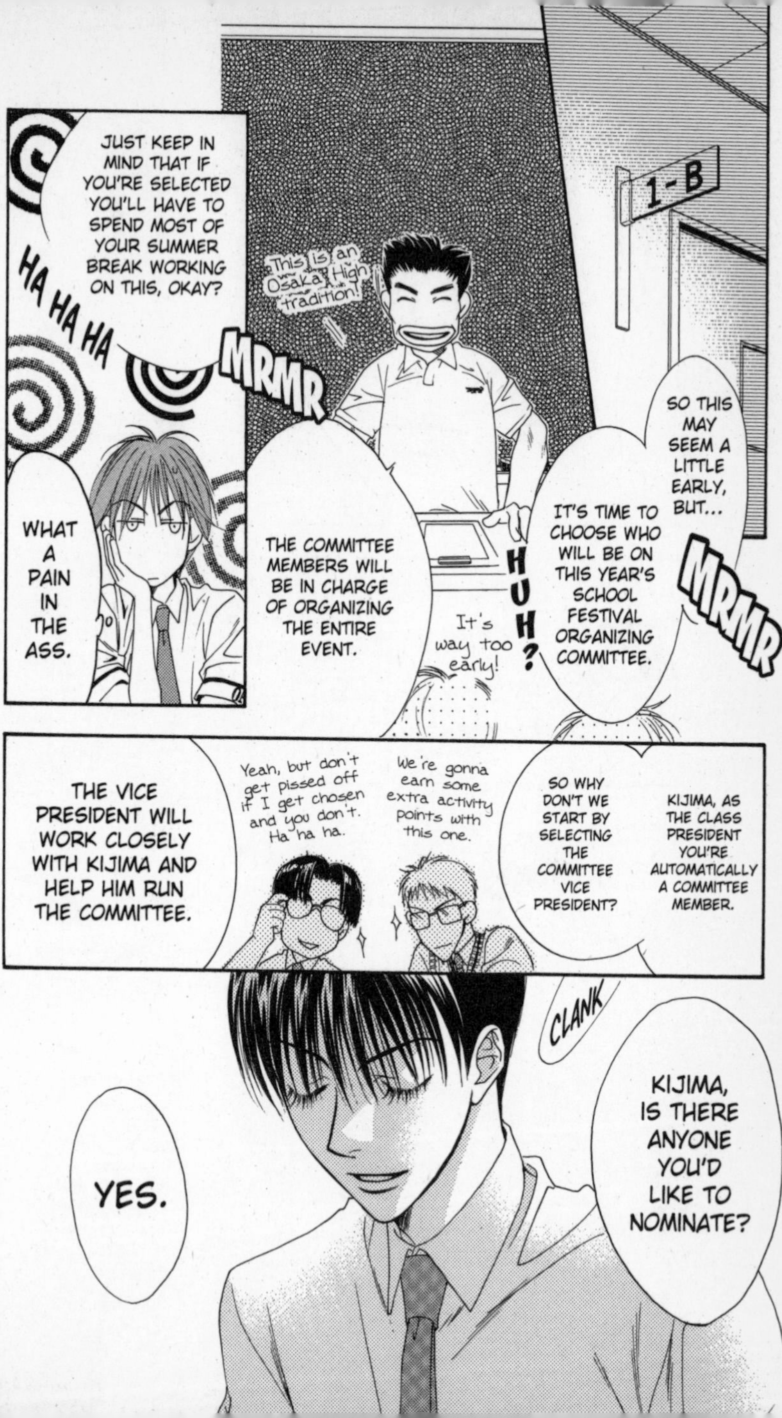
1-B
SO THIS MAY SEEM A LITTLE EARLY, BUT...
IT'S TIME TO CHOOSE WHO WILL BE ON THIS YEAR'S SCHOOL FESTIVAL ORGANIZING COMMITTEE.
MRMR
HUH?
It's way too early!
This is an Osaka High tradition!
THE COMMITTEE MEMBERS WILL BE IN CHARGE OF ORGANIZING THE ENTIRE EVENT.
MRMR
JUST KEEP IN MIND THAT IF YOU'RE SELECTED YOU'LL HAVE TO SPEND MOST OF YOUR SUMMER BREAK WORKING ON THIS, OKAY?
HA HA HA
WHAT A PAIN IN THE ASS.
KIJIMA, AS THE CLASS PRESIDENT YOU'RE AUTOMATICALLY A COMMITTEE MEMBER.
SO WHY DON'T WE START BY SELECTING THE COMMITTEE VICE PRESIDENT?
We're gonna earn some extra activity points with this one.
Yeah, but don't get pissed off if I get chosen and you don't. Ha ha ha.
THE VICE PRESIDENT WILL WORK CLOSELY WITH KIJIMA AND HELP HIM RUN THE COMMITTEE.
CLANK
KIJIMA, IS THERE ANYONE YOU'D LIKE TO NOMINATE?
YES.

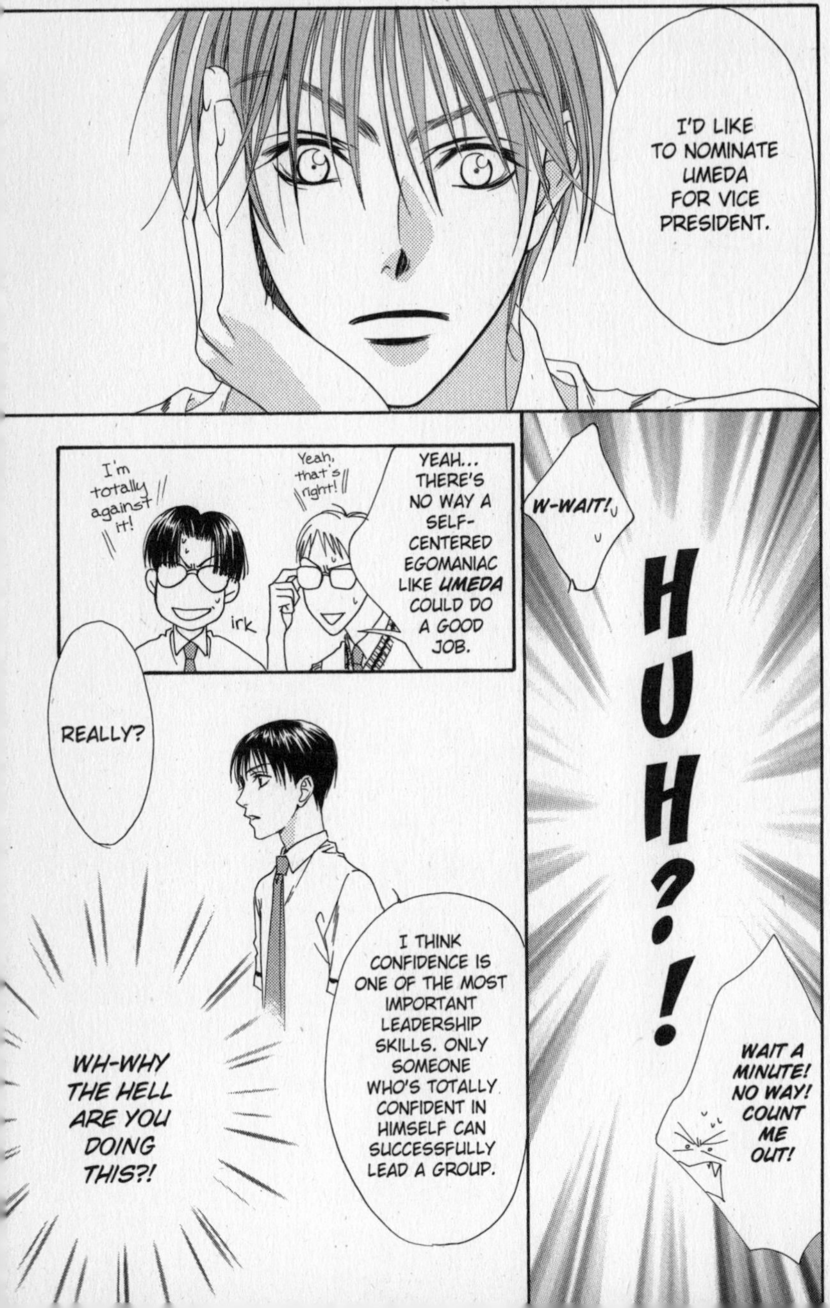
I'D LIKE TO NOMINATE UMEDA FOR VICE PRESIDENT.
W-WAIT!
HUH?!
WAIT A MINUTE! NO WAY! COUNT ME OUT!
YEAH... THERE'S NO WAY A SELF-CENTERED EGOMANIAC LIKE UMEDA COULD DO A GOOD JOB.
Yeah, that's right!
I'm totally against it!
irk
REALLY?
I THINK CONFIDENCE IS ONE OF THE MOST IMPORTANT LEADERSHIP SKILLS. ONLY SOMEONE WHO'S TOTALLY CONFIDENT IN HIMSELF CAN SUCCESSFULLY LEAD A GROUP.
WH-WHY THE HELL ARE YOU DOING THIS?!

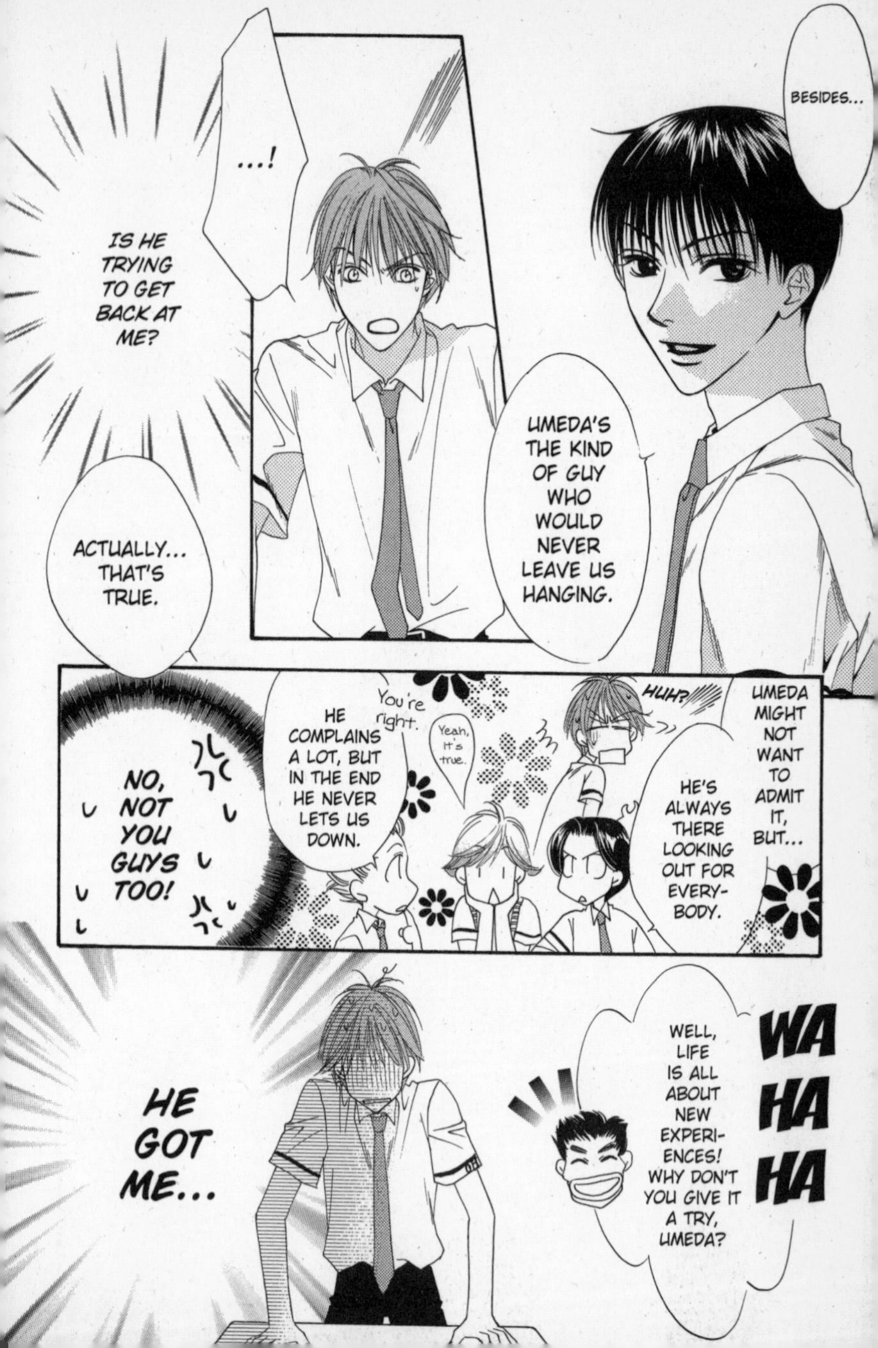
BESIDES...
UMEDA'S THE KIND OF GUY WHO WOULD NEVER LEAVE US HANGING.
...!
IS HE TRYING TO GET BACK AT ME?
ACTUALLY... THAT'S TRUE.
UMEDA MIGHT NOT WANT TO ADMIT IT, BUT...
HUH?
HE'S ALWAYS THERE LOOKING OUT FOR EVERY-BODY.
Yeah, it's true.
You're right.
HE COMPLAINS A LOT, BUT IN THE END HE NEVER LETS US DOWN.
NO, NOT YOU GUYS TOO!
WA HA HA
WELL, LIFE IS ALL ABOUT NEW EXPERI-ENCES! WHY DON'T YOU GIVE IT A TRY, UMEDA?
HE GOT ME...

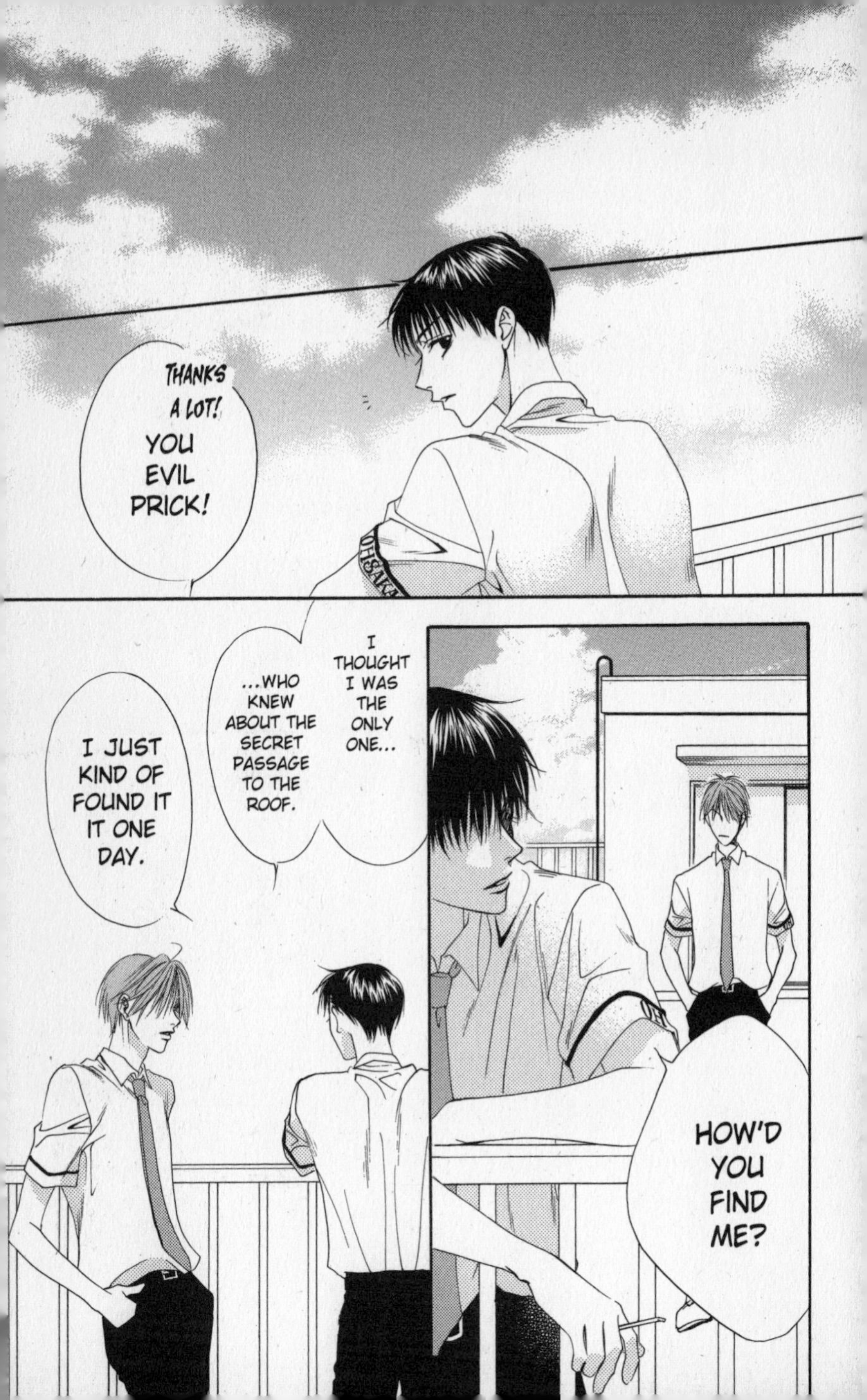
THANKS A LOT! YOU EVIL PRICK!
HOW'D YOU FIND ME?
I THOUGHT I WAS THE ONLY ONE...
...WHO KNEW ABOUT THE SECRET PASSAGE TO THE ROOF.
I JUST KIND OF FOUND IT IT ONE DAY.

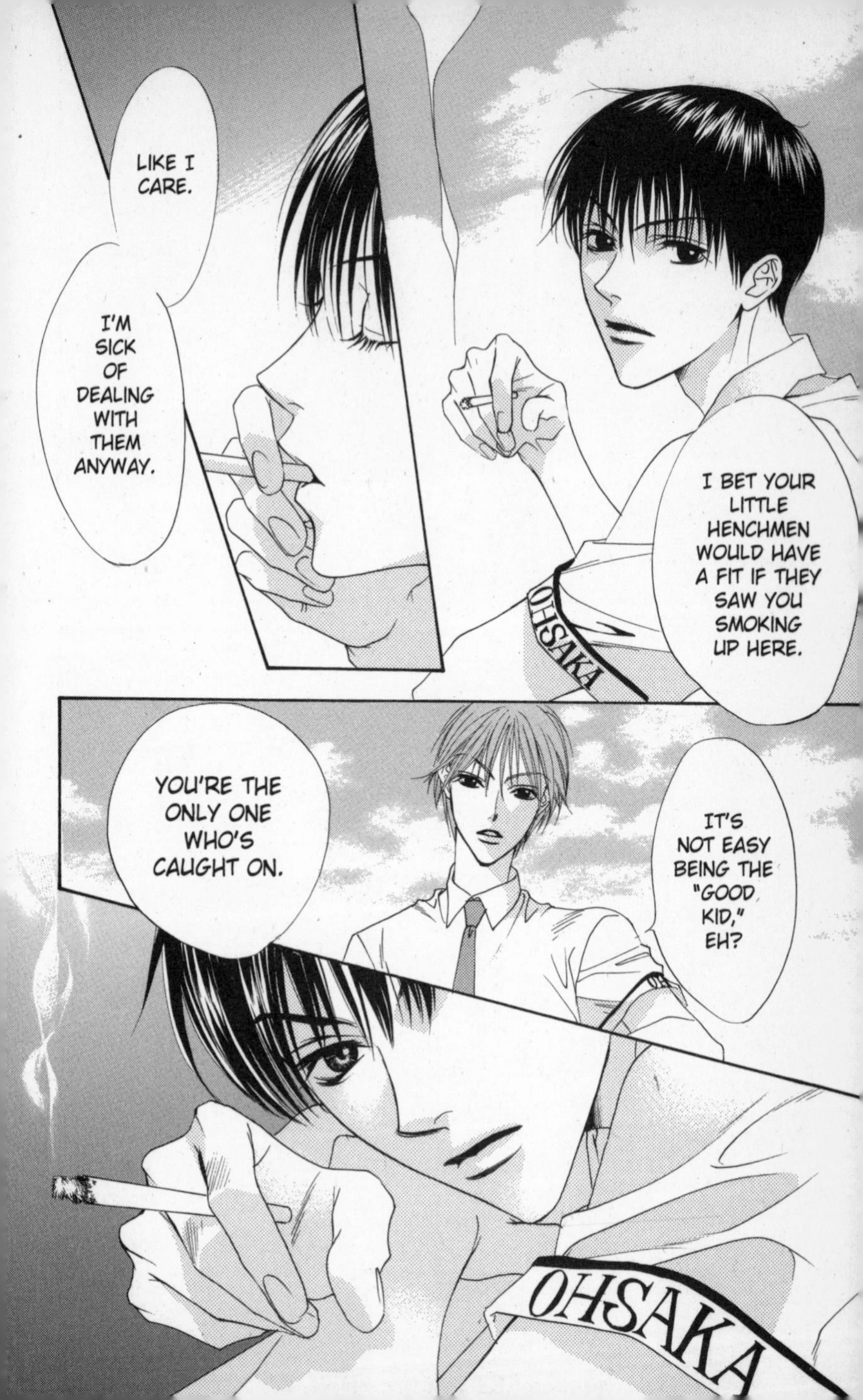
I BET YOUR LITTLE HENCHMEN WOULD HAVE A FIT IF THEY SAW YOU SMOKING UP HERE.
OHSAKA
LIKE I CARE.
I'M SICK OF DEALING WITH THEM ANYWAY.
IT'S NOT EASY BEING THE "GOOD KID," EH?
YOU'RE THE ONLY ONE WHO'S CAUGHT ON.
OHSAKA

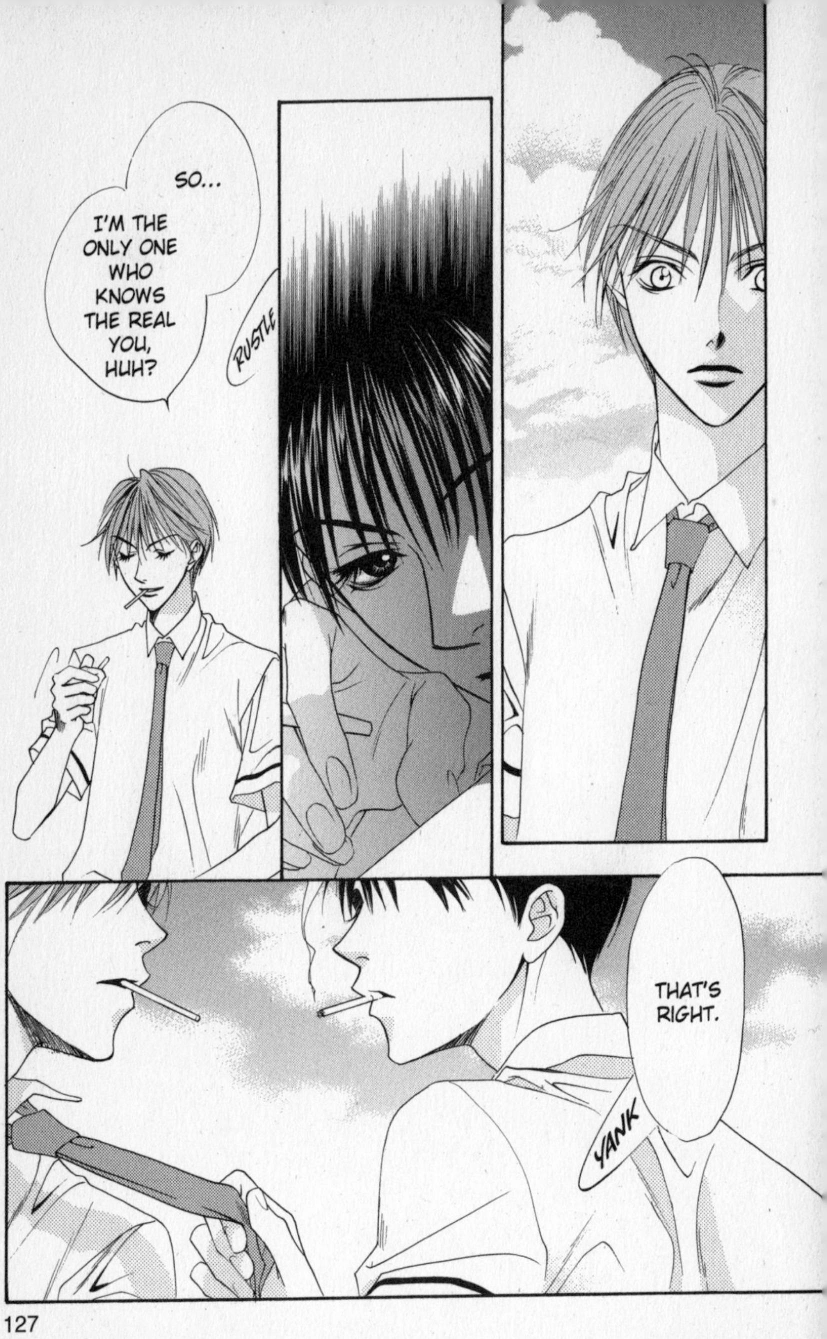
RUSTLE
SO...
I'M THE ONLY ONE WHO KNOWS THE REAL YOU, HUH?
THAT'S RIGHT.
YANK

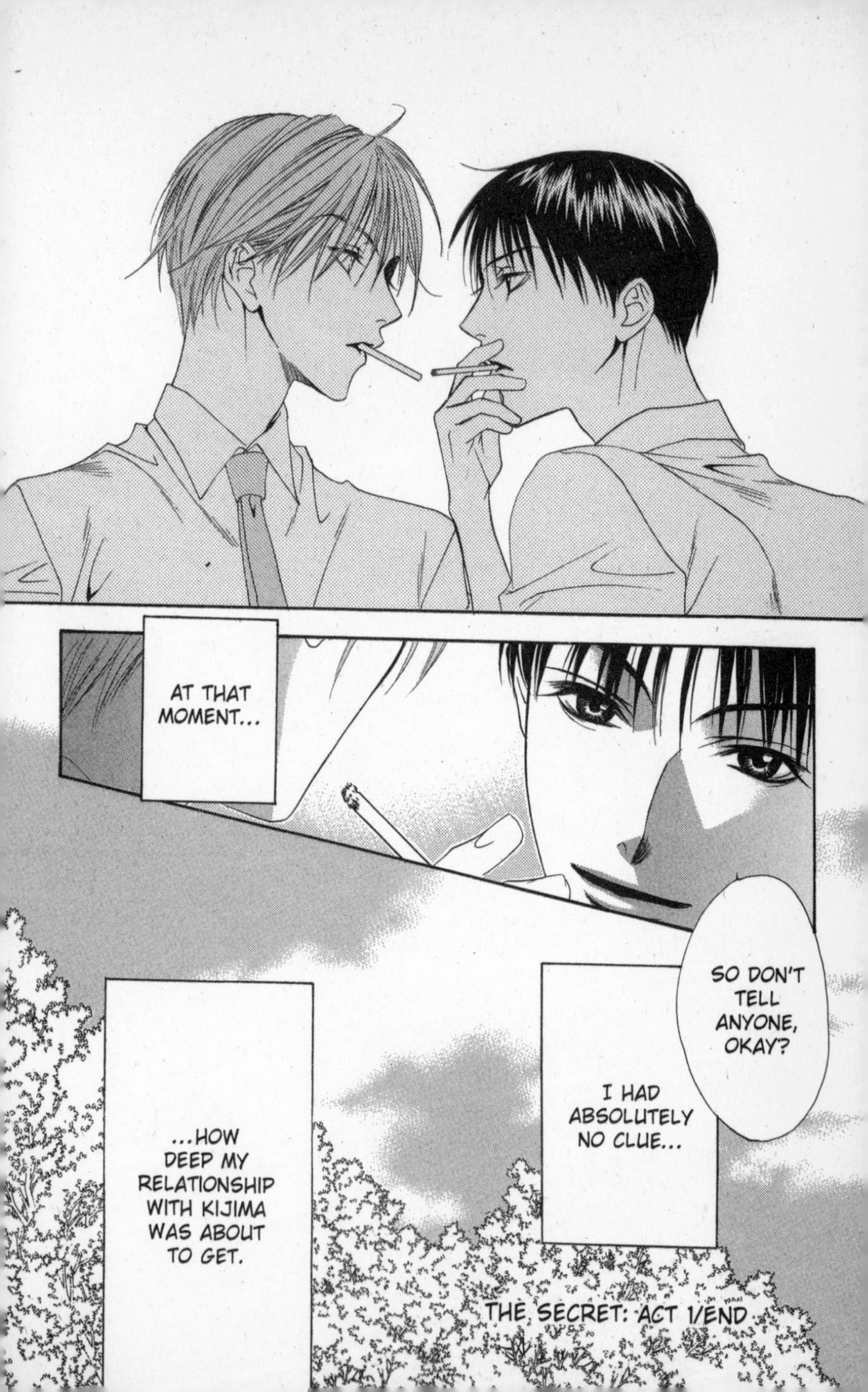
AT THAT MOMENT...
SO DON'T TELL ANYONE, OKAY?
I HAD ABSOLUTELY NO CLUE...
...HOW DEEP MY RELATIONSHIP WITH KIJIMA WAS ABOUT TO GET.
THE SECRET: ACT 1/END

Hana-Kimi

For You in Full Blossom

**Special Episode
The Secret: Act 2**

CHAPTER 78

*LOVE IS KIND OF
LIKE A CAR CRASH...
YOU NEVER SEE
IT COMING.*

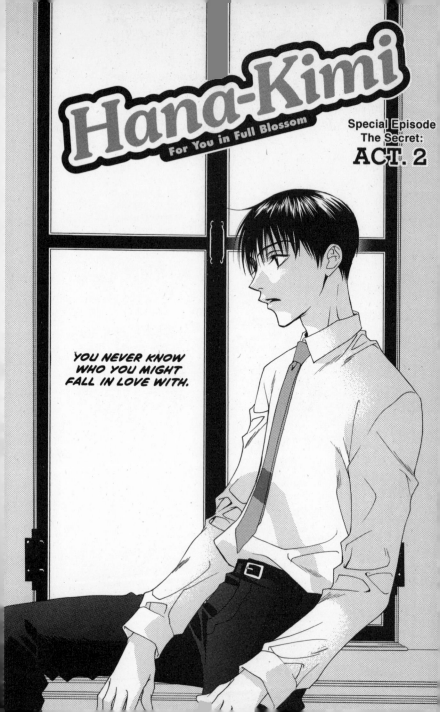

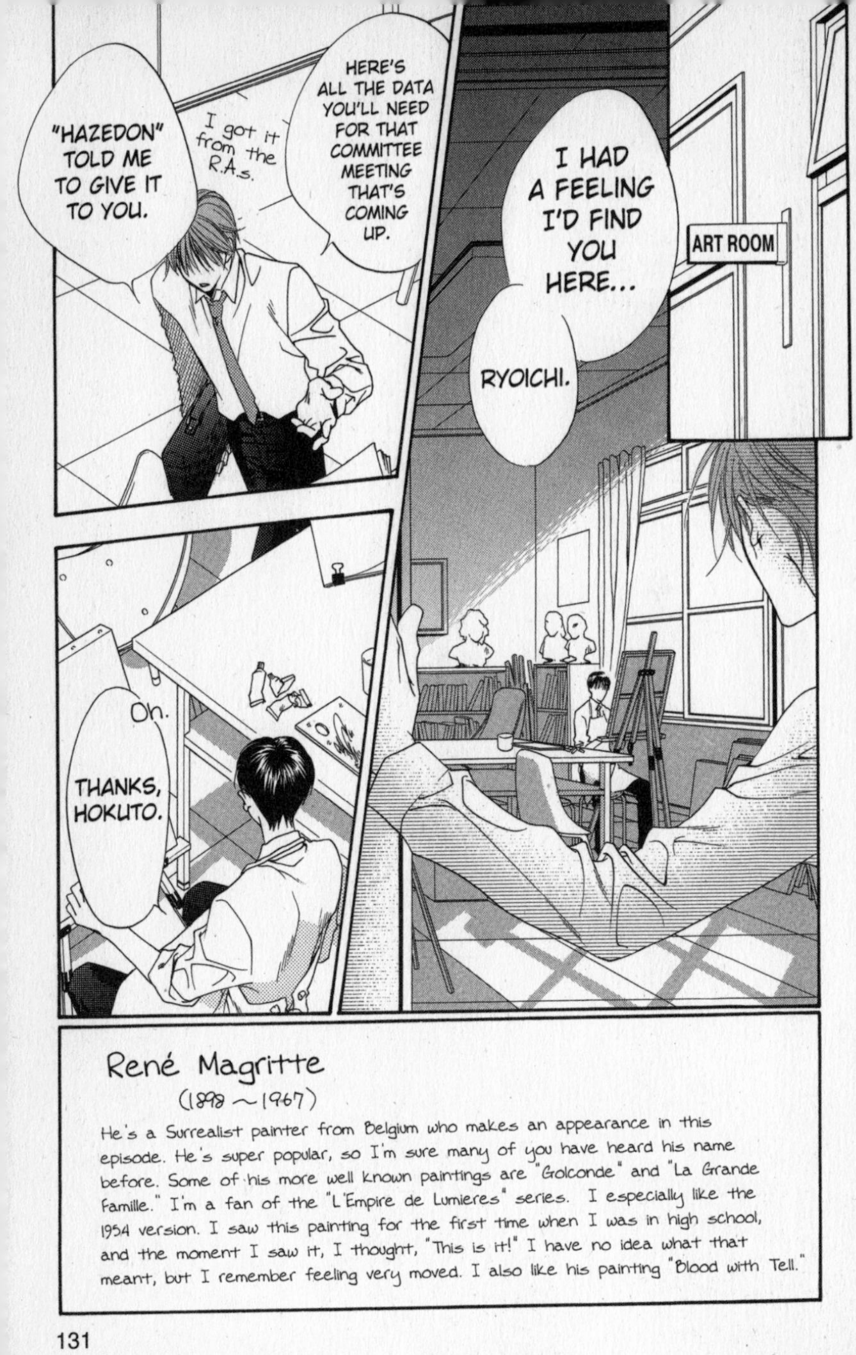
ART ROOM
I HAD A FEELING I'D FIND YOU HERE...
RYOICHI.
HERE'S ALL THE DATA YOU'LL NEED FOR THAT COMMITTEE MEETING THAT'S COMING UP.
I got it from the R.A.s.
"HAZEDON" TOLD ME TO GIVE IT TO YOU.
Oh.
THANKS, HOKUTO.

René Magritte

(1898 ~ 1967)

He's a Surrealist painter from Belgium who makes an appearance in this episode. He's super popular, so I'm sure many of you have heard his name before. Some of his more well known paintings are "Golconde" and "La Grande Famille." I'm a fan of the "L'Empire de Lumieres" series. I especially like the 1954 version. I saw this painting for the first time when I was in high school, and the moment I saw it, I thought, "This is it!" I have no idea what that meant, but I remember feeling very moved. I also like his painting "Blood with Tell."

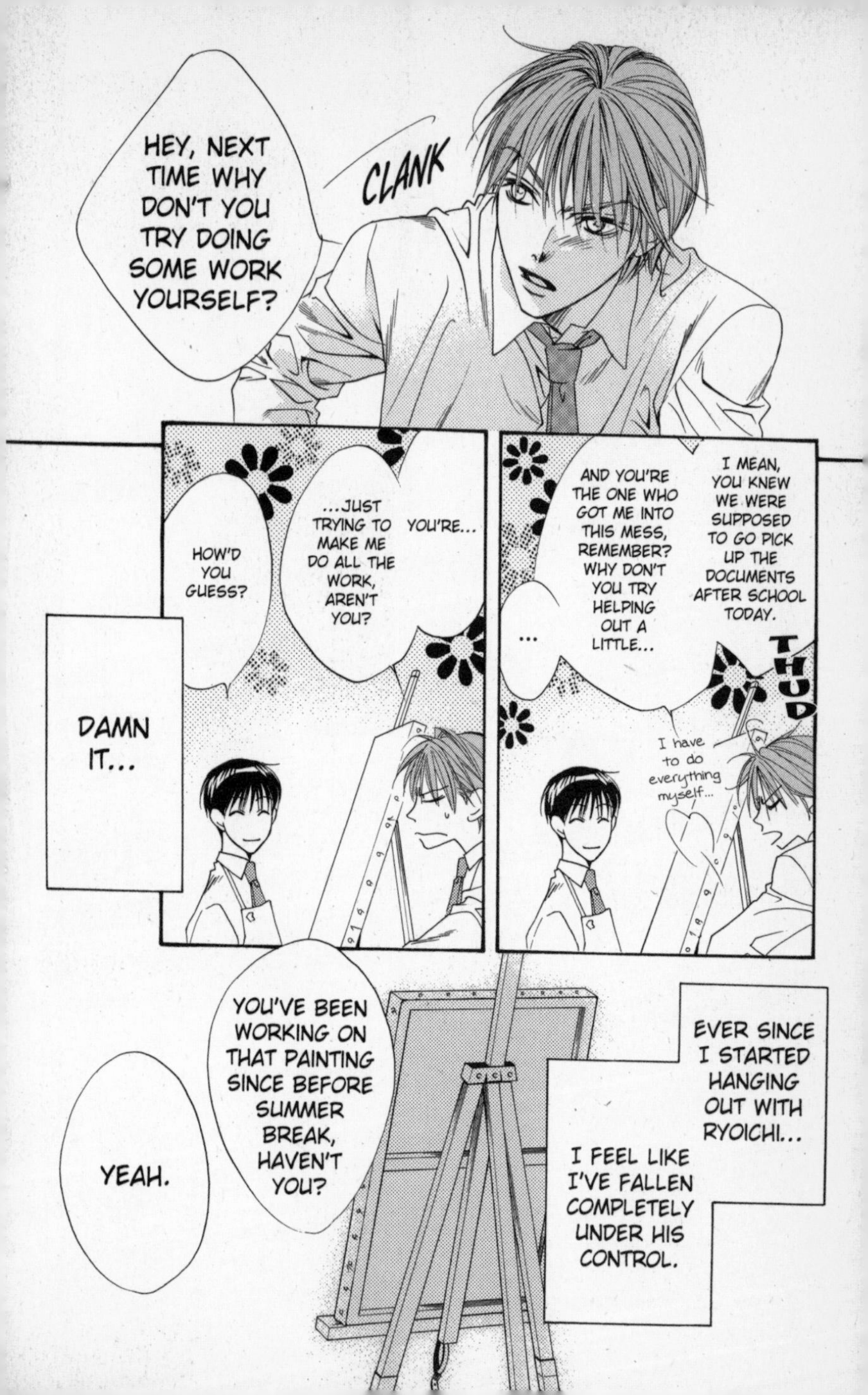
HEY, NEXT TIME WHY DON'T YOU TRY DOING SOME WORK YOURSELF?
CLANK
I MEAN, YOU KNEW WE WERE SUPPOSED TO GO PICK UP THE DOCUMENTS AFTER SCHOOL TODAY.
AND YOU'RE THE ONE WHO GOT ME INTO THIS MESS, REMEMBER? WHY DON'T YOU TRY HELPING OUT A LITTLE...
...
THUD
I have to do everything myself...
YOU'RE...
...JUST TRYING TO MAKE ME DO ALL THE WORK, AREN'T YOU?
HOW'D YOU GUESS?
DAMN IT...
EVER SINCE I STARTED HANGING OUT WITH RYOICHI...
I FEEL LIKE I'VE FALLEN COMPLETELY UNDER HIS CONTROL.
YOU'VE BEEN WORKING ON THAT PAINTING SINCE BEFORE SUMMER BREAK, HAVEN'T YOU?
YEAH.

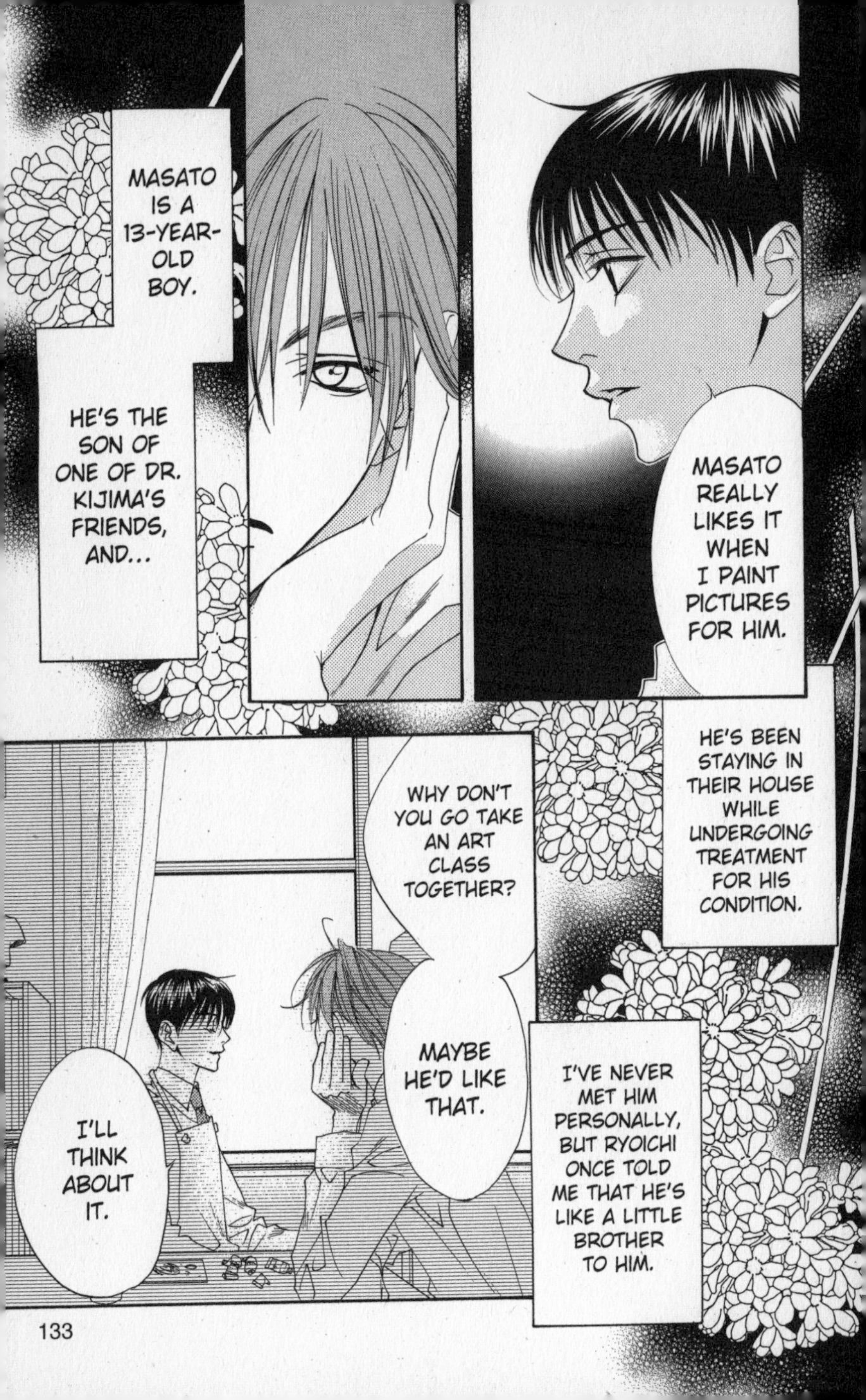
MASATO REALLY LIKES IT WHEN I PAINT PICTURES FOR HIM.
MASATO IS A 13-YEAR-OLD BOY.
HE'S THE SON OF ONE OF DR. KIJIMA'S FRIENDS, AND...
HE'S BEEN STAYING IN THEIR HOUSE WHILE UNDERGOING TREATMENT FOR HIS CONDITION.
I'VE NEVER MET HIM PERSONALLY, BUT RYOICHI ONCE TOLD ME THAT HE'S LIKE A LITTLE BROTHER TO HIM.
WHY DON'T YOU GO TAKE AN ART CLASS TOGETHER?
MAYBE HE'D LIKE THAT.
I'LL THINK ABOUT IT.

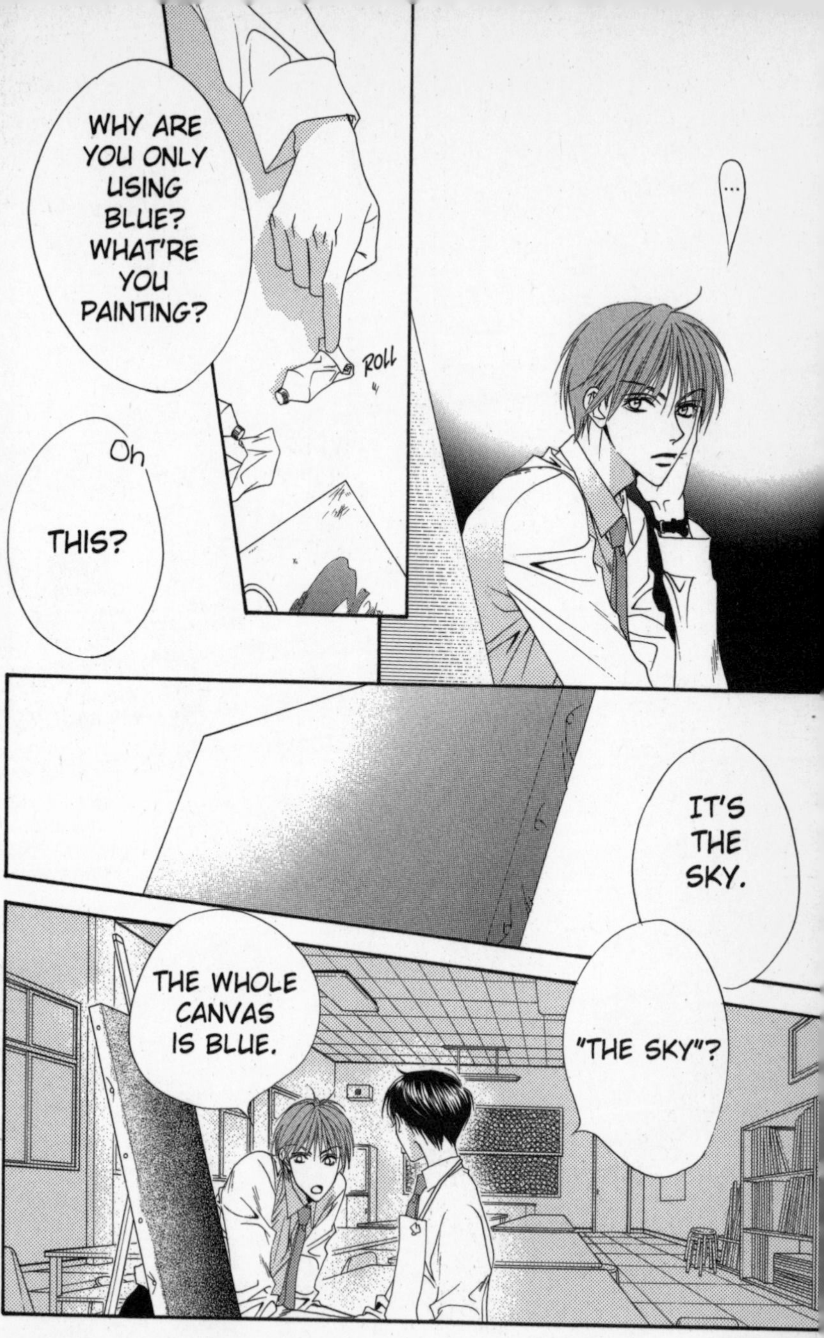
WHY ARE YOU ONLY USING BLUE? WHAT'RE YOU PAINTING?
ROLL
...
Oh THIS?
IT'S THE SKY.
"THE SKY"?
THE WHOLE CANVAS IS BLUE.

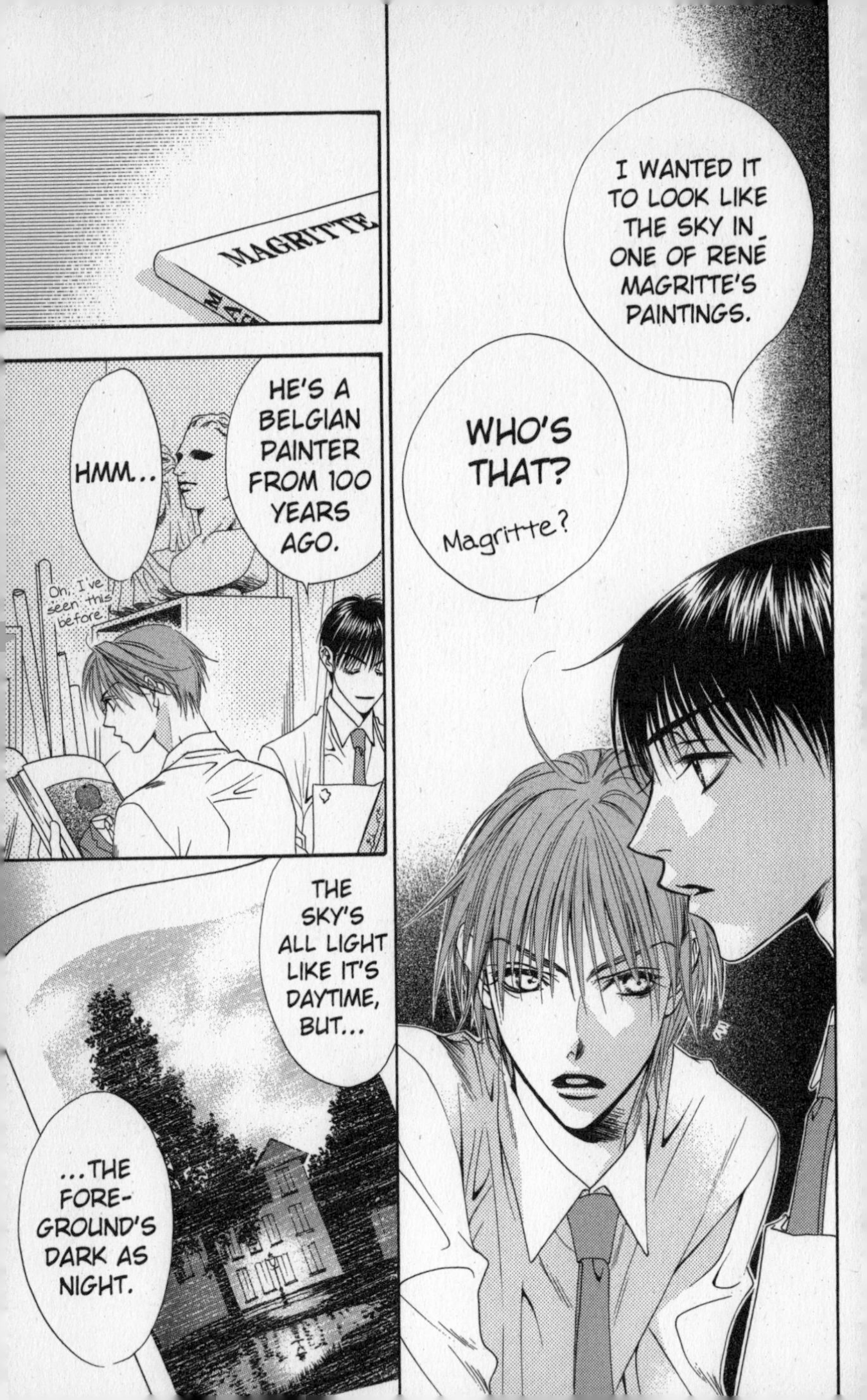
I WANTED IT TO LOOK LIKE THE SKY IN ONE OF RENÉ MAGRITTE'S PAINTINGS.
WHO'S THAT?
Magritte?
MAGRITTE
HE'S A BELGIAN PAINTER FROM 100 YEARS AGO.
HMM...
Oh, I've seen this before.
THE SKY'S ALL LIGHT LIKE IT'S DAYTIME, BUT...
...THE FOREGROUND'S DARK AS NIGHT.

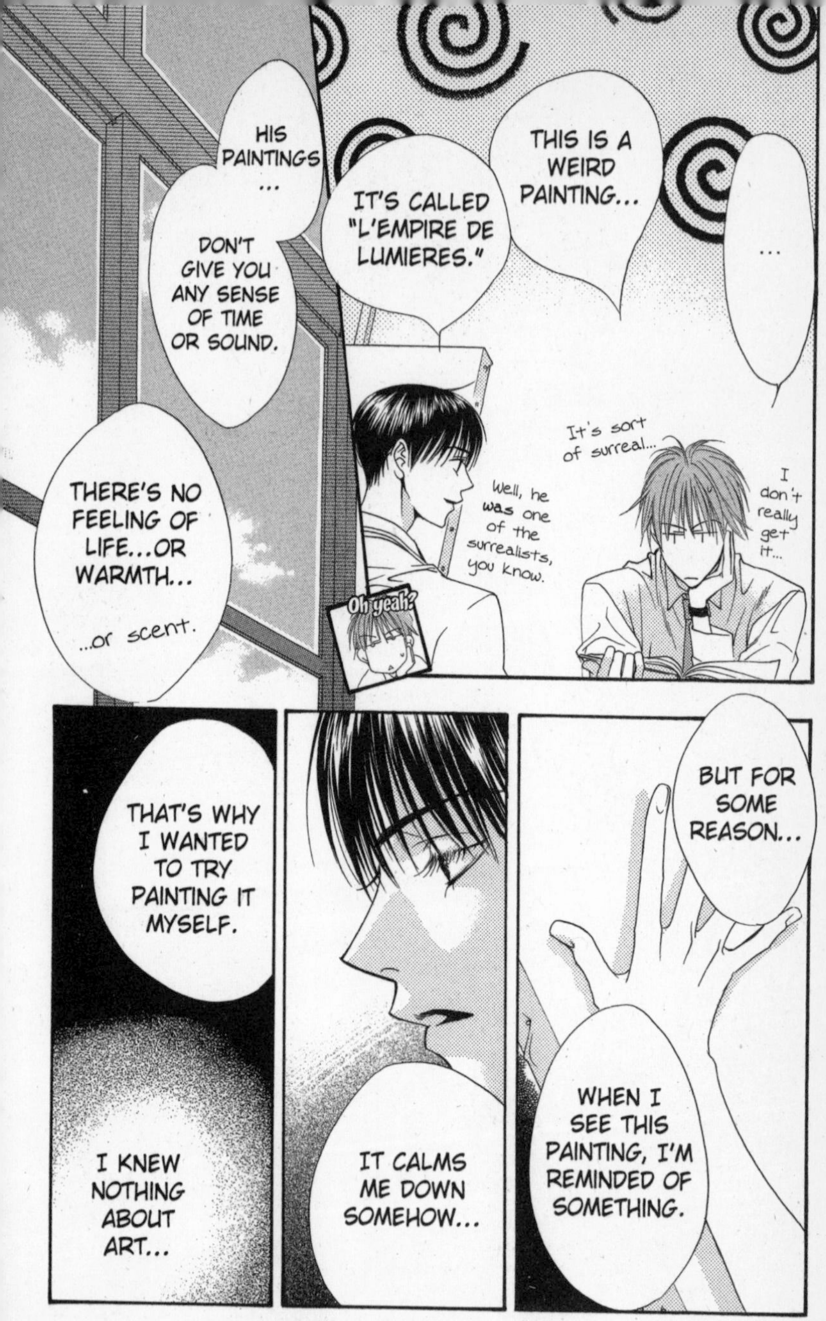
...
THIS IS A WEIRD PAINTING...
IT'S CALLED "L'EMPIRE DE LUMIERES."
It's sort of surreal...
I don't really get it...
Well, he was one of the surrealists, you know.
Oh yeah?
HIS PAINTINGS...
DON'T GIVE YOU ANY SENSE OF TIME OR SOUND.
THERE'S NO FEELING OF LIFE...OR WARMTH...
...or scent.
BUT FOR SOME REASON...
WHEN I SEE THIS PAINTING, I'M REMINDED OF SOMETHING.
IT CALMS ME DOWN SOMEHOW...
THAT'S WHY I WANTED TO TRY PAINTING IT MYSELF.
I KNEW NOTHING ABOUT ART...

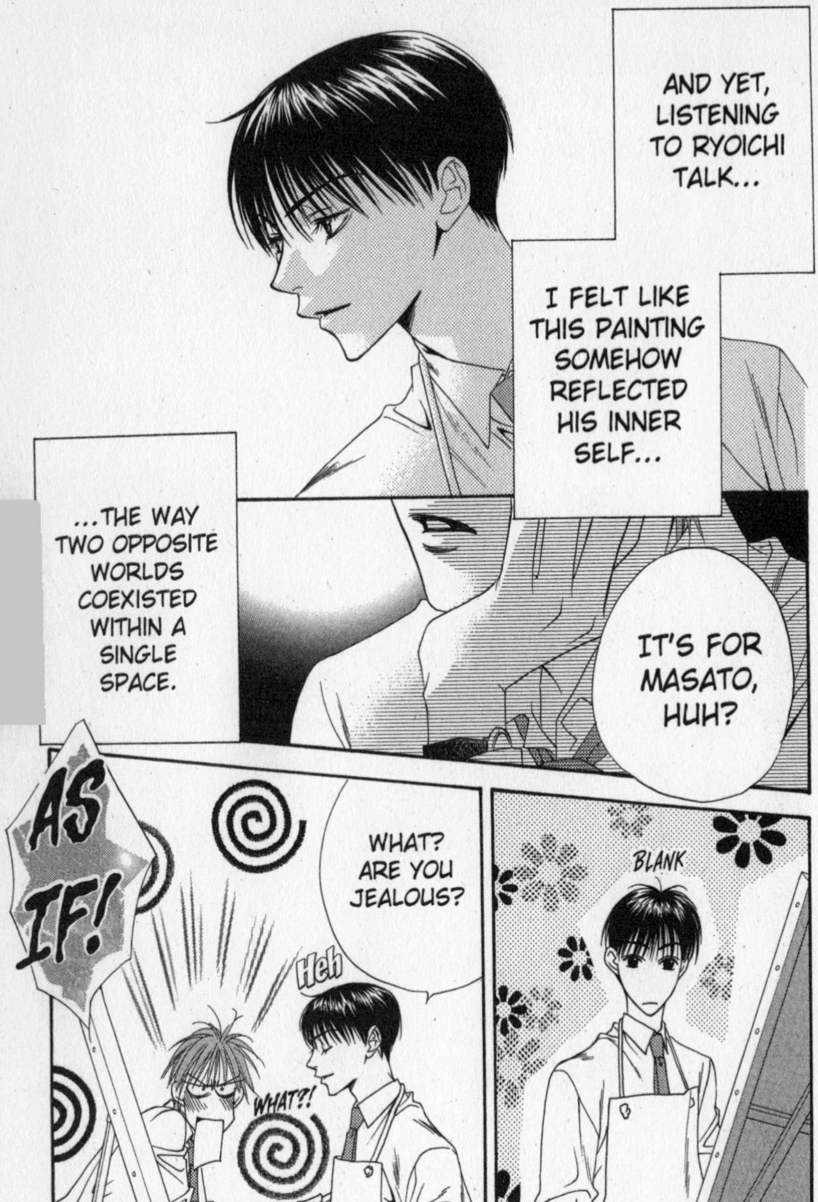
AND YET, LISTENING TO RYOICHI TALK...
I FELT LIKE THIS PAINTING SOMEHOW REFLECTED HIS INNER SELF...
...THE WAY TWO OPPOSITE WORLDS COEXISTED WITHIN A SINGLE SPACE.
IT'S FOR MASATO, HUH?
BLANK
WHAT? ARE YOU JEALOUS?
Heh
WHAT?!
AS IF!

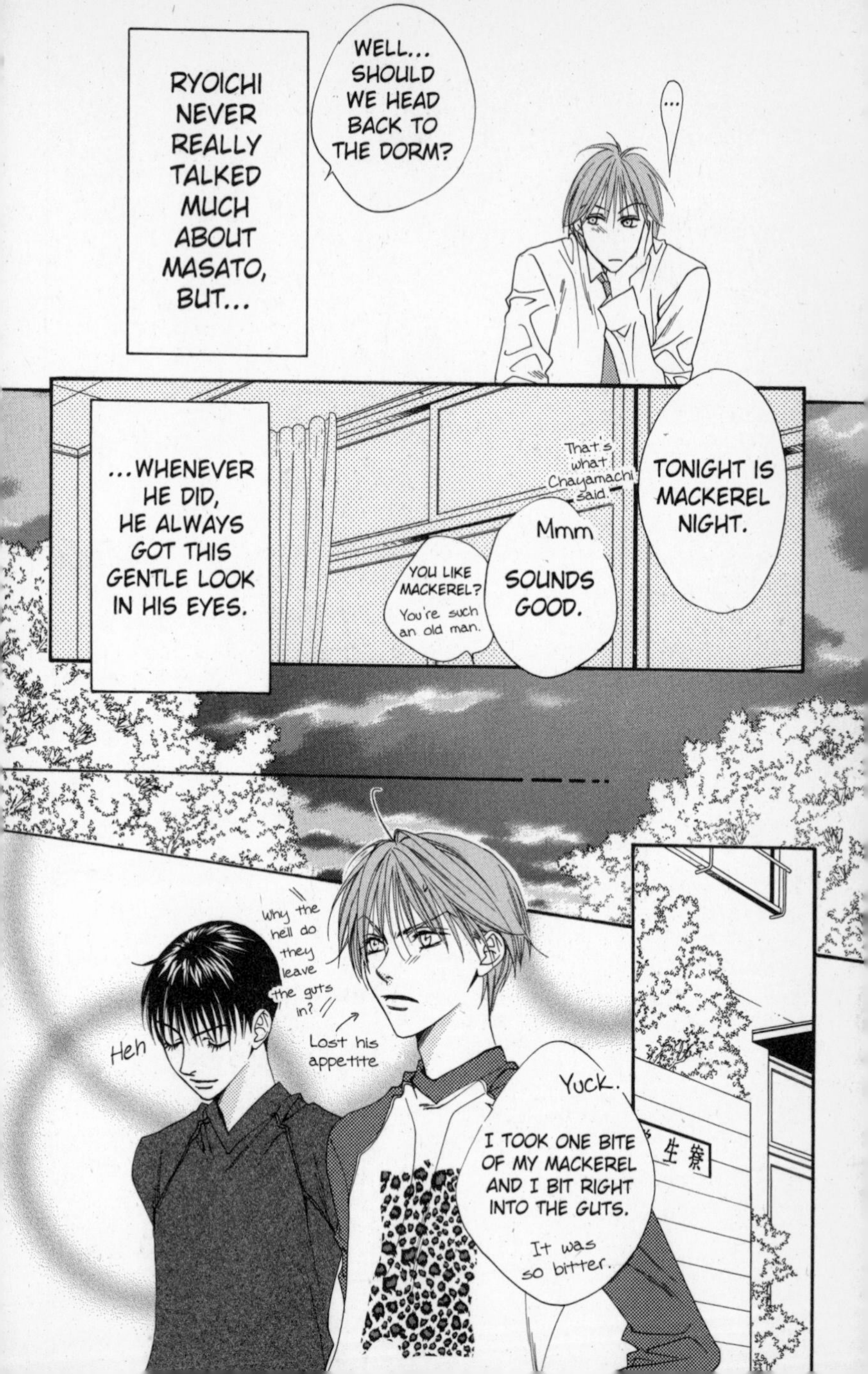
...
WELL... SHOULD WE HEAD BACK TO THE DORM?
RYOICHI NEVER REALLY TALKED MUCH ABOUT MASATO, BUT...
TONIGHT IS MACKEREL NIGHT.
That's what Chayamachi said.
Mmm
SOUNDS GOOD.
YOU LIKE MACKEREL?
You're such an old man.
...WHENEVER HE DID, HE ALWAYS GOT THIS GENTLE LOOK IN HIS EYES.
生寮
Yuck.
I TOOK ONE BITE OF MY MACKEREL AND I BIT RIGHT INTO THE GUTS.
It was so bitter.
Why the hell do they leave the guts in?
Lost his appetite
Heh

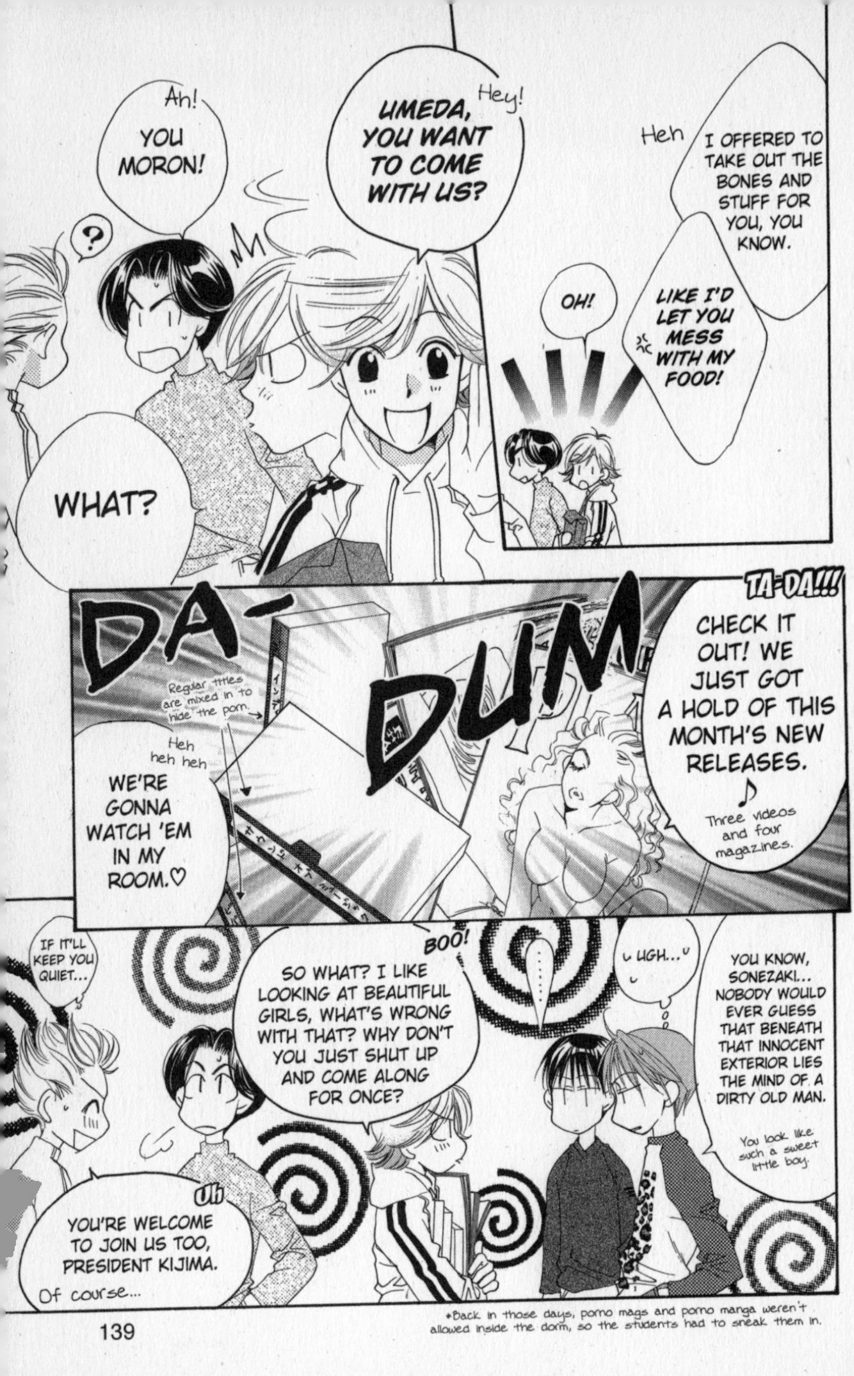
Heh
I OFFERED TO TAKE OUT THE BONES AND STUFF FOR YOU, YOU KNOW.
LIKE I'D LET YOU MESS WITH MY FOOD!
OH!
Hey!
UMEDA, YOU WANT TO COME WITH US?
Ah!
YOU MORON!
?
WHAT?
TA-DA!!!
CHECK IT OUT! WE JUST GOT A HOLD OF THIS MONTH'S NEW RELEASES. ♪
Three videos and four magazines.
DA-DUM
Regular titles are mixed in to hide the porn.
Heh heh heh
WE'RE GONNA WATCH 'EM IN MY ROOM.♡
YOU KNOW, SONEZAKI... NOBODY WOULD EVER GUESS THAT BENEATH THAT INNOCENT EXTERIOR LIES THE MIND OF A DIRTY OLD MAN.
You look like such a sweet little boy.
UGH...
BOO!
SO WHAT? I LIKE LOOKING AT BEAUTIFUL GIRLS, WHAT'S WRONG WITH THAT? WHY DON'T YOU JUST SHUT UP AND COME ALONG FOR ONCE?
IF IT'LL KEEP YOU QUIET...
Oh
YOU'RE WELCOME TO JOIN US TOO, PRESIDENT KIJIMA.
Of course...

*Back in those days, porno mags and porno manga weren't allowed inside the dorm, so the students had to sneak them in.

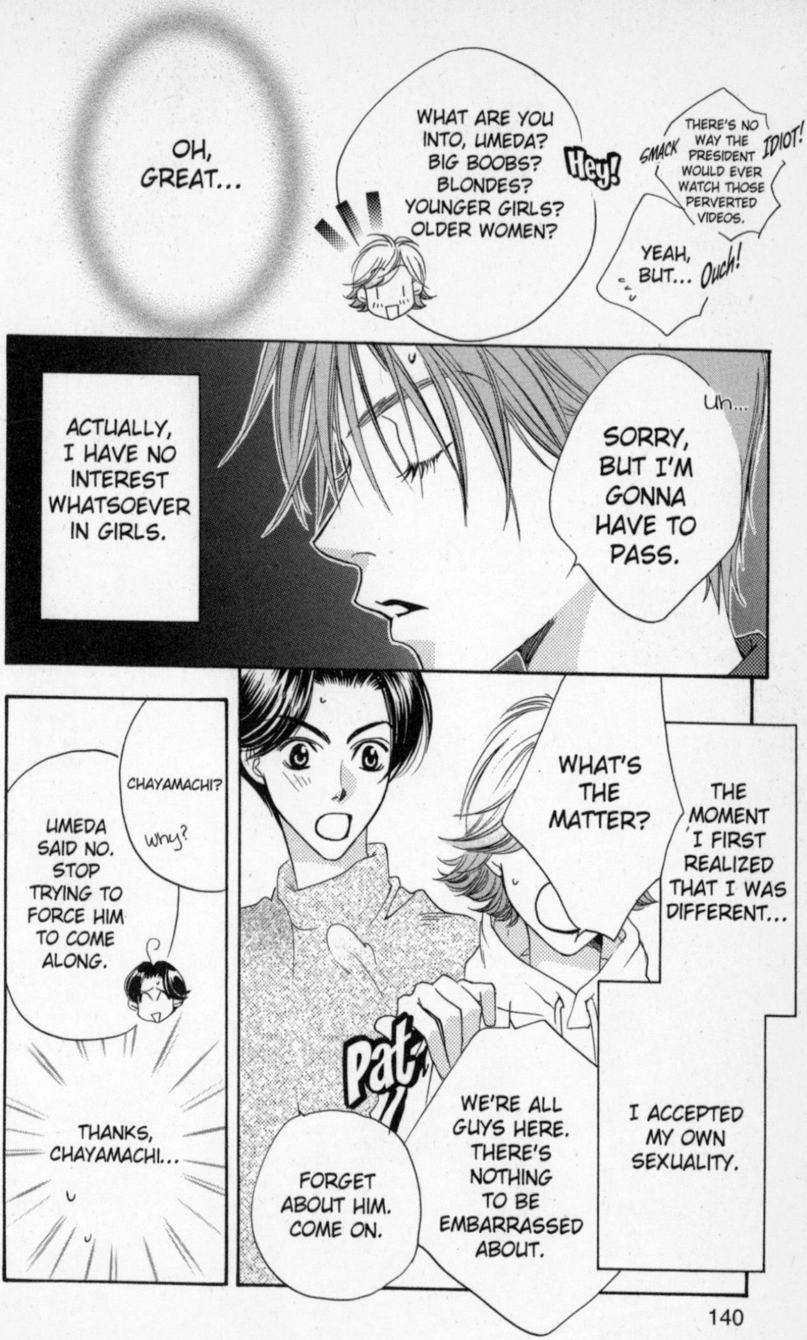
WHAT ARE YOU INTO, UMEDA? BIG BOOBS? BLONDES? YOUNGER GIRLS? OLDER WOMEN?
Hey!
SMACK
THERE'S NO WAY THE PRESIDENT WOULD EVER WATCH THOSE PERVERTED VIDEOS.
IDIOT!
YEAH, BUT...
Ouch!
OH, GREAT...
Uh...
SORRY, BUT I'M GONNA HAVE TO PASS.
ACTUALLY, I HAVE NO INTEREST WHATSOEVER IN GIRLS.
WHAT'S THE MATTER?
THE MOMENT I FIRST REALIZED THAT I WAS DIFFERENT...
I ACCEPTED MY OWN SEXUALITY.
Pat
WE'RE ALL GUYS HERE. THERE'S NOTHING TO BE EMBARRASSED ABOUT.
FORGET ABOUT HIM. COME ON.
CHAYAMACHI?
Why?
UMEDA SAID NO. STOP TRYING TO FORCE HIM TO COME ALONG.
THANKS, CHAYAMACHI...

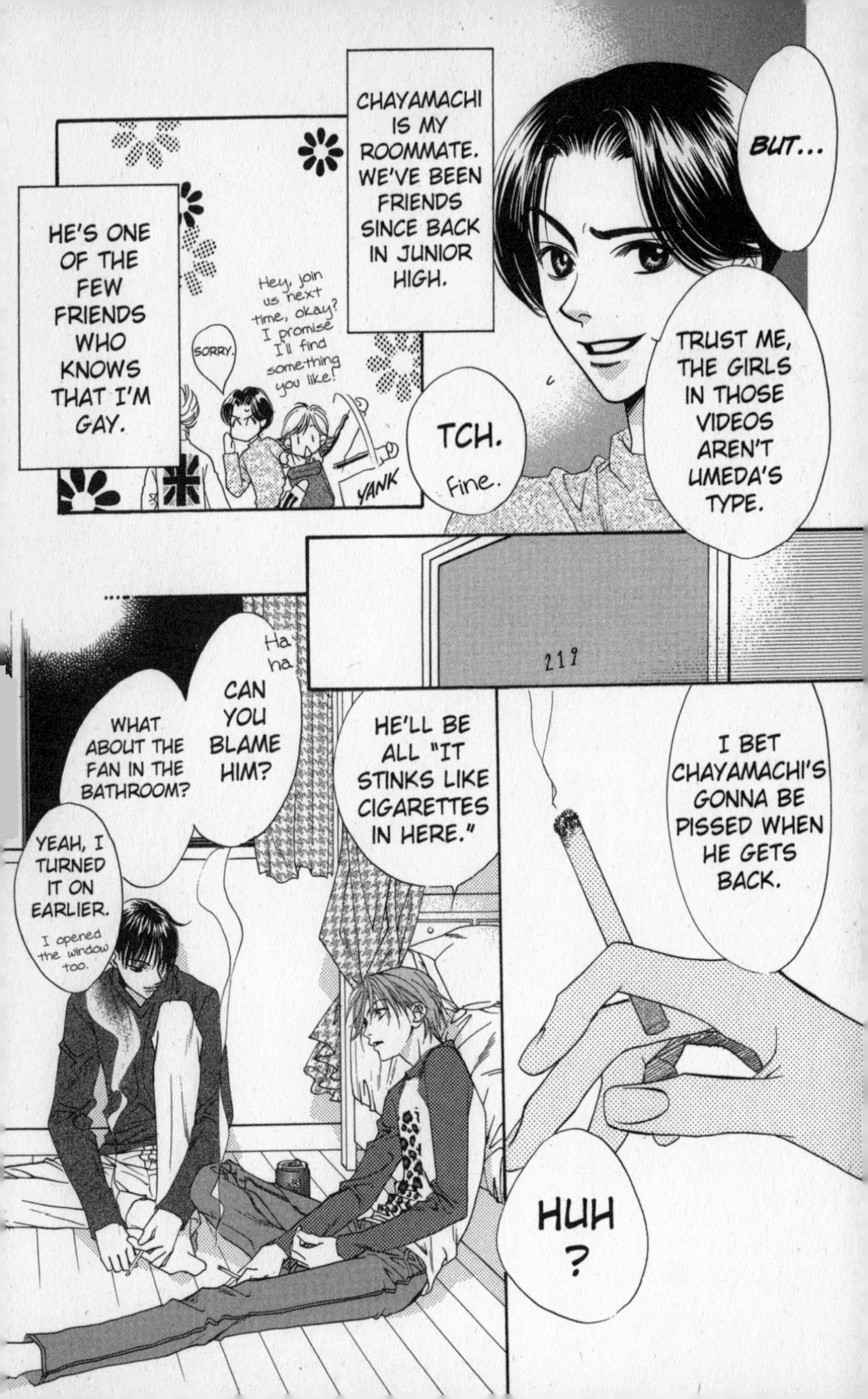

BUT...
TRUST ME, THE GIRLS IN THOSE VIDEOS AREN'T UMEDA'S TYPE.
CHAYAMACHI IS MY ROOMMATE. WE'VE BEEN FRIENDS SINCE BACK IN JUNIOR HIGH.
TCH.
Fine.
Hey, join us next time, okay? I promise I'll find something you like!
SORRY.
YANK
HE'S ONE OF THE FEW FRIENDS WHO KNOWS THAT I'M GAY.
219
I BET CHAYAMACHI'S GONNA BE PISSED WHEN HE GETS BACK.
HUH ?
....
HE'LL BE ALL "IT STINKS LIKE CIGARETTES IN HERE."
Ha ha
CAN YOU BLAME HIM?
WHAT ABOUT THE FAN IN THE BATHROOM?
YEAH, I TURNED IT ON EARLIER.
I opened the window too.

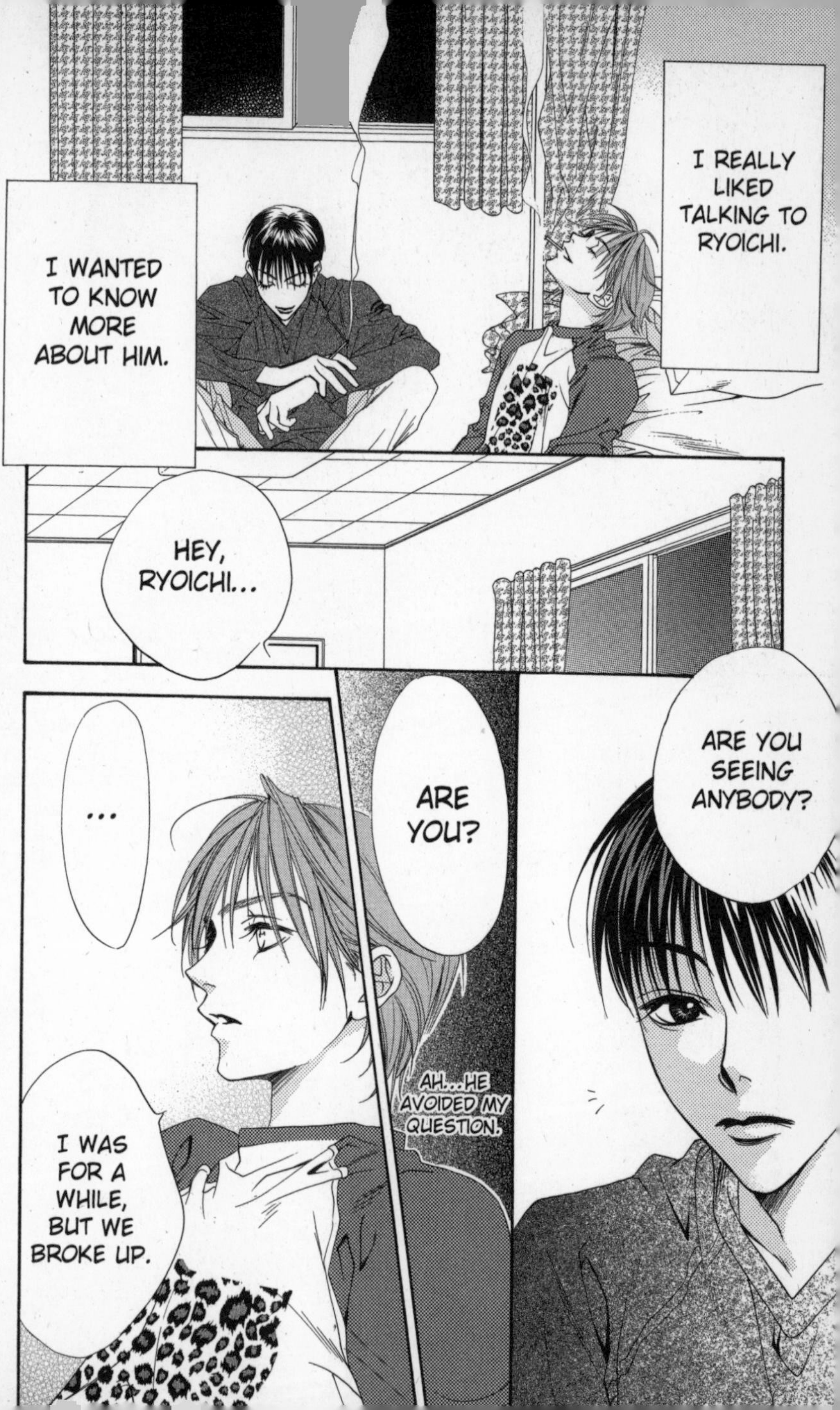
I REALLY LIKED TALKING TO RYOICHI.
I WANTED TO KNOW MORE ABOUT HIM.
HEY, RYOICHI...
ARE YOU SEEING ANYBODY?
ARE YOU?
AH...HE AVOIDED MY QUESTION.
...
I WAS FOR A WHILE, BUT WE BROKE UP.

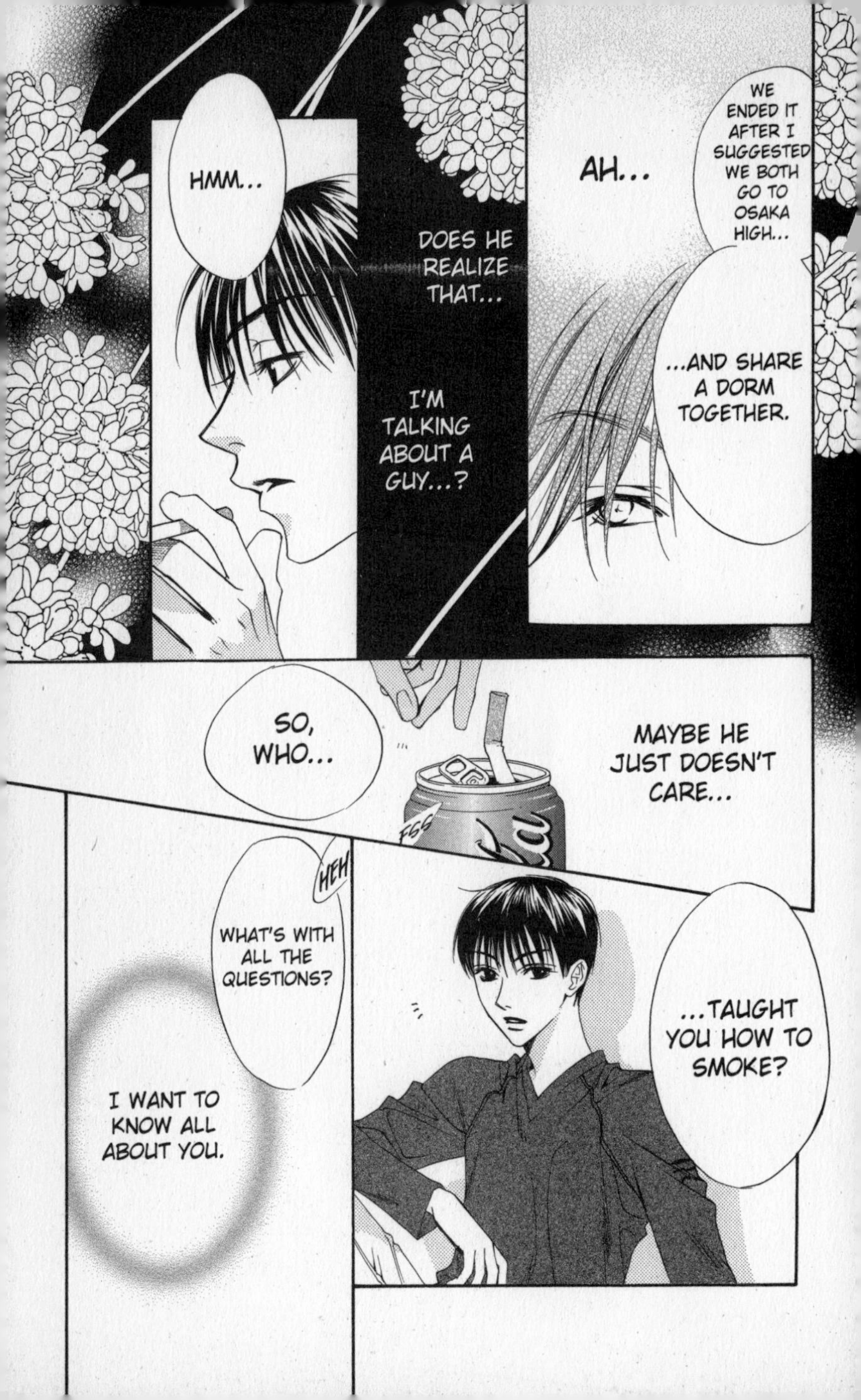
WE ENDED IT AFTER I SUGGESTED WE BOTH GO TO OSAKA HIGH...
...AND SHARE A DORM TOGETHER.
AH...
DOES HE REALIZE THAT...
I'M TALKING ABOUT A GUY...?
HMM...
MAYBE HE JUST DOESN'T CARE...
SO, WHO...
FSS
...TAUGHT YOU HOW TO SMOKE?
HEH
WHAT'S WITH ALL THE QUESTIONS?
I WANT TO KNOW ALL ABOUT YOU.

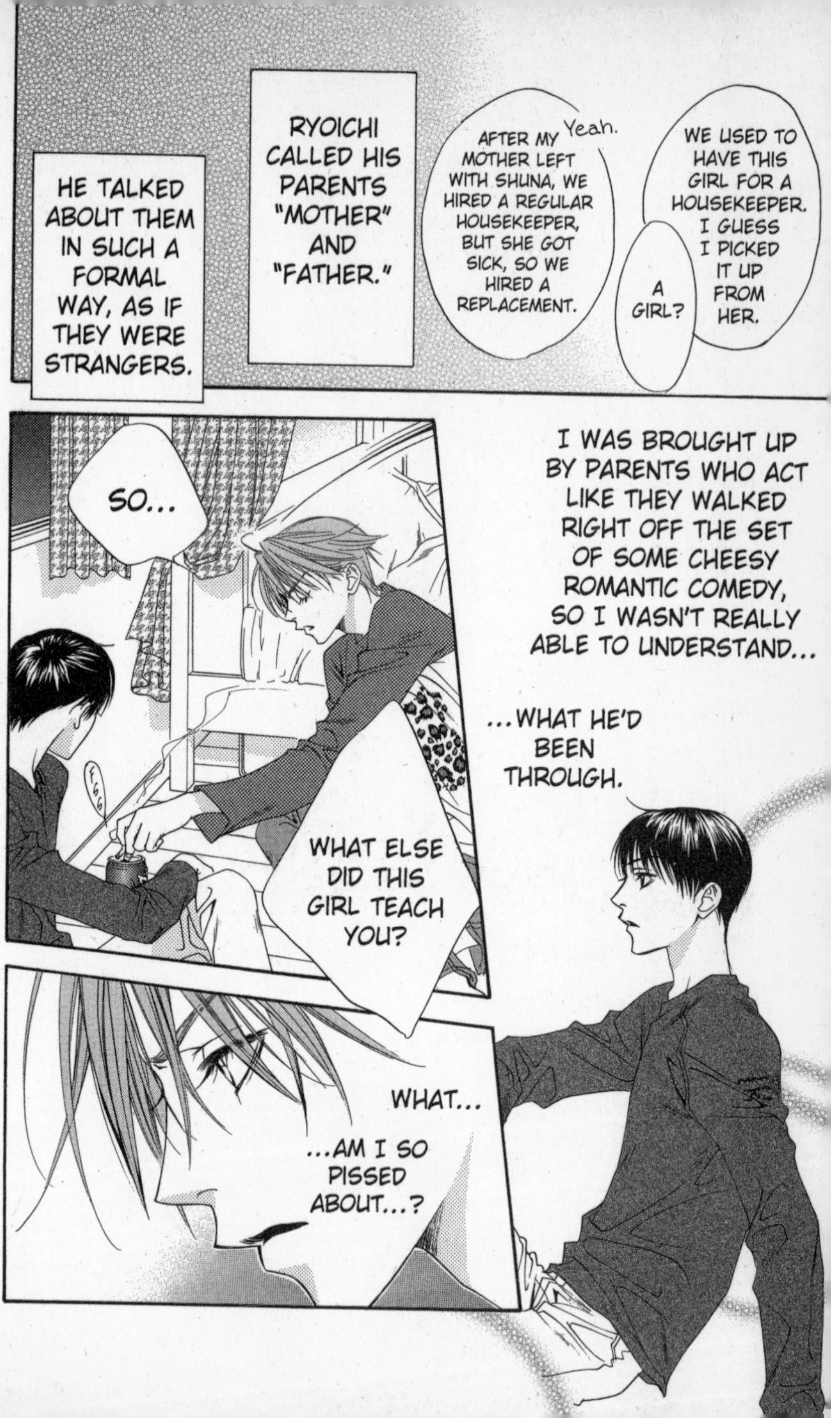
WE USED TO HAVE THIS GIRL FOR A HOUSEKEEPER. I GUESS I PICKED IT UP FROM HER.
A GIRL?
Yeah.
AFTER MY MOTHER LEFT WITH SHUNA, WE HIRED A REGULAR HOUSEKEEPER, BUT SHE GOT SICK, SO WE HIRED A REPLACEMENT.
RYOICHI CALLED HIS PARENTS "MOTHER" AND "FATHER."
HE TALKED ABOUT THEM IN SUCH A FORMAL WAY, AS IF THEY WERE STRANGERS.
I WAS BROUGHT UP BY PARENTS WHO ACT LIKE THEY WALKED RIGHT OFF THE SET OF SOME CHEESY ROMANTIC COMEDY, SO I WASN'T REALLY ABLE TO UNDERSTAND...
...WHAT HE'D BEEN THROUGH.
SO...
WHAT ELSE DID THIS GIRL TEACH YOU?
WHAT...
...AM I SO PISSED ABOUT...?

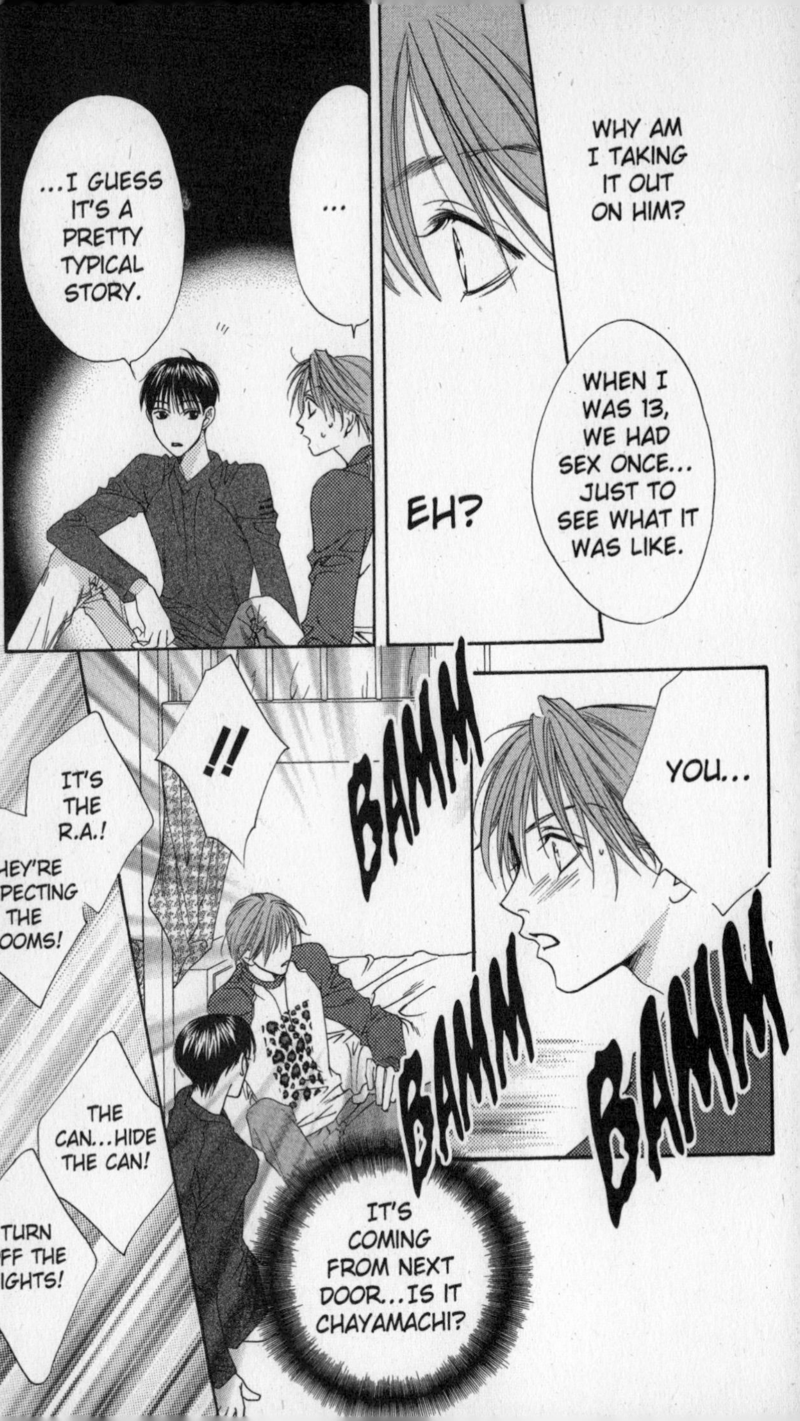
WHY AM I TAKING IT OUT ON HIM?
WHEN I WAS 13, WE HAD SEX ONCE... JUST TO SEE WHAT IT WAS LIKE.
EH?
...I GUESS IT'S A PRETTY TYPICAL STORY.
...
YOU...
BAMM
BAMM
BAMM
BAMM
!!
IT'S COMING FROM NEXT DOOR...IS IT CHAYAMACHI?
IT'S THE R.A.!
THEY'RE INSPECTING THE ROOMS!
THE CAN...HIDE THE CAN!
TURN OFF THE LIGHTS!

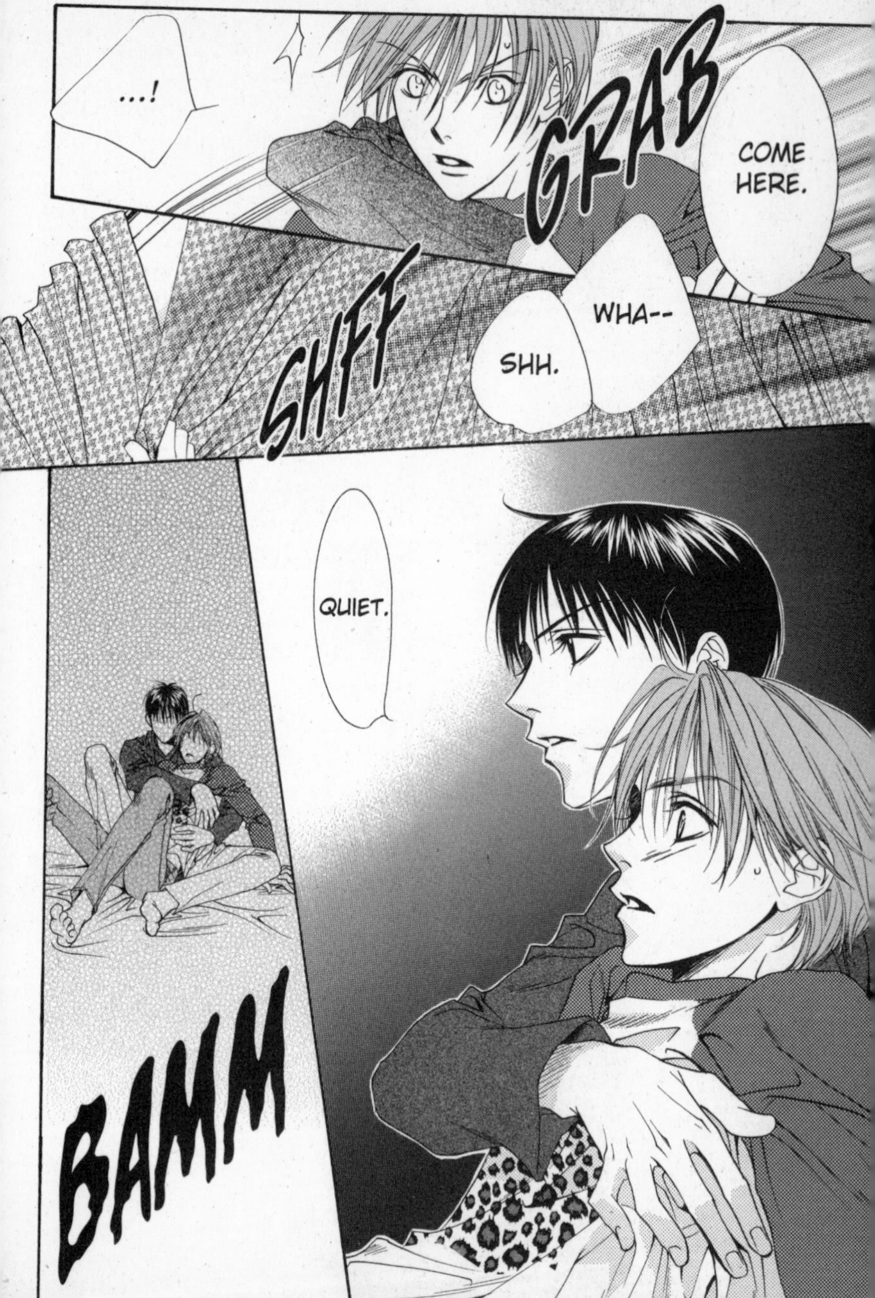
COME HERE.
GRAB
...!
WHA--
SHH.
SHFF
QUIET.
BAMM

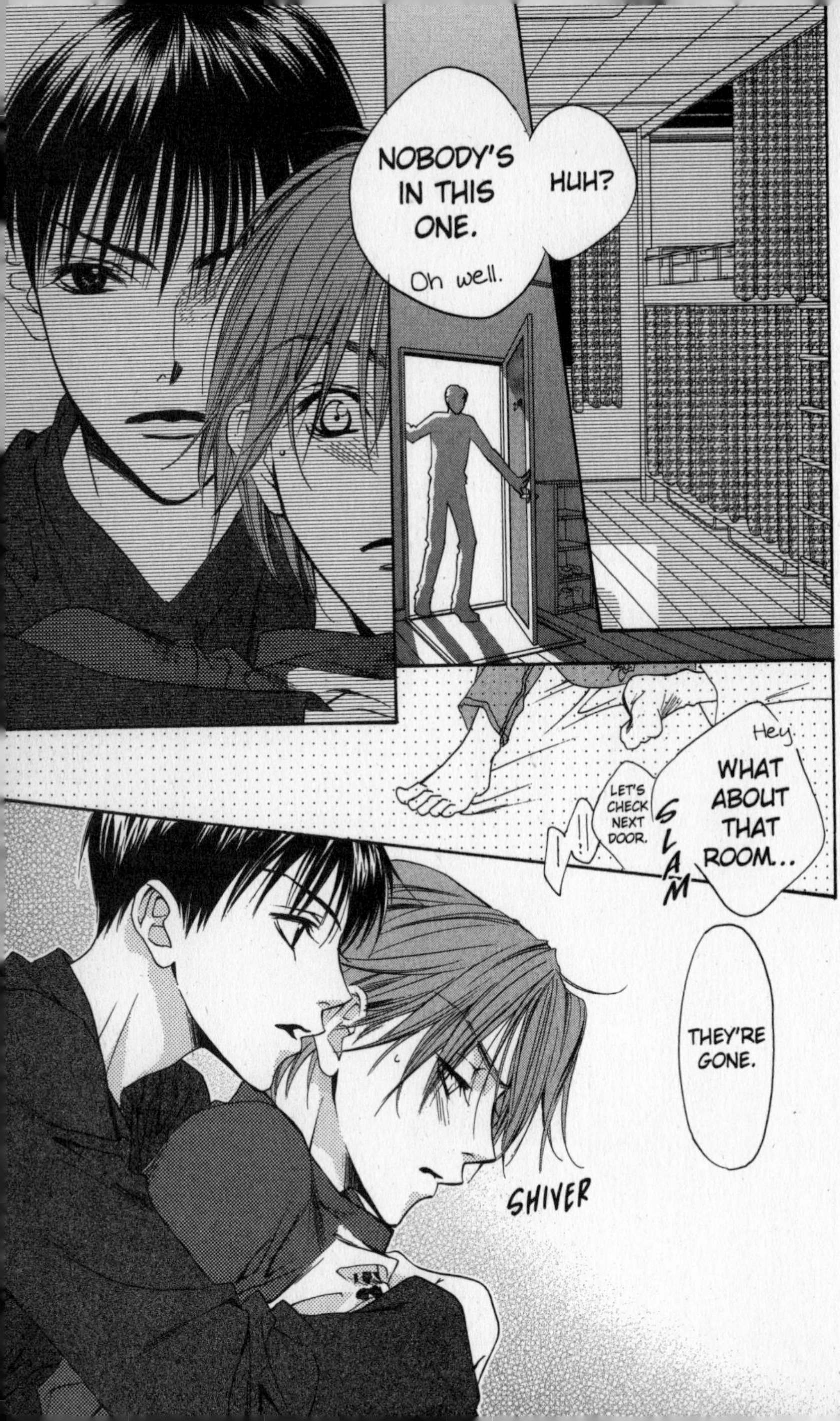
HUH?
NOBODY'S IN THIS ONE.
Oh well.
Hey.
WHAT ABOUT THAT ROOM..
SLAM
LET'S CHECK NEXT DOOR.
!!
THEY'RE GONE.
SHIVER

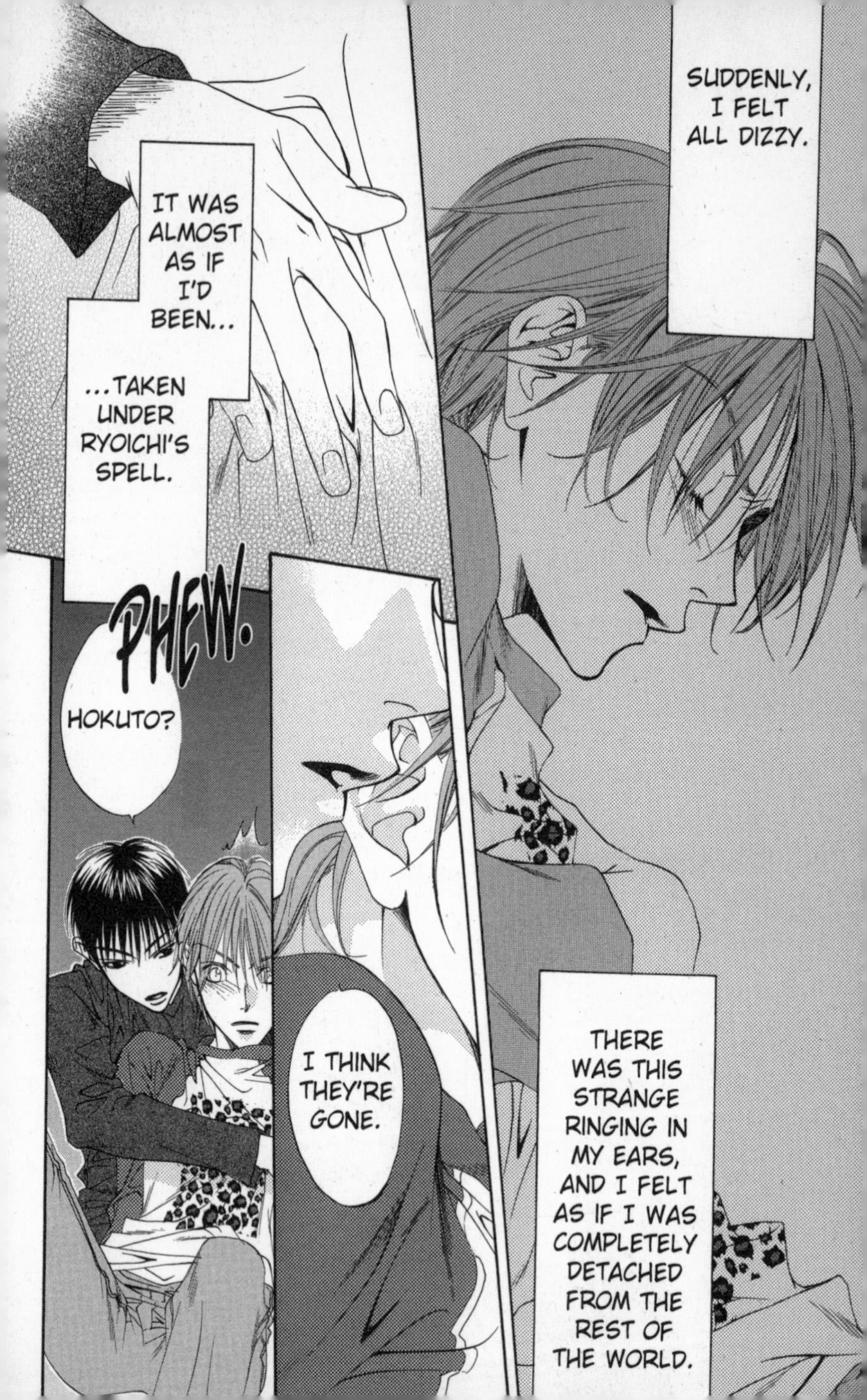
SUDDENLY, I FELT ALL DIZZY.
THERE WAS THIS STRANGE RINGING IN MY EARS, AND I FELT AS IF I WAS COMPLETELY DETACHED FROM THE REST OF THE WORLD.
IT WAS ALMOST AS IF I'D BEEN...
...TAKEN UNDER RYOICHI'S SPELL.
I THINK THEY'RE GONE.
PHEW.
HOKUTO?

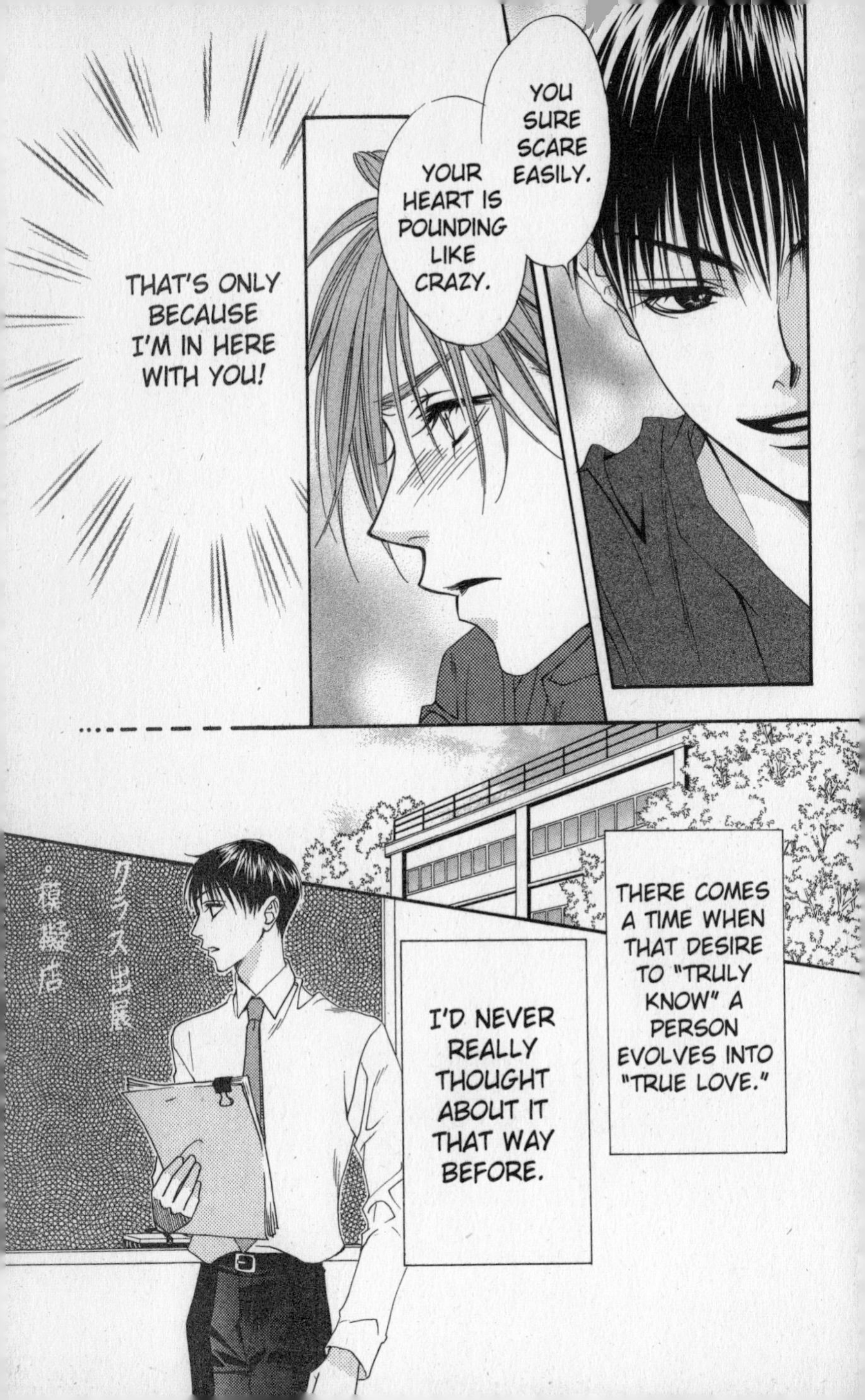
YOU SURE SCARE EASILY.
YOUR HEART IS POUNDING LIKE CRAZY.
THAT'S ONLY BECAUSE I'M IN HERE WITH YOU!
THERE COMES A TIME WHEN THAT DESIRE TO "TRULY KNOW" A PERSON EVOLVES INTO "TRUE LOVE."
I'D NEVER REALLY THOUGHT ABOUT IT THAT WAY BEFORE.
クラス出展
模擬店

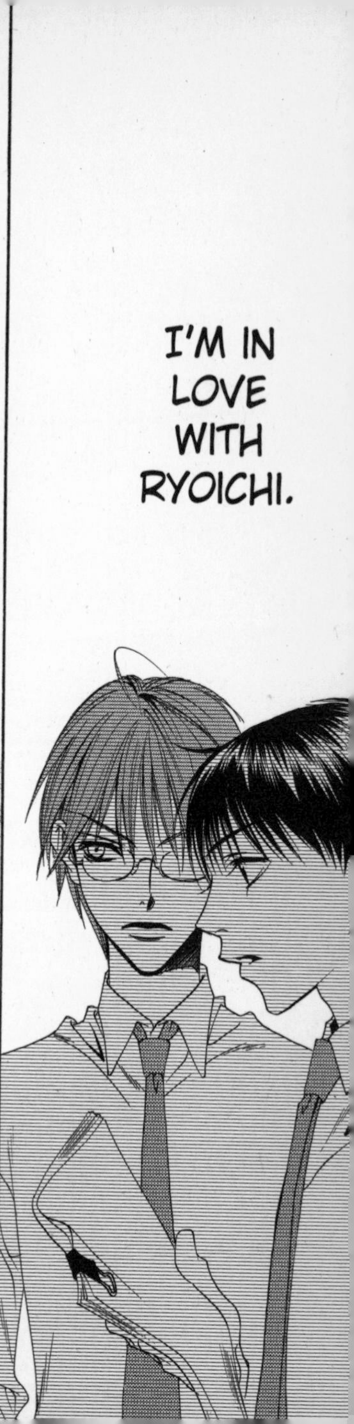
I'M IN LOVE WITH RYOICHI.
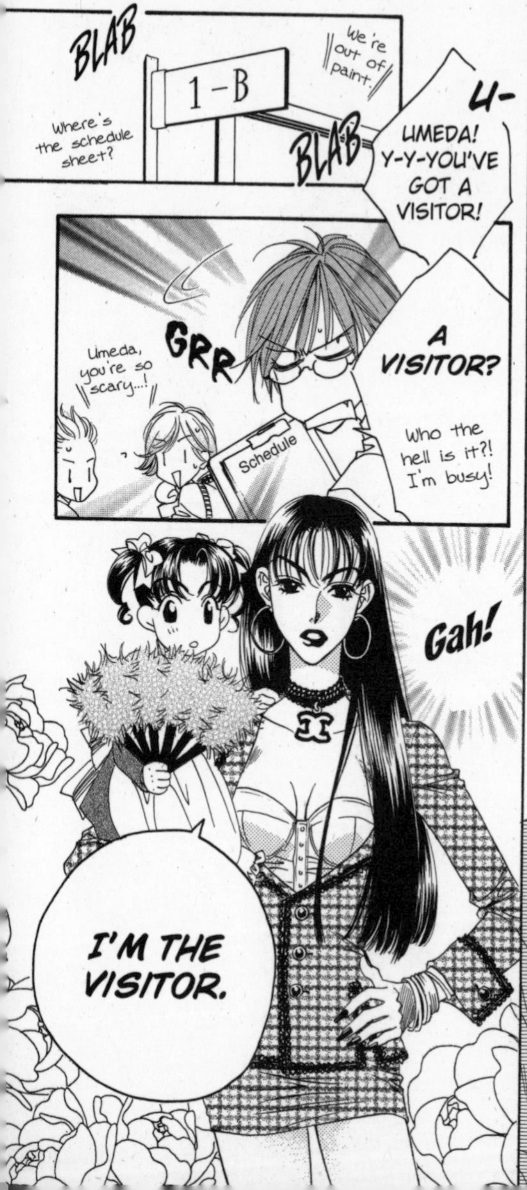
We're out of paint.
BLAB
Where's the schedule sheet?
1-B
BLAB
U-
UMEDA! Y-Y-YOU'VE GOT A VISITOR!
A VISITOR?
Who the hell is it?! I'm busy!
GRR
Schedule
Umeda, you're so scary...!
Gah!
I'M THE VISITOR.

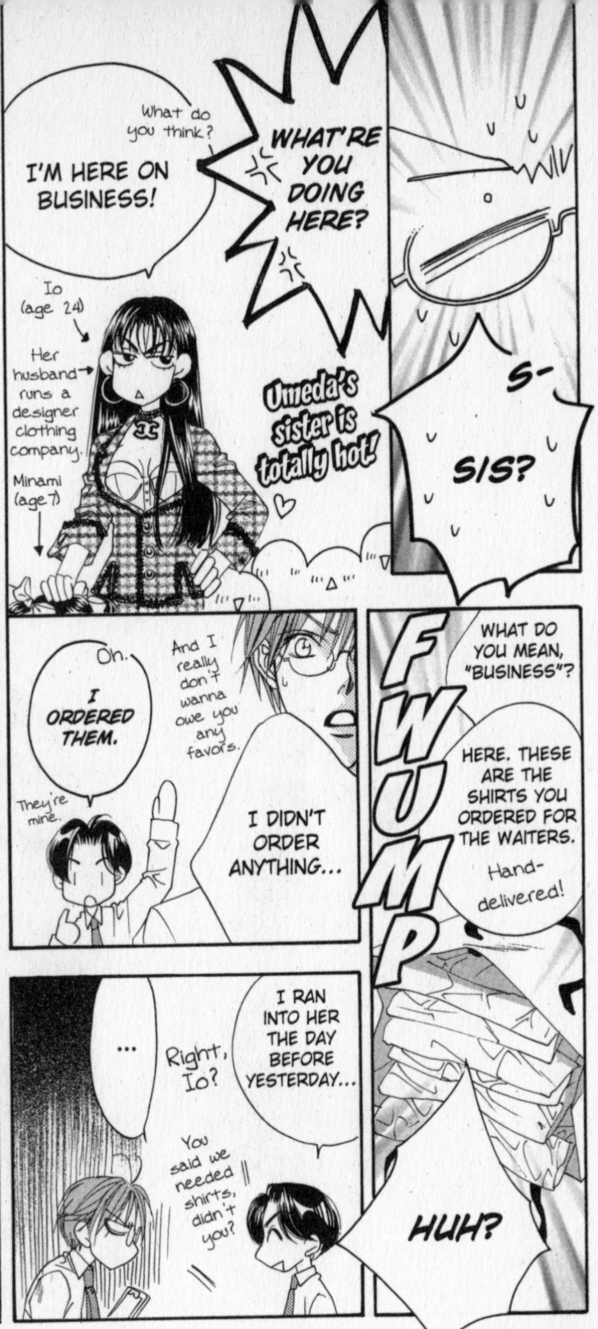
S-
SIS?
WHAT'RE YOU DOING HERE?
What do you think?
I'M HERE ON BUSINESS!
Io (age 24)
Her husband runs a designer clothing company.
Minami (age 7)
Umeda's sister is totally hot!
WHAT DO YOU MEAN, "BUSINESS"?
FWUMP
HERE. THESE ARE THE SHIRTS YOU ORDERED FOR THE WAITERS.
Hand-delivered!
HUH?
I DIDN'T ORDER ANYTHING...
And I really don't wanna owe you any favors.
Oh.
I ORDERED THEM.
They're mine.
I RAN INTO HER THE DAY BEFORE YESTERDAY...
Right, Io?
...
You said we needed shirts, didn't you?

「"SUNSET"」

That's my favorite time of the day. I like foggy early mornings too, but I just love the nostalgic mood you get during sunset. It's nostalgic and eerie at the same time. It makes sense that it's called "Ômagatoki" (the time the demons arrive) in Japanese. Whenever I see René Magritte's "L'Empire de Lumieres" or read Kenji Miyazawa's "Night on the Galactic Railroad," I get the same feeling. I like watching the sunset and seeing the day gradually transform into night. The city starts to light up, and people rush to their homes. Mothers call out for their children, and darkness falls down upon the streets. Mmm...it's such a special time!

Ah! I also felt that way when I read Fuyumi Ono's "Tokyo Ibun" (Unknown Stories of Tokyo)!

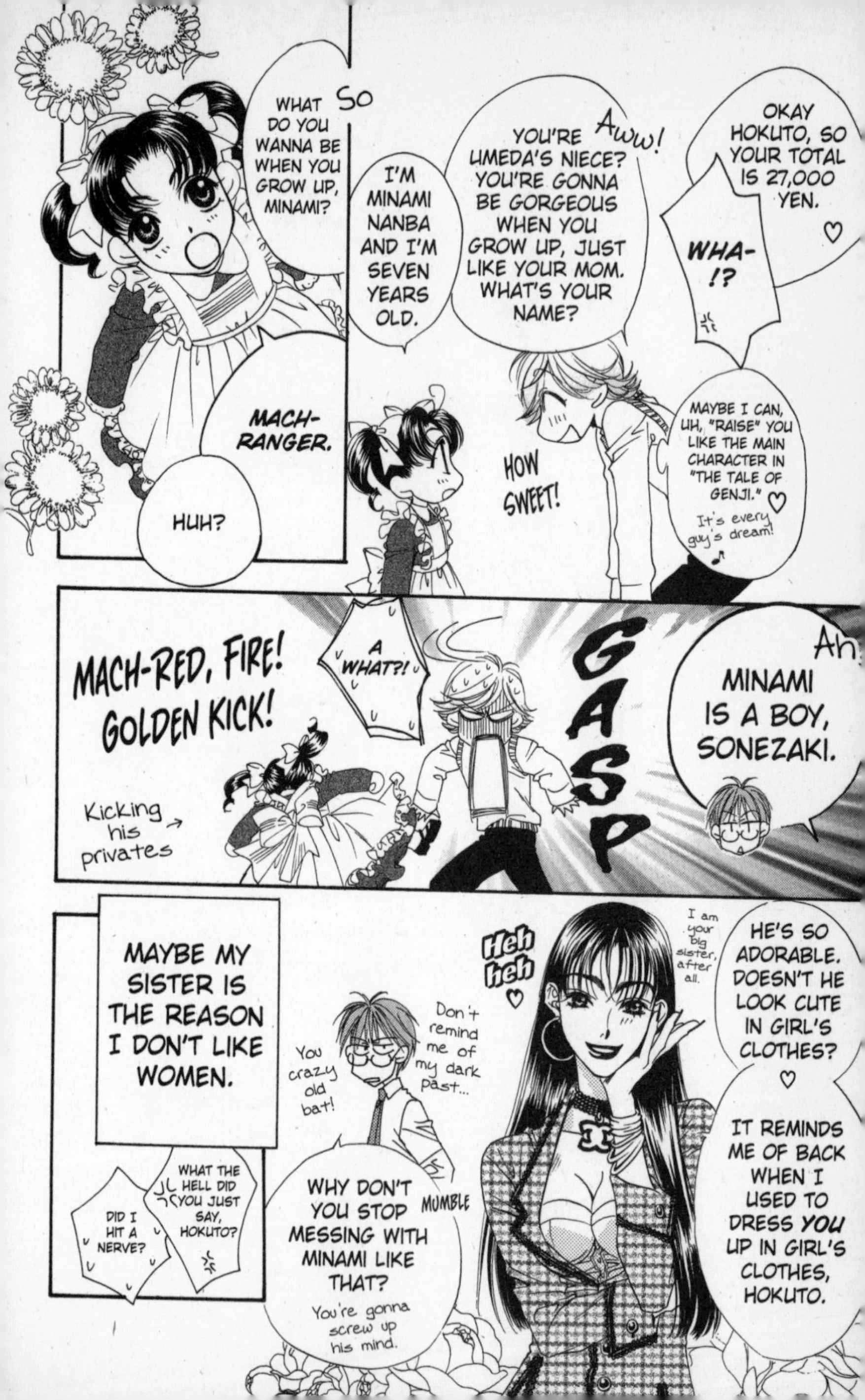
OKAY HOKUTO, SO YOUR TOTAL IS 27,000 YEN. ♡
WHA-!?
Aww!
YOU'RE UMEDA'S NIECE? YOU'RE GONNA BE GORGEOUS WHEN YOU GROW UP, JUST LIKE YOUR MOM. WHAT'S YOUR NAME?
I'M MINAMI NANBA AND I'M SEVEN YEARS OLD.
MAYBE I CAN, UH, "RAISE" YOU LIKE THE MAIN CHARACTER IN "THE TALE OF GENJI." ♡
It's every guy's dream! ♪
HOW SWEET!
So
WHAT DO YOU WANNA BE WHEN YOU GROW UP, MINAMI?
MACH-RANGER.
HUH?
Ah
MINAMI IS A BOY, SONEZAKI.
GASP
A WHAT?!
MACH-RED, FIRE! GOLDEN KICK!
Kicking his privates →
HE'S SO ADORABLE. DOESN'T HE LOOK CUTE IN GIRL'S CLOTHES? ♡
I am your big sister, after all.
IT REMINDS ME OF BACK WHEN I USED TO DRESS *YOU* UP IN GIRL'S CLOTHES, HOKUTO.
Heh heh ♡
Don't remind me of my dark past...
You crazy old bat!
MUMBLE
WHY DON'T YOU STOP MESSING WITH MINAMI LIKE THAT?
You're gonna screw up his mind.
WHAT THE HELL DID YOU JUST SAY, HOKUTO?
DID I HIT A NERVE?
MAYBE MY SISTER IS THE REASON I DON'T LIKE WOMEN.

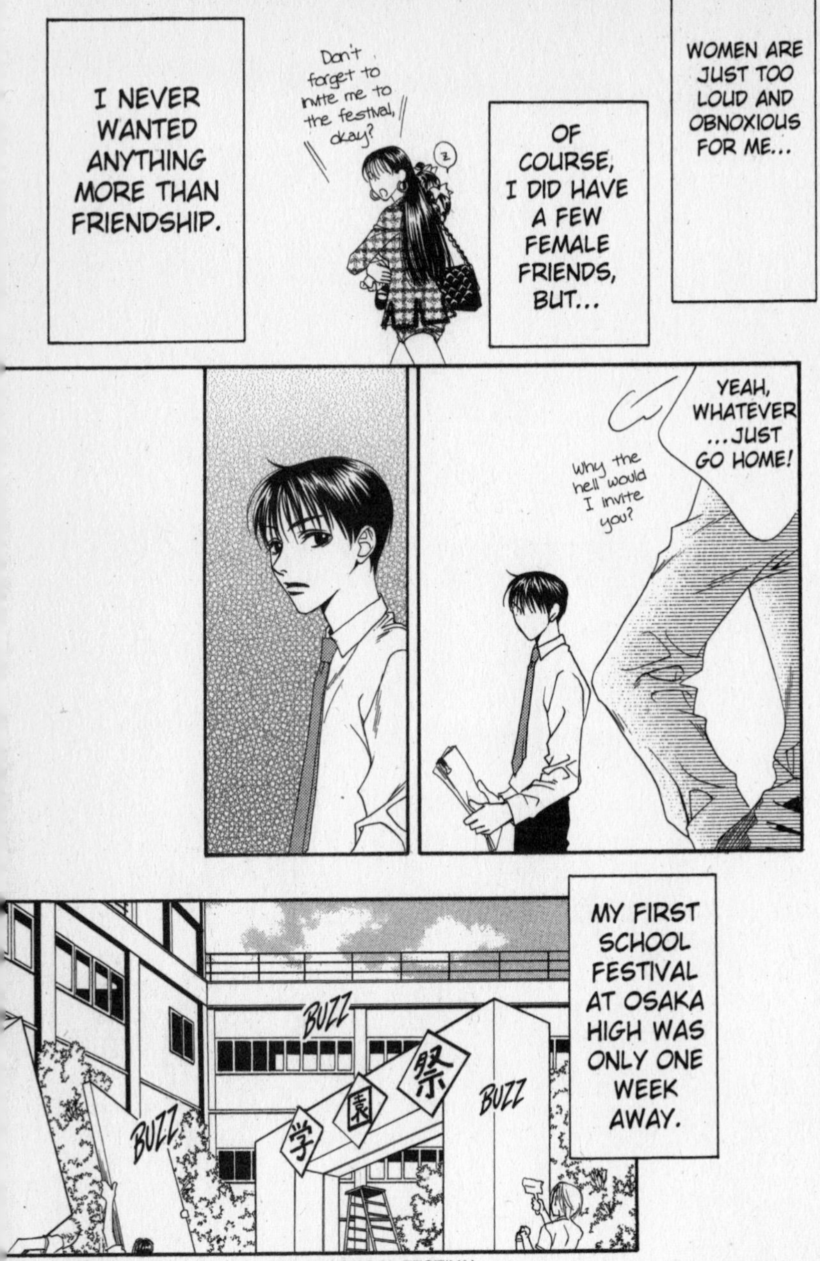
WOMEN ARE JUST TOO LOUD AND OBNOXIOUS FOR ME...
OF COURSE, I DID HAVE A FEW FEMALE FRIENDS, BUT...
Don't forget to invite me to the festival, okay?
I NEVER WANTED ANYTHING MORE THAN FRIENDSHIP.
YEAH, WHATEVER ...JUST GO HOME!
Why the hell would I invite you?
MY FIRST SCHOOL FESTIVAL AT OSAKA HIGH WAS ONLY ONE WEEK AWAY.
BUZZ
BUZZ
学園祭
BUZZ

*SIGN=SCHOOL FESTIVAL

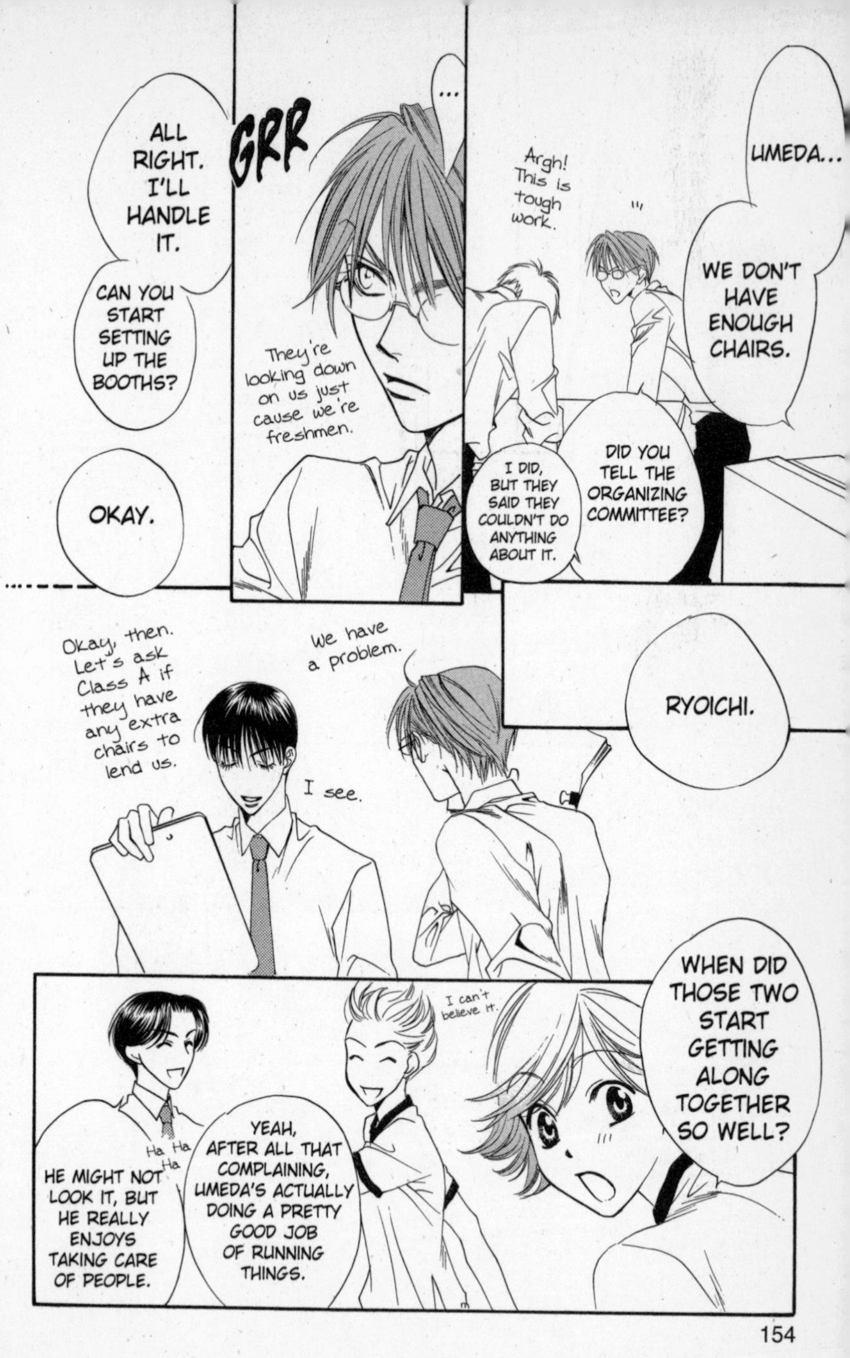
UMEDA...
WE DON'T HAVE ENOUGH CHAIRS.
Argh! This is tough work.
DID YOU TELL THE ORGANIZING COMMITTEE?
I DID, BUT THEY SAID THEY COULDN'T DO ANYTHING ABOUT IT.
...
GRR
They're looking down on us just cause we're freshmen.
ALL RIGHT. I'LL HANDLE IT.
CAN YOU START SETTING UP THE BOOTHS?
OKAY.
RYOICHI.
We have a problem.
Okay, then. Let's ask Class A if they have any extra chairs to lend us.
I see.
WHEN DID THOSE TWO START GETTING ALONG TOGETHER SO WELL?
I can't believe it.
YEAH, AFTER ALL THAT COMPLAINING, UMEDA'S ACTUALLY DOING A PRETTY GOOD JOB OF RUNNING THINGS.
Ha Ha Ha
HE MIGHT NOT LOOK IT, BUT HE REALLY ENJOYS TAKING CARE OF PEOPLE.

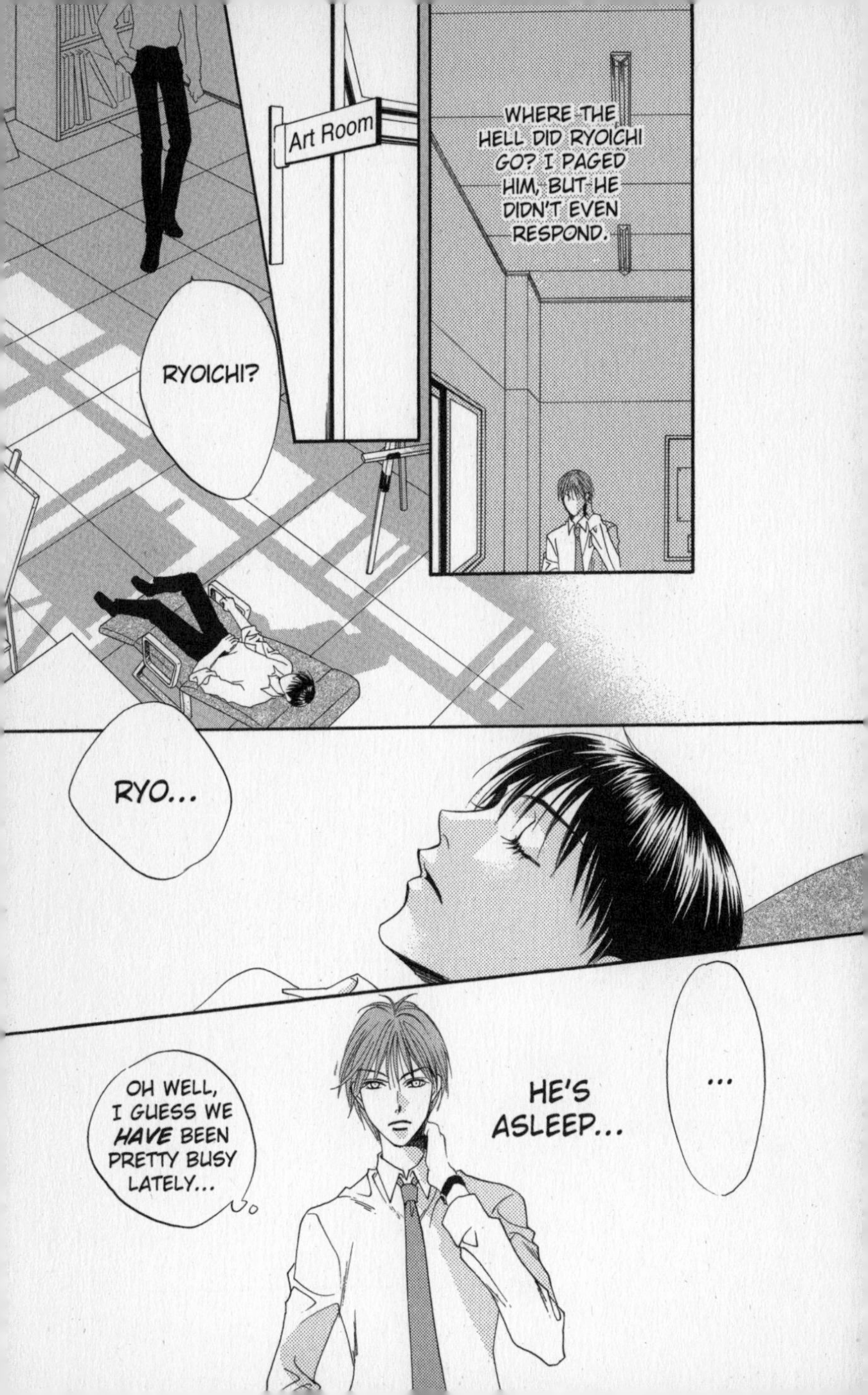

WHERE THE HELL DID RYOICHI GO? I PAGED HIM, BUT HE DIDN'T EVEN RESPOND.
Art Room
RYOICHI?
RYO...
...
HE'S ASLEEP...
OH WELL, I GUESS WE *HAVE* BEEN PRETTY BUSY LATELY...

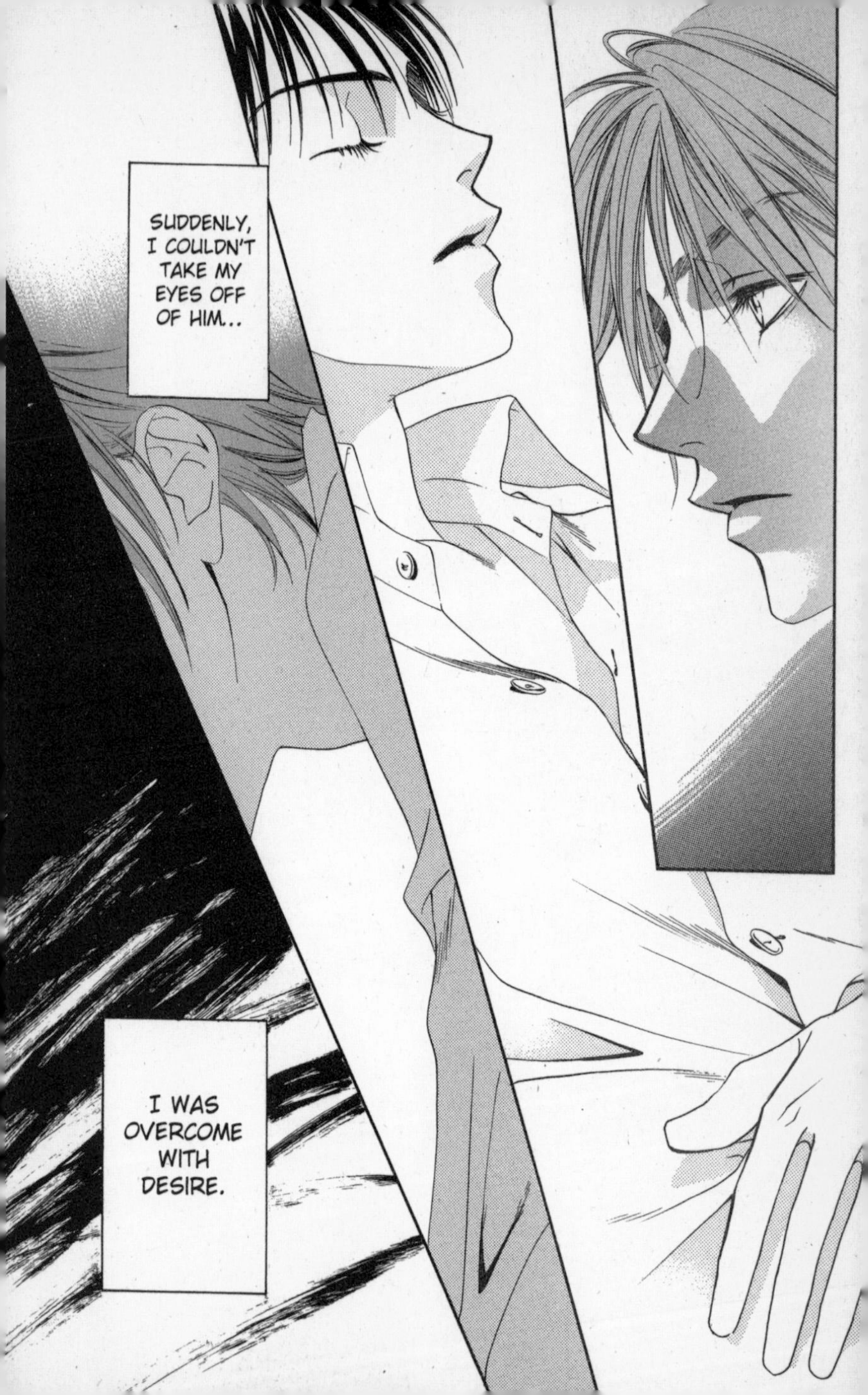
SUDDENLY, I COULDN'T TAKE MY EYES OFF OF HIM...
I WAS OVERCOME WITH DESIRE.

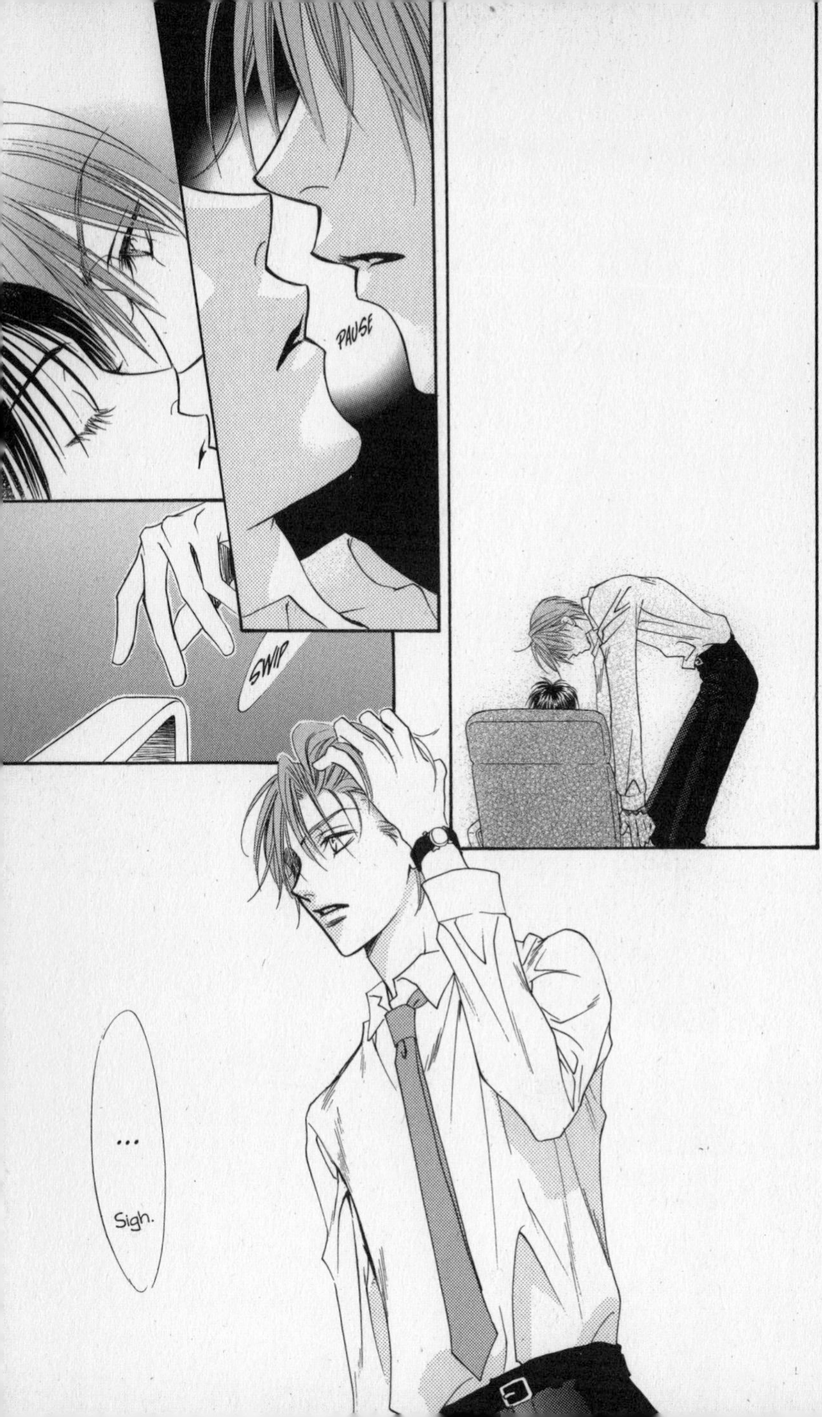
PAUSE
SWIP
...
Sigh.

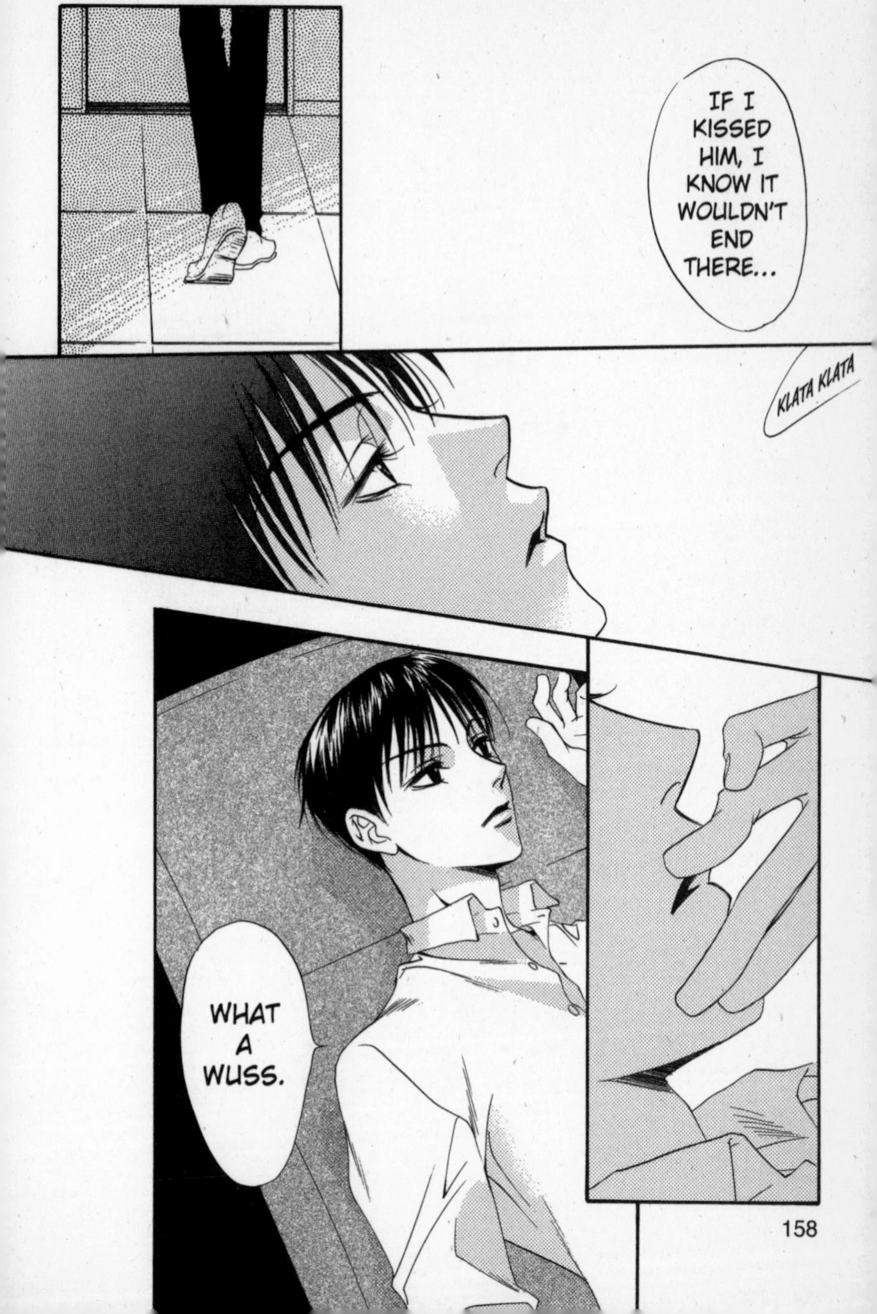
IF I KISSED HIM, I KNOW IT WOULDN'T END THERE...
KLATA KLATA
WHAT A WUSS.

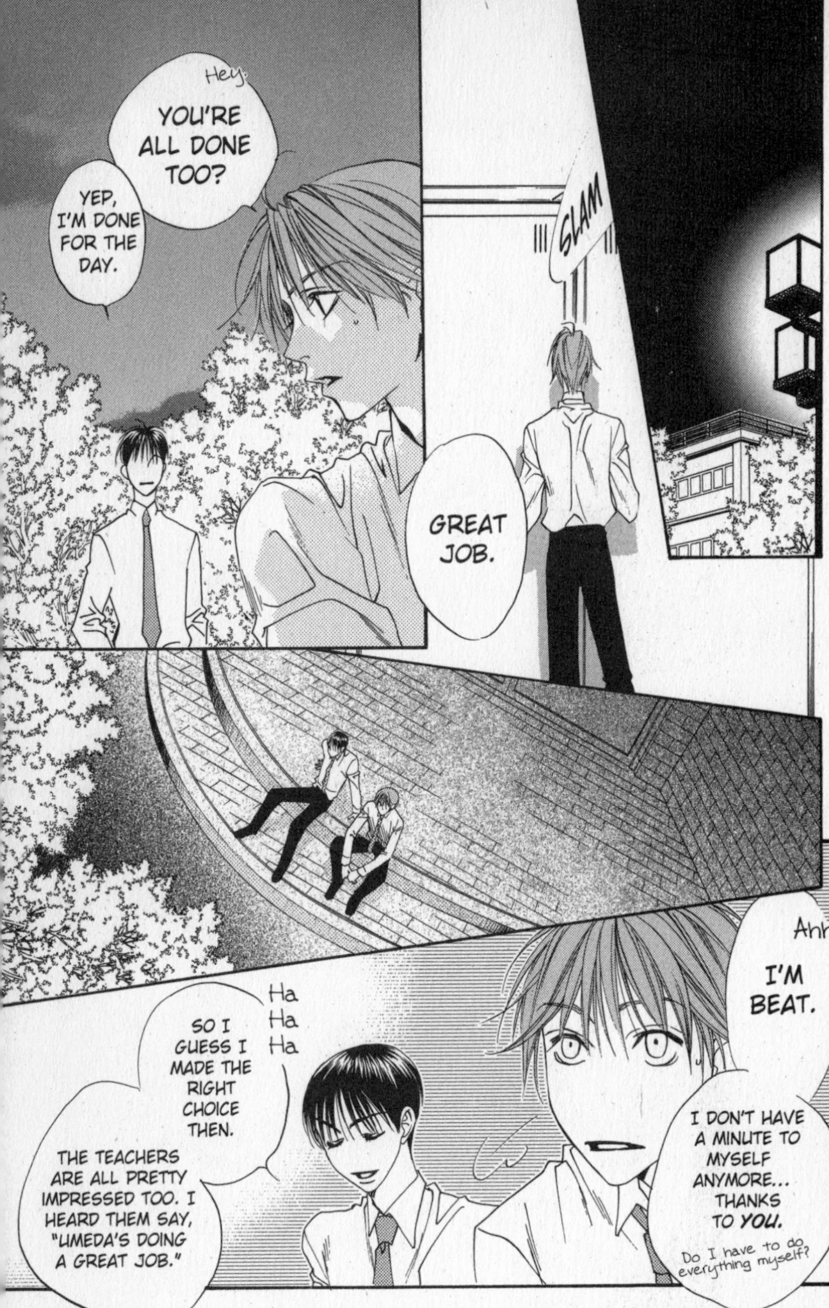
SLAM
GREAT JOB.
Hey.
YOU'RE ALL DONE TOO?
YEP, I'M DONE FOR THE DAY.
Anh.
I'M BEAT.
I DON'T HAVE A MINUTE TO MYSELF ANYMORE... THANKS TO ***YOU.***
Do I have to do everything myself?
Ha Ha Ha
SO I GUESS I MADE THE RIGHT CHOICE THEN.
THE TEACHERS ARE ALL PRETTY IMPRESSED TOO. I HEARD THEM SAY, "UMEDA'S DOING A GREAT JOB."

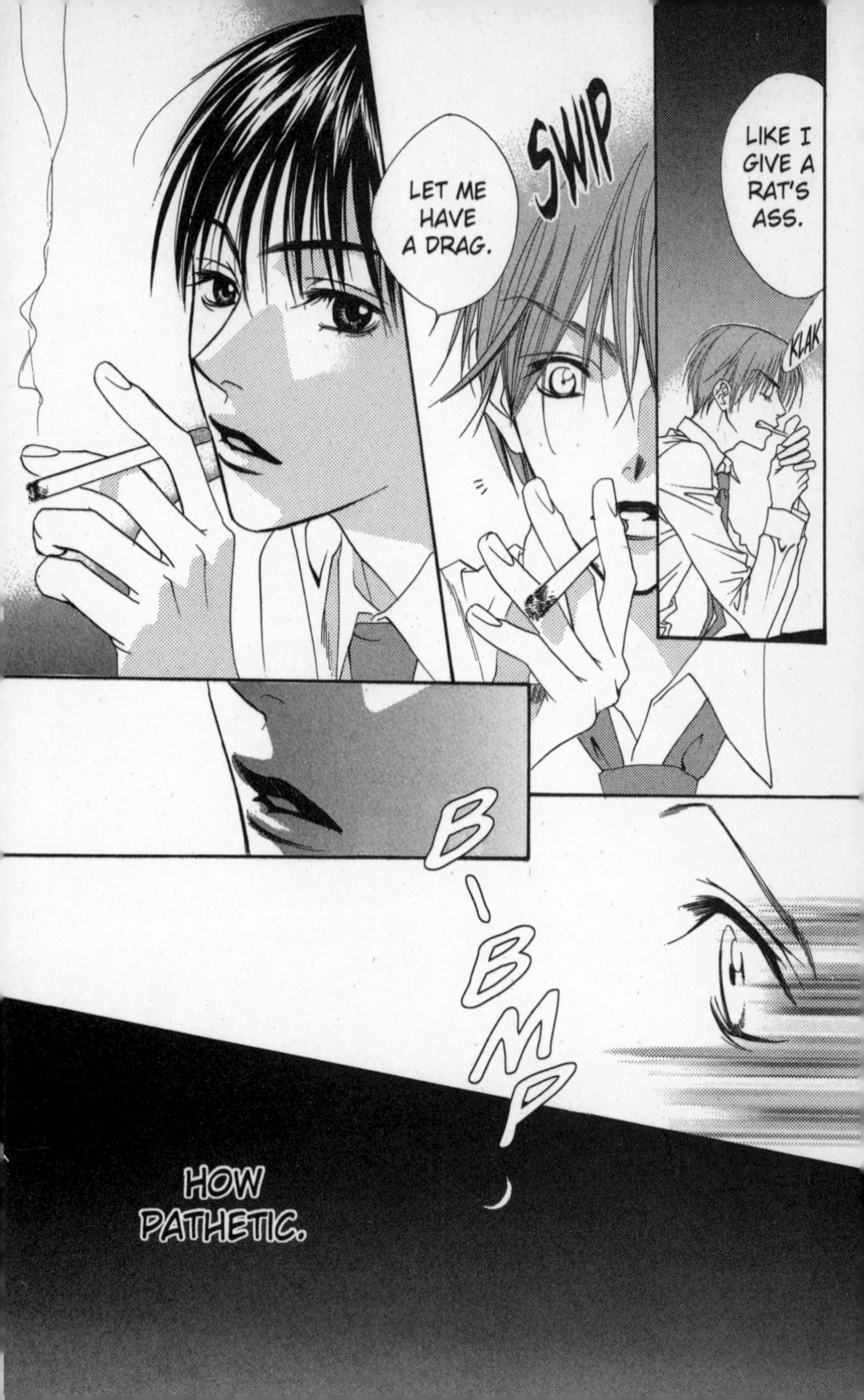
LIKE I GIVE A RAT'S ASS.
KLAK
SWIP
LET ME HAVE A DRAG.
B-BMP
HOW PATHETIC.

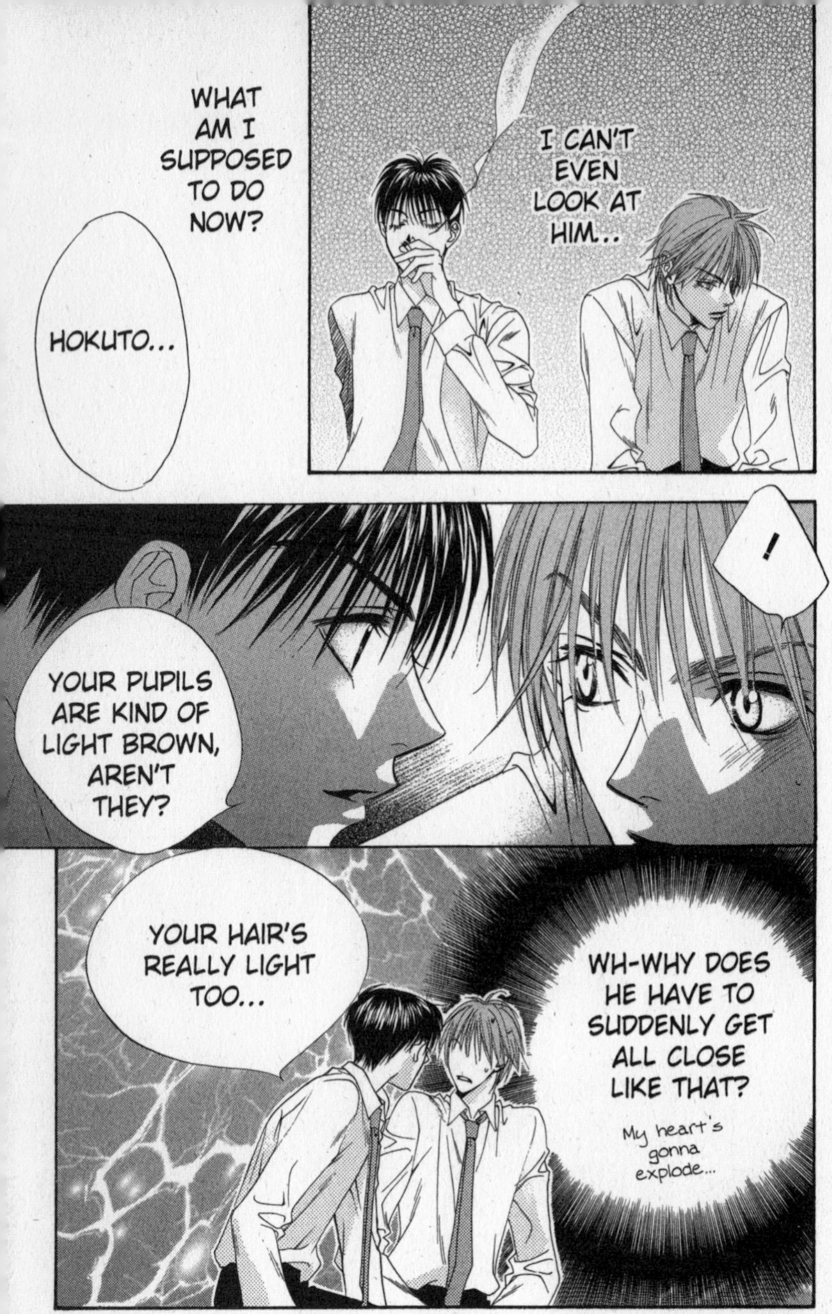
I CAN'T EVEN LOOK AT HIM...
WHAT AM I SUPPOSED TO DO NOW?
HOKUTO...
!
YOUR PUPILS ARE KIND OF LIGHT BROWN, AREN'T THEY?
YOUR HAIR'S REALLY LIGHT TOO...
WH-WHY DOES HE HAVE TO SUDDENLY GET ALL CLOSE LIKE THAT?
My heart's gonna explode...

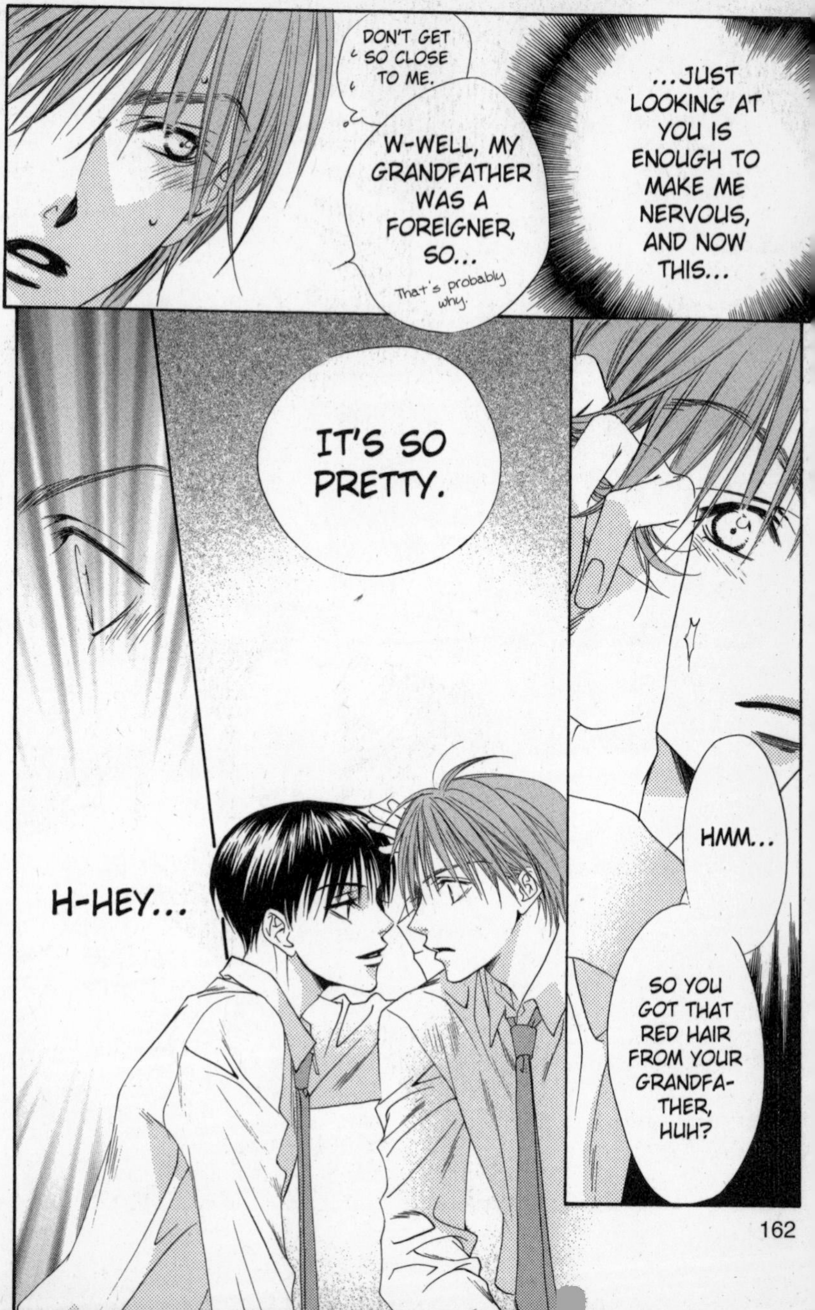
...JUST LOOKING AT YOU IS ENOUGH TO MAKE ME NERVOUS, AND NOW THIS...
DON'T GET SO CLOSE TO ME.
W-WELL, MY GRANDFATHER WAS A FOREIGNER, SO...
That's probably why.
HMM...
SO YOU GOT THAT RED HAIR FROM YOUR GRANDFA-THER, HUH?
IT'S SO PRETTY.
H-HEY...

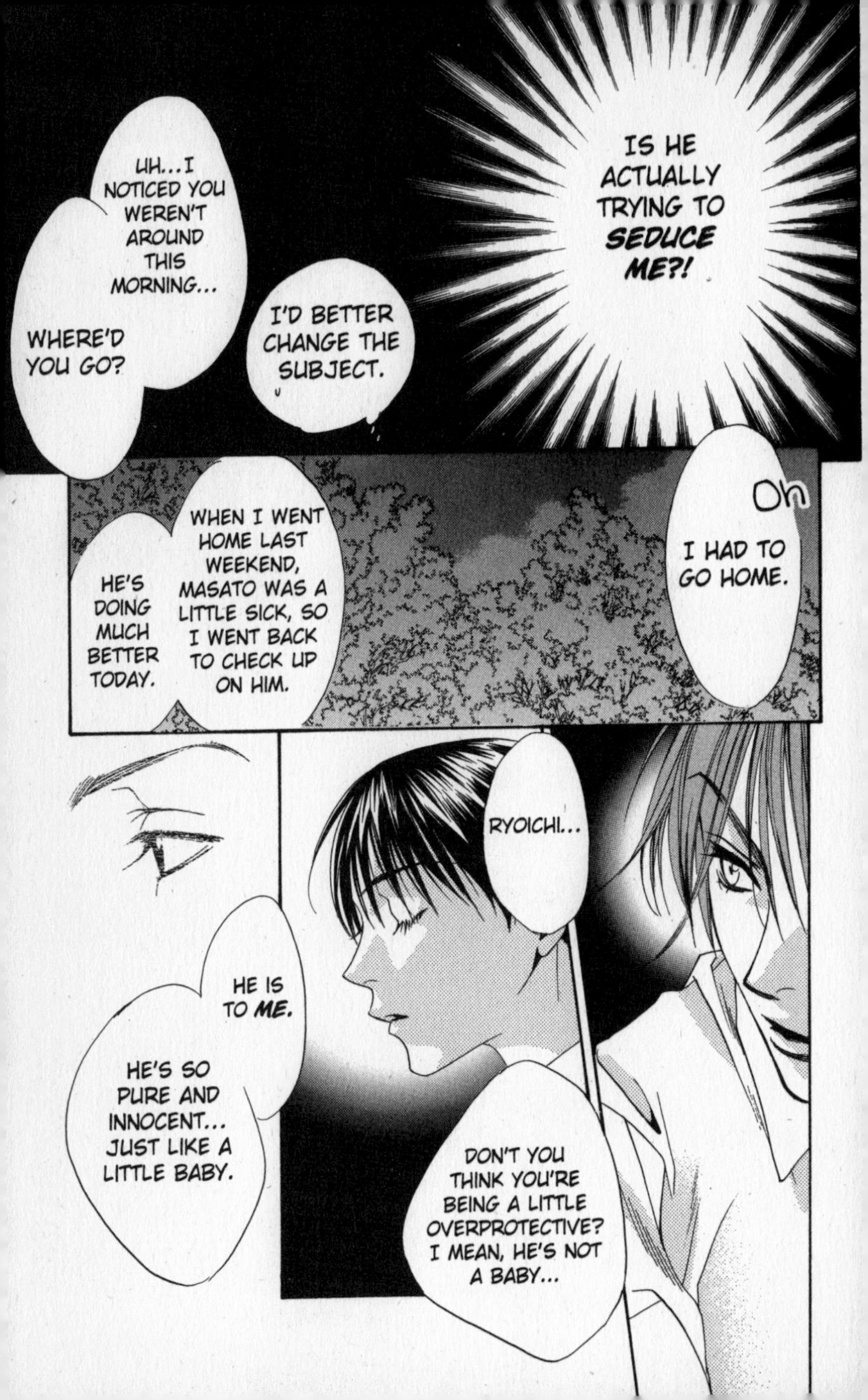
IS HE ACTUALLY TRYING TO **SEDUCE ME?!**
I'D BETTER CHANGE THE SUBJECT.
UH...I NOTICED YOU WEREN'T AROUND THIS MORNING...
WHERE'D YOU GO?
Oh
I HAD TO GO HOME.
WHEN I WENT HOME LAST WEEKEND, MASATO WAS A LITTLE SICK, SO I WENT BACK TO CHECK UP ON HIM.
HE'S DOING MUCH BETTER TODAY.
RYOICHI...
DON'T YOU THINK YOU'RE BEING A LITTLE OVERPROTECTIVE? I MEAN, HE'S NOT A BABY...
HE IS TO **ME.**
HE'S SO PURE AND INNOCENT... JUST LIKE A LITTLE BABY.

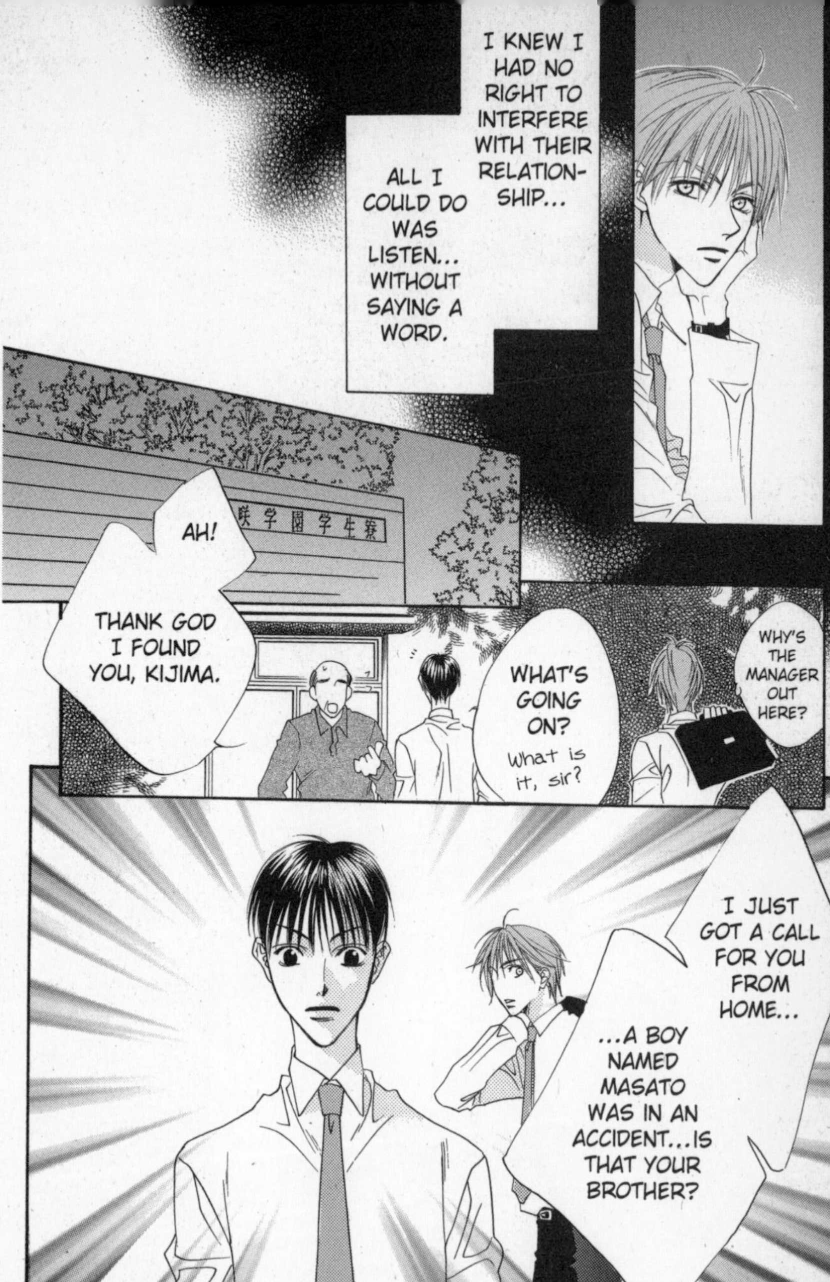
I KNEW I HAD NO RIGHT TO INTERFERE WITH THEIR RELATION-SHIP...
ALL I COULD DO WAS LISTEN... WITHOUT SAYING A WORD.
AH!
THANK GOD I FOUND YOU, KIJIMA.
WHY'S THE MANAGER OUT HERE?
WHAT'S GOING ON?
What is it, sir?
I JUST GOT A CALL FOR YOU FROM HOME...
...A BOY NAMED MASATO WAS IN AN ACCIDENT...IS THAT YOUR BROTHER?

THE SECRET: ACT 2/END

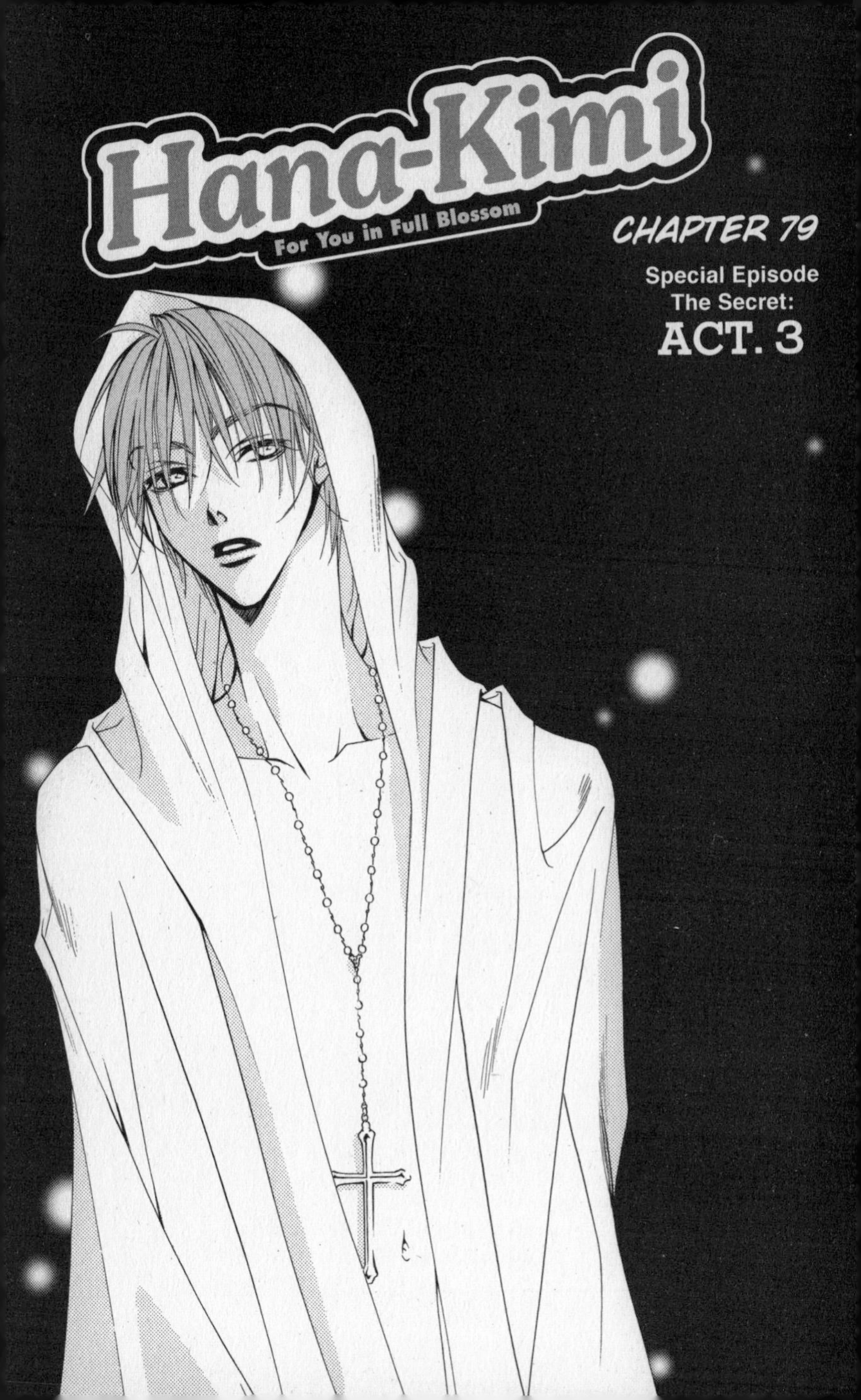
Hana-Kimi
For You in Full Blossom
CHAPTER 79
Special Episode
The Secret:
ACT. 3

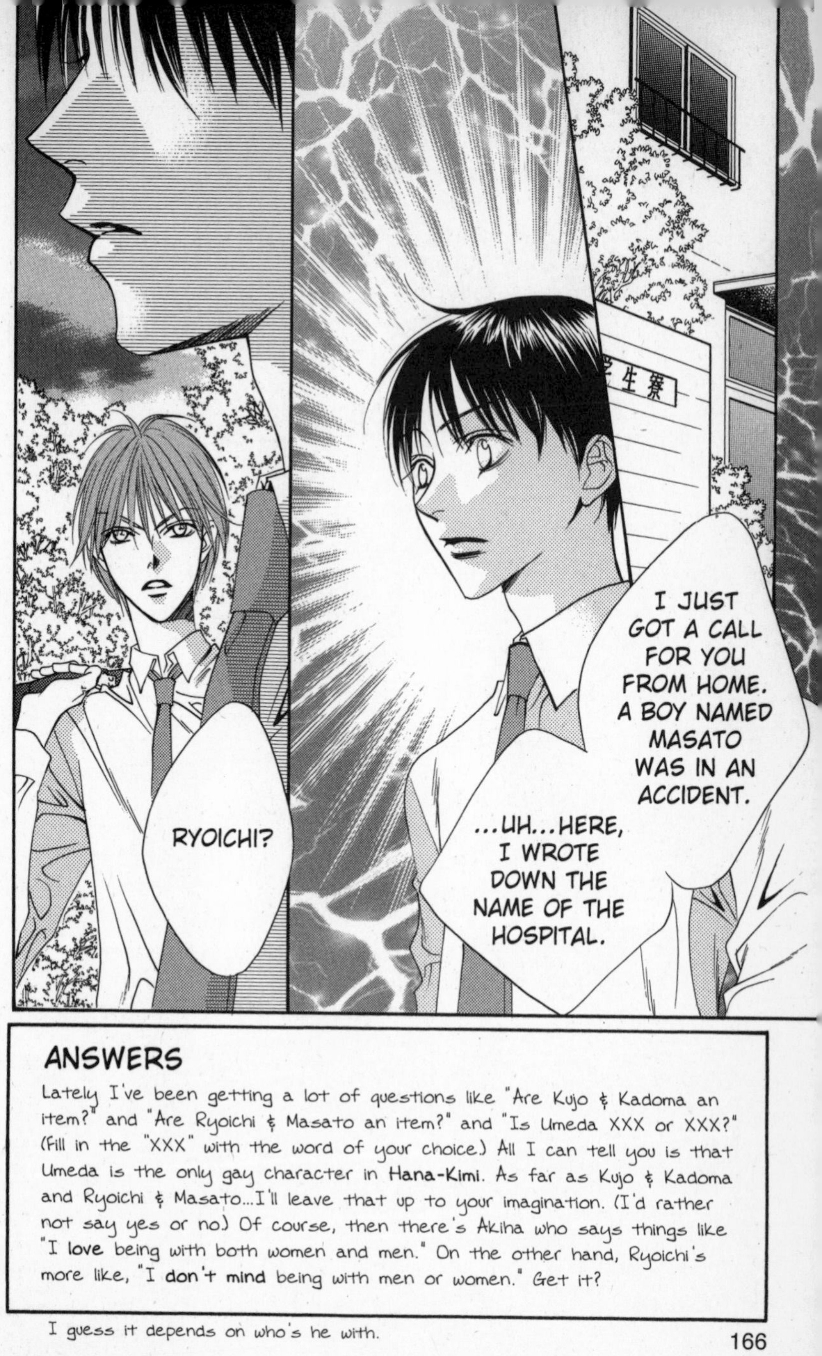
I JUST GOT A CALL FOR YOU FROM HOME. A BOY NAMED MASATO WAS IN AN ACCIDENT.
...UH...HERE, I WROTE DOWN THE NAME OF THE HOSPITAL.
RYOICHI?

ANSWERS

Lately I've been getting a lot of questions like "Are Kujo & Kadoma an item?" and "Are Ryoichi & Masato an item?" and "Is Umeda XXX or XXX?" (Fill in the "XXX" with the word of your choice.) All I can tell you is that Umeda is the only gay character in **Hana-Kimi**. As far as Kujo & Kadoma and Ryoichi & Masato...I'll leave that up to your imagination. (I'd rather not say yes or no.) Of course, then there's Akiha who says things like "I **love** being with both women and men." On the other hand, Ryoichi's more like, "I **don't mind** being with men or women." Get it?

I guess it depends on who's he with.

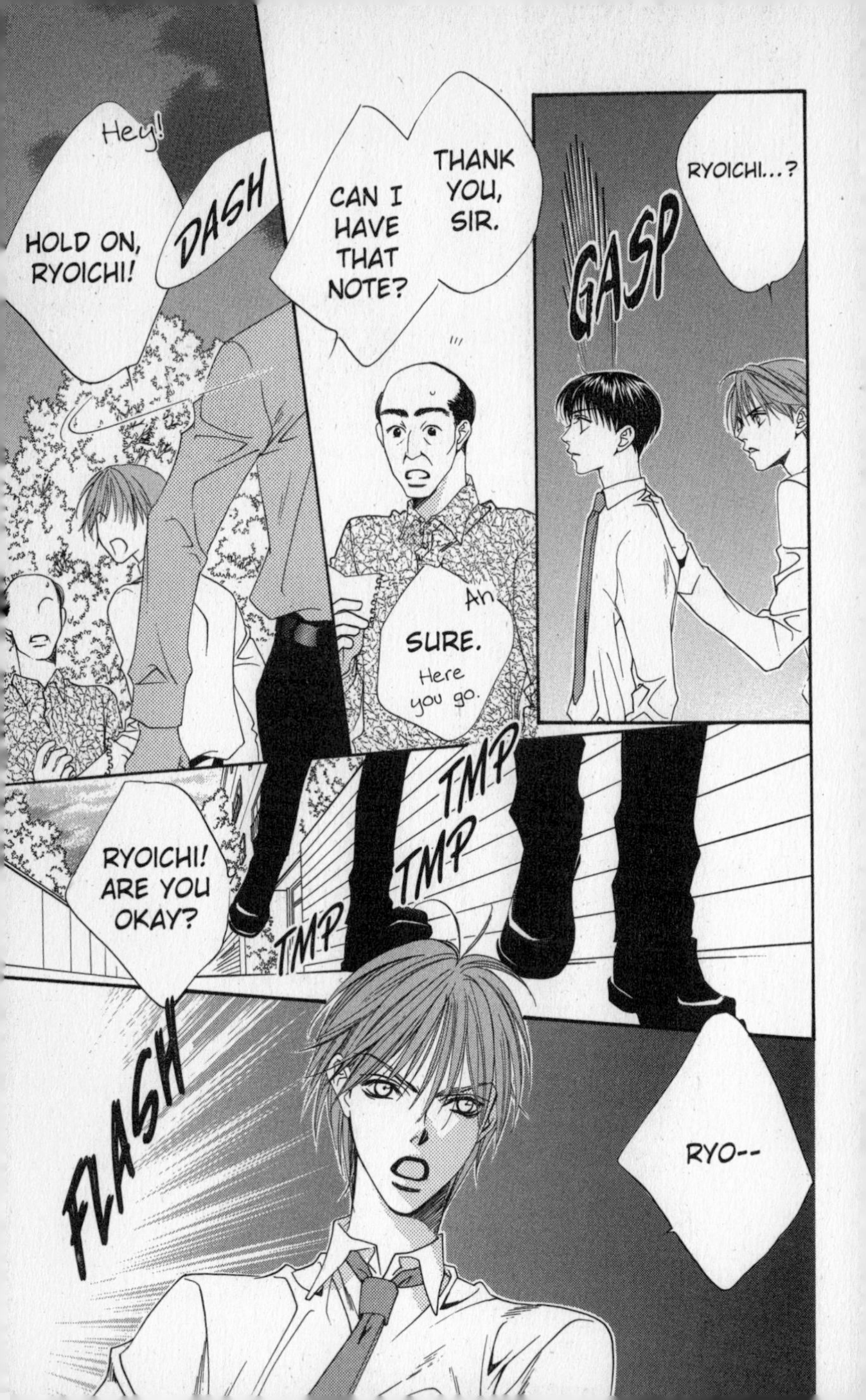
RYOICHI...?
GASP
THANK YOU, SIR.
CAN I HAVE THAT NOTE?
Ah
SURE.
Here you go.
Hey!
HOLD ON, RYOICHI!
DASH
TMP
TMP
TMP
RYOICHI! ARE YOU OKAY?
RYO--
FLASH

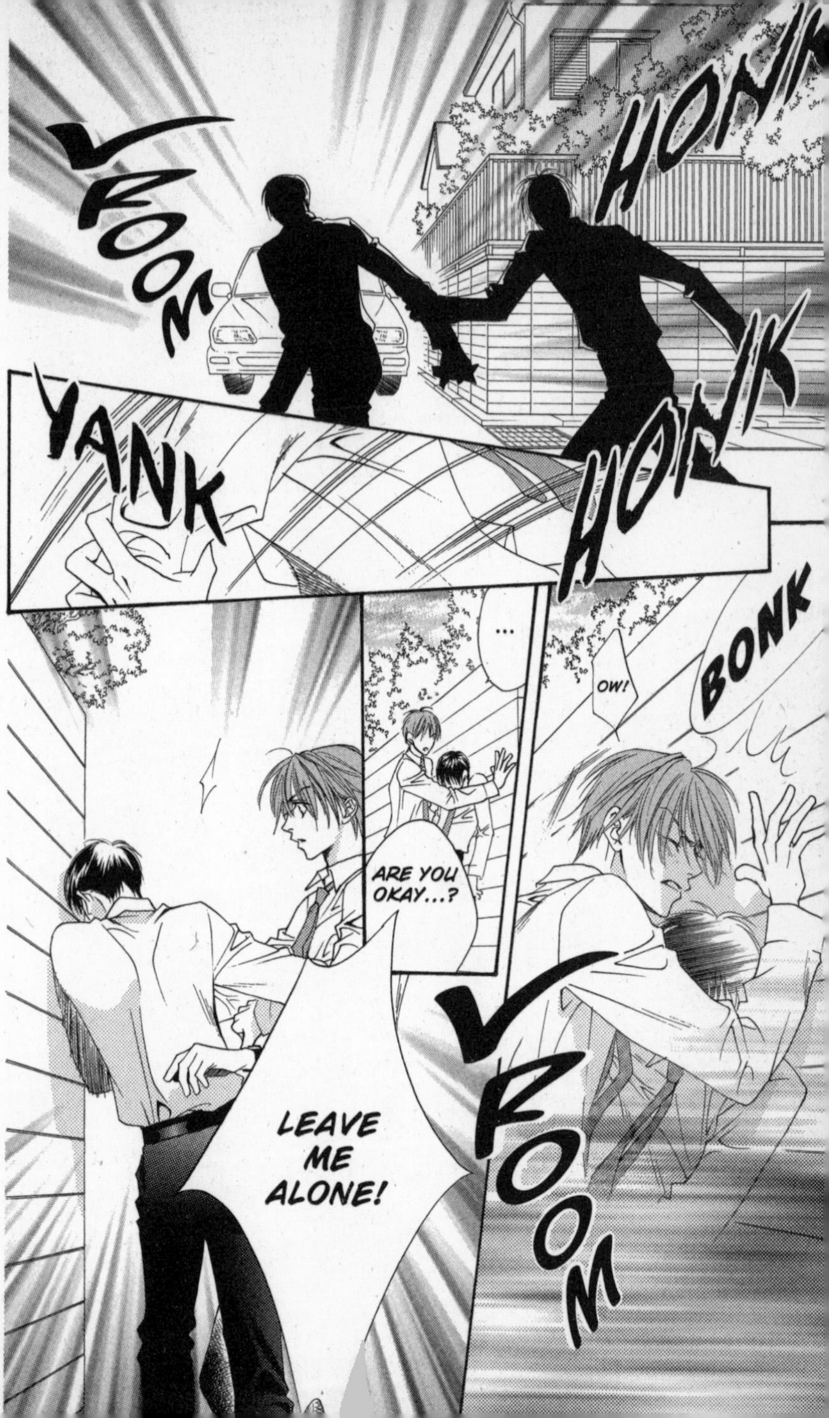
HONK HONK
VROOM
YANK
BONK
OW!
VROOM
...
ARE YOU OKAY...?
LEAVE ME ALONE!

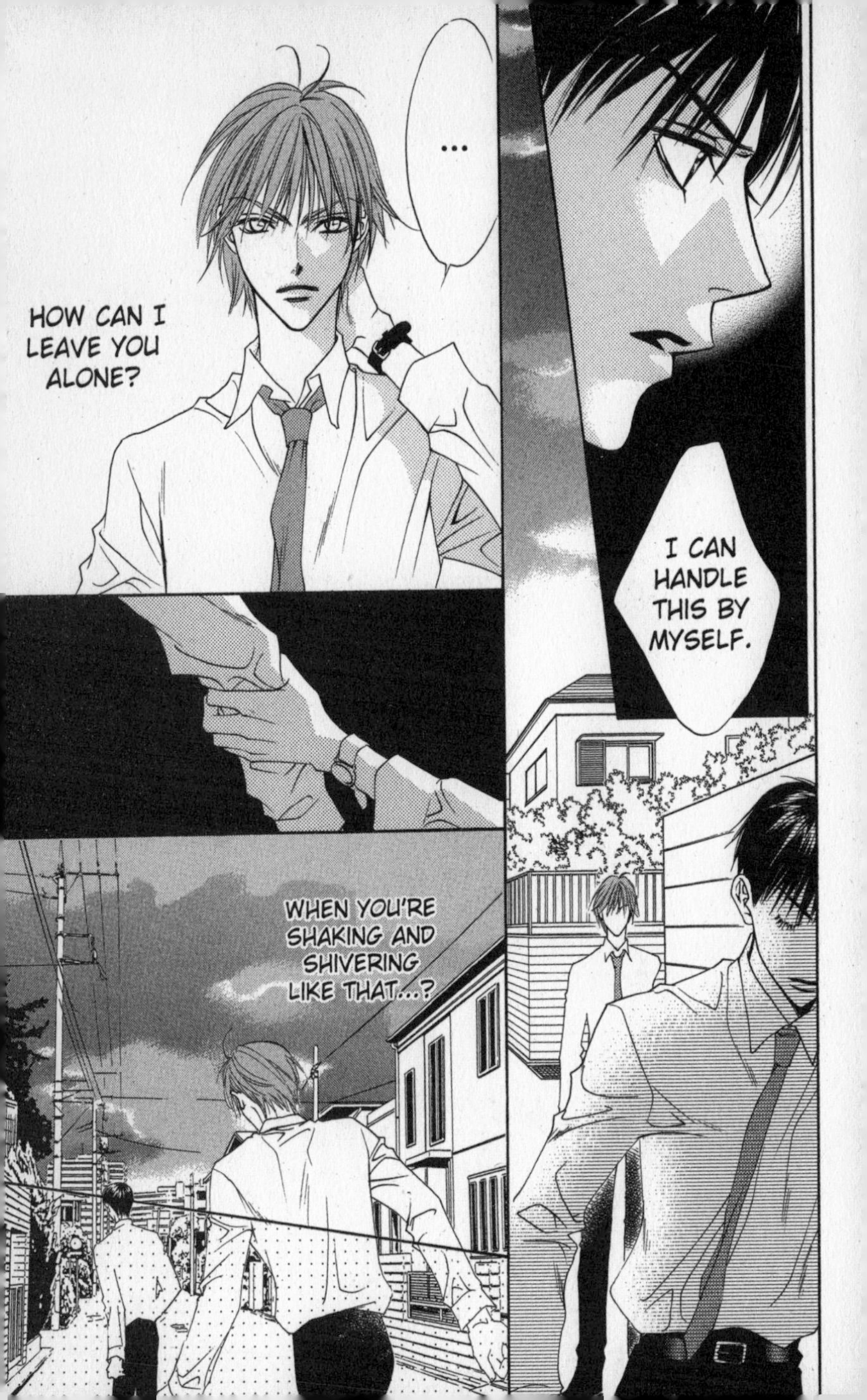
I CAN HANDLE THIS BY MYSELF.
...
HOW CAN I LEAVE YOU ALONE?
WHEN YOU'RE SHAKING AND SHIVERING LIKE THAT...?

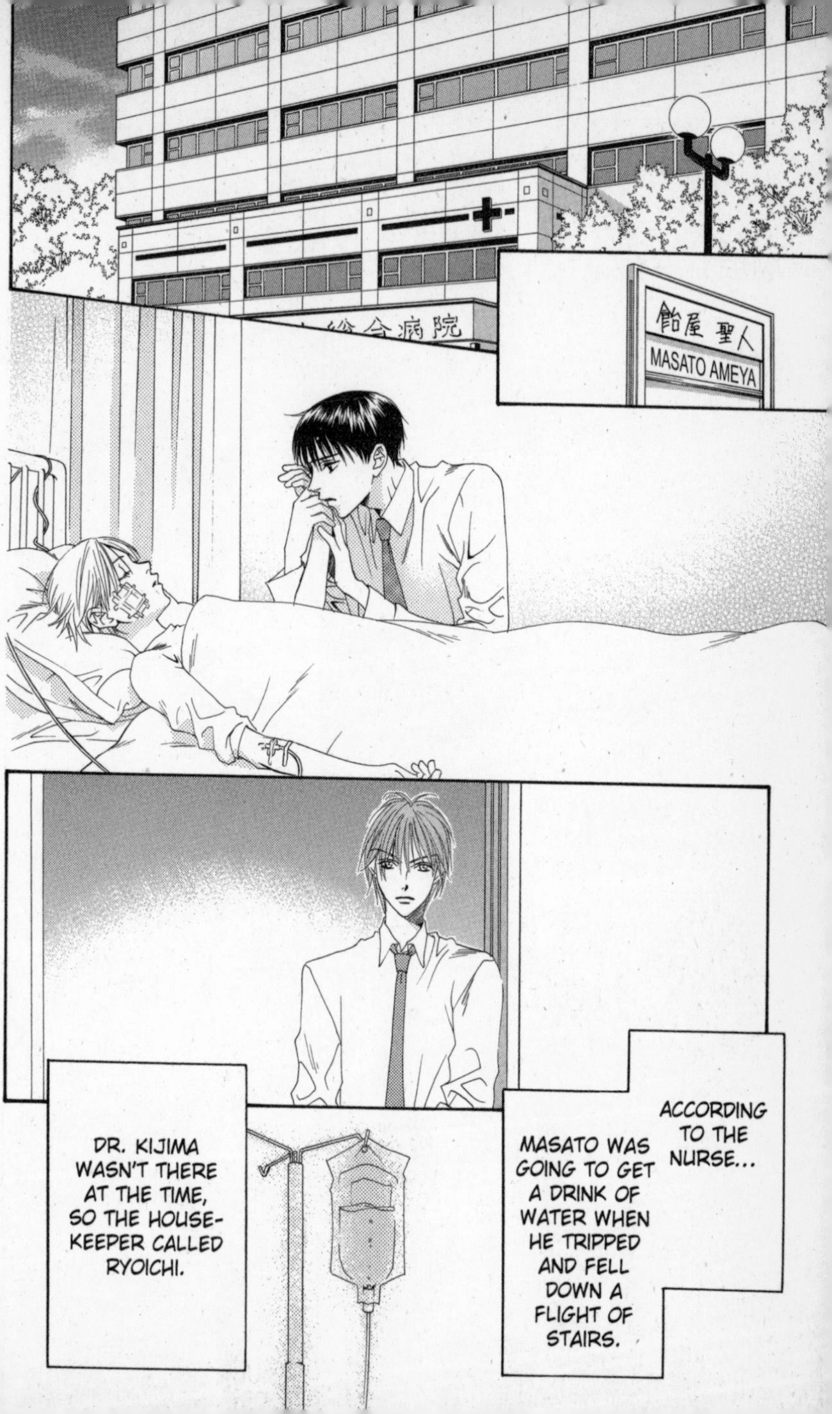
総合病院
飴屋 聖人
MASATO AMEYA
ACCORDING TO THE NURSE...
MASATO WAS GOING TO GET A DRINK OF WATER WHEN HE TRIPPED AND FELL DOWN A FLIGHT OF STAIRS.
DR. KIJIMA WASN'T THERE AT THE TIME, SO THE HOUSE-KEEPER CALLED RYOICHI.

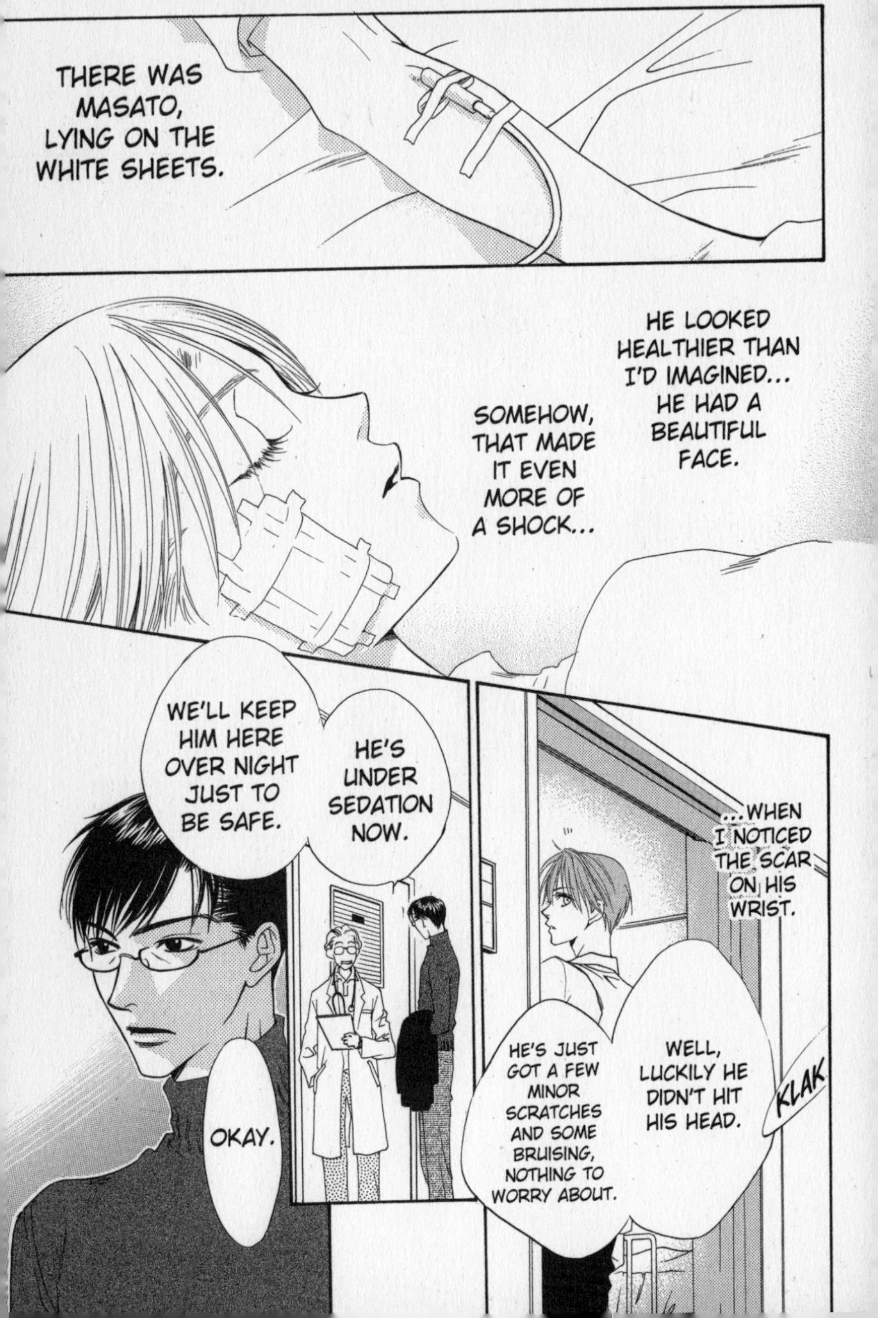
THERE WAS MASATO, LYING ON THE WHITE SHEETS.
HE LOOKED HEALTHIER THAN I'D IMAGINED... HE HAD A BEAUTIFUL FACE.
SOMEHOW, THAT MADE IT EVEN MORE OF A SHOCK...
...WHEN I NOTICED THE SCAR ON HIS WRIST.
KLAK
WELL, LUCKILY HE DIDN'T HIT HIS HEAD.
HE'S JUST GOT A FEW MINOR SCRATCHES AND SOME BRUISING, NOTHING TO WORRY ABOUT.
HE'S UNDER SEDATION NOW.
WE'LL KEEP HIM HERE OVER NIGHT JUST TO BE SAFE.
OKAY.

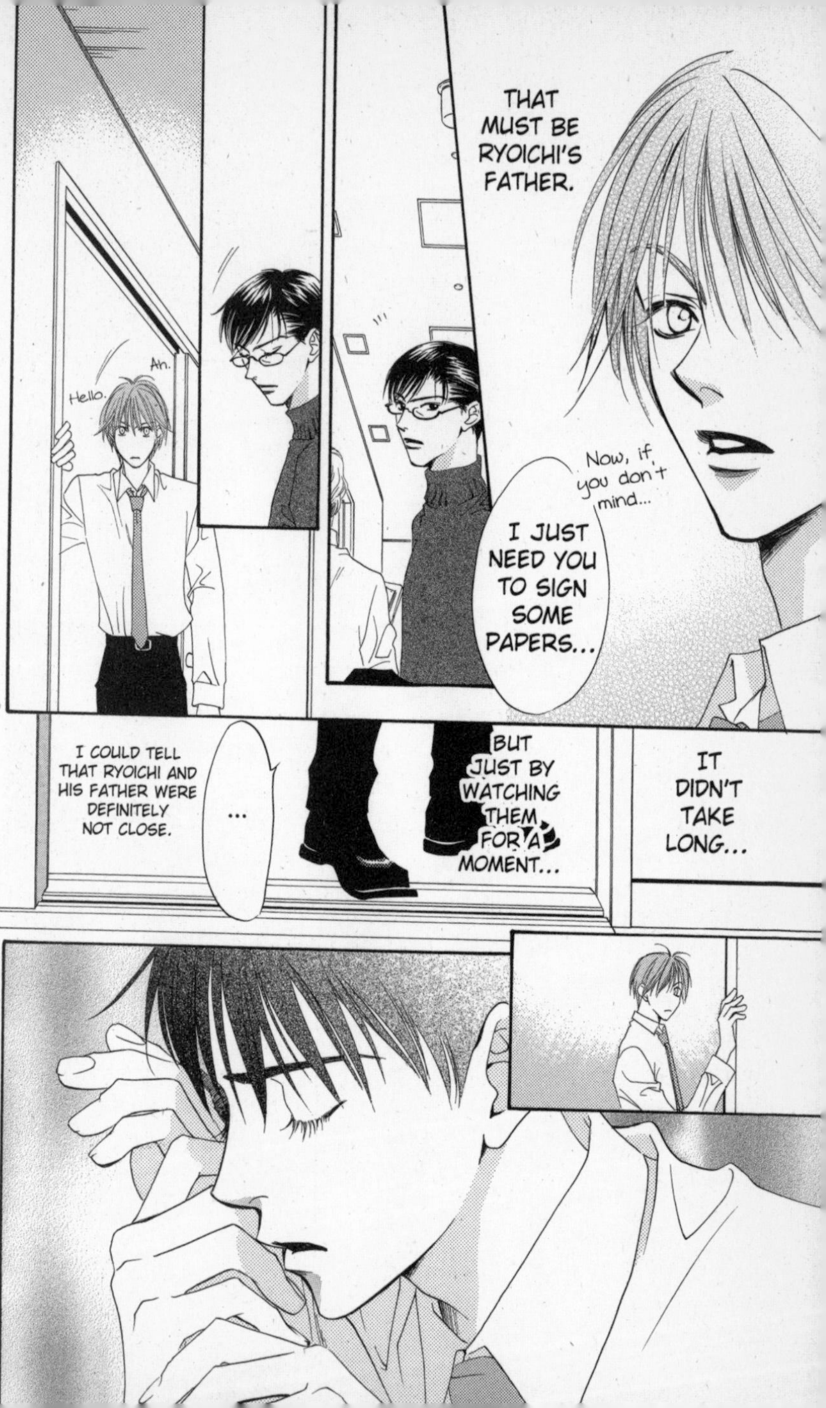
THAT MUST BE RYOICHI'S FATHER.
Now, if you don't mind...
I JUST NEED YOU TO SIGN SOME PAPERS...
Ah.
Hello.
IT DIDN'T TAKE LONG...
BUT JUST BY WATCHING THEM FOR A MOMENT...
...
I COULD TELL THAT RYOICHI AND HIS FATHER WERE DEFINITELY NOT CLOSE.

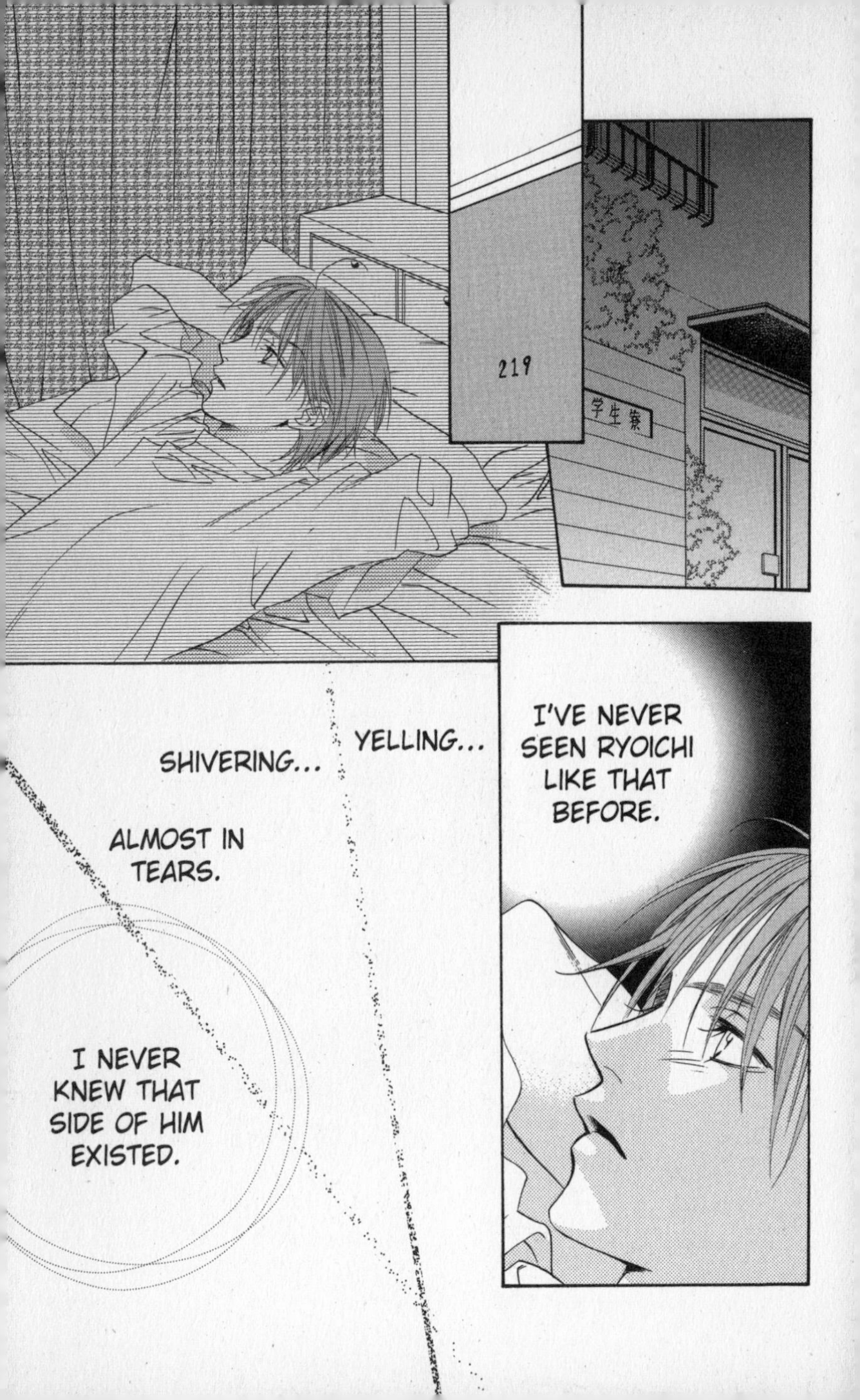
学生寮
219
I'VE NEVER SEEN RYOICHI LIKE THAT BEFORE.
YELLING...
SHIVERING...
ALMOST IN TEARS.
I NEVER KNEW THAT SIDE OF HIM EXISTED.

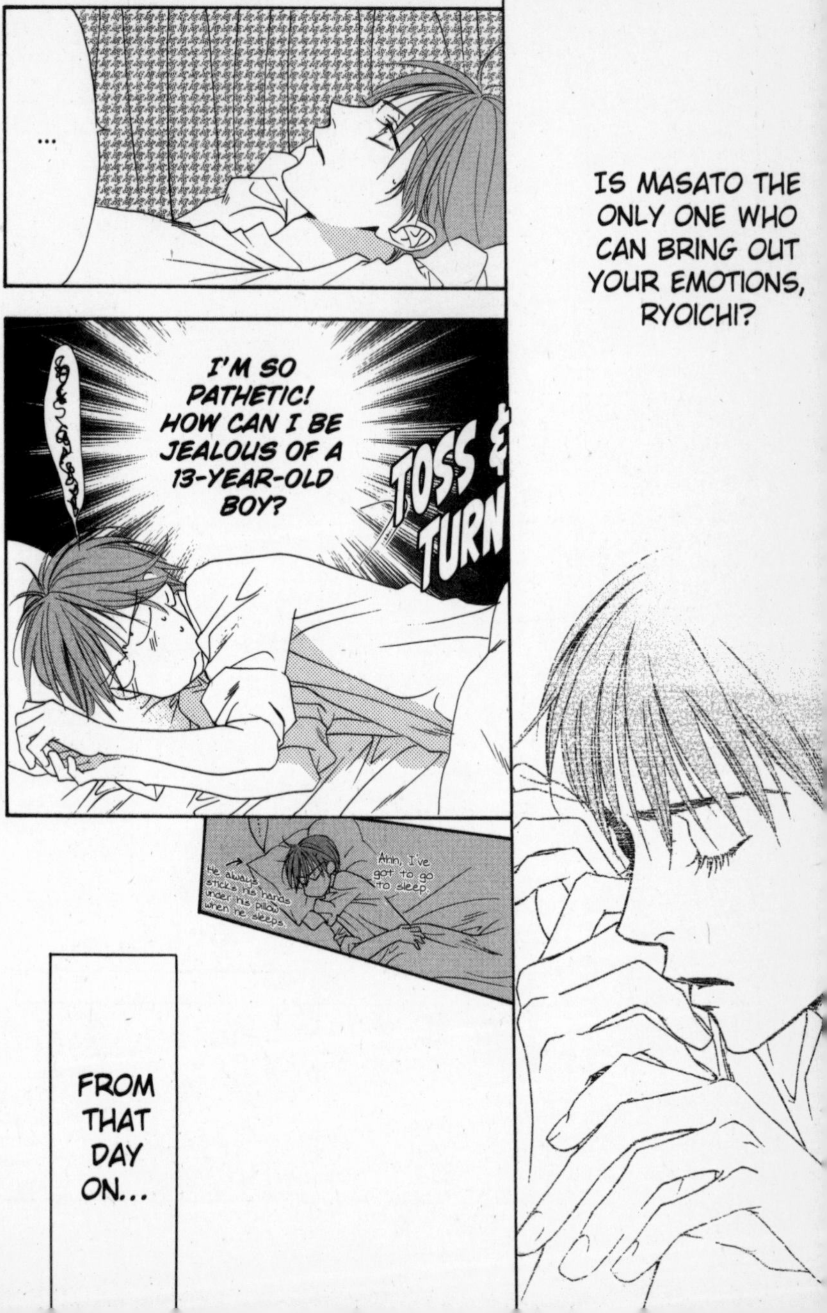
IS MASATO THE ONLY ONE WHO CAN BRING OUT YOUR EMOTIONS, RYOICHI?
...
I'M SO PATHETIC! HOW CAN I BE JEALOUS OF A 13-YEAR-OLD BOY?
TOSS & TURN
Ahh, I've got to go to sleep.
He always sticks his hands under his pillow when he sleeps.
FROM THAT DAY ON...

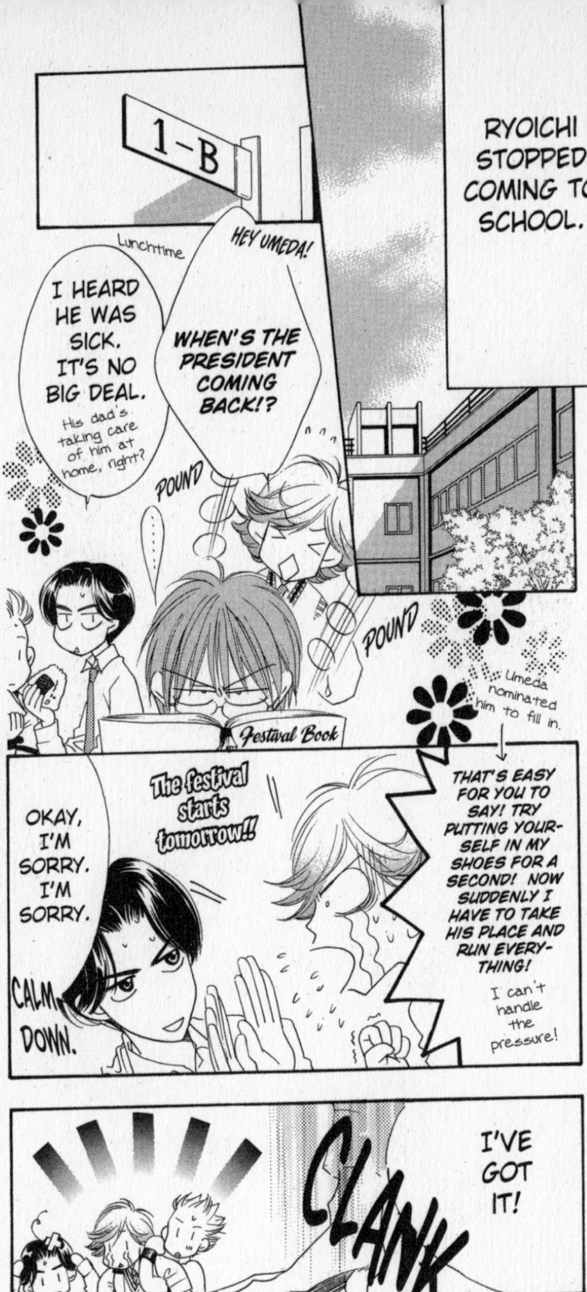
RYOICHI STOPPED COMING TO SCHOOL.
1-B
Lunchtime
HEY UMEDA!
WHEN'S THE PRESIDENT COMING BACK!?
I HEARD HE WAS SICK. IT'S NO BIG DEAL.
His dad's taking care of him at home, right?
POUND
POUND
Festival Book
Umeda nominated him to fill in.
THAT'S EASY FOR YOU TO SAY! TRY PUTTING YOURSELF IN MY SHOES FOR A SECOND! NOW SUDDENLY I HAVE TO TAKE HIS PLACE AND RUN EVERYTHING!
I can't handle the pressure!
The festival starts tomorrow!!
OKAY, I'M SORRY. I'M SORRY.
CALM DOWN.
I'VE GOT IT!
CLANK

「See ya!」

This is the last quarter-page column in this volume! The regular Mizuki & Sano storyline stopped abruptly in the middle, and suddenly Umeda's special episodes took over. If you're reading this thinking "What the heck is going on?" please don't worry...the regular story continues in Volume 15. So, did you enjoy Umeda's special episodes? It's too late to say anything about it now, but I personally was a little unsatisfied with the ending. It worked out fine, but the story actually goes on even further...Wah!...If Hana-Kimi ever ends, and I still feel this way, maybe I'll write the rest of the story. Uh...what do you think? Hmm...

See you in Volume 15! Bye!

2001. Jan

Some of you might have been offended by the "boy on boy" story, but I hope you enjoyed it anyway.

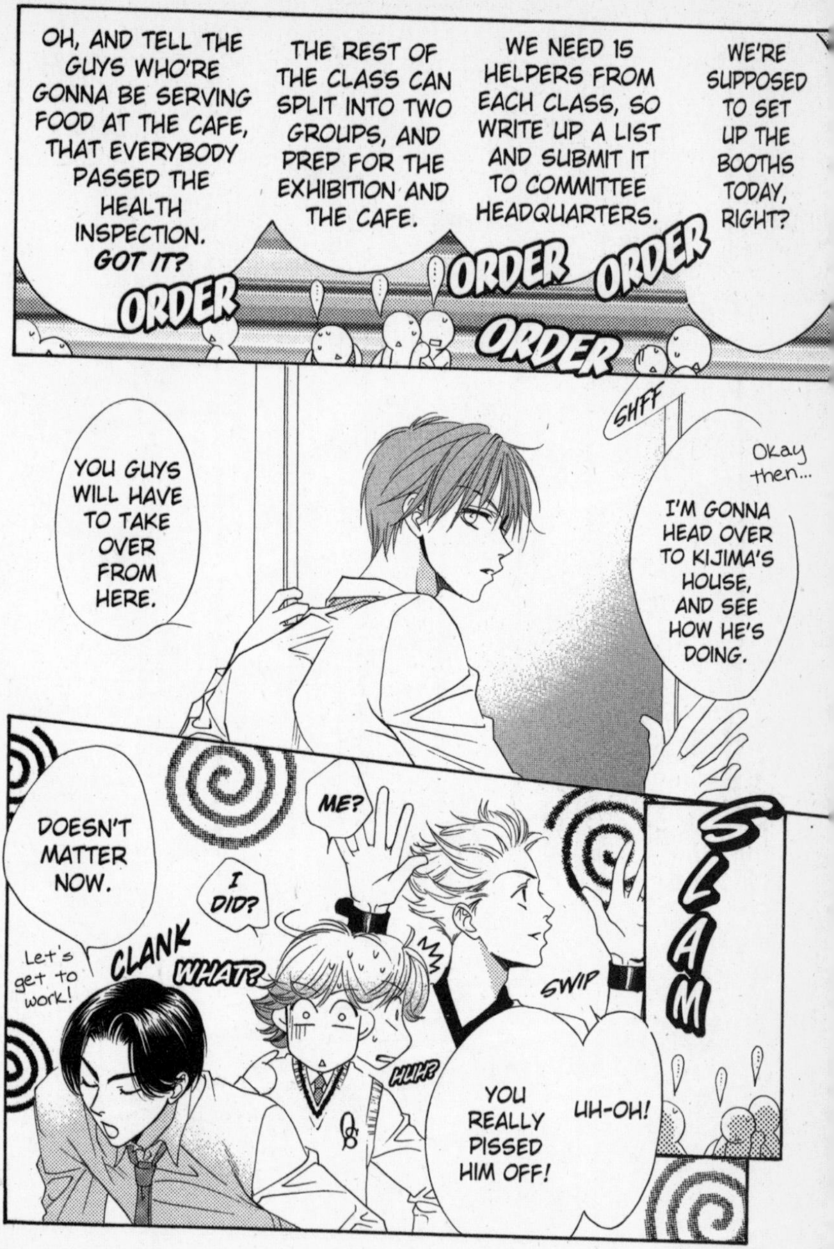
WE'RE SUPPOSED TO SET UP THE BOOTHS TODAY, RIGHT?
WE NEED 15 HELPERS FROM EACH CLASS, SO WRITE UP A LIST AND SUBMIT IT TO COMMITTEE HEADQUARTERS.
THE REST OF THE CLASS CAN SPLIT INTO TWO GROUPS, AND PREP FOR THE EXHIBITION AND THE CAFE.
OH, AND TELL THE GUYS WHO'RE GONNA BE SERVING FOOD AT THE CAFE, THAT EVERYBODY PASSED THE HEALTH INSPECTION. GOT IT?
ORDER
ORDER
ORDER
ORDER
SHFF
Okay then...
I'M GONNA HEAD OVER TO KIJIMA'S HOUSE, AND SEE HOW HE'S DOING.
YOU GUYS WILL HAVE TO TAKE OVER FROM HERE.
SLAM
UH-OH!
YOU REALLY PISSED HIM OFF!
ME?
SWIP
I DID?
HUH?
WHAT?
CLANK
DOESN'T MATTER NOW.
Let's get to work!

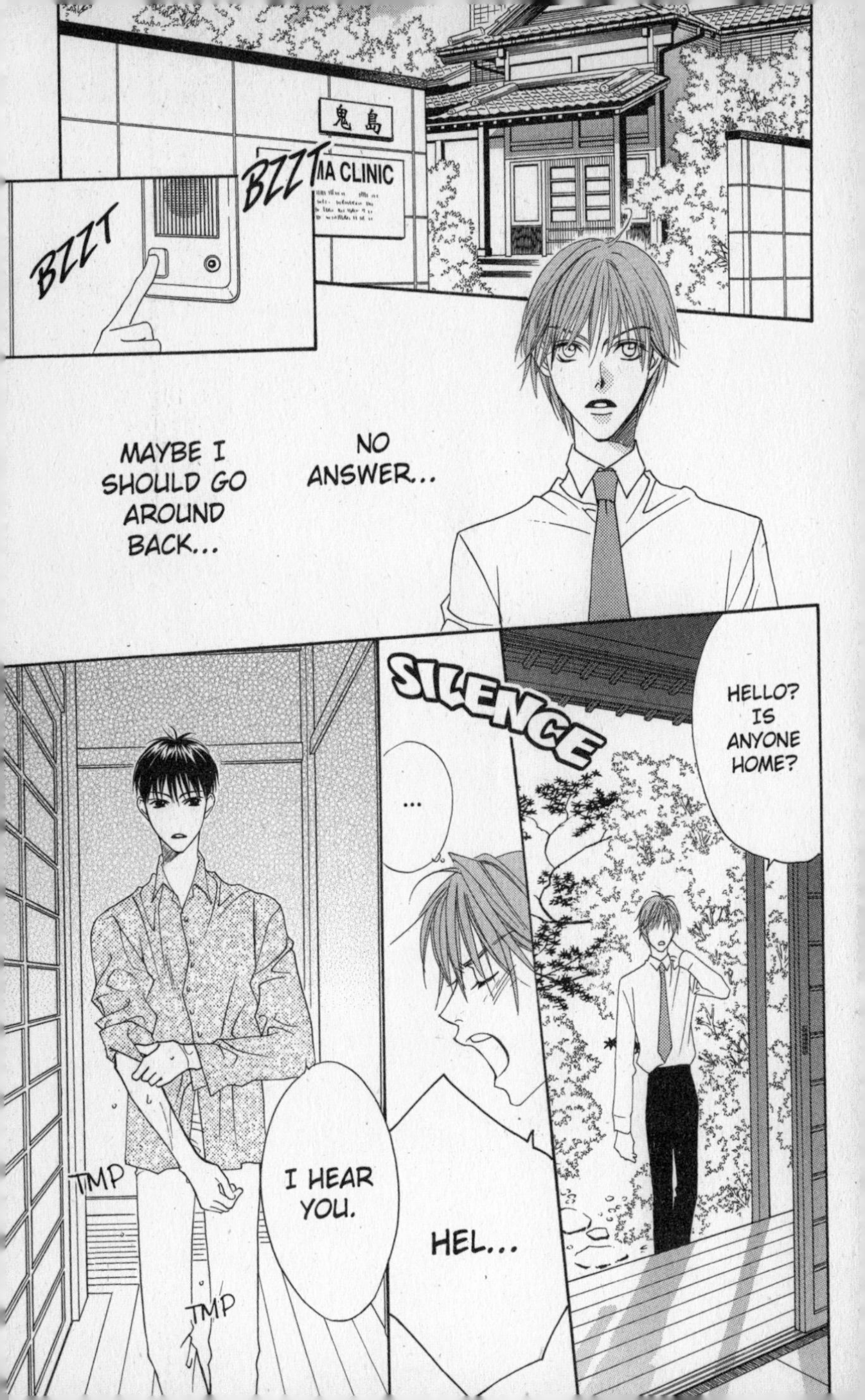

鬼島
MA CLINIC
BZZT
BZZT
NO ANSWER...
MAYBE I SHOULD GO AROUND BACK...
HELLO? IS ANYONE HOME?
SILENCE
...
HEL...
I HEAR YOU.
TMP
TMP

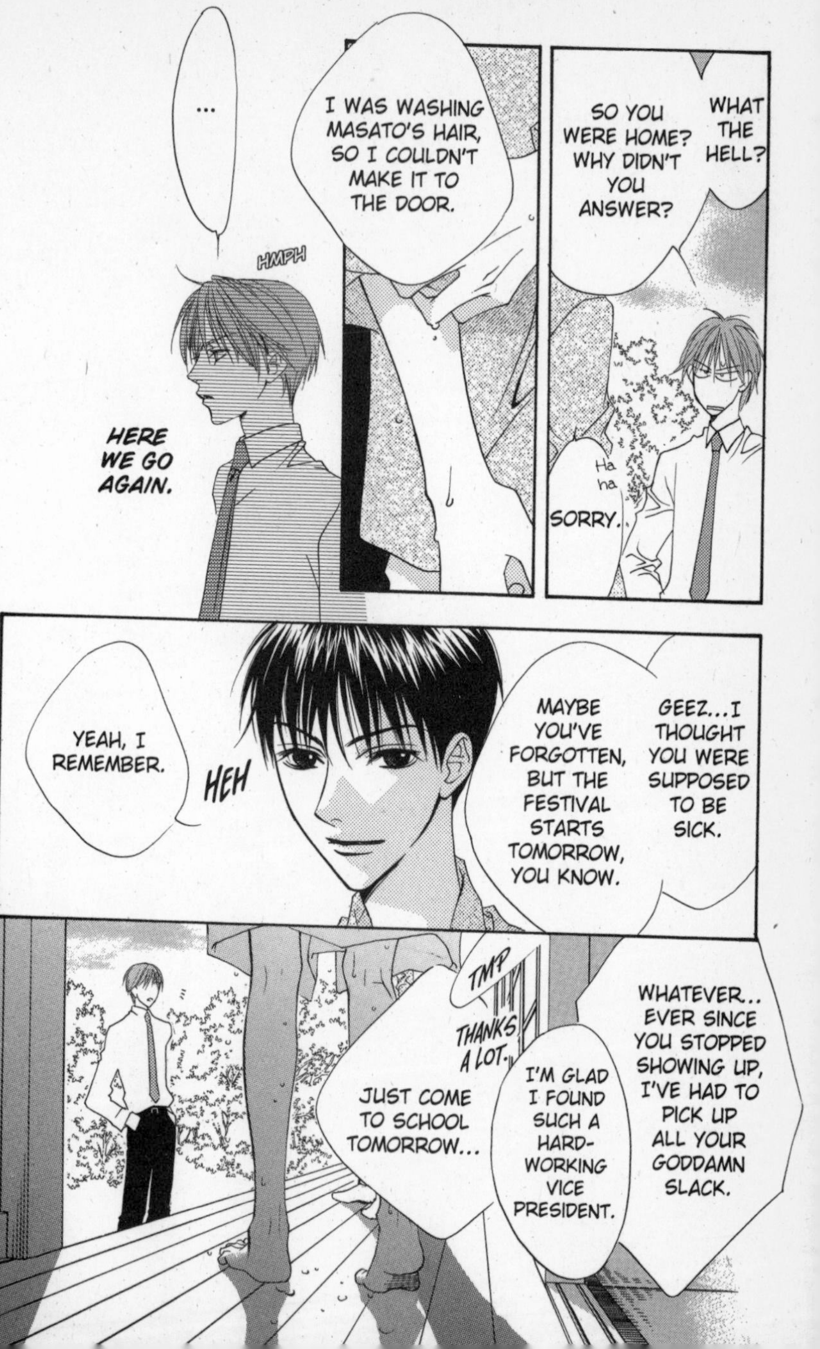
WHAT THE HELL?
SO YOU WERE HOME? WHY DIDN'T YOU ANSWER?
Ha ha
SORRY.
I WAS WASHING MASATO'S HAIR, SO I COULDN'T MAKE IT TO THE DOOR.
...
HMPH
HERE WE GO AGAIN.
GEEZ...I THOUGHT YOU WERE SUPPOSED TO BE SICK.
MAYBE YOU'VE FORGOTTEN, BUT THE FESTIVAL STARTS TOMORROW, YOU KNOW.
HEH
YEAH, I REMEMBER.
WHATEVER... EVER SINCE YOU STOPPED SHOWING UP, I'VE HAD TO PICK UP ALL YOUR GODDAMN SLACK.
TMP
THANKS A LOT.
I'M GLAD I FOUND SUCH A HARD-WORKING VICE PRESIDENT.
JUST COME TO SCHOOL TOMORROW...

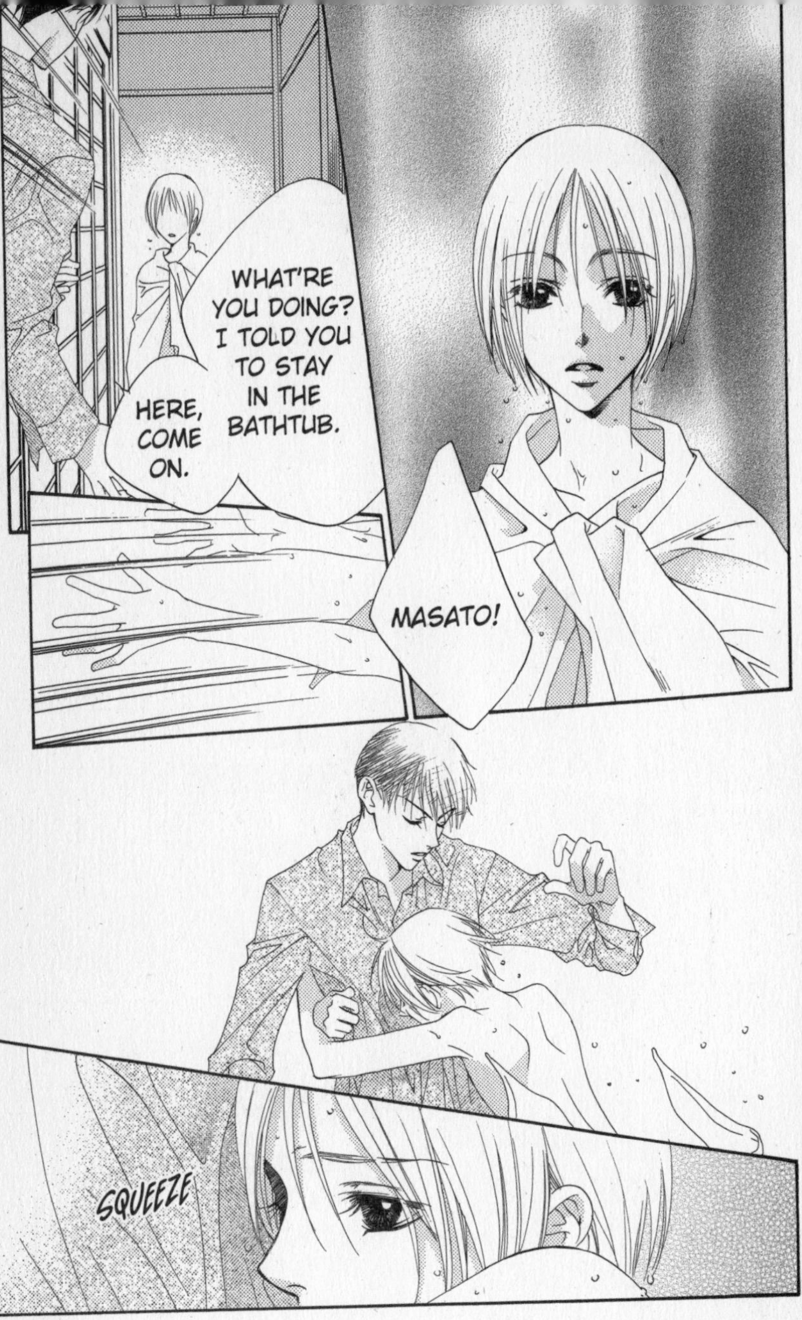
MASATO!
WHAT'RE YOU DOING? I TOLD YOU TO STAY IN THE BATHTUB.
HERE, COME ON.
SQUEEZE

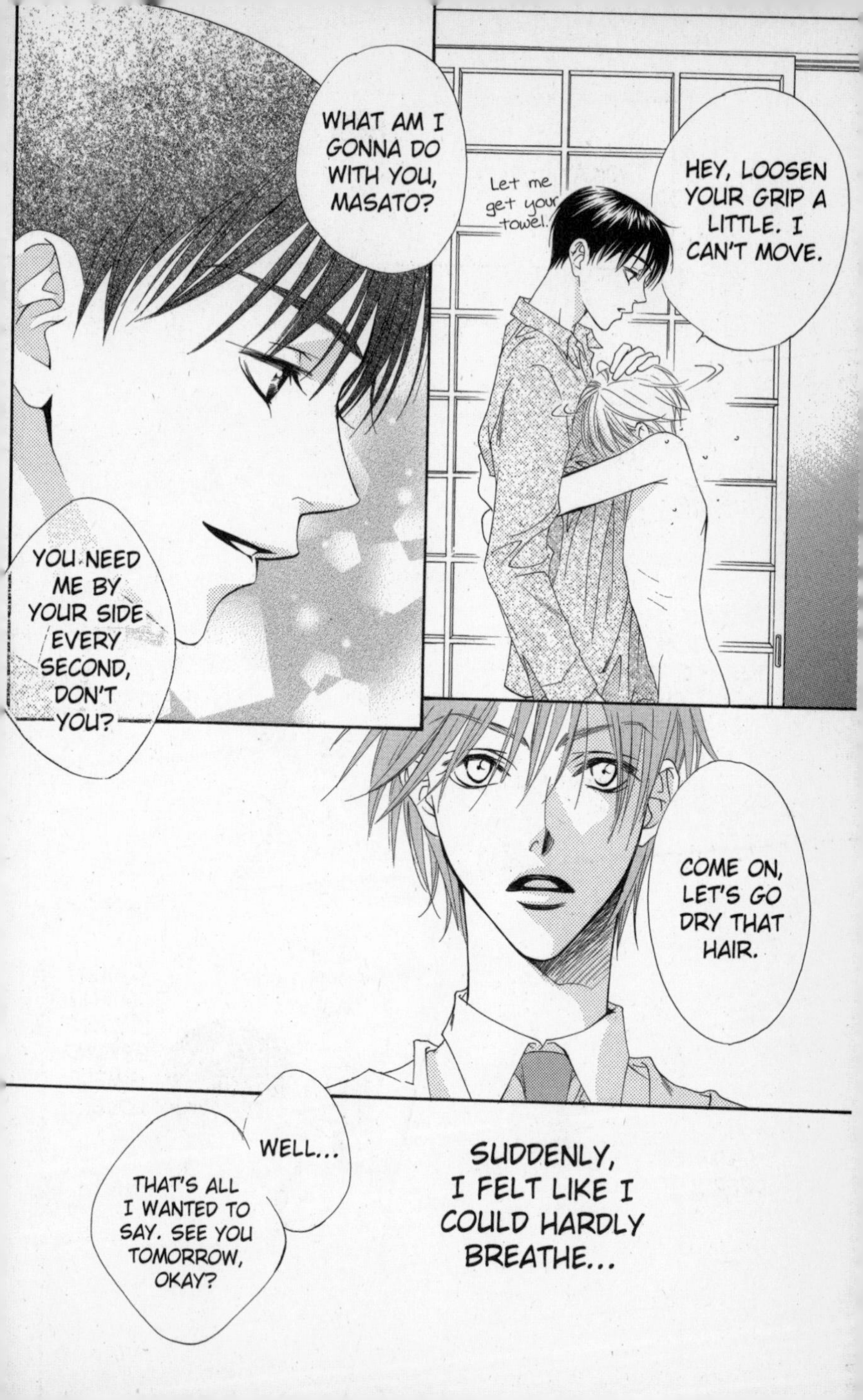
HEY, LOOSEN YOUR GRIP A LITTLE. I CAN'T MOVE.
Let me get your towel.
WHAT AM I GONNA DO WITH YOU, MASATO?
YOU NEED ME BY YOUR SIDE EVERY SECOND, DON'T YOU?
COME ON, LET'S GO DRY THAT HAIR.
WELL...
THAT'S ALL I WANTED TO SAY. SEE YOU TOMORROW, OKAY?
SUDDENLY, I FELT LIKE I COULD HARDLY BREATHE...

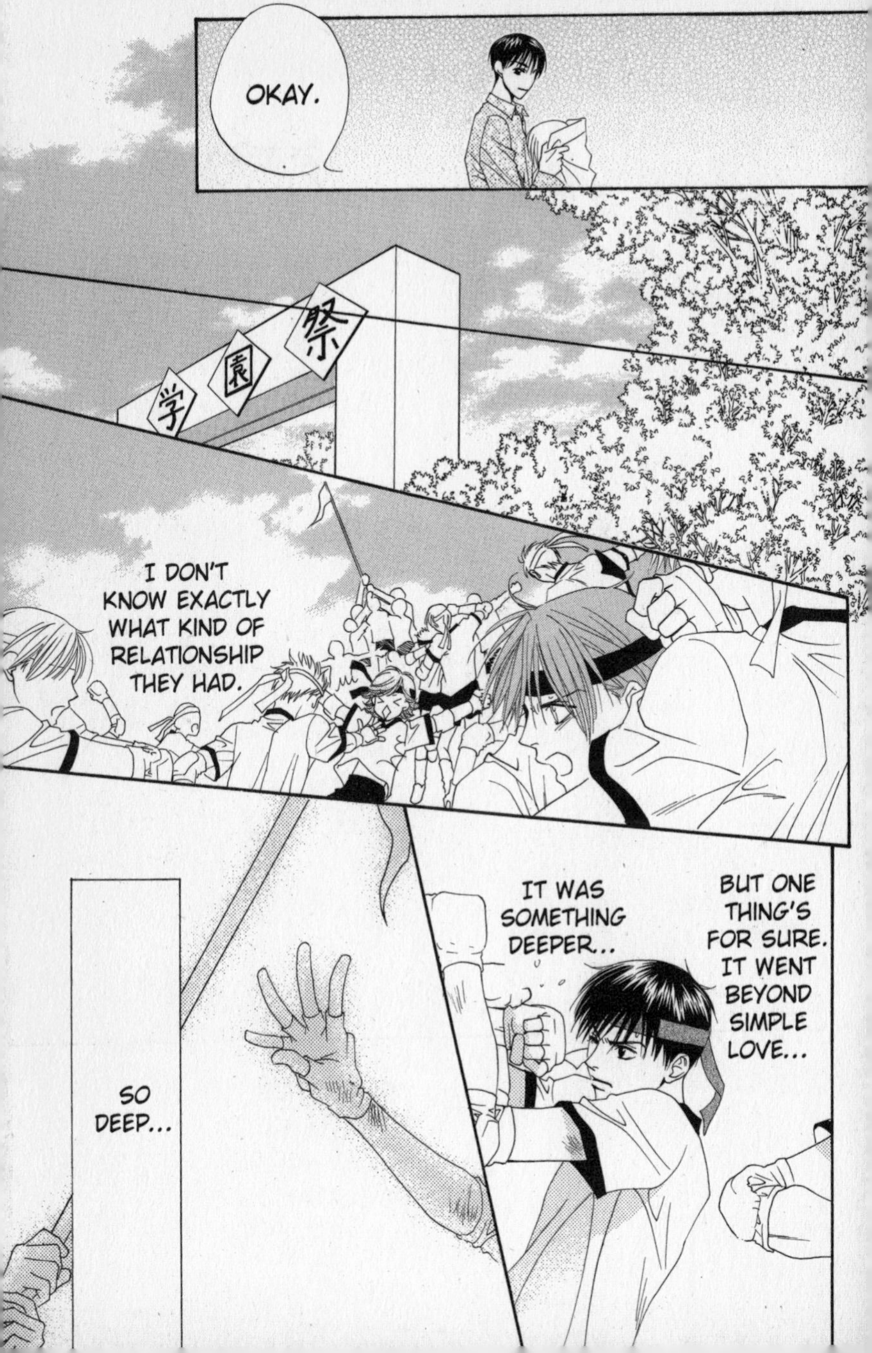
OKAY.
学園祭
I DON'T KNOW EXACTLY WHAT KIND OF RELATIONSHIP THEY HAD.
BUT ONE THING'S FOR SURE. IT WENT BEYOND SIMPLE LOVE...
IT WAS SOMETHING DEEPER...
SO DEEP...

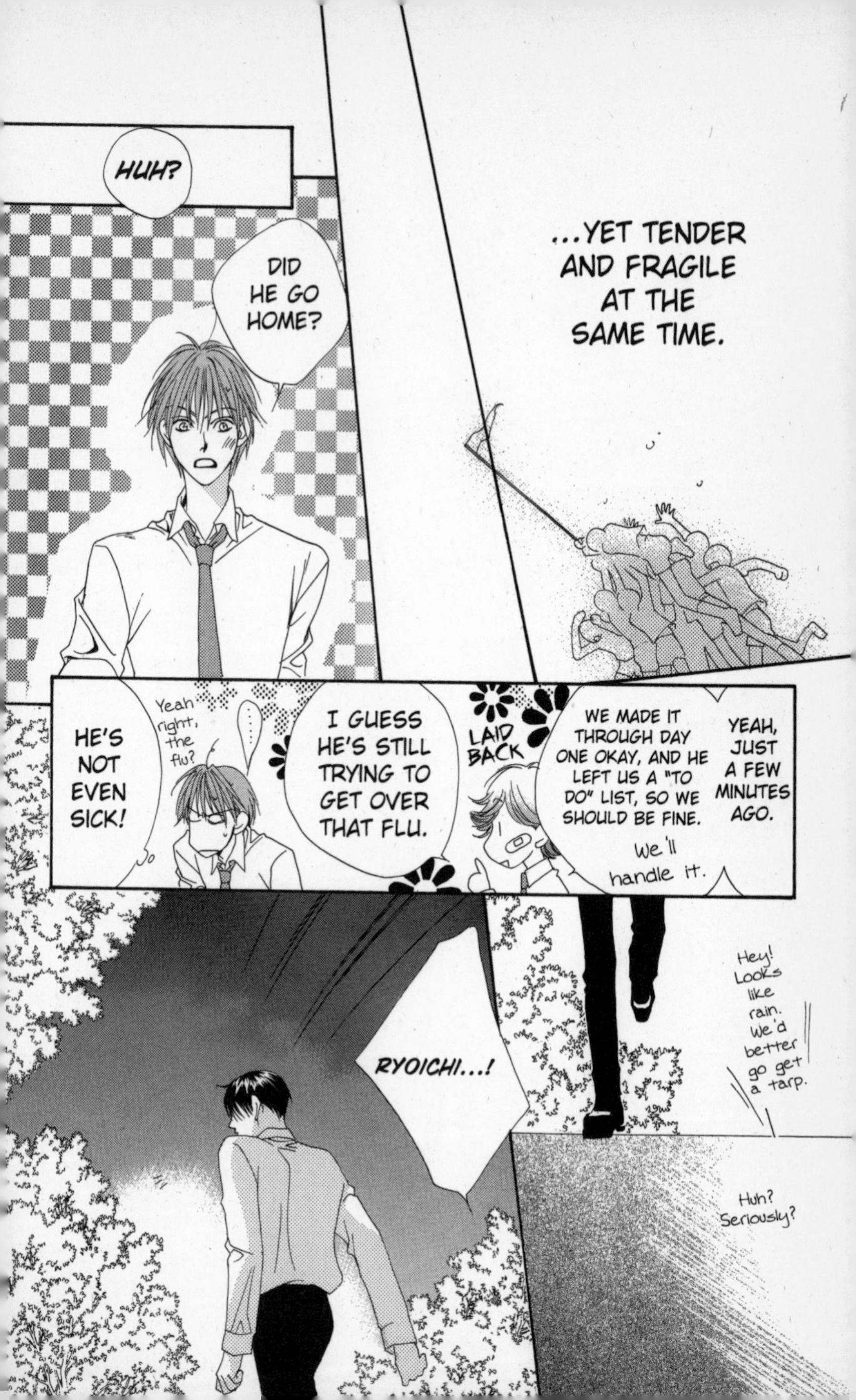
...YET TENDER AND FRAGILE AT THE SAME TIME.
HUH?
DID HE GO HOME?
YEAH, JUST A FEW MINUTES AGO.
WE MADE IT THROUGH DAY ONE OKAY, AND HE LEFT US A "TO DO" LIST, SO WE SHOULD BE FINE.
We'll handle it.
LAID BACK
I GUESS HE'S STILL TRYING TO GET OVER THAT FLU.
...
Yeah right, the flu?
HE'S NOT EVEN SICK!
Hey! Looks like rain. We'd better go get a tarp.
Huh? Seriously?
RYOICHI...!

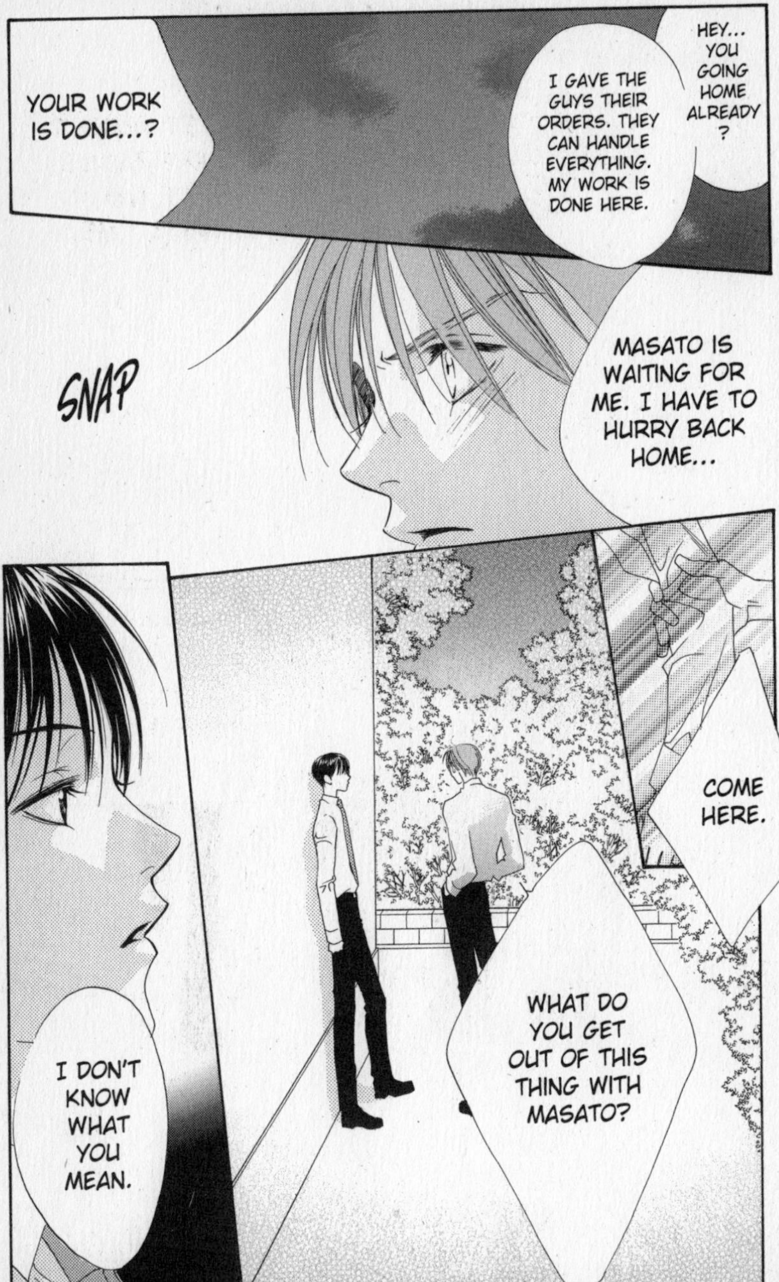
HEY... YOU GOING HOME ALREADY?
I GAVE THE GUYS THEIR ORDERS. THEY CAN HANDLE EVERYTHING. MY WORK IS DONE HERE.
YOUR WORK IS DONE...?
MASATO IS WAITING FOR ME. I HAVE TO HURRY BACK HOME...
SNAP
COME HERE.
WHAT DO YOU GET OUT OF THIS THING WITH MASATO?
I DON'T KNOW WHAT YOU MEAN.

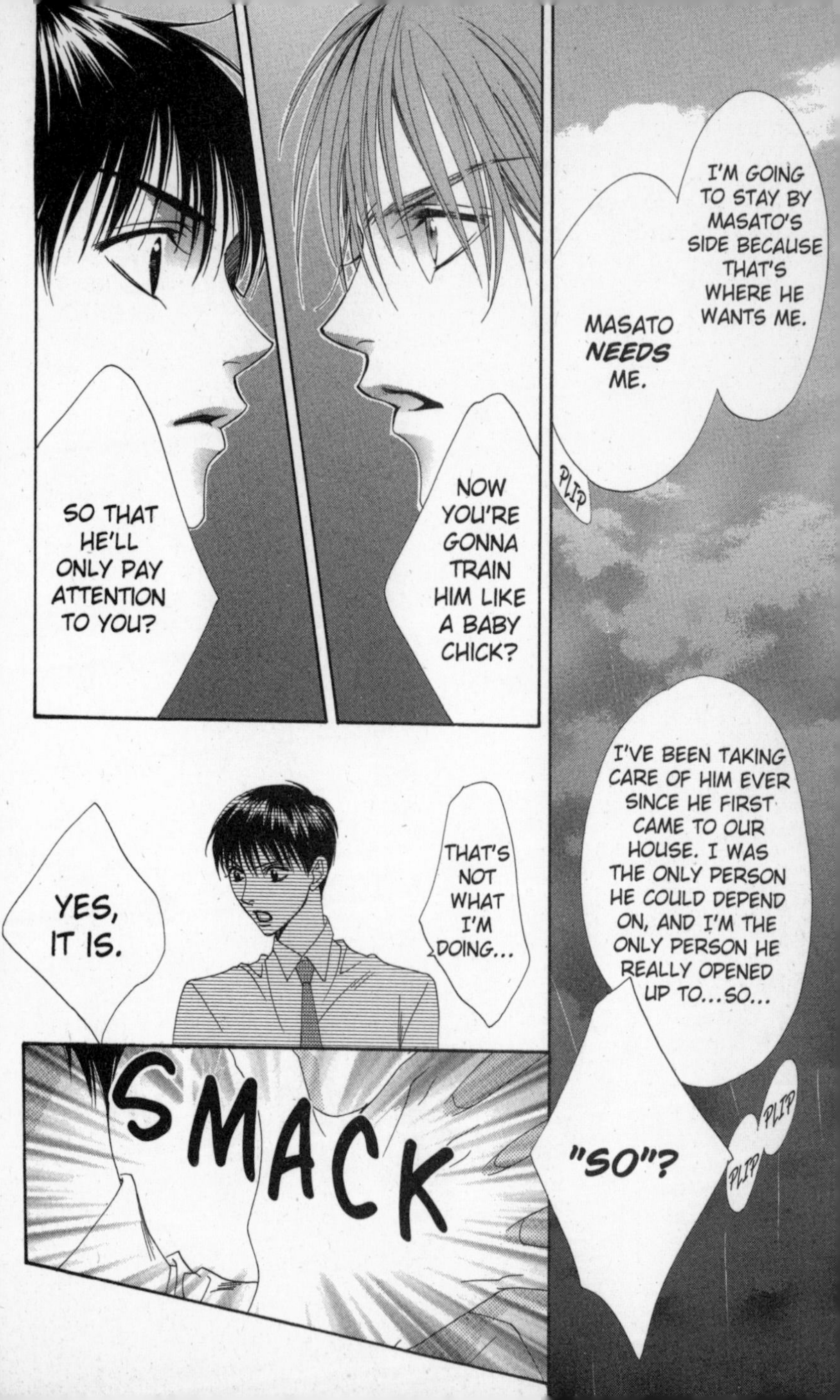
I'M GOING TO STAY BY MASATO'S SIDE BECAUSE THAT'S WHERE HE WANTS ME.
MASATO **NEEDS** ME.
PLIP
I'VE BEEN TAKING CARE OF HIM EVER SINCE HE FIRST CAME TO OUR HOUSE. I WAS THE ONLY PERSON HE COULD DEPEND ON, AND I'M THE ONLY PERSON HE REALLY OPENED UP TO...SO...
"SO"?
PLIP
PLIP
NOW YOU'RE GONNA TRAIN HIM LIKE A BABY CHICK?
SO THAT HE'LL ONLY PAY ATTENTION TO YOU?
THAT'S NOT WHAT I'M DOING...
YES, IT IS.
SMACK

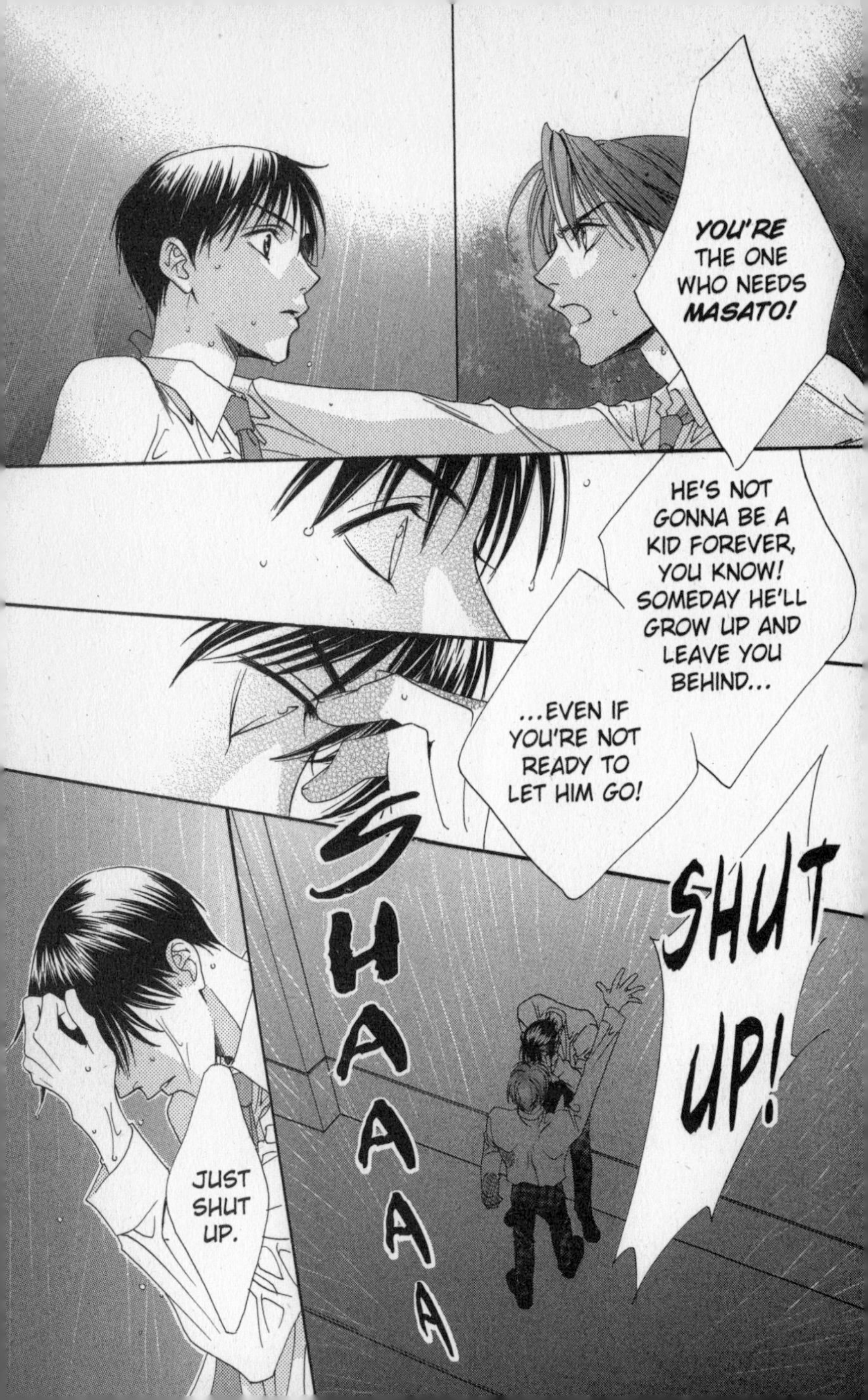
YOU'RE THE ONE WHO NEEDS MASATO!
HE'S NOT GONNA BE A KID FOREVER, YOU KNOW! SOMEDAY HE'LL GROW UP AND LEAVE YOU BEHIND...
...EVEN IF YOU'RE NOT READY TO LET HIM GO!
SHUT UP!
SHAAAAA
JUST SHUT UP.

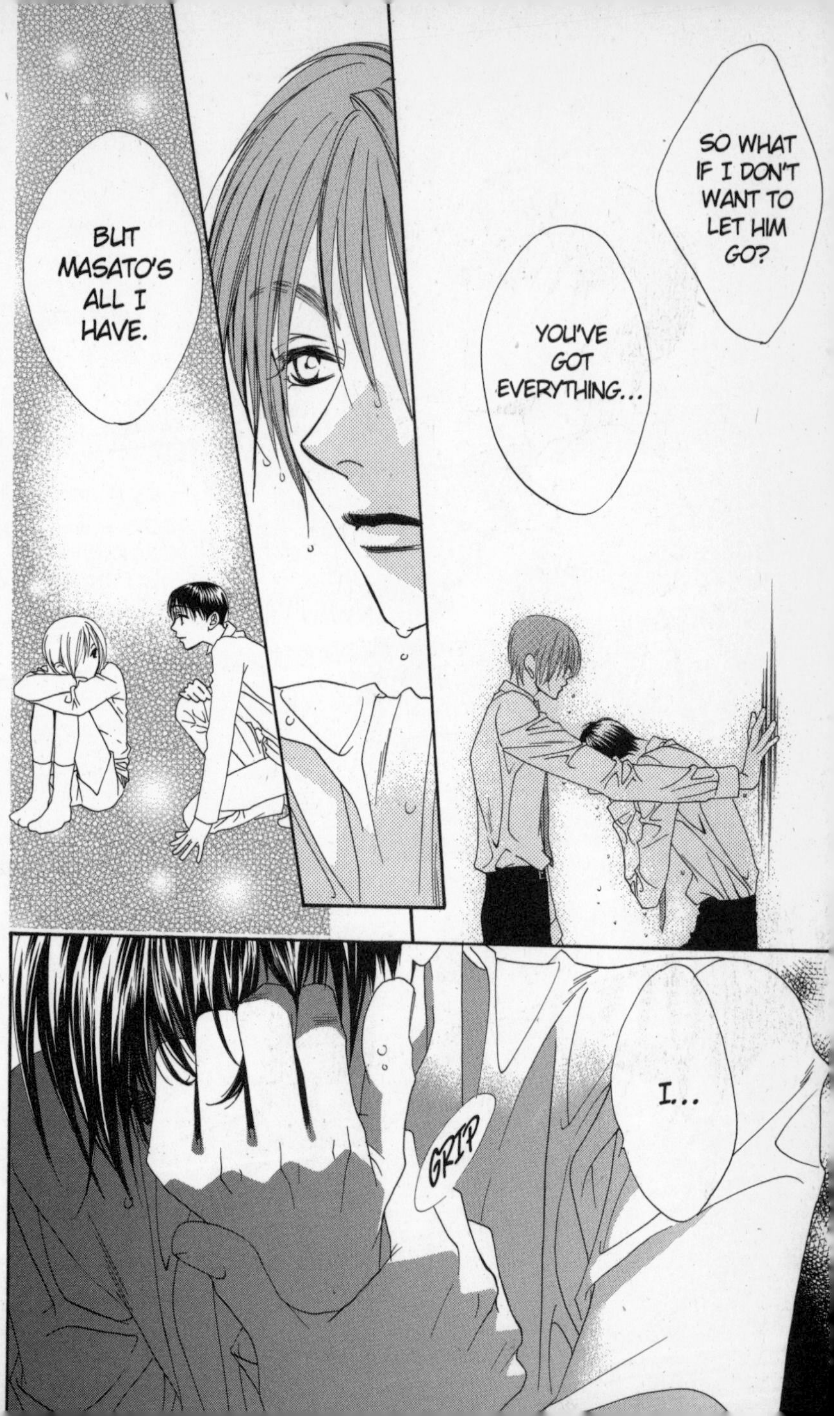
SO WHAT IF I DON'T WANT TO LET HIM GO?
YOU'VE GOT EVERYTHING...
BUT MASATO'S ALL I HAVE.
I...
GRIP

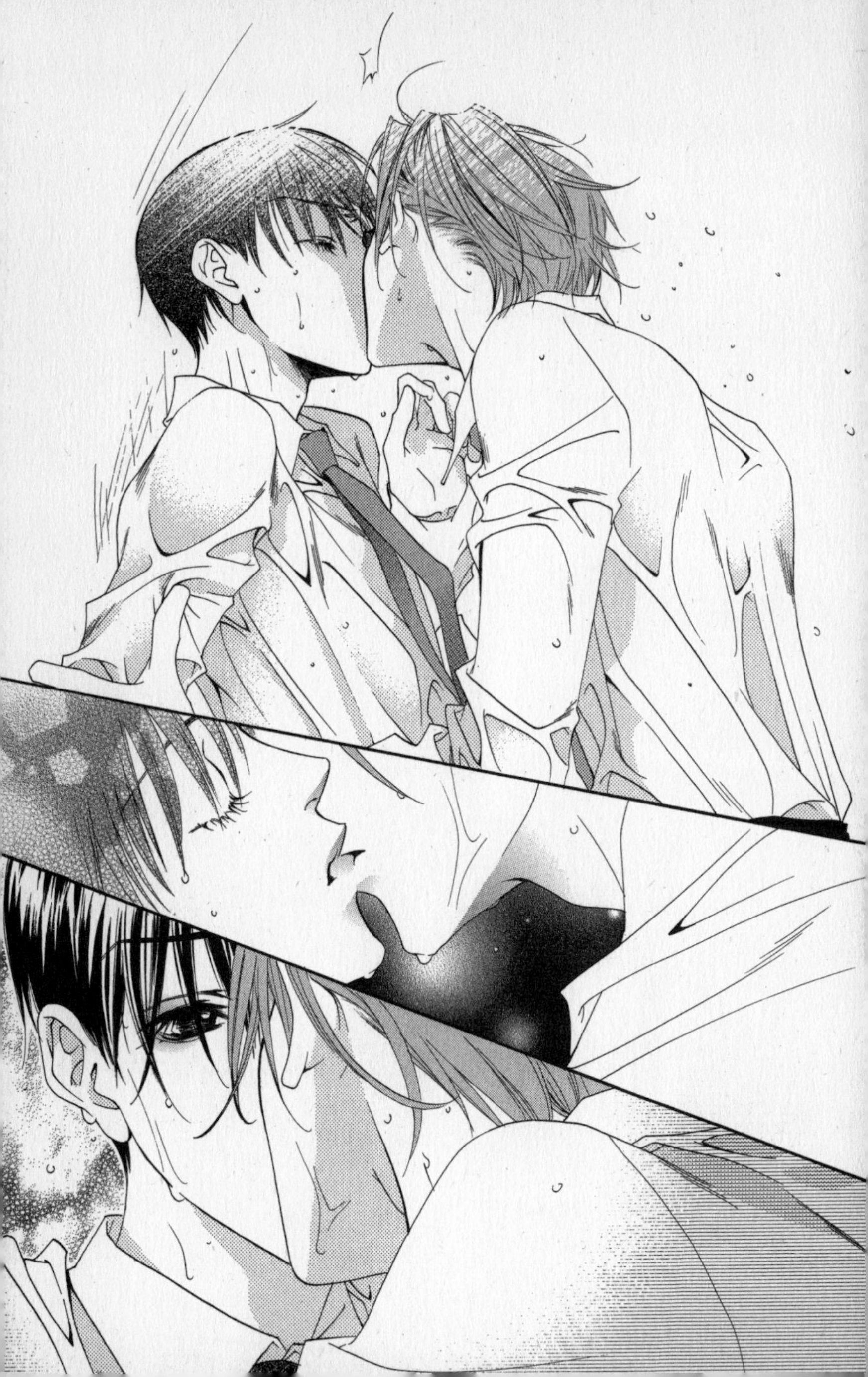

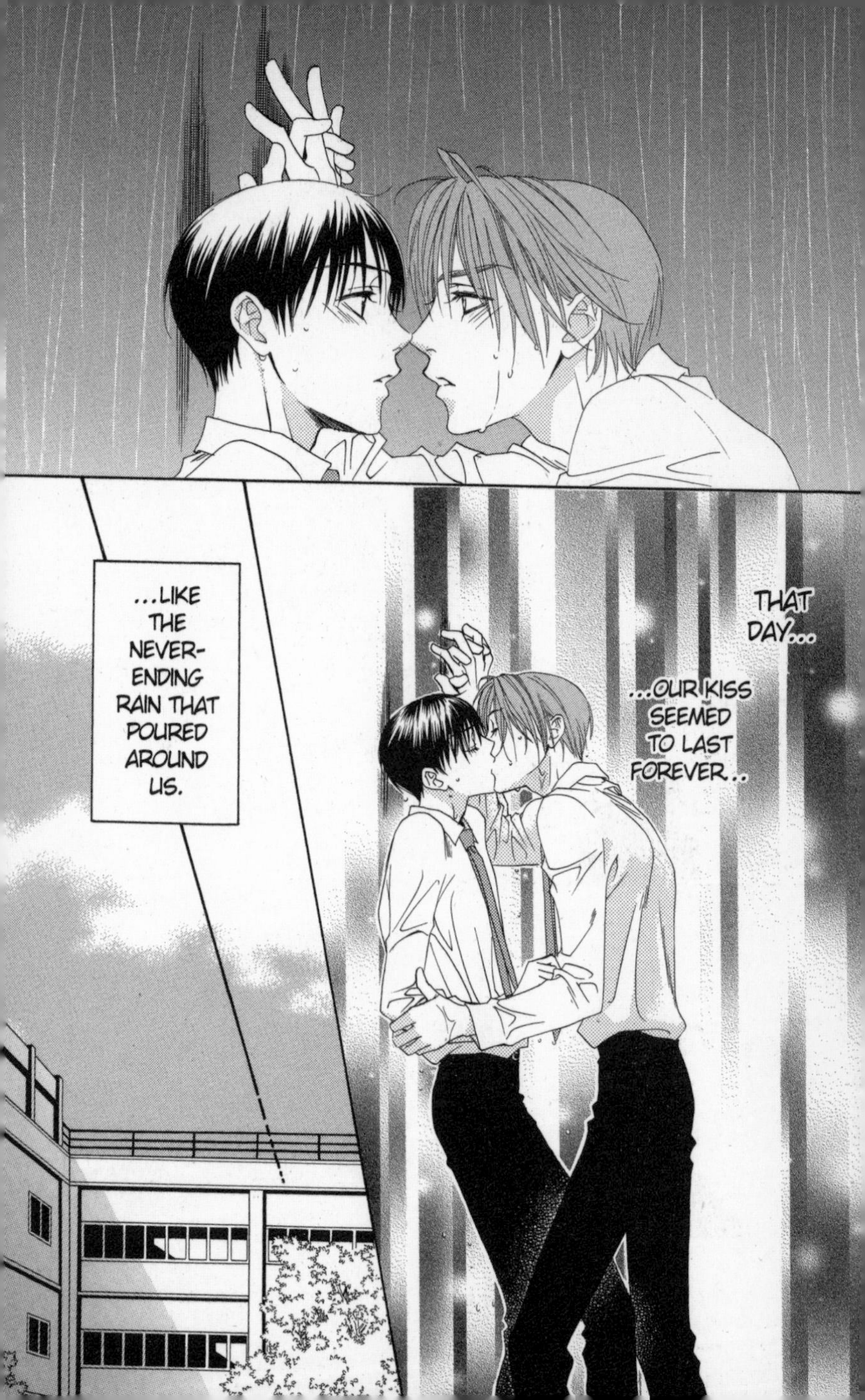
THAT DAY...
...OUR KISS SEEMED TO LAST FOREVER...
...LIKE THE NEVER-ENDING RAIN THAT POURED AROUND US.

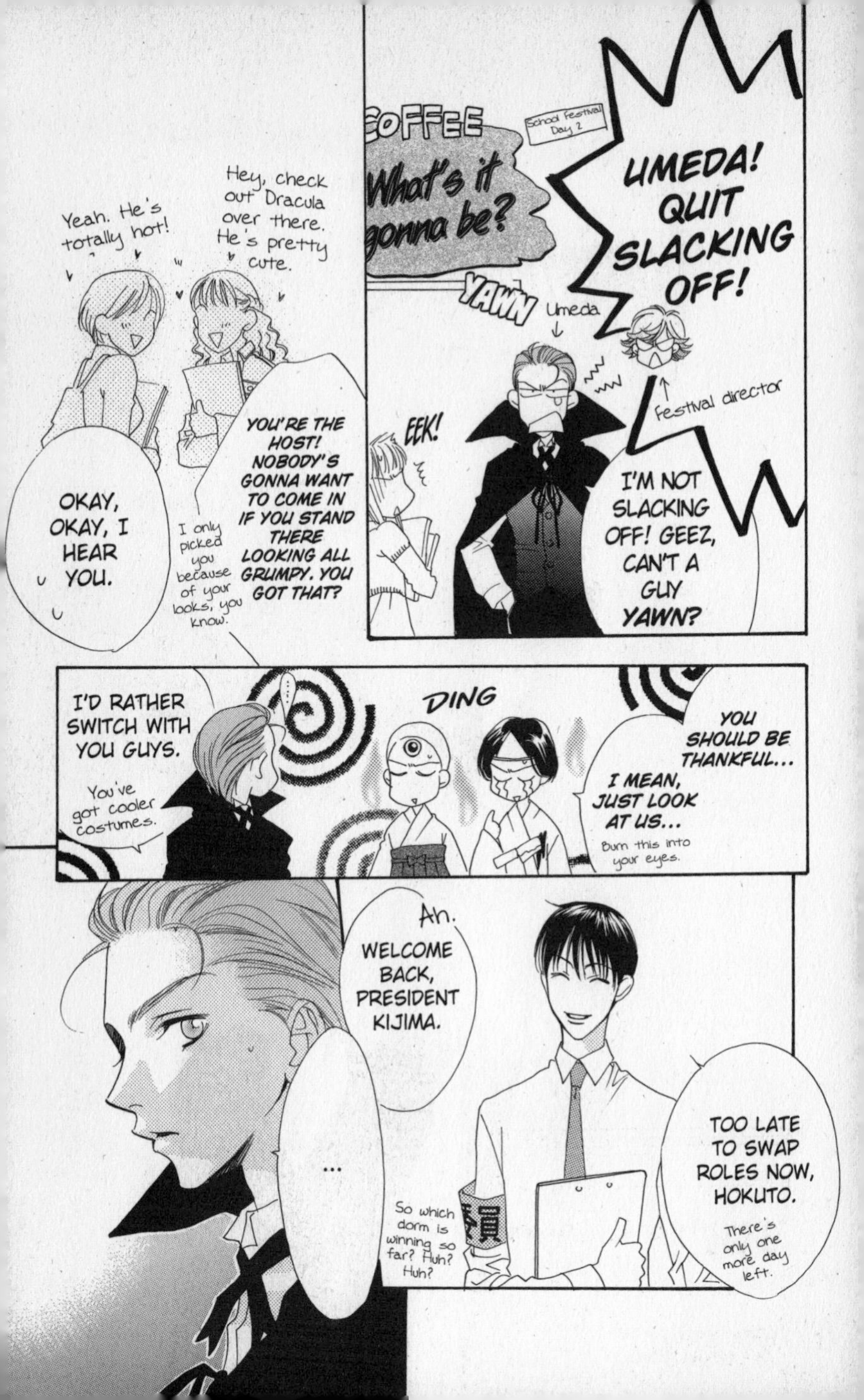
UMEDA! QUIT SLACKING OFF!
School festival Day 2
COFFEE
What's it gonna be?
YAWN
Umeda
Festival director
EEK!
I'M NOT SLACKING OFF! GEEZ, CAN'T A GUY YAWN?
Hey, check out Dracula over there. He's pretty cute.
Yeah. He's totally hot!
YOU'RE THE HOST! NOBODY'S GONNA WANT TO COME IN IF YOU STAND THERE LOOKING ALL GRUMPY. YOU GOT THAT?
I only picked you because of your looks, you know.
OKAY, OKAY, I HEAR YOU.
YOU SHOULD BE THANKFUL... I MEAN, JUST LOOK AT US...
Burn this into your eyes.
DING
I'D RATHER SWITCH WITH YOU GUYS.
You've got cooler costumes.
TOO LATE TO SWAP ROLES NOW, HOKUTO.
There's only one more day left.
So which dorm is winning so far? Huh? Huh?
Ah.
WELCOME BACK, PRESIDENT KIJIMA.
...

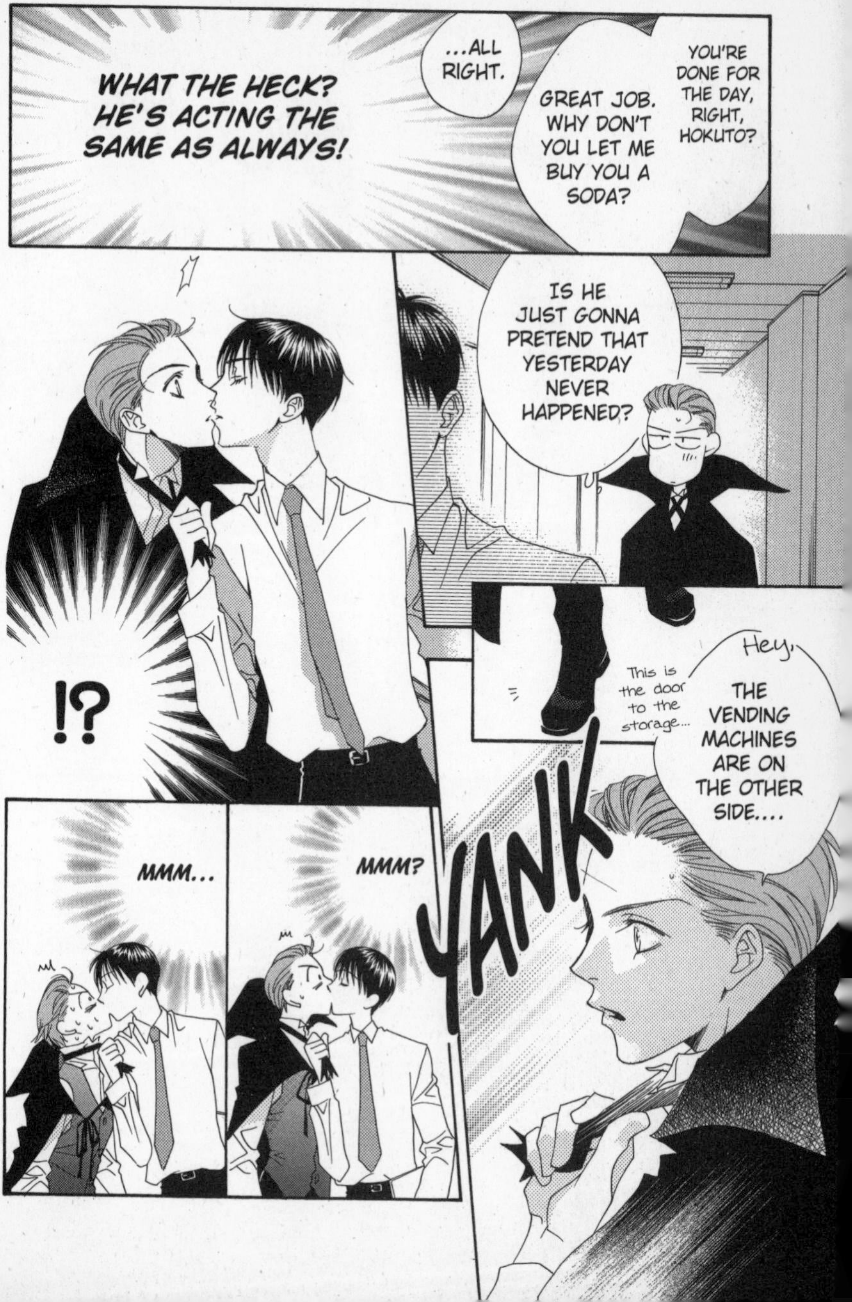
YOU'RE DONE FOR THE DAY, RIGHT, HOKUTO?
GREAT JOB. WHY DON'T YOU LET ME BUY YOU A SODA?
...ALL RIGHT.
WHAT THE HECK? HE'S ACTING THE SAME AS ALWAYS!
IS HE JUST GONNA PRETEND THAT YESTERDAY NEVER HAPPENED?
Hey, THE VENDING MACHINES ARE ON THE OTHER SIDE....
This is the door to the storage...
YANK
!?
MMM?
MMM...

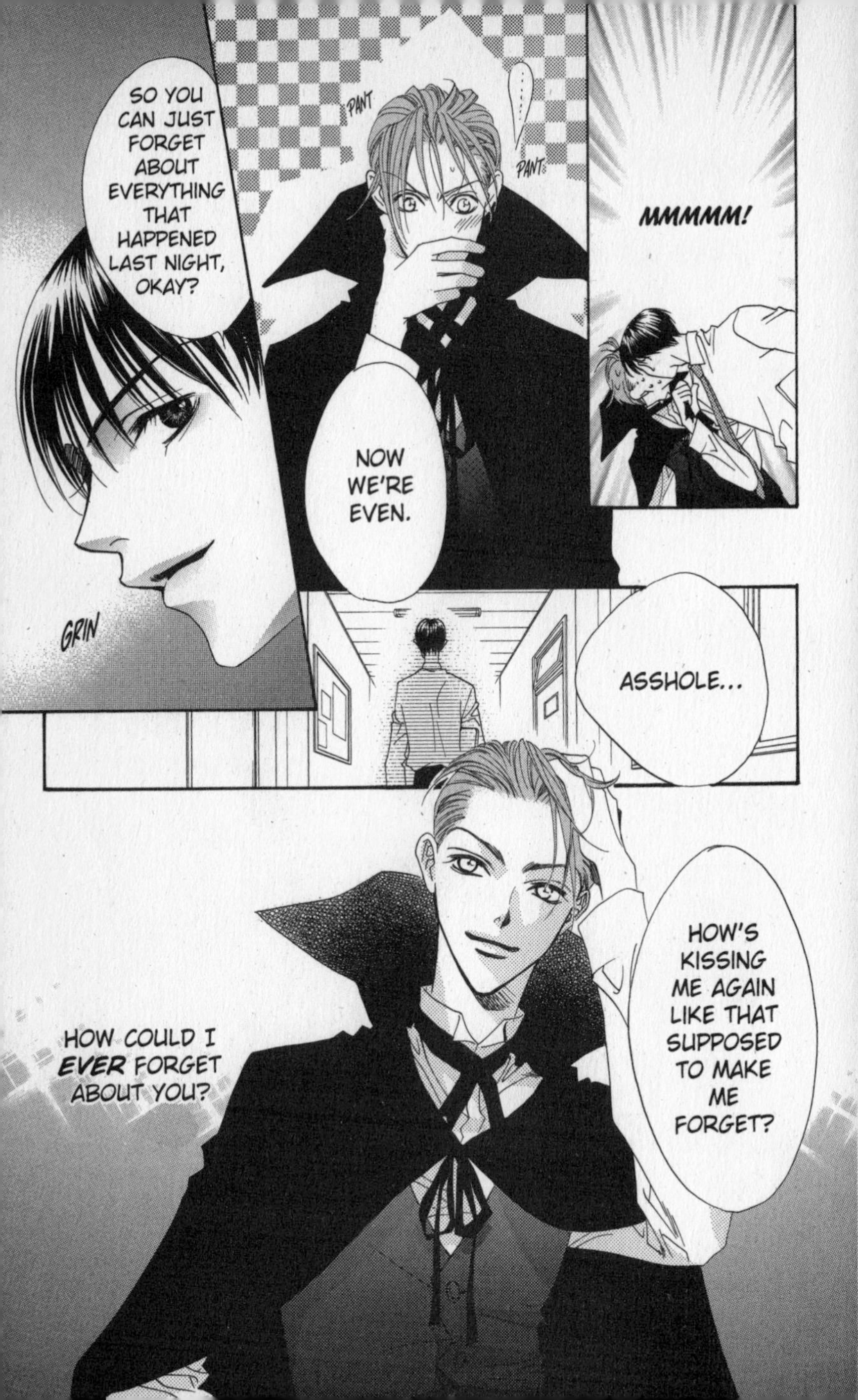
MMMMM!
PANT
PANT
NOW WE'RE EVEN.
SO YOU CAN JUST FORGET ABOUT EVERYTHING THAT HAPPENED LAST NIGHT, OKAY?
GRIN
ASSHOLE...
HOW'S KISSING ME AGAIN LIKE THAT SUPPOSED TO MAKE ME FORGET?
HOW COULD I *EVER* FORGET ABOUT YOU?

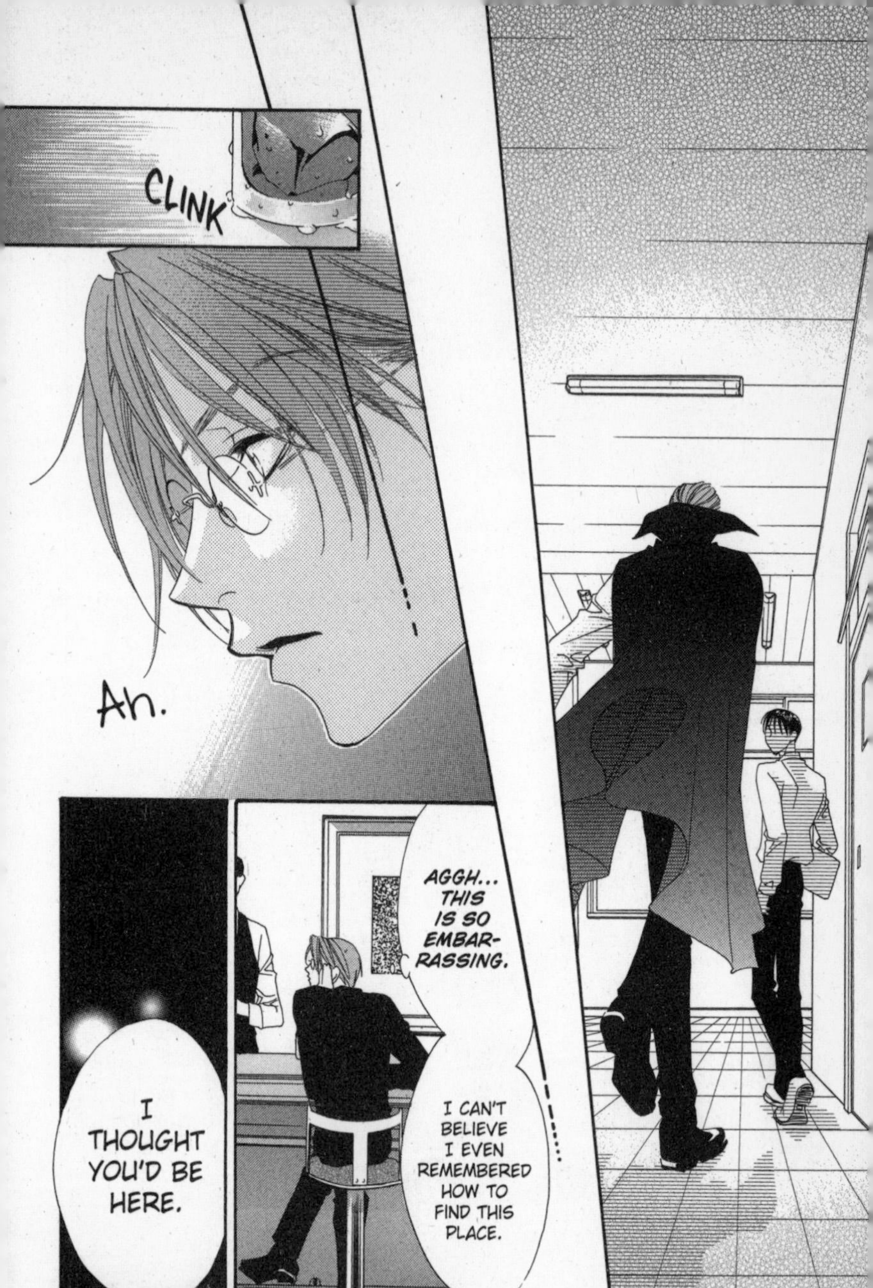
CLINK
Ah.
AGGH... THIS IS SO EMBAR-RASSING.
I CAN'T BELIEVE I EVEN REMEMBERED HOW TO FIND THIS PLACE.
I THOUGHT YOU'D BE HERE.

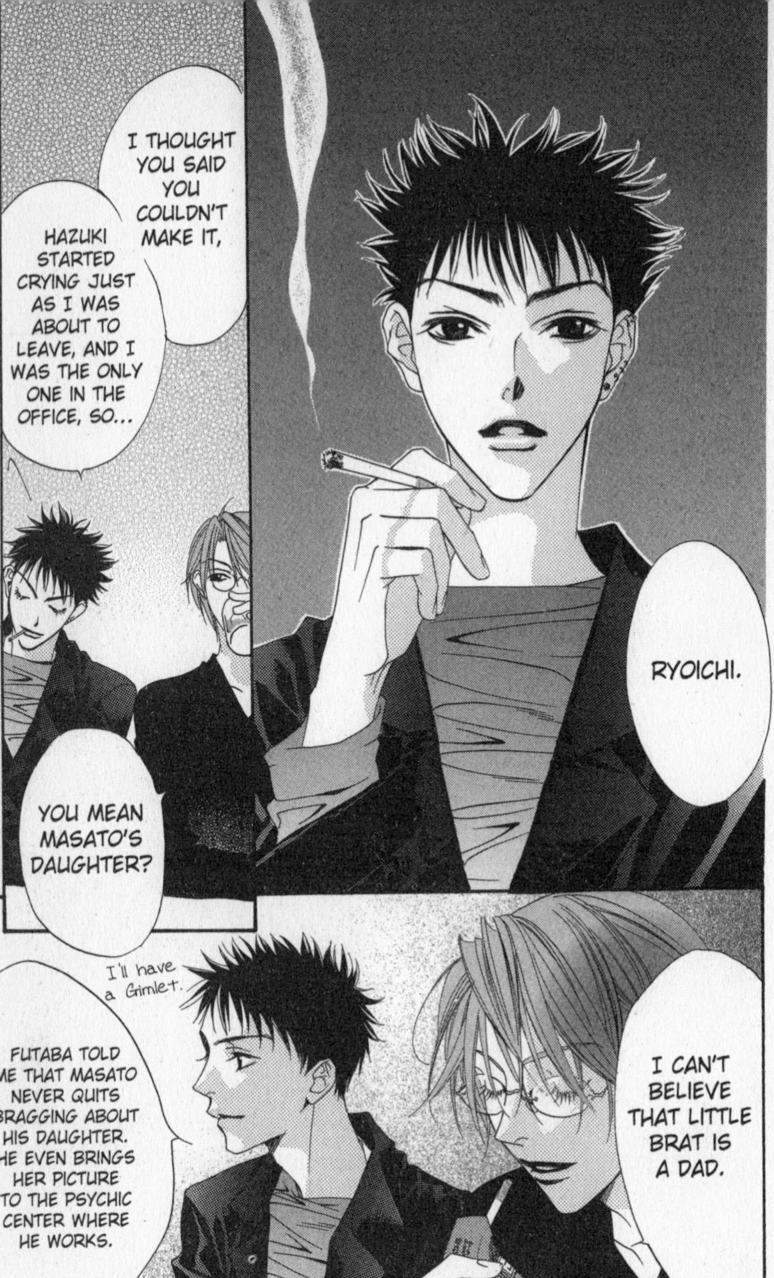
RYOICHI.
I THOUGHT YOU SAID YOU COULDN'T MAKE IT,
HAZUKI STARTED CRYING JUST AS I WAS ABOUT TO LEAVE, AND I WAS THE ONLY ONE IN THE OFFICE, SO...
YOU MEAN MASATO'S DAUGHTER?
I CAN'T BELIEVE THAT LITTLE BRAT IS A DAD.
I'll have a Gimlet.
FUTABA TOLD ME THAT MASATO NEVER QUITS BRAGGING ABOUT HIS DAUGHTER. HE EVEN BRINGS HER PICTURE TO THE PSYCHIC CENTER WHERE HE WORKS.

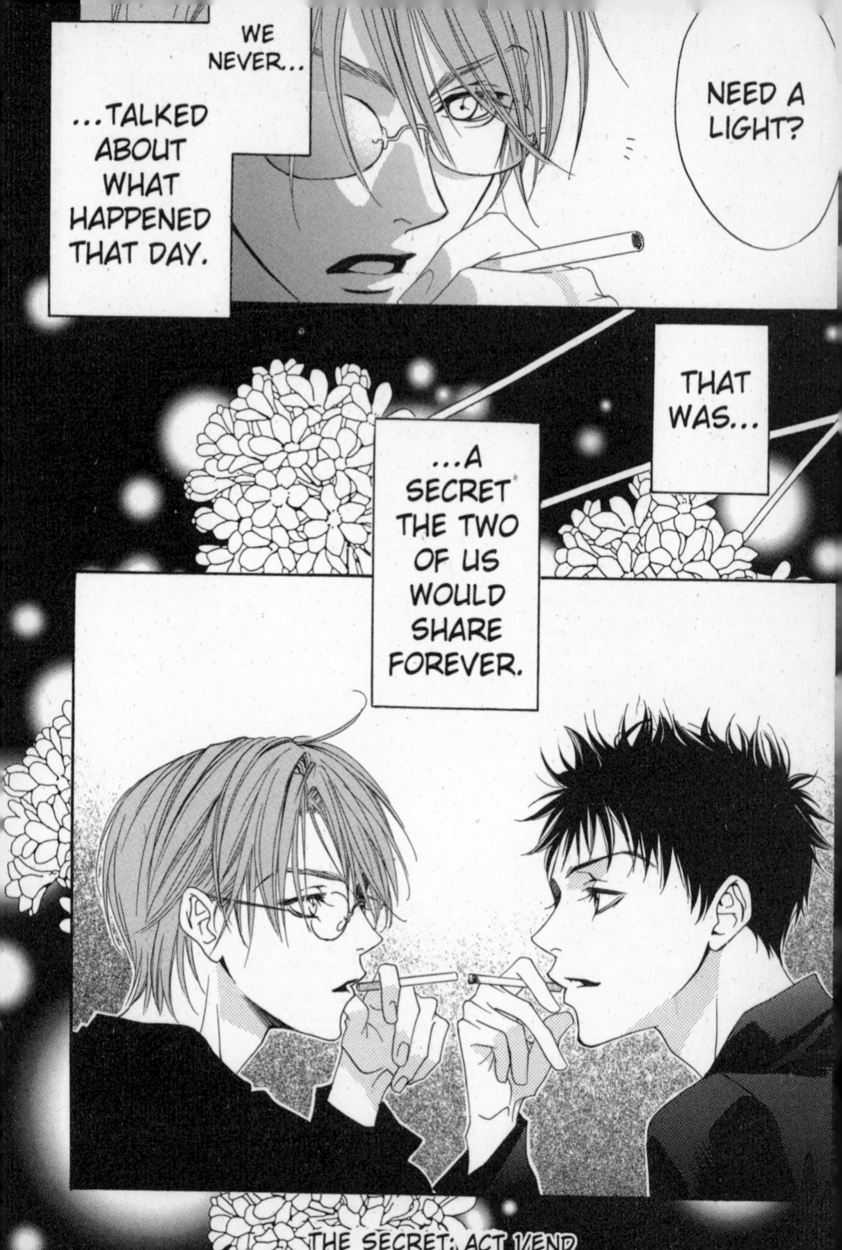
NEED A LIGHT?
WE NEVER...
...TALKED ABOUT WHAT HAPPENED THAT DAY.
THAT WAS...
...A SECRET THE TWO OF US WOULD SHARE FOREVER.
THE SECRET: ACT 1/END

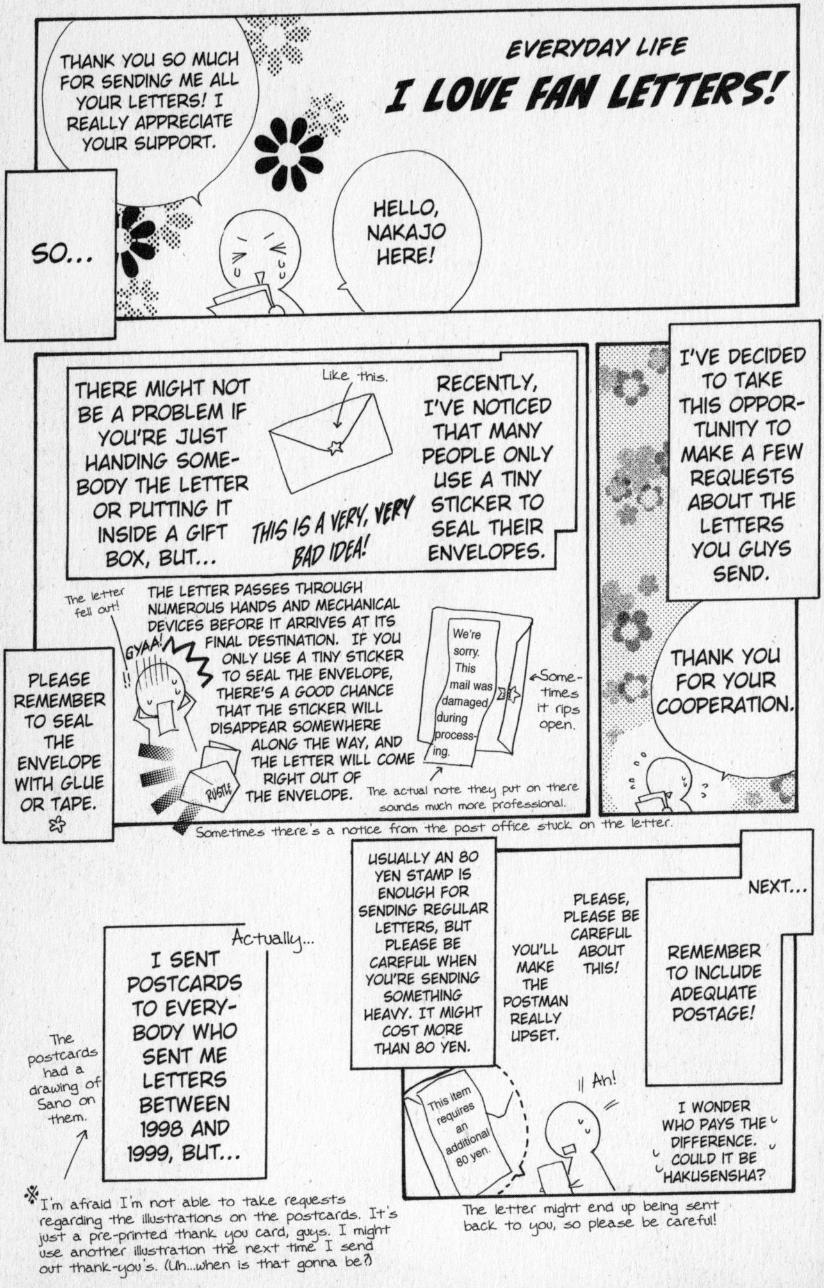
EVERYDAY LIFE
I LOVE FAN LETTERS!
HELLO, NAKAJO HERE!
THANK YOU SO MUCH FOR SENDING ME ALL YOUR LETTERS! I REALLY APPRECIATE YOUR SUPPORT.
SO...
I'VE DECIDED TO TAKE THIS OPPOR-TUNITY TO MAKE A FEW REQUESTS ABOUT THE LETTERS YOU GUYS SEND.
THANK YOU FOR YOUR COOPERATION.
RECENTLY, I'VE NOTICED THAT MANY PEOPLE ONLY USE A TINY STICKER TO SEAL THEIR ENVELOPES.
THIS IS A VERY, VERY BAD IDEA!
Like this.
THERE MIGHT NOT BE A PROBLEM IF YOU'RE JUST HANDING SOME-BODY THE LETTER OR PUTTING IT INSIDE A GIFT BOX, BUT...
Some-times it rips open.
We're sorry. This mail was damaged during process-ing.
The actual note they put on there sounds much more professional.
THE LETTER PASSES THROUGH NUMEROUS HANDS AND MECHANICAL DEVICES BEFORE IT ARRIVES AT ITS FINAL DESTINATION. IF YOU ONLY USE A TINY STICKER TO SEAL THE ENVELOPE, THERE'S A GOOD CHANCE THAT THE STICKER WILL DISAPPEAR SOMEWHERE ALONG THE WAY, AND THE LETTER WILL COME RIGHT OUT OF THE ENVELOPE.
GYAA!!
The letter fell out!
RUSTLE
PLEASE REMEMBER TO SEAL THE ENVELOPE WITH GLUE OR TAPE.
Sometimes there's a notice from the post office stuck on the letter.
NEXT...
REMEMBER TO INCLUDE ADEQUATE POSTAGE!
PLEASE, PLEASE BE CAREFUL ABOUT THIS!
YOU'LL MAKE THE POSTMAN REALLY UPSET.
USUALLY AN 80 YEN STAMP IS ENOUGH FOR SENDING REGULAR LETTERS, BUT PLEASE BE CAREFUL WHEN YOU'RE SENDING SOMETHING HEAVY. IT MIGHT COST MORE THAN 80 YEN.
I WONDER WHO PAYS THE DIFFERENCE. COULD IT BE HAKUSENSHA?
Ah!
This item requires an additional 80 yen.
The letter might end up being sent back to you, so please be careful!
Actually...
I SENT POSTCARDS TO EVERY-BODY WHO SENT ME LETTERS BETWEEN 1998 AND 1999, BUT...
The postcards had a drawing of Sano on them.
※I'm afraid I'm not able to take requests regarding the illustrations on the postcards. It's just a pre-printed thank you card, guys. I might use another illustration the next time I send out thank-you's. (Uh...when is that gonna be?)

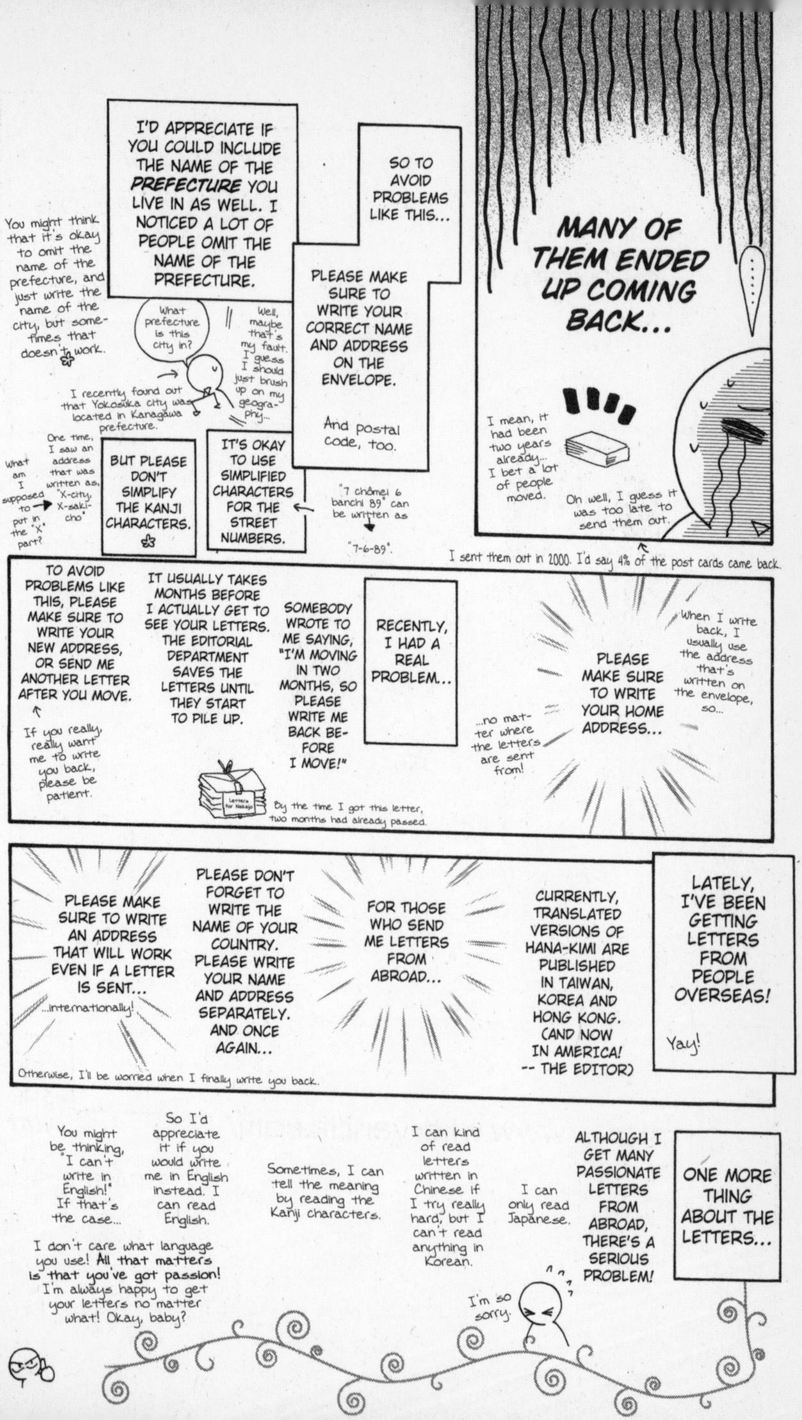
MANY OF THEM ENDED UP COMING BACK...
I mean, it had been two years already... I bet a lot of people moved.
Oh well, I guess it was too late to send them out.
I sent them out in 2000. I'd say 4% of the post cards came back.
SO TO AVOID PROBLEMS LIKE THIS...
PLEASE MAKE SURE TO WRITE YOUR CORRECT NAME AND ADDRESS ON THE ENVELOPE.
And postal code, too.
I'D APPRECIATE IF YOU COULD INCLUDE THE NAME OF THE PREFECTURE YOU LIVE IN AS WELL. I NOTICED A LOT OF PEOPLE OMIT THE NAME OF THE PREFECTURE.
You might think that it's okay to omit the name of the prefecture, and just write the name of the city, but sometimes that doesn't work.
Well, maybe that's my fault. I guess I should just brush up on my geography...
What prefecture is this city in?
I recently found out that Yokosuka city was located in Kanagawa prefecture.
IT'S OKAY TO USE SIMPLIFIED CHARACTERS FOR THE STREET NUMBERS.
"7 chômei 6 banchi 89" can be written as "7-6-89".
BUT PLEASE DON'T SIMPLIFY THE KANJI CHARACTERS.
One time, I saw an address that was written as, "X-city, X-saki-cho"
What am I supposed to put in the "X" part?
PLEASE MAKE SURE TO WRITE YOUR HOME ADDRESS...
When I write back, I usually use the address that's written on the envelope, so...
...no matter where the letters are sent from!
RECENTLY, I HAD A REAL PROBLEM...
SOMEBODY WROTE TO ME SAYING, "I'M MOVING IN TWO MONTHS, SO PLEASE WRITE ME BACK BEFORE I MOVE!"
By the time I got this letter, two months had already passed.
IT USUALLY TAKES MONTHS BEFORE I ACTUALLY GET TO SEE YOUR LETTERS. THE EDITORIAL DEPARTMENT SAVES THE LETTERS UNTIL THEY START TO PILE UP.
Letters for Nakajo
TO AVOID PROBLEMS LIKE THIS, PLEASE MAKE SURE TO WRITE YOUR NEW ADDRESS, OR SEND ME ANOTHER LETTER AFTER YOU MOVE.
If you really, really want me to write you back, please be patient.
LATELY, I'VE BEEN GETTING LETTERS FROM PEOPLE OVERSEAS!
Yay!
CURRENTLY, TRANSLATED VERSIONS OF HANA-KIMI ARE PUBLISHED IN TAIWAN, KOREA AND HONG KONG. (AND NOW IN AMERICA! -- THE EDITOR)
FOR THOSE WHO SEND ME LETTERS FROM ABROAD...
PLEASE DON'T FORGET TO WRITE THE NAME OF YOUR COUNTRY. PLEASE WRITE YOUR NAME AND ADDRESS SEPARATELY. AND ONCE AGAIN...
PLEASE MAKE SURE TO WRITE AN ADDRESS THAT WILL WORK EVEN IF A LETTER IS SENT...
...internationally!
Otherwise, I'll be worried when I finally write you back.
ONE MORE THING ABOUT THE LETTERS...
ALTHOUGH I GET MANY PASSIONATE LETTERS FROM ABROAD, THERE'S A SERIOUS PROBLEM!
I'm so sorry.
I can only read Japanese.
I can kind of read letters written in Chinese if I try really hard, but I can't read anything in Korean.
Sometimes, I can tell the meaning by reading the Kanji characters.
So I'd appreciate it if you would write me in English instead. I can read English.
You might be thinking, "I can't write in English!" If that's the case...
I don't care what language you use! All that matters is that you've got passion! I'm always happy to get your letters no matter what! Okay, baby?

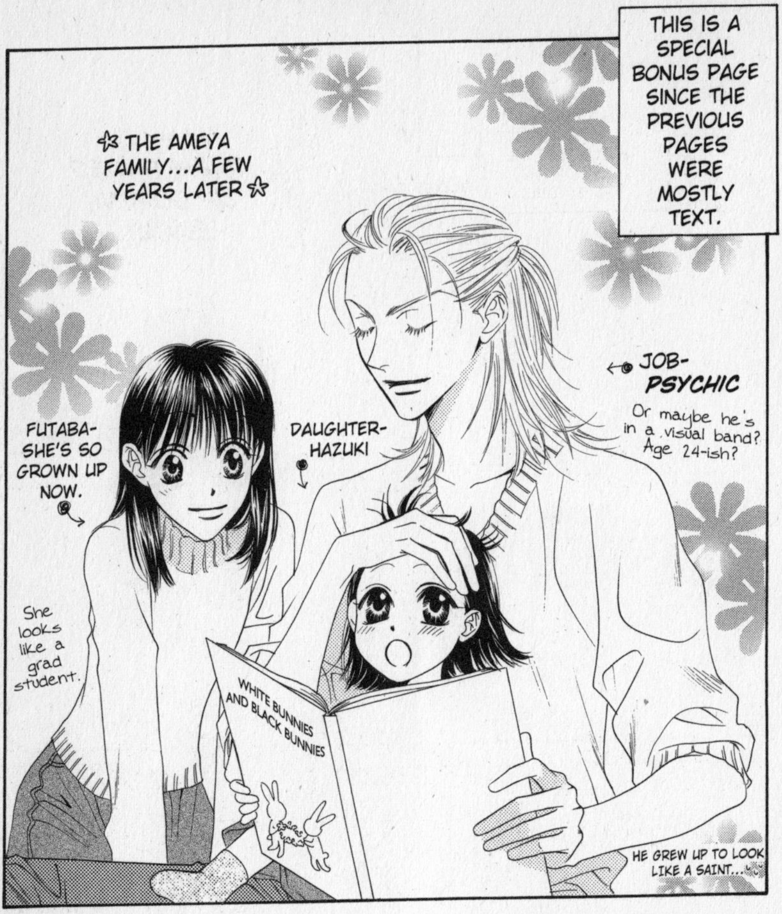
THIS IS A SPECIAL BONUS PAGE SINCE THE PREVIOUS PAGES WERE MOSTLY TEXT.
THE AMEYA FAMILY...A FEW YEARS LATER
JOB-PSYCHIC
Or maybe he's in a visual band? Age 24-ish?
DAUGHTER-HAZUKI
FUTABA-SHE'S SO GROWN UP NOW.
She looks like a grad student.
WHITE BUNNIES AND BLACK BUNNIES
HE GREW UP TO LOOK LIKE A SAINT...
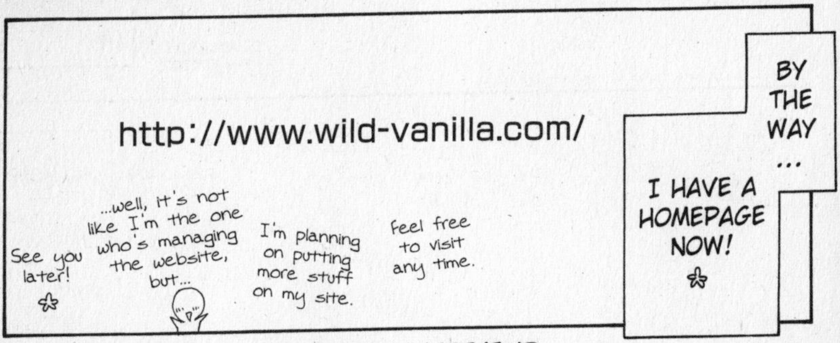
BY THE WAY...
I HAVE A HOMEPAGE NOW!
http://www.wild-vanilla.com/
Feel free to visit any time.
I'm planning on putting more stuff on my site.
...well, it's not like I'm the one who's managing the website, but...
See you later!

EVERYDAY LIFE/END

SPECIAL, SPECIAL BONUS

Hey there, my dear!
If you're having
problems with your
relationship, why
not try a tarot
card reading?

↓
Grin

MASATO AT
WORK.

ABOUT THE AUTHOR

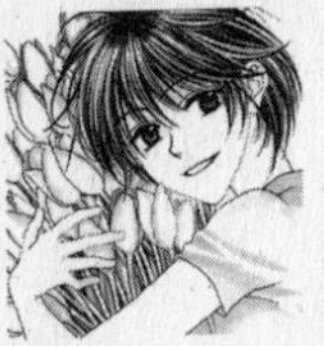

Hisaya Nakajo's manga series **Hanazakari no Kimitachi he** (For You in Full Blossom, casually known as **Hana-Kimi**) has been a hit since it first appeared in 1997 in the shôjo manga magazine **Hana to Yume** (Flowers and Dreams). In Japan, two **Hana-Kimi** art books and several "drama CDs" have been released. Her other manga series include **Missing Piece** (2 volumes) and **Yumemiru Happa** (The Dreaming Leaf, 1 volume).

Hisaya Nakajo's website:
www.wild-vanilla.com

IN THE NEXT VOLUME ...

Unable to forget her near-kiss experience, Mizuki finds herself drawing ever closer to Sano. But Nakatsu is lovesick too, and the tension builds when he asks Sano point-blank: *Do you like Mizuki?* Can Nakatsu and Sano's friendship survive the answer? Meanwhile, Sano's old high-jump rival Kagurazaka returns, bringing news of a surprising new challenger!

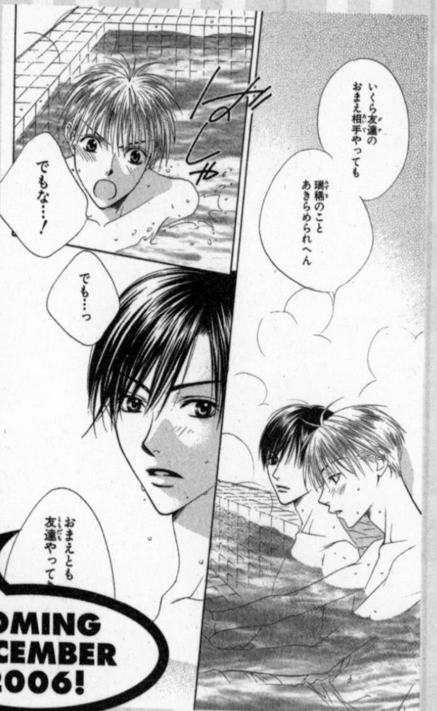

いくら友達のおまえ相手やっても
瑞稀のことあきらめられへん
でもな…!
でも…っ
おまえとも友達やって

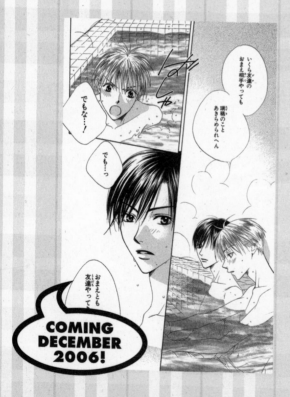

COMING DECEMBER 2006!

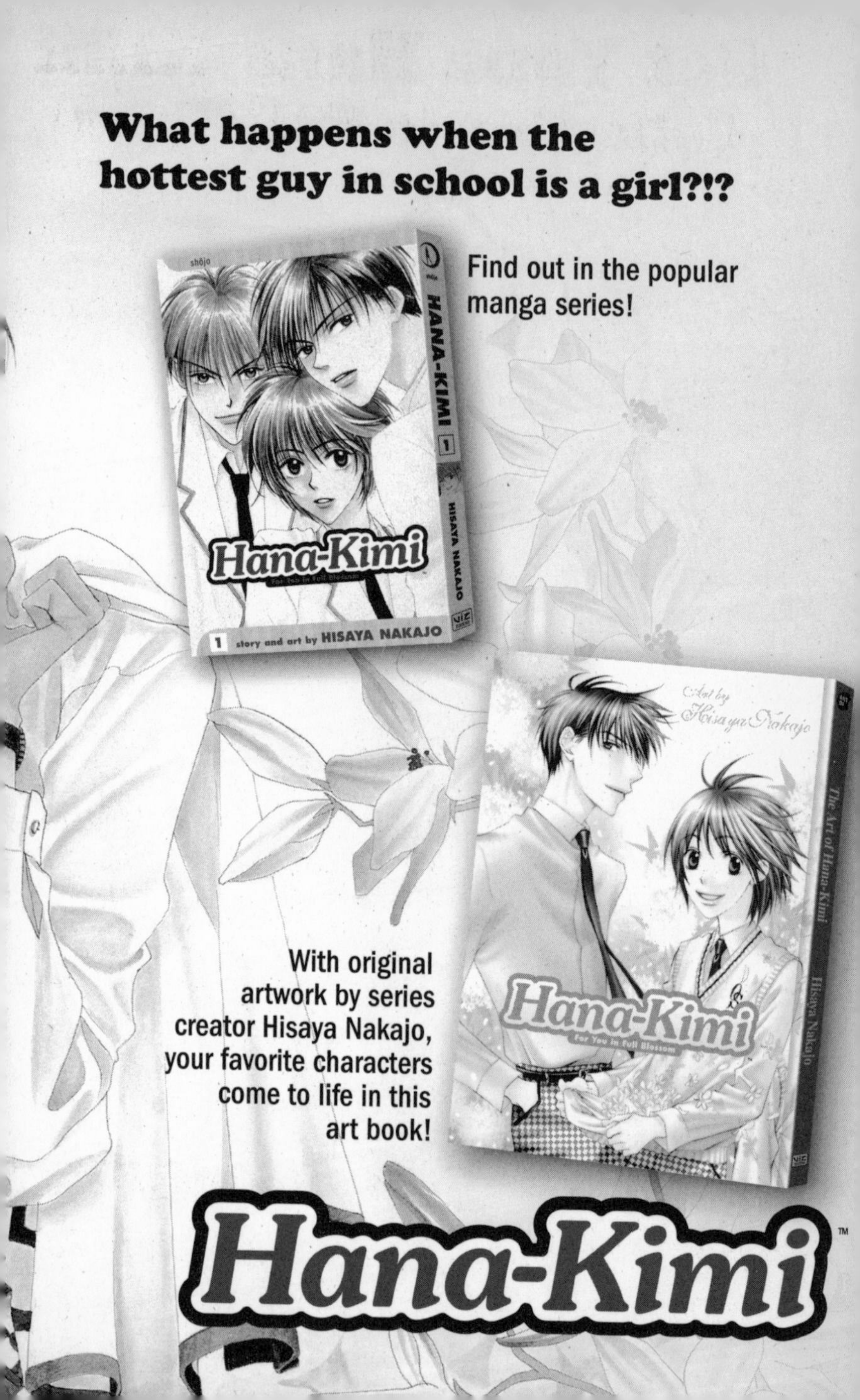

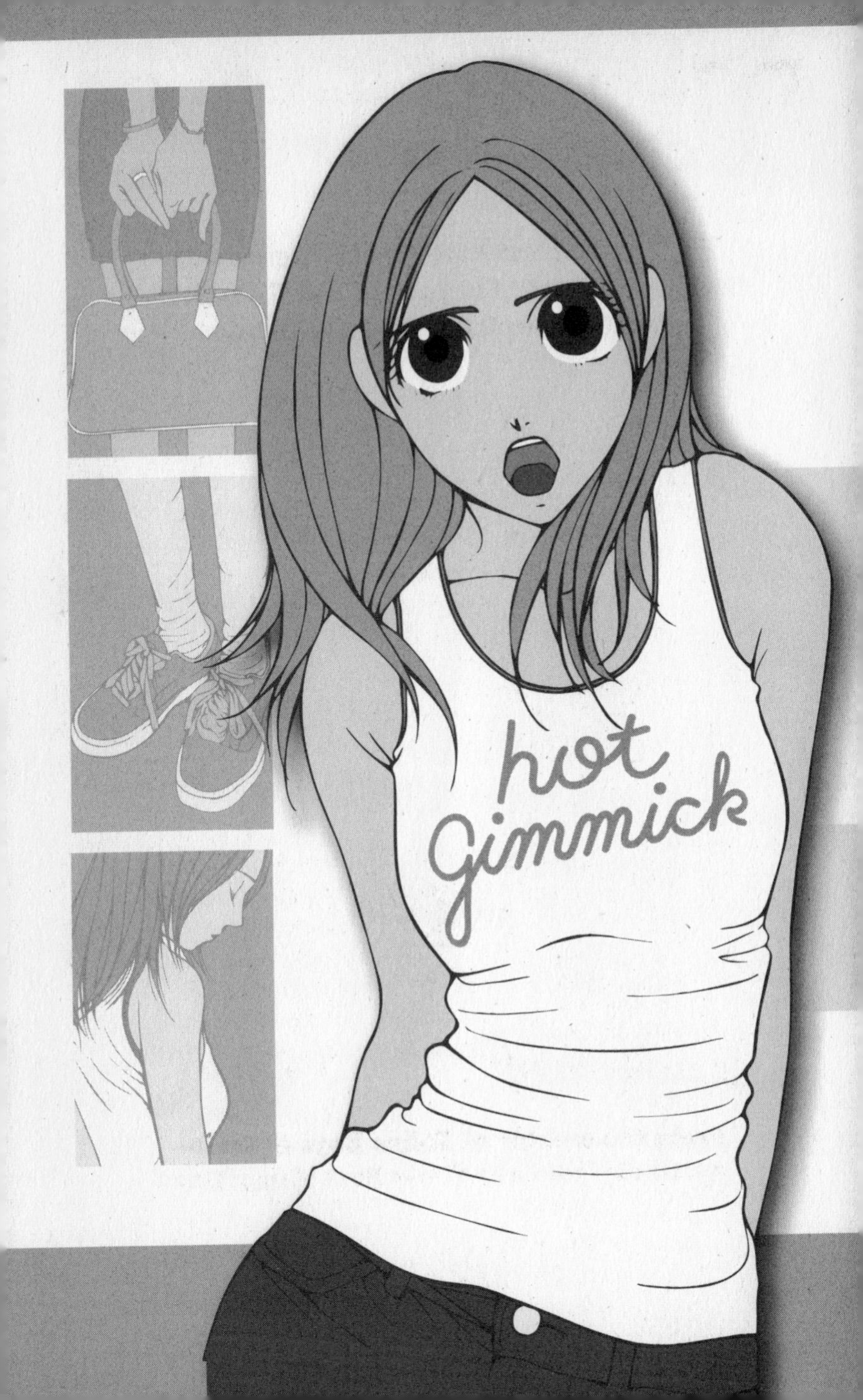
hot
Gimmick

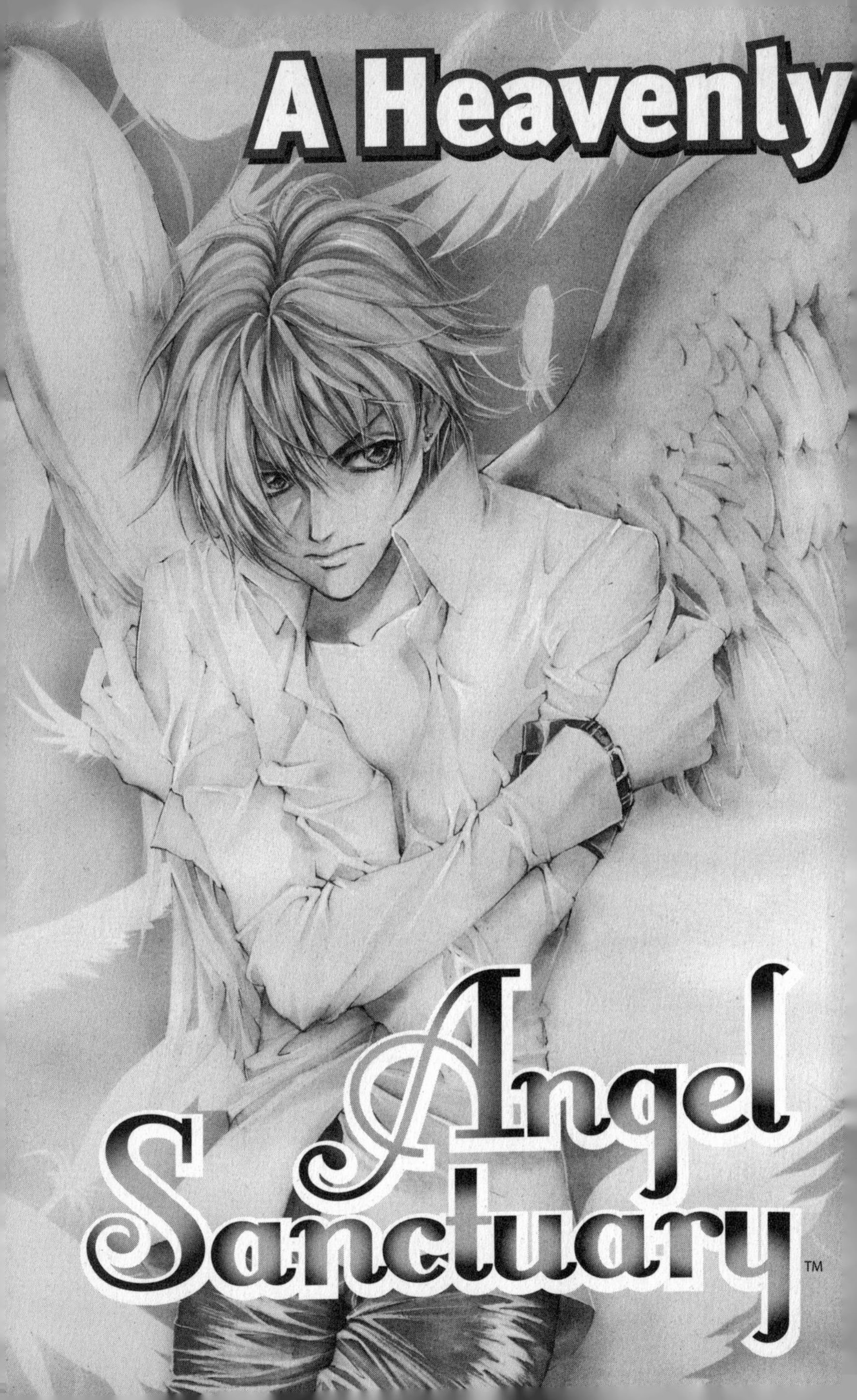
A Heavenly
Angel Sanctuary™